Introduction to **Statistics with SPSS for Social Science**

Visit the *Introduction to Statistics with SPSS for Social Science* Companion Website at **www.pearsoned.co.uk/norris** to find valuable **student** learning material:

- Datasets from the book allowing you to analyse and practise.

PEARSON

At Pearson, we take learning personally. Our courses and resources are available as books, online and via multi-lingual packages, helping people learn whatever, wherever and however they choose.

We work with leading authors to develop the strongest learning experiences, bringing cutting-edge thinking and best learning practice to a global market. We craft our print and digital resources to do more to help learners not only understand their content, but to see it in action and apply what they learn, whether studying or at work.

Pearson is the world's leading learning company. Our portfolio includes Penguin, Dorling Kindersley, the Financial Times and our educational business, Pearson International. We are also a leading provider of electronic learning programmes and of test development, processing and scoring services to educational institutions, corporations and professional bodies around the world.

Every day our work helps learning flourish, and wherever learning flourishes, so do people.

To learn more please visit us at: www.pearson.com/uk

Introduction to Statistics with SPSS for Social Science

Gareth Norris   Aberystwyth University

Faiza Qureshi   City University London

Dennis Howitt   University of Loughborough

Duncan Cramer   University of Loughborough

Harlow, England • London • New York • Boston • San Francisco • Toronto • Sydney • Auckland • Singapore • Hong Kong
Tokyo • Seoul • Taipei • New Delhi • Cape Town • São Paulo • Mexico City • Madrid • Amsterdam • Munich • Paris • Milan

Pearson Education Limited
Edinburgh Gate
Harlow
Essex CM20 2JE
England

and Associated Companies throughout the world

Visit us on the World Wide Web at:
www.pearson.com/uk

First published 2012

© Pearson Education Limited 2012

ISBN: 978-1-4082-3759-5

British Library Cataloguing-in-Publication Data
A catalogue record for this book is available from the British Library

Library of Congress Cataloging-in-Publication Data
  Norris, Gareth.
    Introduction to statistics with SPSS for social science / Gareth Norris, Faiza Qureshi. -- 1st ed.
      p. cm.
    Includes bibliographical references and index.
    ISBN 978-1-4082-3759-5
    1. SPSS (Computer file)   2. Social sciences--Statistical methods--Computer programs.
  I. Qureshi, Faiza, 1981-   II. Title.
    HA32.N64 2012
    005.5'5--dc23
                                                                    2011052975

10 9 8 7 6 5 4 3 2 1
16 15 14 13 12

Typeset in 9.5/12pt Sabon by 35
Printed and bound by Rotolito Lombarda, Italy

Brief contents

Contents

Part 4   More advanced statistics and techniques   275

Guided tour

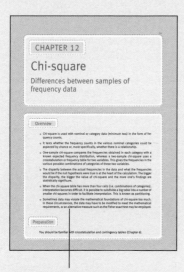

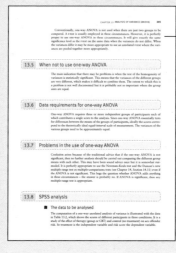

Background details

Outlines the background to the techniques discussed in each chapter to encourage a deeper understanding. This includes:

- What the technique is
- When you should use it
- When you should not use it
- The data required for the analysis
- Typical problems to be aware of

Clear Overview

Introduces the chapter to give students a feel for the topics covered.

Calculation

Provides step-by-step instruction for working through a calculation.

Step-by-step illustrations and screenshots of SPSS

This presents the stages of data entry and data analysis visually, to help you gain confidence in the processes and procedures of SPSS.

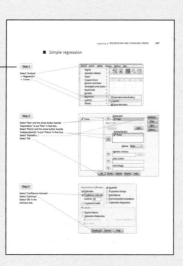

Reporting the output

Explains how you should
present output from SPSS.

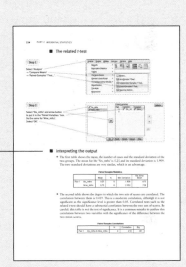

Interpreting the output

Offers a simple explanation of
what the important parts of the
output mean. SPSS statistical
output is presented exactly as
it appears on the screen to help
you become familiar with it.

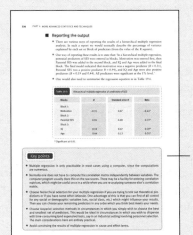

Key Points

Each chapter concludes with
a set of key points to help
summarise chapter coverage
and serve as a useful reminder
when revising a topic.

Website

Datasets from the book allow
you to analyse and practise.

Introduction

The current text is an adaptation of a leading text in statistics from the field of psychology. While psychology may fall under the umbrella of the social sciences, many of its subjects are very specific to its unique field of inquiry. For many instructors in wider social science subjects (e.g. criminology, sociology, political science, etc.), textbooks on quantitative research methods have been limited in both scope and number, and many of the examples in psychology are not relevant for teaching in other disciplines. Hence, this book will go some way to alleviate this disparity and provide the detailed step-by-step guide to empirical research that our colleagues in psychology have enjoyed for some time. The other key aspect of this book is that it integrates within each chapter a walk-through guide to analysing data using SPSS (Statistical Package for the Social Sciences). This invaluable resource enables students and instructors to put theory into practice without the need for an additional text.

Statistics are a subject often endured rather than enjoyed. This is particularly so for social science students who are often more interested in social phenomena (people, places, actions, etc.) rather than numerical interpretations of these events. However, as students ourselves in the past and current instructors of research methods courses, we recognise the importance of this aspect of social science degrees. We feel that many students are instantly turned off by the thought of numbers and believe it is a skill that they simply do not possess. However, more and more degree programs are integrating quantitative methods into the syllabus as the demands of employers are requiring high levels of statistical literacy in today's data driven societies. It is hoped that this book will go some way to reduce this anxiety and provide a readily accessible guide through the full process, from initial data collection right through to analysis with SPSS.

■ Structure

This textbook is intended to cover most of the statistics that students need in a first-degree course in the social sciences and well beyond, including:

- Basic descriptive statistics from tables and diagrams through to the correlation co-efficient and simple regression.

- Inferential statistics and significance testing.

- Analysis of variance (ANOVA) including one-way related and unrelated ANOVAs, two-way unrelated ANOVAs, mixed designs and the analysis of covariance. The computation of appropriate significance levels for multiple comparisons is given special attention.

- Advanced correlational statistics such as partial correlation, multiple regression and factor analysis.

- Advanced techniques including meta-analysis, log-linear analysis, reliability and confidence intervals. Note: confidence intervals have been advocated increasingly in recent years as an alternative to conventional statistical significance testing.

- Analysis of complex qualitative, nominal or category data. It features log-linear analysis together with two sorts of logistic regression – multinomial logistic regression and binomial logistic regression. Logistic regression can use score variables as independent variables, of course, but we have emphasised nominal or category independent variables.

■ Level of difficulty

Throughout, the book is designed to remain at a relatively simple level even when complex statistics are being explained. The material is aimed at the vast majority of students who, although having some mathematical skills, nevertheless do not relish complex formulae and abstract explanations of obscure mathematical procedures.

Nevertheless, rigour is not sacrificed to this end. Students following our advice and recommendations carefully will be able to analyse virtually any data effectively and to a competent standard. To this end we have been scrupulous in ensuring that alternative statistical procedures are mentioned when the limits of applicability of a statistical technique are breached. A good example of this is the inclusion of the Fisher exact probability test when chi-square is not applicable because of small expected frequencies. Students' data sets are often fairly small and must be analysed as they are because the option of collecting more data is not available.

■ Flexibility

The textbook is designed as a menu of statistical techniques, not all of which need be sampled. Chapters 1 to 12 constitute a thorough but compact basic introduction to statistics; they are suitable for use as a basic-level course as they cover descriptive statistics and common inferential statistics. Flexibility was an important feature, planned into the text for the following reasons:

- All instructors teach courses differently. The textbook covers most of the commonly taught techniques and many less common ones too. Instructors may omit some chapters without causing difficulties. The textbook contains pertinent basic and revision information within each chapter wherever possible. In other words, instructors will be able to select their favoured route through the material.

- Some instructors prefer to teach statistics practically through the use of computers. This is made easy by this book which contains both a textbook and a computer manual in one place.

- Many students will have little difficulty in self-study of most chapters. Supervisors of student practical classes and projects may find this particularly appealing as they can direct students to appropriate parts of the textbook.

- However, the flexibility is far greater than this. The text can serve as an introduction to statistics or as a book for an intermediate-level course. Not only is this better value for students; it means that the problems of transferring from one textbook to another are bypassed.

There is no right or wrong way of structuring modules in social science statistics courses. What is appropriate depends on what students know already, the aims and objectives of the module and, most importantly, the other modules that the students are taking, especially those involving practical research. If statistics is taught as part of practical classes then it may be difficult to include formal lectures on the use of statistics. For these reasons and many others, this text is itself modular in construction. The physical order of the chapters in the text is merely one of several possibilities. Our aim is to give a thorough grounding in descriptive statistics before moving on to the basic principles of significance testing. This is partly because we feel that descriptive statistics is not always handled well by students who too often regard statistical significance as equivalent to statistical analysis, at the expense of understanding and describing their data.

Most lecturers will choose their own route through the material. For example, the chapters on correlation and regression may be omitted or deferred if the lecturer wishes to teach basic experimental design and analysis. For this reason, each chapter lists essential prerequisites in terms of the students' knowledge and also refers to later chapters if these are particularly relevant.

■ Professional relevance

It is increasingly obvious that the statistics taught to students and the statistics contained in journal articles and books are drawing apart. For that reason, the book contains introductions to techniques such as factor analysis, multiple regression, path analysis and logistic regression which are common in professional publications and generally easy to do using computer packages. Again, this section of the textbook may form part of an intermediate course.

■ Other features

- Tables of statistical significance have been simplified extensively wherever possible for pedagogic reasons. Students find some books hard and confusing to use because the statistical tables are so obscurely or badly presented. Nevertheless, the book contains among the most extensive selection of tables possible, and some tables not available elsewhere.

- Statistical formulae have been kept to a minimum. This is relatively easy since not too many formulae are necessary anyway.

- Every calculation is illustrated with a step-by-step example for students to follow. Where hand calculation is too difficult, the student is advised that it is essential to use a computer package (e.g. SPSS).

- We have preferred to use methods and descriptions that communicate clearly and effectively to students even if they are at times not the most formally rigorous explanations. This introduces a degree of informality that might annoy the most statistically precise thinkers. We think it is for the greater good to avoid too abstract an approach.

- We have tried to provide insight into the ways in which social scientists use statistics.

- Practical advice on the learning and use of statistics is given at the end of every chapter of the textbook.

■ Web resources

There is a website (www.pearsoned.co.uk/norris) associated with this textbook offering datasets used in the analysis and other resources. However, it is worthwhile emphasising that there are extensive web resources available to do many of the calculations described in this textbook. If a comprehensive statistical analysis package is not available, these sites are an attractive resource. These are constantly becoming available. The quick way of tracking them is simply to enter the name of the statistic into a favourite search engine.

List of figures

List of tables

List of boxes

List of calculation boxes

Acknowledgements

■ Authors' acknowledgements

As this book is an adaptation of two existing texts (*Introduction to Statistics in Psychology* and *Introduction to SPSS in Psychology*), it seems fitting we begin our thanks to the original authors of these books, Dennis Howitt and Duncan Cramer. They have been extremely generous in allowing us relatively free reign to pick and choose the material we deemed necessary to expand these texts into the wider social science market as one volume. On occasion, we both felt some nervousness at this process as we cast a critical eye over the work of two leading figures in psychology research methods. However, they have been supportive of our endeavours and – so we are led to believe – pleased with the outcome.

The second debt of gratitude must go to Andrew Taylor at Pearson Education, who has patiently steered this project along. With two authors based some distance apart this has not always been easy. Luckily our shared passion for Formula 1 motor racing has ensured that we have in constant contact and Andrew has intuitively recognised those times when we have needed some encouragement and support.

Many people work behind the scenes on these productions – we are thankful for all of the assistance we have received along the way, but in particular we would like to mention (in no particular order): Mary Lince (desk editor), Jane Lawes (editorial assistance), Patrick Bonham (copy editing) and Helen MacFadyen (proofreading). Like most academics, we have little knowledge of the editorial process and we have been amazed at how well they have been able to extract the relevant information from us with the minimum of pain.

Finally, we would like to thank all the reviewers who have provided us with vital feedback on the chapters they have been sent.

Gareth Norris and Faiza Qureshi

■ Publisher's acknowledgements

The publishers would like to thank the anonymous panel of reviewers for their support with the development of the manuscript. The publishers would further like to thank the authors for the dedication, effort and skill they demonstrated in producing this book, and also the authors of the originating psychology texts for supporting the adaptation.

We are grateful to the following for permission to reproduce copyright material:

Screenshots

Screenshots from PASW Statistics 19.0 screengrabs. Reprint courtesy of International Business Machines Corporation, copyright © SPSS, Inc., an IBM Company

Photographs

Reuters/ Wolfgang Rattay, p. 50

In some instances we have been unable to trace the owners of copyright material, and we would appreciate any information that would enable us to do so.

PART 1

Descriptive statistics

Chapter 1

Why you need statistics

Types of data

Overview

- Statistics is a word used to describe data but also to assess what reliance we can place on information based on samples.

- A variable is any concept that we can measure and that varies between individuals or cases.

- Variables should be identified as nominal (also known as category, categorical or qualitative) variables, or score (also known as numerical or quantitative) variables.

- Nominal variables are simply named categories.

- Score variables are measured in the form of a numerical scale which indicates the quantity of the variable.

1.1   Introduction

Every day we are bombarded with statistical information, most times without realising. Simply by reading a newspaper, watching the television or even going out shopping, the chances are you will come across some form of statistical information, such as stories on crime rates, figures on how well or badly your football team has played in recent matches, discounts on clothes during the sales (10% off), television adverts stating that nine out of ten cats prefer a certain brand of cat food, opinion polls on how the three main political parties in the UK are viewed by the public, and so forth. The list is endless.

Statistics is a tool that can be used to answer a researcher's questions, as research (such as dissertation projects) is very varied and can be quite complex. Only the researcher can fully know what they want their research to achieve – what issues they want resolving through collecting research data and analysing it. Unless the researcher clearly understands what they want the research to achieve, statistics can be of little help. Very often, when approached for statistical advice, we find that we have to clarify the objectives of the research first of all – and then try to unravel how the researcher thought that the data collected would help them. These are *not* statistical matters but issues to do with developing research ideas and planning appropriate data collection. So the first thing is to list the questions that the data were intended to answer. Too often, sight of the purpose of the research is lost in the forest of the research practicalities.

There are three types of statistical techniques:

1. *Descriptive statistics* provide ways of summarising and describing information that we collect from different sources. This is achieved using tables and diagrams to summarise data, and simple formulae which turn fairly complex data into simple indexes that describe numerically the main features of the data (Part 1).

2. *Inferential statistics* is about generalising from a sample to the entire population, such as from the British Crime Survey (BCS). The current BCS sample stands at 51,000 people aged 16 or over (The National Archives, 2011). The data can be weighted to make the analysis representative of the entire population of England and Wales (Part 2).

3. *Data exploration techniques* simplify large amounts of data that otherwise would be much too confusing. They allow researchers to clarify trends in their data (Parts 3 and 4).

1.2   Variables and measurement

A variable is anything that varies and can be measured. So, the age, height and hair or eye colour of a person are variables. There are only two different types of measurement in statistics – category and numerical measurements.

1. *Category (nominal/qualitative) measurement* is deciding to which category of a variable a particular case belongs. If we were carrying out research looking into the legal marital status (variable) of people, we would have to decide whether or not they were never married, married, divorced or widowed (categories). There are no numbers involved in the process of categorisation.

    However, you need to be warned of a possible confusion that can occur. If you have 100 people whose legal marital status is known, you might wish to count how

Table 1.1	Frequencies of legal marital status
Legal marital category	**Number of frequency in set**
Never married	27
Married	10
Divorced	15
Widowed	48

many are never married, married, and so forth. These counts could be entered into a data table like Table 1.1. Notice that the numbers this time correspond to a count of the *frequency* or number of cases falling into each of the four categories. *They are not scores*, but frequencies. The numbers do not correspond to a single measurement but are the aggregate of many separate measurements.

2. *Numerical (score/quantitative) measurement* is giving a *numerical* value to a measurement. We could record the penalty points received by five people for a range of motoring offences, as in Table 1.2. Each of the numerical values in the table indicates the named individual's *score* on the variable.

    The distinction between numerical scores and frequencies is important, so always take care to check whether what appear to be numerical scores in a table are actually frequencies.

Table 1.2	Penalty points received by five named individuals
Individual	**Penalty points**
Gemma	0
Theresa	5
Martha	6
Michael	11
Tom	3

Make a habit of mentally labelling variables as numerical scores or nominal categories. If you do this, it is a big step forward in thinking statistically. This is all you really need to know about types of measurement. However, you should be aware that others use more complex systems. Read the following section to learn more about scales of measurement.

■ Levels of measurement

You may find it unnecessary to learn the contents of this section in detail. However, it does contain terms with which you ought to be familiar, since other people might make reference to them.

The levels of measurement were developed by Stevens (1946) who held that all measurement could be carried out using four different types of scales: nominal, ordinal, interval and ratio. The four 'theoretical' scales of measurement are as follows. The scales numbered 2, 3 and 4 are different types of *numerical* scores.

1. **Nominal categorisation,** as already discussed above, places cases into *named* categories (see Table 1.1).

2. **Ordinal (rank) measurement** places the scores in order (hence *ordinal*) from the smallest to the largest. For example, in a Grand Prix, drivers will be ranked according to where they finished, so first, second, third, fourth, fifth and so forth.

3. **Interval (equal interval) measurement** is often used in surveys. If a survey was being carried out in relation to feelings of safety at night, you may be asked to rate your feelings of safety on a 7-point scale, from very safe (1) to very unsafe (7). This is an *interval* scale because it has equidistant points between each of the seven points. Thus, we can understand the differences in the answers of respondents along the scale.

4. **Ratio measurement** is exactly the same as the interval scale measurement but with one important distinction. A ratio scale of measurement has an absolute zero point that is measured as 0, for example distance, height and length. So, 0 kilometre is the smallest distance one can have. However, ratio measurement is not often used in social research.

1.3   Statistical significance

Statistical significance is a term you will come across frequently in statistics. A crucial fact about research is that it is carried out on samples of cases rather than all possible cases. This is due to time and financial constraints. Sometimes, it is very difficult to specify what the population is in words (e.g. when one collects a sample of participants from a coffee shop on the high street). The realisation that research could be done on relatively small samples was the initial stimulus for many of the statistical techniques described in this book.

For many, statistics means tests of significance. This is a mistaken emphasis since, in terms of importance in any analysis, basic descriptive statistics are key to understanding your data. Statistical significance is about a very limited question – is it reasonably safe to generalise from my sample?

In order to do this, in statistics usually we take information based on the sample(s) of data we have collected and generalise to the population from which we might assume the sample is drawn. Sometimes, one simply takes the sample characteristics and assumes that the population characteristics are the same. On other occasions, the sample characteristics have to be slightly modified to obtain the best estimate of the population characteristics. Whichever applies, you then use these estimated population characteristics to plot the distribution of characteristics of random samples taken from the estimated population. The most important characteristic that is estimated from samples is the variation of scores in the data.

The distribution of these random samples forms a baseline against which the characteristic of our sample obtained in our research can be compared with what happens under conditions of randomness. If our actual sample characteristic is unlikely to have occurred as a consequence of randomness then we say that it is *statistically significant*. All we mean is that it is at the extremes of the distribution of random samples. If our sample is very typical of what happens by random sampling, then we say that our sample characteristic is *not statistically significant*.

Often, in social research, this is put in terms of accepting or rejecting the *null hypothesis*. The null hypothesis is basically that there is no relationship or no difference in our data. Usually, the population is specified in terms of the null hypothesis. That is, in our population there is no correlation, or in our population there is no difference.

Statistical significance is often set at the 0.05 or 5% significance level. This is purely arbitrary and is not actually set in stone. Sometimes, one would require a more stringent significance level (say 0.01 or 1%) and in some circumstances one could relax the criterion a little. However, unless you are very experienced you perhaps ought to stick with the 0.05 or 5% level of statistical significance. This level of significance means that there is a 1 in 20 chance of getting a result as extreme as ours by random sampling from the estimated population.

One-tailed significance testing is used when the direction of the trend in the data is predicted on the basis of strong theory or consistent previous research. The prediction is made prior to collecting the data. Such conditions are rarely met in student research and it is recommended that you stick to two-tailed testing.

Finally, notice that the precision of this approach is affected by how representative the sample characteristics are of the population characteristics. One cannot know this, of course. This may help you understand that despite the mathematical sophistication of statistics, in fact it should be used as a guide rather than a seal of approval.

1.4 SPSS guide: an introduction

■ What is SPSS?

Learning to use SPSS is a transferable skill which is often a valuable asset in the job market. The program is used at all levels from students to specialist researchers, and in a great many academic fields and practical settings. One big advantage is that once the basics are learnt, SPSS is just as easy to use for simple analyses as for complex ones. The purpose of this introductory chapter is to enable beginners quickly to take advantage of the facilities of SPSS. However, users who have familiarity with, say, word processing will find much of this relevant to using SPSS – opening programs, opening files and saving files, for instance. Do not be afraid to experiment.

■ To access SPSS

SPSS for Windows is generally accessed using buttons and menus in conjunction with clicks of the mouse. Consequently the quickest way of learning is simply to follow our steps and screenshots on a computer.

Step 1

Double left click on the SPSS icon with the mouse if it appears anywhere in the window, otherwise click the 'Start' button (bottom left corner of screen) to find the list of programs, open the list of programs and click on SPSS.

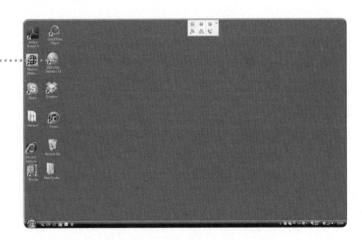

Step 2

This screen eventually appears after a few moments. You could choose any of the options in the window. However, it is best to close down the superimposed menu by clicking on the close-down button or on 'Cancel'. The superimposed menu may not appear as it can be permanently closed down.

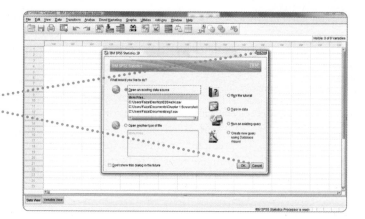

■ To enter data

Step 1

The SPSS Data Editor can now be seen unobstructed by the menu. The Data Editor is a spreadsheet into which data are entered. The columns are used to represent different variables; the rows are the different cases (participants) for which you have data.

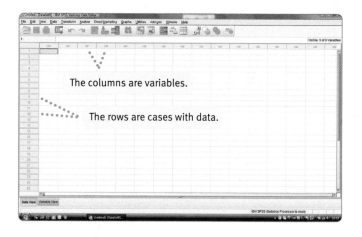

The columns are variables.

The rows are cases with data.

Step 2

To enter data into SPSS simply highlight one of the cells by clicking on that cell – SPSS always has one cell highlighted.

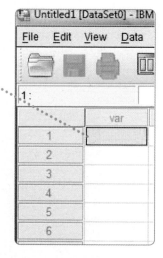

Step 3

Then type a number using the computer keyboard. On pressing Return on the keyboard or selecting another cell with the mouse, this number will be entered into the spreadsheet as shown here. The value 6.00 is the entry for the first row (first case) of the variable VAR00001.

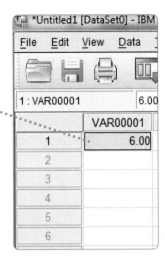

Step 4

Correcting errors: simply highlight the cell where the error is using your mouse and type in the correction. On pressing Return or moving to another cell, the correction will be entered.

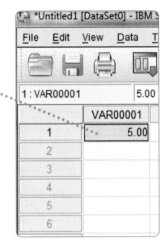

■ Moving within a window with the mouse

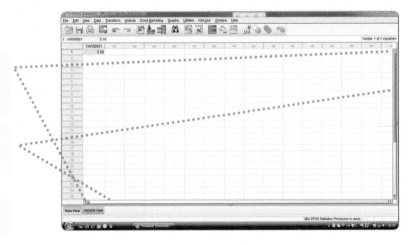

One can now move a row or column at a time by clicking on the arrow-headed buttons near the vertical and horizontal scroll bars.

For major movements, drag the vertical and horizontal scroll bars to move around the page.

The relative position of the scroll bar indicates the relative position in the file.

■ Moving within a window using the keyboard keys with the mouse

One can move one page up or down on the screen by pressing the Pg Up and Pg Dn keyboard keys.

The cursor keys on the keyboard move the cursor one space or character according to the direction of the arrow.

■ Saving data to disk

Step 1

By selecting 'File' then 'Save As...' it is possible to save the data as a file.
The saved data is automatically given the extension '.sav' by SPSS. A distinctive file name is helpful such as 'eg1' so that its contents will be clear.

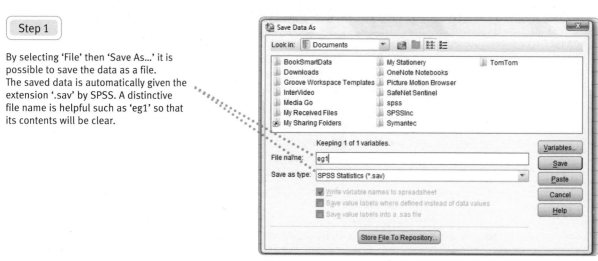

Step 2

To choose the place where the data file will be saved, indicate this place in the 'Look in' box. Use the arrow to browse to the selected location.

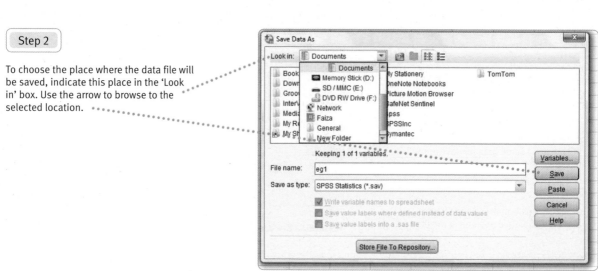

■ Opening up a data file

Step 1

To open an existing file,
click 'File', 'Open' and 'Data...'.
Look in 'Look in' if the file is not in
the 'Open File' box (which it will be
if you have just saved it), type in the
file name ('eg1') and then 'Open'.

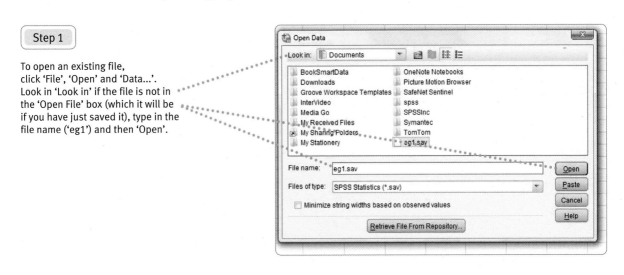

Step 2

To open a new file, click 'File', 'New'
and 'Data'. This file can be saved as
in Step 1 in the previous section.

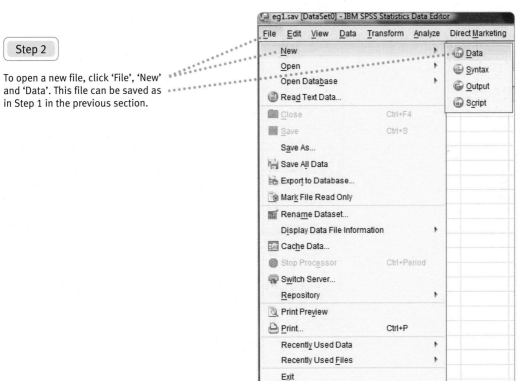

■ Using Variable View to create and label variables

Step 1

Clicking on the 'Variable View' tab at the bottom changes the 'Data View' (the data spreadsheet) screen to one in which information about your variables may be entered conveniently.

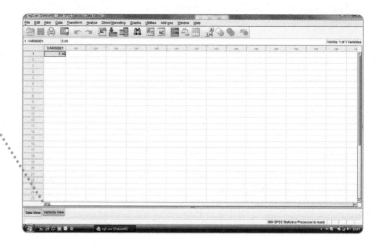

Step 2

This is the 'Variable View' spreadsheet. In this case one variable is already listed. We entered it in Step 3 in 'To enter data' above. But we can rename it and add extra variables quite simply by highlighting the appropriate cell and typing in a new or further variable names.

Step 3

There is no practical limit to the length of the variable names. Highlight one of the cells under 'Name' and type in a distinct variable name. The rest of the columns are given default values but may be changed. These renamed and newly defined variables will appear on the 'Data View' screen when this is selected. That is, new variables have been created and specified.

Step 4

It is important to note that other columns are easily changed too.

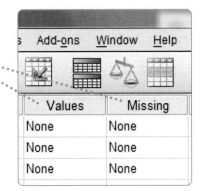

Step 5

This 'button' appears. Click on it.

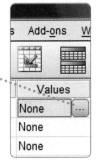

Step 6

This small window appears. Follow the next few steps. They show how male and female would be entered using the codes 1 for male and 2 for female.

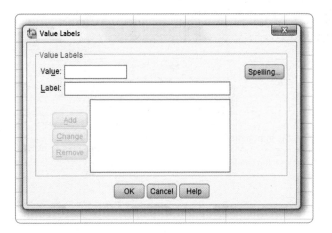

Step 7

Type 1 next to 'Value:' and male next to 'Label:'. Then click 'Add'.

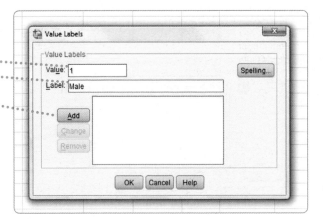

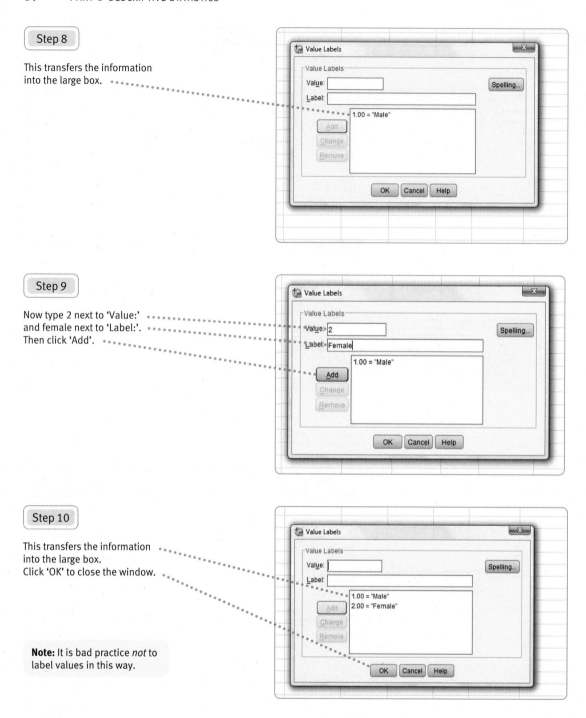

Step 8

This transfers the information into the large box.

Step 9

Now type 2 next to 'Value:' and female next to 'Label:'. Then click 'Add'.

Step 10

This transfers the information into the large box.
Click 'OK' to close the window.

Note: It is bad practice *not* to label values in this way.

■ More on Data View

Step 1

To return to 'Data View' click on this tab at the bottom left of the screen.

Step 2

This is how 'Data View' looks now.
The data can be entered for all of the variables
and cases. Remember that the value 5.00 was
entered earlier along with the variable names.
We can start entering the data in full now.

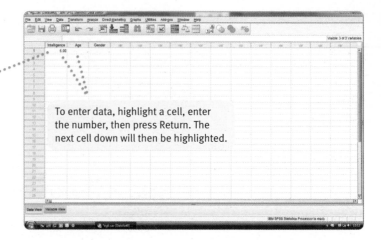

To enter data, highlight a cell, enter
the number, then press Return. The
next cell down will then be highlighted.

Step 3

This shows how a typical data spreadsheet
appears. Notice how the values for gender are
coded as 1.00 and 2.00. It is possible to reveal
their value labels instead. Click on the icon
that contains a triangle and the number 1 on
the task bar at the top.

Step 4

Now the values are given as male and female.

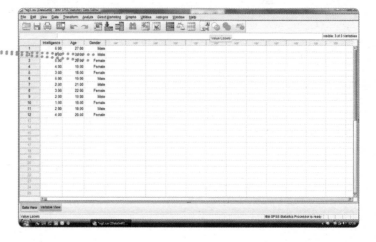

Select 'Data' to insert extra variables, extra cases, select cases and other data manipulations.

Select 'Window' to switch between the data spreadsheet and any output calculated on the data.

Step 5

There are many options available to you, including statistical analyses. Some of these options are shown here.

Select 'Transform' for a range of things that can be done with the data – such as recoding the values and computing combinations of variables.

Select 'Analyze' to access the full range of statistical calculations that SPSS calculates.

Select 'Graphs' for bar charts, scatterplots, and many other graphical representation methods.

■ A simple statistical calculation

Step 1

To calculate the average (i.e. mean) age, follow the following stages:
Click 'Analyze'.
Select 'Descriptive Statistics'.
Select 'Descriptives...'.

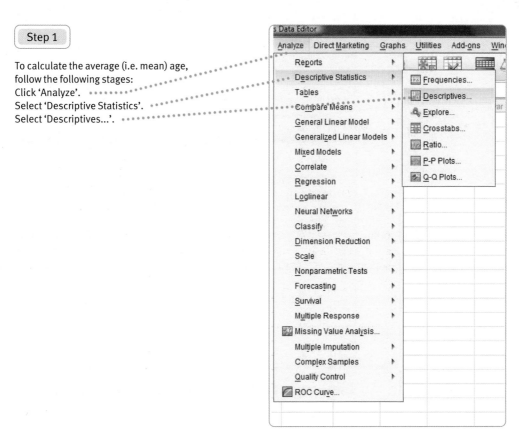

Step 2

This box appears. Highlight 'Intelligence' with mouse.

Click on arrowed button to move 'Intelligence' over into the 'Variable(s):' box.

Then click 'OK'.

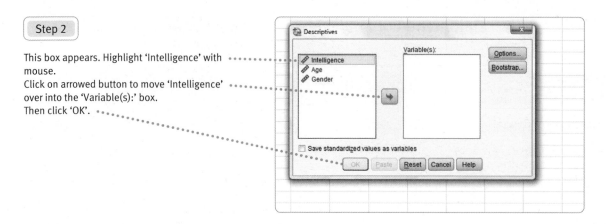

■ The SPSS output

The 'Data Editor' window is replaced in view by the SPSS Output window.

The first part of the output is a list of commands that can be used to run this procedure.

The second part is a table of statistics.

The average (mean) intelligence score is circled here for clarity.

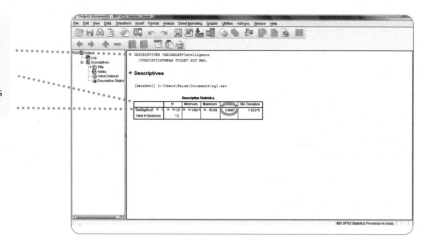

It is worth spending an hour or so simply practising with SPSS. You will find that this is the quickest way to learn. It is also advisable to use the tutorial offered by SPSS. The option to go through the tutorial appears when SPSS is first opened.

■ Major types of analysis and suggested SPSS procedures

Table 1.3	Types of analysis and SPSS procedures	
Type/purpose of analysis	**Suggested procedures**	**Chapter**
All types of study	Descriptive statistics, tables and diagrams	2–6
Assessing the relationship between two variables	Correlation coefficient	7
	Regression	8
Comparing two sets of scores for differences	Unrelated t-test	10
	Related t-test	11
	F-ratio test	13
	Unrelated ANOVA	13
	Related ANOVA	13
Comparing the means of two or more sets of scores	Unrelated ANOVA	13
	Related ANOVA	13
	Multiple comparisons	14
Comparing the means of two or more sets of scores (ANOVAs) while controlling for spurious variables influencing the data	ANCOVA	15
Complex experiments, etc. with *two* or more unrelated independent variables and *one* dependent variable:	Two (or more)-way ANOVA	14
● if you have related *and* unrelated measures	Mixed-design ANOVA	14
● if other variables may be affecting scores on the dependent variable	Analysis of covariance	15
ANOVA designs with several conceptually relevant dependent variables	MANOVA	16
Eliminating third variables which may be affecting a correlation coefficient	Partial correlation	17
Finding predictors for a score variable	Simple regression	8
	Stepwise multiple regression	19
	Hierarchical multiple regression	19
Finding predictors for a category variable	Multinomial logistic regression	20
	Binomial logistic regression	21
Analysing a questionnaire		9
Comparing frequency data	Chi-square	12
	Fisher exact test	12
	Log-linear analysis	22
Factor analysis		18

Key points

- Always ask yourself what sort of measurement it is you are considering – is it a numerical score on a variable or is it putting individuals into categories?

- Never assume that a number is necessarily a numerical score. Without checking, it could be a *frequency* of observations in a named category.

- Clarity of thinking is a virtue in statistics – you will rarely be expected to demonstrate great creativity in your statistical work. Understanding precisely the meaning of terms is an advantage in statistics.

CHAPTER 2

Describing variables

Tables and diagrams

Overview

- Tables and diagrams are important aspects of descriptive statistics (the description of the major features of the data). Examining data in this sort of detail is a vital stage of any statistical analysis and should never be omitted. This chapter describes how to create and present tables and diagrams for individual variables.

- Statistical tables and diagrams should effectively communicate information about your data. Beware of complexity.

- The type of data (nominal versus score) largely determines what an appropriate table and diagram will be.

- If the data are nominal, then simple frequency tables, bar charts or pie charts are most appropriate. The frequencies are simply the numbers of cases in each of the separate categories.

- If the data are scores, then frequency tables or histograms are appropriate. However, to keep the presentation uncluttered and to help clarify trends, it is often best to put the data into bands (or ranges) of adjacent scores.

Preparation

Remind yourself what a variable is from Chapter 1. Similarly, if you are still not sure of the nominal (categorisation) form of measurement and the use of numerical scores in measurement, then revise these too. Familiarise yourself with SPSS from Chapter 1 too, as the present chapter will show you the steps to produce tables and diagrams using SPSS.

2.1   Introduction

You probably know a lot more about statistics than you think. The mass media regularly feature statistical tables and diagrams; children become familiar with statistical tables and diagrams at school. Skill with these methods is essential because researchers collect large amounts of data from numerous people. If we asked 100 people their age, sex, marital status, number of children and occupation, this would yield 500 separate pieces of information, as there are five variables to consider. However, it is not very helpful to present these 500 measurements in your research report. This unprocessed information is called *raw data*. Statistical analysis has to be more than describing the raw ingredients. It requires the data to be structured in ways that *effectively communicate* the major trends. If you fail to structure your data, you may as well just give the reader copies of your questionnaires or observation schedules to interpret themselves.

Box 2.1   Research design issue

One of the easiest mistakes to make in research is to allow respondents in your research to give more than one answer to a question. So, for example, if you ask people to name their favourite television programme and allow each person more than one answer, you will find that the data can be very tricky to input into SPSS as it does not handle multiple responses very well. The data may also be very tricky to analyse thoroughly. Certainly it is possible to draw up tables and diagrams *only* if you intend to carry out a basic analysis, as the more advanced statistical procedures will become difficult to apply. You will sometimes read comments to the effect that the totals in a table exceed the number of respondents in the research. So, if you asked *n* = 100 respondents the following question:

In what ways can Stop and Search have an impact upon tackling crime and disorder (check all that apply)?

- Deterrence
- Crime detection
- Identifying crime hotspot areas
- Other _____

you may generate more than *n* = 100 answers (unless all tick only one answer) as you are allowing the respondents to tick multiple options to a single variable.

But if you asked *n* = 100 police officers the following question:

How many years have you worked with the police service?

- 0–1 year
- 2–5 years
- 6–10 years
- 11–20 years
- 21 or more years

you should generate *n* = 100 responses (unless some decide not to answer the question) as the respondents can tick only one option to a single variable.

See Chapter 9 on the analysis of a questionnaire/survey project. If you plan your data analysis in detail before you collect your data, you should be able to anticipate any difficulties.

2.2   Choosing tables and diagrams

There are very few rules regulating the production of tables and diagrams in statistics, so long as:

- They are clear and concise

- They communicate quickly the important trends in the data.

There is absolutely no point in using tables and diagrams that do not ease the task of communication. Probably the best way of deciding whether your tables and diagrams do their job well is to ask other people to interpret what they mean. Tables which are unclear to other people are generally useless.

Descriptive statistics are, by and large, relatively simple visual and numerical techniques for describing the major features of one's data. Descriptive statistics can be used by researchers:

- To understand the distribution of respondents' answers in the research

- To communicate the major characteristics of the data to others (such as through reports, dissertations and journal articles).

Never regard descriptive statistical analysis as an unnecessary or trivial stage in research. It is probably more informative than any other aspect of data analysis.

- As long as you are able to decide whether your data are either numerical scores or nominal (category) data, there are few other choices to be made, since the available tables and diagrams are essentially dependent upon this distinction.

■ Tables and diagrams for nominal (category) data

One of the main characteristics of tables and diagrams for nominal (category) data is that they have to show the *frequencies* of cases in each category used. While there may be as many categories as you wish, it is *not* the function of statistical analysis to communicate all of the data's detail; the task is to identify the major trends. For example, imagine you are researching the public's attitudes towards young people and anti-social behaviour. If you ask respondents in your research their occupations then you might find that they mention tens if not hundreds of different job titles – newsagents, homemakers, company executives and so forth. Simply counting the frequencies with which different job titles are mentioned results in a vast number of categories. You need to think of relevant and meaningful ways of reducing this vast number into a smaller number of much broader categories that might reveal important trends. For example, since the research is about a criminal justice issue, you might wish to form a category made up of those involved in criminal justice – some might be youth justice officers, some youth workers, some social workers, and so forth. Instead of keeping these as different categories, they might be combined into a category 'youth worker'. There are no hard-and-fast rules about combining to form broader categories. The following might be useful rules of thumb:

- Keep your number of categories low, especially when you have only small numbers of respondents in your research.

- Try to make your 'combined' categories meaningful and sensible in the light of the purposes of your research. It would be nonsense, for example, to categorise jobs by the letter of the alphabet with which they start – nurses, nuns, nursery teachers and national footballers all have jobs beginning with the same letter, but it is very difficult to see any other common thread which allows them to be combined meaningfully.

Table 2.1	Occupational status of respondents in the research expressed as frequencies and percentage frequencies	
Occupation	**Frequency**	**Percentage frequency**
Administrator	17	21.25
Florist	3	3.75
Police officer	23	28.75
Student	20	25.00
Other	17	21.25

In terms of drawing tables, all we do is to list the categories we have chosen and give the frequency of cases that fall into each of the categories, as in Table 2.1. The frequencies are presented in two ways in this table – *simple* frequencies and *percentage* frequencies. A percentage frequency is the frequency expressed as a percentage of the total of the frequencies (or total number of cases, usually).

Notice also that one of the categories is called 'other'. This consists of those cases which do not fit into any of the main categories. Generally, all other things being equal, it is best to have a small number of cases in the 'other' category.

Calculation 2.1

Percentage frequencies

Many readers will not need this, but if you are a little rusty with simple maths, it might be helpful.

The percentage frequency for a particular category, say for students, is the frequency in that category expressed as a percentage of the total frequencies in the data table.

Step 1 What is the category frequency? For students in Table 2.1:

$$\text{category frequency}_{[students]} = 20$$

Step 2 Add up all of the frequencies in Table 2.1:

$$\text{total frequencies} = \text{administrators} + \text{florists} + \text{police officers} + \text{students} + \text{other}$$
$$= 17 + 3 + 23 + 20 + 17$$
$$= 80$$

Step 3

$$\text{percentage frequency}_{[students]} = \frac{\text{category frequency}_{[students]} \times 100}{\text{total frequencies}}$$
$$= \frac{20 \times 100}{80} = \frac{2000}{80} = 25\%$$

One advantage of using computers is that they enable experimentation with different schemes of categorising data in order to decide which is best for your purposes. In this you would use initially narrow categories for coding your data. Then you can tell the computer which of these to combine into broader categories.

■ Pie diagrams

Sometimes it is preferable to turn frequency tables into diagrams. Good diagrams are quickly understood and add variety to the presentation. The main types of diagram for nominal (category) data are *pie diagrams* and *bar charts*. A pie diagram is a very familiar form of presentation – it simply expresses each category as a slice of a pie which represents all cases (see Figure 2.1).

Notice that the *number* of slices is small – a multitude of slices can be confusing. Each slice is clearly marked with its category name, and the percentage frequency in each category also appears.

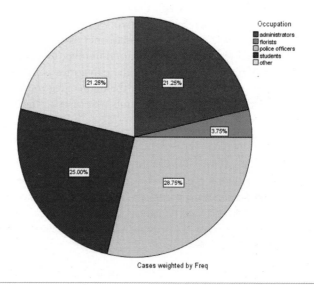

| FIGURE 2.1 | A simple pie diagram showing type of occupation |

Calculation 2.2

Slices for a pie diagram

There is nothing difficult in constructing a pie diagram. Our recommendation is that you turn each of your frequencies into a percentage frequency. Since there are 360 degrees in a circle, if you multiply each percentage frequency by 3.6 you will obtain the angle (in degrees) of the slice of the pie which you need to mark out. In order to create the diagram you will require a protractor to measure the angles. However, computer graph packages are standard at any university or college and do an impressive job.

In Table 2.1, 25.00% of cases were students. In order to turn this into the correct angle for the slice of the pie, you simply need to multiply 25.00 by 3.6 to give an angle of 90 degrees.

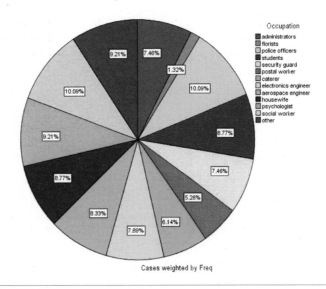

Cases weighted by Freq

FIGURE 2.2   A poor pie diagram showing respondents' occupations

---

Figure 2.2 shows a *bad* example of a pie diagram for purposes of comparison. There are several problems with this pie diagram:

● There are too many small slices identified by different shading patterns and the legend takes time to decode.

● It is not too easily seen what each slice concerns, and the relative sizes of the slices are difficult to judge. We have the size of the slices around the figure and a separate legend or key to identify the components to help cope with the overcrowding problem. In other words, too many categories have resulted in a diagram which is far from easy to read – a cardinal sin in any statistical diagram.

A simple frequency table might be more effective in this case.

■ Bar charts

Another very familiar form of statistical diagram for nominal (category) data is the *bar chart*. Again these charts are very common in the media. Basically they are diagrams in which bars represent the size of each category. An example is shown in Figure 2.3.

The relative lengths (or heights) of the bars quickly reveal the main trends in the data. With a bar chart there is very little to remember other than that the bars have a standard space separating them. The spaces indicate that the categories are not in a numerical order; they are frequencies of categories, *not* scores.

It is hard to go wrong with a bar chart (that is not a challenge!) so long as you remember the following:

● The heights of the bars represent frequencies (number of cases) in a category.

● Each bar should be clearly labelled as to the category it represents.

● Too many bars make bar charts hard to follow.

● Avoid having *many* empty or near-empty categories which represent very few cases. Generally, the information about substantial categories is the most important. (Small categories can be combined together as an 'other' category.)

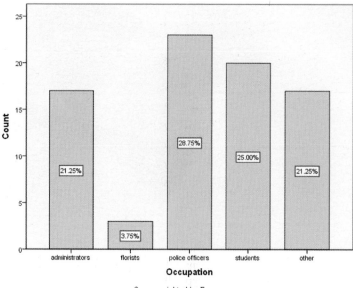

Cases weighted by Freq

FIGURE 2.3   Bar chart showing occupational categories in Table 2.1

- Nevertheless, if *important* categories have very few entries then this needs recording. So, for example, a researcher who is particularly interested in opportunities for women surveys people in top management and finds very few women employed in such jobs. It is important to draw attention to this in the bar chart of males and females in top management. Once again, there are no hard-and-fast rules to guide you – common sense will take you a long way.

- Make sure that the vertical axis (the heights of the bars) is clearly marked as being frequencies or percentage frequencies.

- The bars should be of equal width.

In newspapers and on television you are likely to come across a variant of the bar chart called the *pictogram*. In this, the bars of the bar chart are replaced by varying sized drawings of something eye-catching to do with your categories. Thus, pictures of men or women of varying heights, for example, replace the bars. Pictograms are rarely used in professional presentations. The main reason is that pictures of things get wider as well as taller as they increase in size. This can misrepresent the relative sizes of the categories, given that readers forget that it is only the height of the picture that counts.

◼ Tables and diagrams for numerical score data

One crucial consideration when deciding what tables and diagrams to use for score data is the number of separate scores recorded for the variable in question. This can vary markedly. So, for example, age in the general population can range from newly born to over 100 years of age. If we merely recorded ages to the nearest whole year then a table or diagram may have entries for 100 different ages. Such a table or diagram would look horrendous. If we recorded age to the nearest month, then we could multiply this number of ages by 12. Such scores can be grouped into bands or ranges of scores to allow effective tabulation (Table 2.2).

Table 2.2	Ages expressed as age bands

Age range	Frequency
0–9 years	19
10–19 years	33
20–29 years	17
30–39 years	22
40–49 years	17
50 years and over	3

In social science research, it is also fairly common to use questions which pre-specify just a few response alternatives. The so-called Likert-type questionnaire item is a good case in point. Typically this looks something like this:

Statistics is my favourite university subject:
Strongly agree   Agree   Neither agree nor disagree   Disagree   Strongly disagree

Respondents completing this questionnaire circle the response alternative which best fits their personal opinion. It is conventional in this type of research to code these different response alternatives on a 5-point scale from 1 to 5. This scale will have only five possible values, so:

Strongly agree will be coded as 1.
Neither agree nor disagree will be coded as 3.
Strongly disagree will be coded as 5.

Tabulating such data is quite straightforward. Indeed, you can simply report the numbers or frequencies of replies for each of the different categories or scores as in Table 2.3.

A *histogram* might be the best form of statistical diagram to represent these data. At first sight histograms look very much like bar charts but without gaps between the bars. This is because the histogram does not represent distinct unrelated categories but different points on a *numerical* measurement scale. So a histogram of the above data might look like Figure 2.4.

Table 2.3	Distribution of students' attitudes towards statistics

Response category	Value	Frequency
Strongly agree	1	17
Agree	2	14
Neither agree nor disagree	3	6
Disagree	4	2
Strongly disagree	5	1

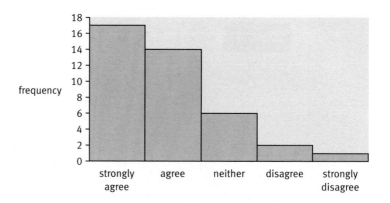

Tables and diagrams should present major features of your data in a simple and easily assimilated form. So sometimes you will have to use *bands of scores* rather than individual score values just as you did for Table 2.2. So if we asked 100 people their ages we could categorise their replies into bands such as 0–9 years, 10–19 years, 30–39 years, 40–49 years and a final category of those 50 years and over. By using bands we reduce the risk of empty parts of the table and allow any trends to become clear (Figure 2.5).

How one chooses the bands to use is an important question. The answer is a bit of luck and judgement, and a lot of trial and error. It is very time-consuming to rejig the ranges of the bands when one is analysing the data by hand. One big advantage of computers is that they will recode your scores into bands repeatedly until you have tables which seem to do the job as well as possible. The criterion is still whether the table communicates information effectively.

The one rule is that the bands ought to be of the same size – that is, they should cover, for example, equal ranges of scores. Generally this is easy except at the upper and lower ends of the distribution. Perhaps you wish to use 'over 70' as your upper range. This, in modern practice, can be done as a bar of the same width as the others, but it must be very carefully marked.

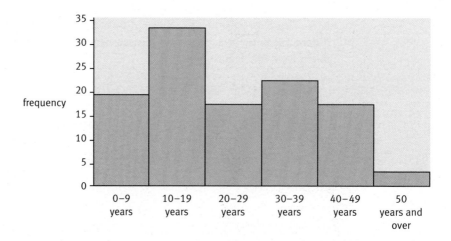

FIGURE 2.5   Use of bands of scores to enable simple presentation

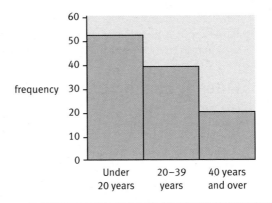

| FIGURE 2.6 | Histogram showing 'collapsed' categories |

You might want to redefine the bands of scores and generate another histogram based on identical data but a different set of bands (Figure 2.6). It requires some thought to decide which of the diagrams is best for a particular purpose. There are no hard-and-fast rules.

2.3   Errors to avoid

There are a few mistakes that you can make in drawing up tables and diagrams:

- *Do not* forget to head the table or diagram with a succinct description of what it concerns. You will notice that we have done our best throughout this chapter to supply each table and diagram with a clear title.

- Label everything on the table or diagram as clearly as possible. What this means is that you have to mark your bar charts and histograms in a way that tells the reader what each bar means. Then you must indicate what the height of the bar refers to – probably either frequency or percentage frequency.

Note that this chapter has concentrated on describing a *single* variable as clearly as possible. In Chapter 6, methods of making tables and diagrams showing the relationships between two or more variables are described.

2.4   SPSS analysis

■ The data to be analysed

SPSS is generally used to summarise raw data but it can use data that have already been summarised as shown in Table 2.1. In other words, since the data in Table 2.1 are based on 80 people, the data would occupy 80 cells of one column in the 'Data Editor' window and each occupation would be coded with a separate number, so that administrators might be coded 1, florists 2 and so on. Thus, one would need 17 rows containing 1 to represent administrators, three rows containing 2 to represent florists, and so on. However, it is possible to carry out certain analyses on summarised data provided that we appropriately weight the categories by the number of frequency of cases in them.

■ Entering summarised categorical or frequency data by weighting

It seems better practice to define your variables in 'Variable View' of the 'Data Editor' before entering the data in 'Data View' because we can remove the decimal places where they are not necessary. So we always do this first. For this table we need two columns in 'Data View': one to say what the categories are, and the other to give the frequencies for these categories. In 'Variable View' variables are presented as rows.

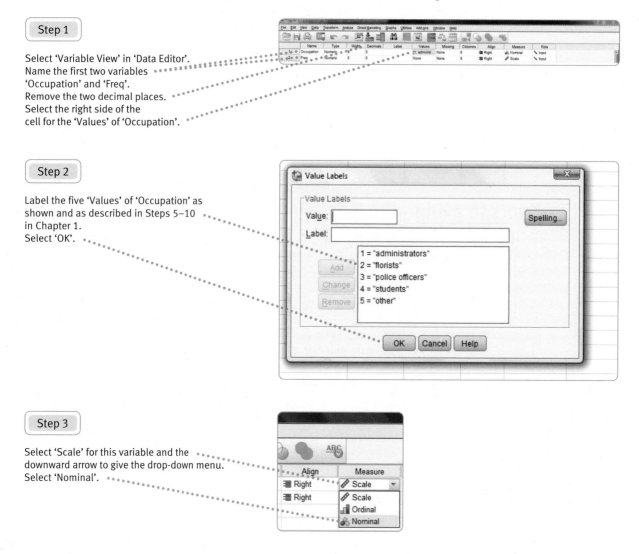

Step 1

Select 'Variable View' in 'Data Editor'.
Name the first two variables
'Occupation' and 'Freq'.
Remove the two decimal places.
Select the right side of the
cell for the 'Values' of 'Occupation'.

Step 2

Label the five 'Values' of 'Occupation' as
shown and as described in Steps 5–10
in Chapter 1.
Select 'OK'.

Step 3

Select 'Scale' for this variable and the
downward arrow to give the drop-down menu.
Select 'Nominal'.

Step 4

Select 'Data View'. Enter the data as shown.

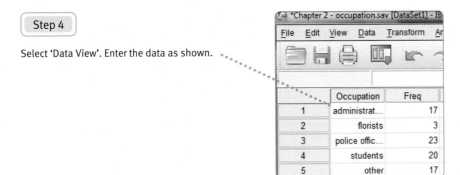

Step 5

Select 'Data' and 'Weight Cases...'.

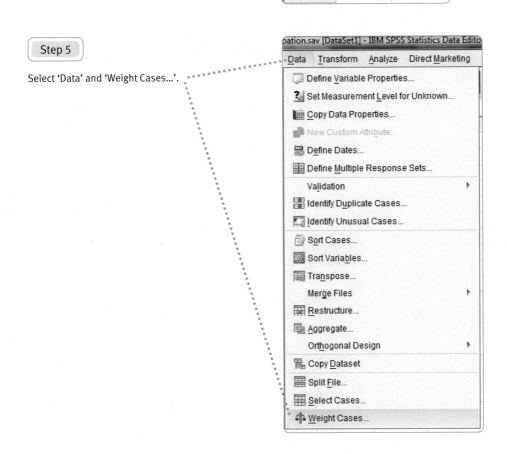

Step 6

Select 'Freq', 'Weight cases by' and click on the arrow button to put it in the 'Frequency Variable:' box.
Select 'OK'.

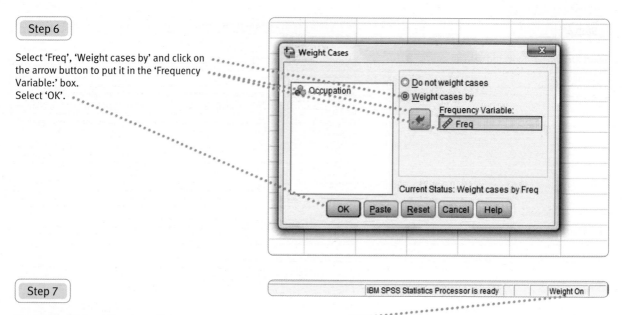

Step 7

The cases, which are the occupations, are now weighted by the frequencies as shown by the 'Weight On' message in the lower right-hand corner of the Data Editor.

■ Percentage frequencies

Step 1

Select 'Analyze'
→ 'Descriptive Statistics'
→ 'Frequencies...'.

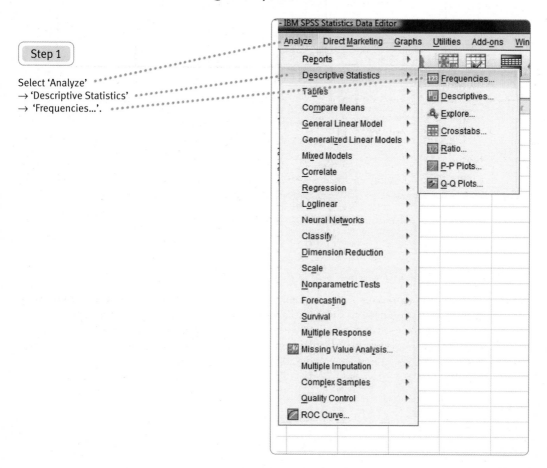

Step 6

Select 'Occupation' and click on the arrow button to put 'Occupation' in the 'Variable(s):' box.
Select 'OK'.

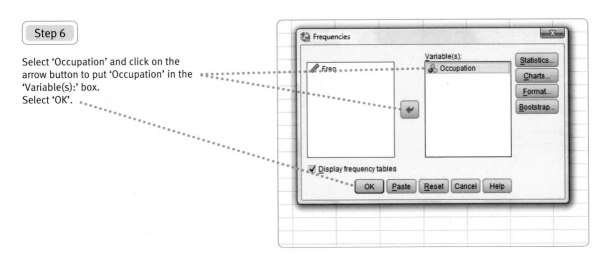

Interpreting the output

Occupation

		Frequency	Percent	Valid Percent	Cumulative Percent
Valid	administrators	17	21.3	21.3	21.3
	florists	3	3.8	3.8	25.0
	police officers	23	28.8	28.8	53.8
	students	20	25.0	25.0	78.8
	other	17	21.3	21.3	100.0
	Total	80	100.0	100.0	

- The first column of this table gives the labels of the five categories, and the second column gives their actual fequencies.

- The third column gives the percentage frequency of each category, including any missing values of which there are none. So 17 is 21.3% of a total of 80.

- The fourth column gives the percentage frequency, excluding any missing values. As there are none, these percentages are the same as those in the third column.

- The fifth column adds the percentages down the table, so 25.0% of the cases are florists.

Reporting the output

Only the category labels, the frequency and percentage frequency need to be reported; consequently you need to simplify this table if you are going to present it. If the occupation was missing for some of the cases you would need to decide whether you would present percentages including or excluding them. There is no need to present both sets of figures. Also omit the term 'Valid' in the first column as its meaning may only be familiar to SPSS users.

2.5   Pie diagram of category data

Step 1

Select 'Graphs'
→ 'Legacy Dialogs'
→ 'Pie...'.

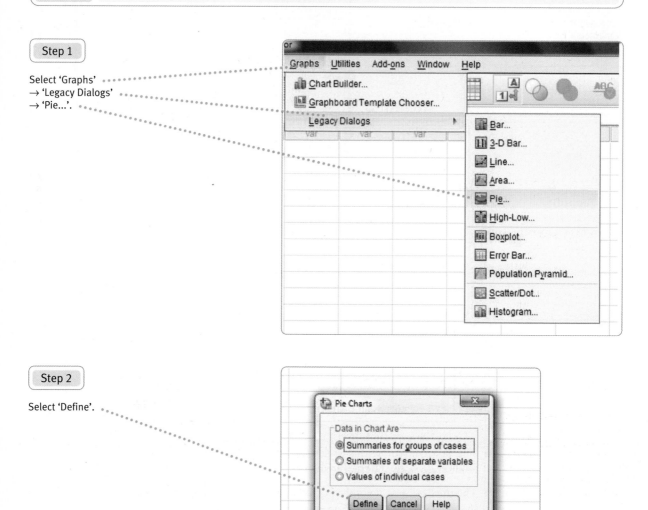

Step 2

Select 'Define'.

Step 3

Highlight 'Occupation' and click on the arrow
to place it into the 'Define Slices by:' box.
Select 'OK'.

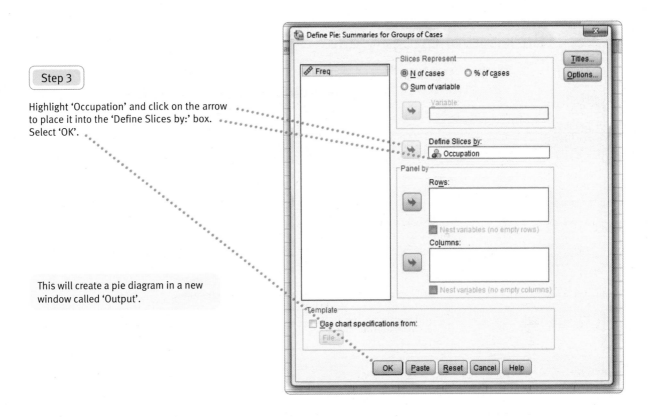

This will create a pie diagram in a new
window called 'Output'.

Step 4

Click twice on the pie diagram to bring up
the 'Chart Editor'.
Select 'Elements' → 'Show Data Labels'
to add percentage frequencies.
This brings up a 'Properties' pop-up
box where you can change the data
labels from 'Percent' to 'Count'.

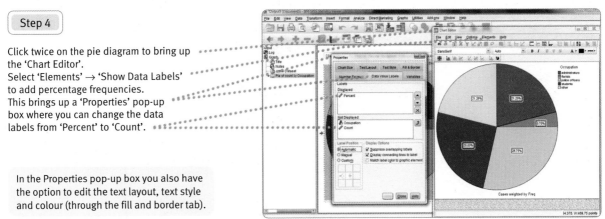

In the Properties pop-up box you also have
the option to edit the text layout, text style
and colour (through the fill and border tab).

2.6 Bar chart of category data

Step 1

Select 'Graphs'
→ 'Legacy Dialogs'
→ 'Bar...'.

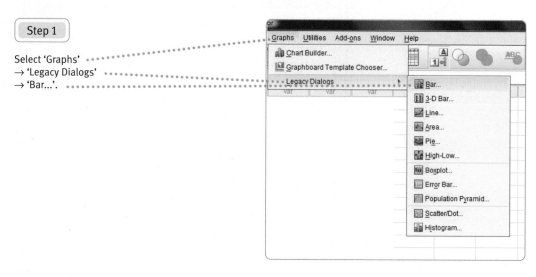

Step 2

Select 'Define'.

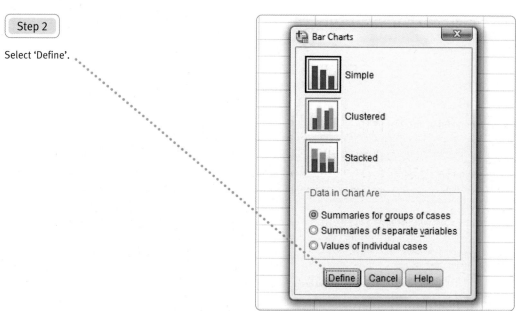

Step 3

Highlight 'Occupation' and click on the arrow to place it into the 'Category Axis:' box. Select 'OK'.

This will create a bar chart in a new window called 'Output'.

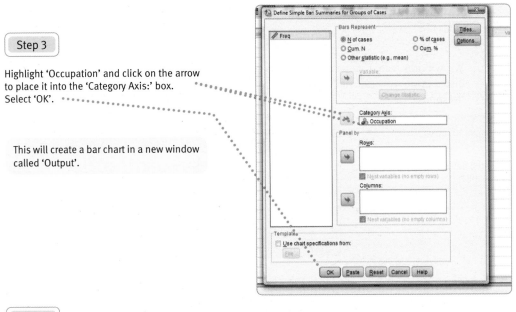

Step 4

Click twice on the bar chart to bring up the 'Chart Editor'. Follow the same procedure as for the pie diagram to edit the bar chart (Figure 2.7).

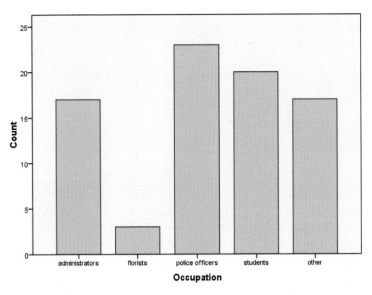

Cases weighted by Freq

FIGURE 2.7   Bar chart of category data

2.7 Histograms

We will illustrate the making of a histogram with the data in Table 2.3 which shows the distribution of students' attitudes towards statistics. We have labelled this variable 'Response'.

Step 1

In the 'Data Editor' enter the data, weight and label them as described earlier.

	Response	Freq	Va
1	1	17	
2	2	14	
3	3	6	
4	4	2	
5	5	1	

Step 2

Select 'Graphs'
→ 'Legacy Dialogs'
→ 'Histogram...'.

Step 3

Highlight 'Response' and click on the arrow to place it in the 'Variable:' box. Select 'OK'.

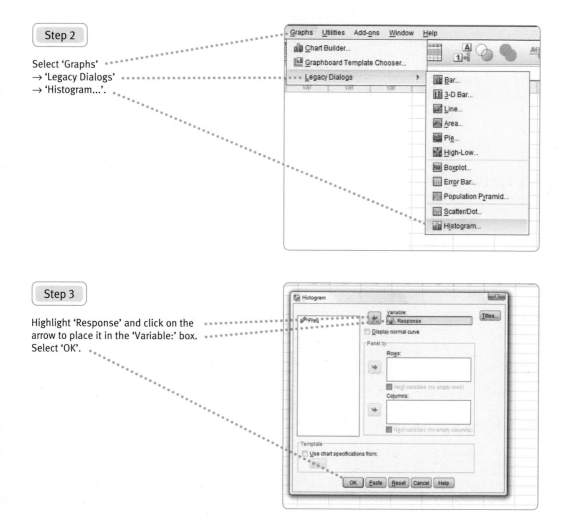

Figure 2.8 is the histogram that you can edit using the 'Chart Editor'.

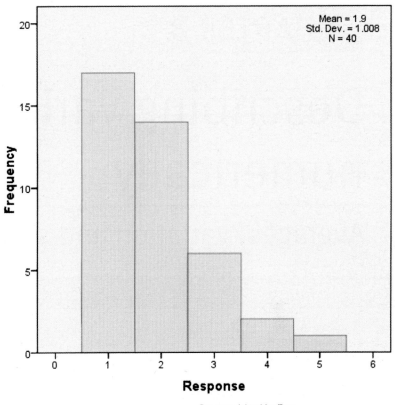

Cases weighted by Freq

FIGURE 2.8	Histogram of students' responses (5-point scale)

Key points

- Try to make your tables and diagrams useful. It is not usually their purpose to record the data as you collected it in your research. Of course you can list your data in the appendix of projects that you carry out, but this is not useful as a way of illustrating trends. It is part of a researcher's job to make the data accessible to the reader in a structured form that is easily understood.

- Especially when using computers, it is very easy to generate *useless* tables and diagrams. This is usually because computer analysis encourages you not to examine your raw data in any detail. This implies that you should always regard your first analyses as tentative and merely a step towards something better.

- If a table is not clear to you, it is unlikely to be any clearer to anyone else.

- Check each table and diagram for clear and full labelling of each part. Especially, check that frequencies are clearly marked as such.

- Check that there is a clear, helpful title to each table and diagram.

CHAPTER 3

Describing variables numerically

Averages, variation and spread

- Scores can be described numerically – for example, the average of a sample of scores can be given.

- There are several measures of central tendency – the most typical or most likely score.

- The mean score is simply the average score assessed by the total of the scores divided by the number of scores.

- The mode is the numerical value of the most frequently occurring score.

- The median is the score in the middle if the scores are ordered from smallest to largest.

- The spread of scores can be expressed as the range, which is the difference between the largest and the smallest score.

- Variance (an indicator of variability around the average) indicates the spread of scores in the data. Unlike the range, variance takes into account all of the scores. It is a ubiquitous statistical concept.

- Nominal data can only be described in terms of the numbers of cases falling in each category. The mode is the only measure of central tendency that can be applied to nominal (category) data.

Preparation

Revise the meaning of nominal (category) data and numerical score data.

3.1 Introduction: mean, median and mode

The concept of the central tendency of a set of scores refers to the most typical and likely scores in the distribution of measurements. There are three main measures of the typical scores: the arithmetic mean, the mode and the median. These are quite distinct concepts but generally simple enough in themselves.

■ The arithmetic mean

The arithmetic mean is calculated by summing all of the scores in a distribution and dividing by the number of scores. This is the everyday concept of average. In statistical notation we can express this mean as follows:

$$\bar{X}_{mean} = \frac{\sum X_{[scores]}}{N_{[number\ of\ scores]}}$$

As this is the first statistical formula we have presented, you should take very careful note of what each symbol means:

X is the statistical symbol for a score
$\sum$ is the summation or sigma sign
$\sum X$ means add up all of the scores X
N is the number of scores
$\bar{X}$ is the statistical symbol for the arithmetic mean of a set of scores.

We have added a few comments in small square brackets [just like this]. Although mathematicians may not like them very much, you might find they help you to interpret a formula a little more quickly.

Although you probably do not need the formula to work out the arithmetic mean, it is useful at this stage to make sure that you understand how to decode the symbols (Calculation 3.1). This is a simple example but contains several of the important elements of statistical formulae. It is good preparation to go through the calculation using this formula.

Calculation 3.1

The numerical or arithmetic mean

To illustrate the calculation of the arithmetic mean we can use the following six scores:

$X_1 = 7$ $X_3 = 4$ $X_5 = 7$
$X_2 = 5$ $X_4 = 7$ $X_6 = 5$

The subscripts following the Xs above define a particular score.

$$\bar{X}_{mean} = \frac{\sum X_{[scores]}}{N_{[number\ of\ scores]}}$$

$$= \frac{X_1 + X_2 + X_3 + X_4 + X_5 + X_6}{N} = \frac{7 + 5 + 4 + 7 + 7 + 5}{6} = \frac{35}{6} = 5.83$$

Therefore, the arithmetic mean of the six scores is $M = 5.83$ (M = mean).

■ The median

The median is the middle score of a set if the scores are organised from the smallest to the largest. Thus the scores 7, 5, 4, 7, 7, 5, 3, 4, 6, 8, 5 become 3, 4, 4, 5, 5, 5, 6, 7, 7, 7, 8 when put in order from the smallest to the largest. Since there are 11 scores and the median is the middle score from the smallest to the largest, the median has to be the sixth score, i.e. 5.

With odd numbers of scores all of which are different, the median is easily calculated since there is a single score that corresponds to the middle score in the set of scores. However, if there is an even number of all different scores in the set then the mid-point will not be a single score but two scores. So if you have 12 different scores placed in order from smallest to largest, the median will be somewhere between the sixth and seventh score from smallest. There is no such score, of course, by definition – the 6.5th score just does not exist. What we could do in these circumstances is to take the average of the sixth and seventh scores to give us an estimate of the median.

For the distribution of 40 scores shown in Table 3.1 (remember the frequency is the number of times the score appears), the middle score from the smallest is somewhere between the 20th and 21st scores. Thus the median is somewhere between score 5 (the 20th score) and score 6 (the 21st score). One could give the average of these two as the median score – that is, the median is 5.5. For most purposes this is good enough.

You may find that computer programs give different values from this. The computer program is making adjustments since there may be several identical scores near the median. SPSS will calculate the mean.

Table 3.1	Frequency distribution of 40 scores	
Score		**Frequency (f)**
1		1
2		2
3		4
4		6
5		7
6		8
7		5
8		3
9		2
10		1
11		0
12		1

■ The mode

The mode is the most frequently occurring category of score. It is merely the most common score or most frequent category of scores. In other words, you can apply the mode to any category of data and not just scores. In the above example where the scores were 7, 5, 4, 7, 7, 5 we could represent the scores in terms of their frequencies of occurrence (Table 3.2).

Table 3.2	Frequencies of scores	
Score		**Frequency (f)**
4		1
5		2
6		0
7		3

Table 3.3	A bimodal frequency distribution	
Score		**Frequency (f)**
3		1
4		2
5		3
6		1
7		3
8		1

Frequencies are often represented as f in statistics. It is very easy to see in this example that the most frequently occurring score is 7 with a frequency of 3. So the mode of this distribution is 7.

If we take the slightly different set of scores 7, 5, 4, 7, 7, 5, 3, 4, 6, 8, 5, the frequency distribution of these scores is shown in Table 3.3. Here there is no single mode since scores 5 and 7 jointly have the highest frequency of 3. This sort of distribution is called bimodal and the two modes are 5 and 7. The general term multimodal implies that a frequency distribution has several modes.

The mode is the only measure in this chapter that applies to nominal (category) data as well as numerical score data.

Box 3.1	Key concepts

Identifying outliers statistically

Outliers are a few scores which are out of step with the rest of the data and can mislead the researcher. Routinely, good researchers examine their data for possible outliers simply by inspecting tables of frequencies or scatterplots, for example. This is normally sufficient but does involve an element of judgement which you may not be comfortable with. There are more objective ways of identifying outliers which reduce this subjective element. Essentially what is done is to define precise limits beyond which a score is suspected of being an outlier. One simple way ➡

of doing this is based on the interquartile range (see Section 3.3) which is not affected by outliers, since it is based on the middle 50% of scores put in order of their size.

To calculate the interquartile range, essentially the scores on a variable are arranged from smallest to largest and the 25% of smallest scores and the 25% of largest scores are ignored. This leaves the 50% of scores in the middle of the original distribution. The difference between the largest and the smallest score in this middle 50% is the interquartile range. Outliers, which by definition are unusually large or small scores, cannot affect the interquartile range, since they will be in the top or bottom 25% of scores and thus eliminated in calculating the interquartile range.

Imagine that we had the following scores for the IQs (Intelligence Quotients) from a sample of 12 individuals:

120, 115, 65, 140, 122, 142, 125, 135, 122, 138, 144, 118

Common sense would suggest that the score of 65 is uncharacteristic of the sample's IQs in general so we would probably identify it as a potential outlier anyway.

To calculate the interquartile range we would first rearrange the scores from smallest to largest (or get a computer to do all of the work for us). This gives us:

65, 115, 118, 120, 122, 122, 125, 135, 138, 140, 142, 144

Since there are 12 scores, to calculate the interquartile range we delete the three (i.e. 25%) lowest scores and also delete the three (i.e. 25%) highest scores. The three lowest scores are 65, 115 and 118 and the three highest scores are 140, 142 and 144. With the extreme quarters deleted, we have the following six scores which are the middle 50% of scores:

120, 122, 122, 125, 135, 138

The interquartile range is the largest of these scores minus the smallest. Thus the interquartile range is $138 - 120 = 16$ in this case. This interquartile range is multiplied by 1.5 which gives us $1.5 \times 16 = 24$.

Outliers among the low scores are defined as any score which is smaller than the smallest score in the interquartile range $- 24 = 120 - 24 = 96$. Outliers among the high scores are defined as any score which is bigger than the largest score in the interquartile range $+ 24 = 138 + 24 = 162$. In other words, scores which are not between 96 and 162 are outliers in this example. The IQ of 65 is thus regarded as an outlier. On the assumption that the scores are normally distributed, less than 1% of scores would be defined as outliers. This method identifies the moderate outliers.

Extreme outliers are identified in much the same way but the interquartile range is multiplied by 3 (rather than 1.5). This gives us $3 \times 16 = 48$. Extreme outliers among the low scores are scores which are smaller than $120 - 48 = 72$. Extreme outliers among the high scores are scores larger than $138 + 48 = 186$. Thus the participant who has an IQ of 65 would be identified as an extreme outlier. In normally distributed scores, extreme outliers will occur only about once in half a million scores.

It would be usual practice to delete outliers from your data. You might also wish to compare the outcome of the analysis with the complete data and with outliers excluded. If you delete the outliers from your data, it is common practice to stipulate this in your research.

3.2   Comparison of mean, median and mode

Usually the mean, median and mode will give different values of the central tendency when applied to the same set of scores. It is only when a distribution is perfectly symmetrical and the distribution peaks in the middle that they coincide completely. Regard big differences between the mean, median and mode as a sign that your distribution of scores is rather asymmetrical or lopsided. Distributions of scores do not have to be perfectly symmetrical for statistical analysis.

3.3   The spread of scores: variability

The concept of variability is essential in statistics. It is related to (but is not identical with) the statistical term variance. Variance is nothing more nor less than a mathematical formula that serves as a useful indicator of variability.

The following set of ages of 12 university students can be used to illustrate some different ways of measuring variability in our data:

18 years	21 years	23 years	18 years	19 years	19 years
19 years	33 years	18 years	19 years	19 years	20 years

These 12 students vary in age from 18 to 33 years. In other words, the range covers a 15-year period. The interval from youngest to oldest (or tallest to shortest, or fattest to thinnest) is called the *range* – a useful statistical concept. As a statistical concept, range is always expressed as a single number such as 20 years and seldom as an interval, say from 19 to 24 years.

One trouble with range is that it can be influenced by outliers/extreme cases. Thus the 33-year-old student in the above set of ages is having a big influence on the range of ages of the students. This is because s/he is much older than most of the students. For this reason, the interquartile range has advantages. To calculate the interquartile range we split the age distribution into quarters and take the range of the middle two quarters (or middle 50%), ignoring the extreme quarters. Since we have 12 students, we delete the three youngest (the three 18-year-olds) and the three oldest (aged 33, 23 and 21). This leaves us with the middle two quarters (the middle 50%) which includes five 19-year-olds and one 20-year-old. The range of this middle two quarters, or the interquartile range, is one year (from 19 years to 20 years). The interquartile range is sometimes a better indicator of the variability of, say, age than the full range, because extreme ages are excluded.

Although the range has a number of useful advantages, it does ignore a lot of information. For example, it does not consider all the scores in the set, only the extreme ones. For this reason, there are other techniques which can measure the spread/variability of scores and how they differ from the mean score of the set. These measures are called the *mean deviation* and *variance*.

■ Mean deviation

To calculate mean deviation, we have to work out the mean of the set of scores and how much each score in the set differs from that mean. These deviations are then added up, ignoring the negative signs, to give the total of deviations from the mean. Finally, we can divide by the number of scores to give the average or mean deviation from the mean of the set of scores. If we take the ages of the students listed above, we find that the total of the ages is $18 + 21 + 23 + 18 + 19 + 19 + 19 + 33 + 18 + 19 + 19 + 20 = 246$. Divide this total by 12 and we get the average age in the set to be 20.5 years. Now if we subtract 20.5 years from the age of each of the students we get the figures in Table 3.4.

The average amount of deviation from the mean (ignoring the sign) is known as the mean deviation. For the deviations in Table 3.4 this would give a value of 2.6 years.

■ Variance

Variance is calculated in an almost identical way to mean deviation but for one thing. When we draw up a table to calculate the variance, we *square* each deviation from the mean before summing the total of these squared deviations, as shown in Table 3.5.

Table 3.4	Deviations from the mean
Score − mean	**Deviation from mean**
18 − 20.5	−2.5
21 − 20.5	0.5
23 − 20.5	2.5
18 − 20.5	−2.5
19 − 20.5	−1.5
19 − 20.5	−1.5
19 − 20.5	−1.5
33 − 20.5	12.5
18 − 20.5	−2.5
19 − 20.5	−1.5
19 − 20.5	−1.5
20 − 20.5	−0.5

Table 3.5	Squared deviations from the mean	
Score − mean	**Deviation from mean**	**Square of deviation from mean**
18 − 20.5	−2.5	6.25
21 − 20.5	0.5	0.25
23 − 20.5	2.5	6.25
18 − 20.5	−2.5	6.25
19 − 20.5	−1.5	2.25
19 − 20.5	−1.5	2.25
19 − 20.5	−1.5	2.25
33 − 20.5	12.5	156.25
18 − 20.5	−2.5	6.25
19 − 20.5	−1.5	2.25
19 − 20.5	−1.5	2.25
20 − 20.5	−0.5	0.25
Total	**0**	**193**

The total of the squared deviations from the mean is 193. If we divide this by the number of scores (12), it gives us the value of the variance, which equals 16.08 in this case.

Expressing variance as a formula (see Calculation 3.2):

$$\text{Variance} = \frac{\sum(X - \bar{X})^2}{N}$$

The calculation of variance above corresponds to this formula. However, in statistics there are often quicker ways of doing calculations. These quicker methods involve computational formulae. The computational formula for variance is important and worth memorising as it occurs in many contexts.

> **Box 3.2   Focus on**

Using negative (−) values

Some statistical techniques can generate data involving negative signs. Negative values occur in statistical analyses because working out differences between scores is common. The mean is often taken away from scores, or one score is subtracted from another. Negative values are not a problem since either the computer or the calculator will do them for you. A positive value is one which is bigger than zero. Often the + sign is omitted as it is taken for granted.

A negative value (or minus value or − value) is a number which is smaller than (less than) zero. The negative sign is never omitted. A value of −20 is a smaller number than −3 (whereas a value of +20 is a bigger number than +3).

Negative values should cause few problems in terms of calculations – the calculator or computer has no difficulties with them. With a calculator you will need to enter that a number is a negative. A key labelled +/− is often used to do this. On a computer, the number must be entered with a − sign.

Probably, the following are the only things you need to know to be able to understand negative numbers in statistics:

- If a negative number is multiplied by another negative number the outcome is a positive number. So $-2 \times -3 = +6$. This is also the case when a number is squared. Thus $-3^2 = +9$. You need this information to understand how the standard deviation and variance formulae work.

- If you have got negative values for your scores, it is usually advantageous to add a number of sufficient size to make all of the scores positive. This normally makes absolutely no difference to the outcome of your statistical analysis. For example, the variance and standard deviation of −2, −5 and −6 are exactly the same if we add 6 to each of them. That is, calculate the variance and standard deviation of +4, +1 and 0 and you will find them to be identical to those for −2, −5 and −6. It is important that the same number is added to all of your scores. Doing this is helpful, since many of us experience anxiety about negative values and prefer it if they are not there.

> # Calculation 3.2

Variance using the computational formula

The computational formula for variance speeds the calculation, since it saves having to calculate the mean of the set of scores and subtract this mean from each of the scores. The formula is:

$$\text{Variance}_{[\text{computational formula}]} = \frac{\sum X^2 - \dfrac{(\sum X)^2}{N}}{N}$$

Take care with elements of this formula:

X = the general symbol for each member of a set of scores
$\sum$ = sigma or the summation sign, i.e. add up all the things which follow
$\sum X^2$ = the sum of the squares of each of the scores
$(\sum X)^2$ = sum all the scores and square that total
N = the number of scores.

→

Step 1 Applying this formula to our set of scores, it is useful to draw up a table (Table 3.6) consisting of our scores and some of the steps in the computation. N (number of scores) equals 12.

Table 3.6	A set of scores and their squares for use in computing the formula for variance

Score X	Squared score X^2
18	324
21	441
23	529
18	324
19	361
19	361
19	361
33	1089
18	324
19	361
19	361
20	400
$\sum X = 246$	$\sum X^2 = 5236$
$(\sum X)^2 = 246^2 = 60{,}516$	

Step 2 Substituting these values in the computational formula:

$$\text{Variance}_{[\text{computational formula}]} = \frac{\sum X^2 - \frac{(\sum X)^2}{N}}{N} = \frac{5236 - \frac{60{,}516}{12}}{12} = \frac{5236 - 5043}{12} = \frac{193}{12} = 16.08$$

Interpreting the results Variance is difficult to interpret in isolation from other information about the data, since it is dependent on the measurement in question. Measures which are based on a wide numerical scale for the scores will tend to have higher variance than measures based on a narrow scale. Thus if the range of scores is only 10 then the variance is likely to be less than if the range of scores is 100.

Reporting the results Usually variance is routinely reported in tables which summarise a variable or a number of variables along with other statistics such as the mean and range. This is shown in Table 3.7.

Table 3.7	Illustrating the table for descriptive statistics

Variable	N	Mean	Variance	Range
Age	12	20.50 years	16.08	15 years

| Box 3.3 | Key concepts |

Variance estimate

There is a concept called the *variance estimate* (or estimated variance) which is closely related to variance. The difference is that the variance estimate is your best guess as to the variance of a population of scores *if* you only have the data from a small set of scores from that population on which to base your estimate. The variance estimate is described in Chapter 5. It involves a slight amendment to the variance formula in that instead of dividing by N, one divides by N – 1.

The formula for the estimated variance is:

Some textbooks and some computer programs give you calculations based on this formula rather than the one we used in Calculation 3.2. Since virtually all statistical analyses in social sciences are based on samples and we normally wish to generalise from these samples to all cases, then the estimated variance is likely to be used in practice. Hence it is reasonable to use the estimated variance as the general formula for variance. The drawback to this is that if we are merely describing the data, this practice is theoretically imprecise.

$$\text{Estimated variance} = \frac{\sum X^2 - \frac{(\sum X)^2}{N}}{N - 1}$$

3.4 Probability

From time to time, researchers need to be able to calculate the probabilities (or the chance) associated with certain patterns of events. For example, a spiritual medium who addresses a crowd of 500 people is doing nothing spectacular if in Britain she claims to be speaking to a dead relative of someone and that relative is Mary or Martha or Margaret. The probability of someone in the 500 having such a relative is very high.

The principles of probability

When any of us use a test of significance we are utilising probability theory. This is because most statistical tests are based on it. We have been using probability in previous chapters on significance testing when we talked about the 5% level of significance, the 1% level of significance and the 95% confidence intervals. Basically what we meant by a 5% level of significance is that a particular event (or outcome) would occur on five occasions out of 100. Although we have adopted the percentage system of reporting probabilities in this book, statisticians would normally not write of a 5% probability. Instead they would express it as being out of a *single* event rather than 100 events. Thus:

- 0.05 (or just .05) is an alternative way of writing 5%.
- 0.10 (or .10) is an alternative way of writing 10%.
- 1.00 is an alternative way of writing 100%.

The difficulty for some of us with this alternative, more formal, way of writing probability is that it leaves everything in decimals, which does not appeal to the less mathematically skilled. However, you should be aware of the alternative notation since it appears in many research reports. Furthermore, much computer output can give probabilities to several decimal places, which can be confusing. For example, what does a probability of 0.00001 mean? The answer is one chance in 100,000 or a 0.001% probability $(1/100,000 \times 100 = 0.001\%)$.

Box 3.4   Focus on

Probability example

An interesting example of probability took place during the 2010 World Cup in South Africa. Paul the Octopus gained international stardom for correctly predicting the winner of Germany's seven matches at the 2010 World Cup, including the final. Paul's career initially began during UEFA Euro 2008. In Euro 2008, Paul correctly predicted the outcome of four out of six of Germany's matches (66.6% accuracy). During the World Cup 2010, Paul the Octopus was presented with two boxes, each containing mussels (an Octopus's favourite food). Each box had a flag of the national football team that was to play in the forthcoming match placed on the front. Paul would eat the mussel from the box with the flag of the winning team. His predictions were 100% correct for the World Cup in 2010. However, Paul's predictions are not that extraordinary. Paul had a 50-50 chance (probability) of predicting any single result, as he had a choice of two boxes filled with his favourite food. As he was predicting only two possible outcomes (win or lose – there was no

option for a draw) he had a 1 in 64 chance of predicting six correct outcomes and a 1 in 2 chance of predicting the first game correctly. Sadly, Paul the Octopus died peacefully of old age in October 2010.

Paul the Octopus predicting Germany's win over England: World Cup 2010 (South Africa)

Source: Reuters/Wolfgang Rattay

There are two rules of probability with which social scientists ought to be familiar. They are the *addition rule* and the *multiplication rule*.

- The *addition rule* is quite straightforward. It merely states that for a number of mutually exclusive outcomes the sum of their probabilities adds up to 1.00. So if you have a set of 150 people of whom 100 are women and 50 are men, the probability of picking a woman at random is 100/150 or 0.667, and the probability of picking a man at random is 50/150 or 0.333. However, the probability of picking either a man or a woman at random is 0.667 + 0.333 or 1.00. In other words, it is certain that you will pick either a man or a woman. In statistical probability theory, one of the two possible outcomes is usually denoted p and the other is denoted q, so $p + q = 1.00$.

- The *multiplication rule* is about a set of events. It can be illustrated by our set of 150 men and women in which 100 are women and 50 are men. Again the assumption is that the categories or outcomes are mutually exclusive. We could ask how likely it is that the first five people that we pick at random will all be women, given that the probability of choosing a woman on a single occasion is 0.667. The answer is that we multiply the probability associated with the first person being a woman by the probability that the second person will be a woman by the probability that the third person will be a woman by the probability that the fourth person will be a woman by the probability that the fifth person will be a woman:

Probability of all five being women $= p \times p \times p \times p \times p$
$$= 0.667 \times 0.667 \times 0.667 \times 0.667 \times 0.667$$
$$= 0.13$$

Therefore there is a 13% probability (0.13) that we will choose a sample of five women at random. That is not a particularly rare outcome. However, picking a sample of all men from our set of men and women is much rarer:

Probability of all five being men $= p \times p \times p \times p \times p$
$$= 0.333 \times 0.333 \times 0.333 \times 0.333 \times 0.333$$
$$= 0.004$$

Therefore there is a 0.4% probability (0.004) of choosing all men.

3.5   Confidence intervals

The idea of confidence intervals is an important one. The confidence interval approach gives the most likely range of the population values of the statistics and, thanks to SPSS, involves little or no labour. In inferential statistics (Part 2), we use all sorts of statistics from a sample or samples to estimate the characteristics of the population from which the sample was drawn. Few of us will have any difficulty understanding that if the mean age of a sample of participants is 23.5 years then our best estimate of the mean age of the population is exactly the same at 23.5 years. This estimate is known as a point estimate simply because it consists of a single figure (or point). Most of us will also understand that this single figure is simply the best estimate and that it is likely that the population mean will be, to a degree, different. We know this because we know that when we randomly sample from a population, the sample mean is likely to be similar to the population mean but generally will be a little different. So it follows that if we use a sample to estimate a population characteristic then our estimate will be subject to the variation due to sampling.

Confidence intervals simply are the most likely spread of values of a population characteristic (parameter) when it is estimated from a sample characteristic (statistic). So instead of an estimate of the mean population age of 23.5 one would get a confidence interval of, say, 20.0 years to 27.0 years. Actually the confidence interval gives the spread of the middle 95% of means in the case of the 95% confidence interval, or the middle 99% of means in the case of the 99% confidence interval.

The value of the confidence interval is essentially dependent on the spread of scores in the original sample of data – the bigger the spread of scores, the wider will be the confidence interval. So the variability in the scores is used to estimate the standard deviation of the population. This standard deviation can then be used to estimate the standard error of the population (see Chapter 5). Then it is simply a matter of working out the number of standard errors that cover the middle 95% of the distribution of sample means which could be drawn from that population.

3.6   SPSS analysis

■ The data to be analysed

We will illustrate the computation of the mean, median and mode on the ages of university students – see Table 3.8. You will see from the dialogue box in Step 5 that there are many additional statistical values that may be calculated. You should have little difficulty obtaining these by adapting the steps presented below.

Table 3.8	Ages of 12 university students

| 18 years | 21 years | 23 years | 18 years | 19 years | 19 years |
| 19 years | 33 years | 18 years | 19 years | 19 years | 20 years |

■ Entering the data

Step 1

In 'Variable View' of the 'Data Editor' name the first variable 'Age'. Remove the two decimal places.

	Name	Type	Width	Decimals
1	Age	Numeric	8	0

Step 2

In 'Data View' of the 'Data Editor' enter the ages in the first column.

	Age
1	18
2	21
3	23
4	18
5	19
6	19
7	19
8	33
9	18
10	19
11	19
12	20

■ Conducting the analysis

Step 3

Select 'Analyze'
→ 'Descriptive Statistics'
→ 'Frequencies...'.

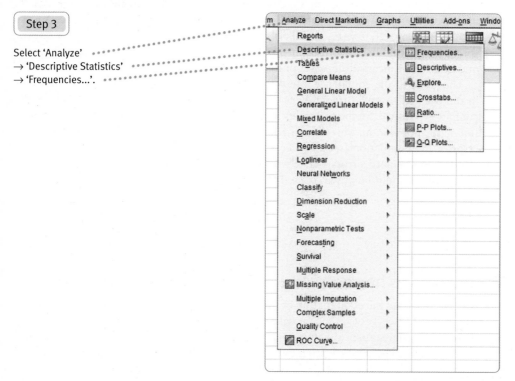

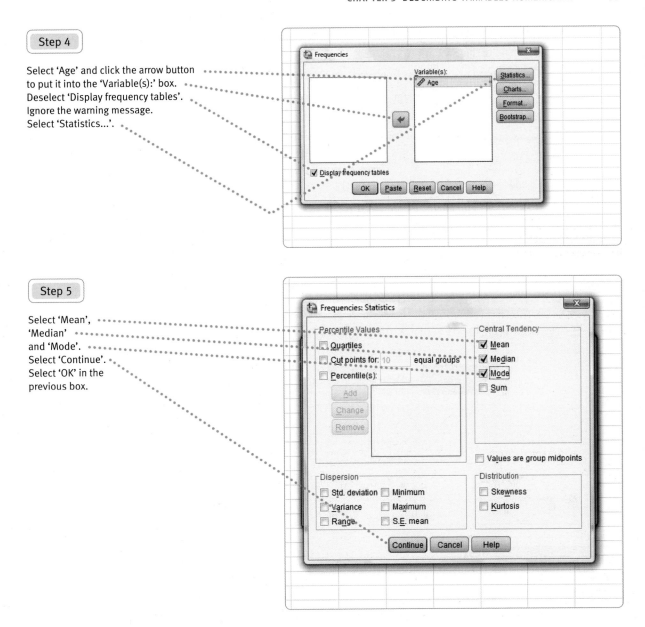

Step 4

Select 'Age' and click the arrow button
to put it into the 'Variable(s):' box.
Deselect 'Display frequency tables'.
Ignore the warning message.
Select 'Statistics...'.

Step 5

Select 'Mean',
'Median'
and 'Mode'.
Select 'Continue'.
Select 'OK' in the
previous box.

■ Interpreting the output

Statistics

Age

N	Valid	12
	Missing	0
Mean		20.50
Median		19.00
Mode		19

- There are 12 cases with valid data on which the analysis is based.
- There is no (0) missing data.
- The mean age (mathematical average) = 20.50 years.
- The median age (the age of the person halfway up a list of ages from smallest to largest) is 19.00.
- The modal (most common) age is 19. Check the next table on the output. This gives frequencies for each value. A variable may have more than one mode.

Reporting the output

- The mean, median and mode can be presented in tabular form such as in Table 3.9.
- Two decimal places are more than enough for most data. Most measurement is approximate, and the use of several decimal places tends to imply an unwarranted degree of precision.
- For the median, it is probably less confusing if you do not report values as 19.00 but as 19. However, if the decimal places were anything other than .00 then this should be reported, since it indicates that the median is estimated and does not correspond to any actual scores for these particular data.

Table 3.9	Mean, median and mode of ages of students	
		Age of students ($N = 12$)
	Mean	20.50 years
	Median	19 years
	Mode	19 years

Key points

- Because they are routine ways of summarising the typical score and the spread of a set of scores, it is important always to report the following information for each of your variables:
  - Mean, median and mode
  - Range and variance
  - Number of scores in the set of scores.

- *The above does not apply to nominal categories*. For these, the frequency of cases in each category exhausts the main possibilities.

- When using a computer, look carefully for variables that have zero variance. They can cause problems and generally ought to be omitted from your analyses. Normally the computer will not compute the calculations you ask for in these circumstances. The difficulty is that if all the scores of a variable are the same, it is impossible to calculate many statistical formulae. If you are calculating by hand, variables with all the scores the same are easier to spot.

- If you need to know more on probability theory, especially if you need to estimate precisely the likelihood of a particular pattern or sequence of events occurring, we suggest that you consult books such as Kerlinger (1986) for more complete accounts of mathematical probability theory.

CHAPTER 4

Shapes of distributions of scores

Overview

- The shape of the distribution of scores is a major consideration in statistical analysis. It simply refers to the characteristics of the frequency distribution (i.e. histogram) of the scores.

- The normal distribution is an ideal because it is the theoretical basis of many statistical techniques. It is best remembered as a bell-shaped frequency diagram.

- The normal distribution is a symmetrical distribution. That is, it can be folded perfectly on itself at the mean. Symmetry is another ideal in many statistical analyses. Distributions which are not symmetrical are known as skewed distributions.

- Kurtosis indicates how steep or flat a curve is compared with the normal (bell-shaped) curve.

- Cumulative frequencies are ones which include all of the lower values on an accumulating basis. So the highest score will always have a cumulative frequency of 100% since it includes all of the smaller scores.

- Percentiles are the numerical values of the score that cut off the lowest 10%, 30%, 95%, or what have you, of the distribution of scores.

Preparation

Be clear about numerical scores and how they can be classified into ranges of scores (Chapter 2).

4.1   Introduction

The final important characteristic of sets of scores is the particular shape of their distribution. It is useful for a researcher to be able to describe this shape concisely.

4.2   Histograms and frequency curves

Histograms are the plots of the frequency of scores (the vertical dimension) against a numerical scale (the horizontal dimension). Figure 4.1 is an example of a histogram based on a relatively small set of scores. This histogram has quite severe steps from bar to bar. In other words, it is quite angular and not a smooth shape at all, as the horizontal numerical scale moves along in discrete steps, so resulting in this pattern. Things would be different if we measured on a *continuous scale* on which every possible score could be represented to the smallest fraction. For example, we might decide to measure people's weights in kilograms to the nearest whole kilogram. But we know that weights do not really conform to this set of discrete steps or points; people who weigh 69 kilograms actually differ in weight by up to a kilogram from each other. Weight can be measured in fractions of kilograms, not just whole kilograms. In other words, weight

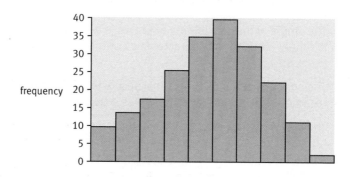

FIGURE 4.1   Histogram showing steep steps

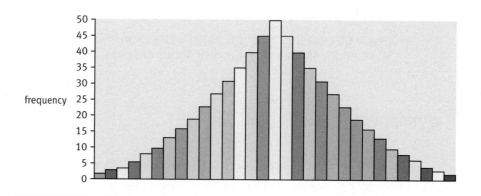

FIGURE 4.2   A smooth curve based on small blocks

is a continuous measurement with infinitesimally small steps between measures so long as we have sufficiently precise measuring instruments.

So a histogram of weights measured in kilograms is at best an approximation to reality. Within each of the blocks of the histogram is a possible multitude of smaller steps. For this reason, it is conventional when drawing frequency curves for theoretical purposes to smooth out the blocks to a continuous curve. In essence, this is like taking much finer and more precise measurements and redrawing the histogram. Instead of doing this literally, we approximate it by drawing a smooth curve through imaginary sets of extremely small steps. When this is done our histogram is 'miraculously' turned into a continuous unstepped curve (Figure 4.2).

4.3   The normal curve

The normal curve describes a particular shape of the frequency curve. It is sufficient to regard it as a symmetrical bell shape (Figure 4.3). It is called the 'normal' curve because it was once believed that distributions in the natural world corresponded to this shape. However, the normal curve is not universal, but it is important because many distributions are more or less this shape – at least sufficiently so for most practical purposes. Don't forget that for the perfectly symmetrical, bell-shaped (normal) curve the values of the mean, median and mode are identical. Disparities between the three are indications that you have an asymmetrical curve.

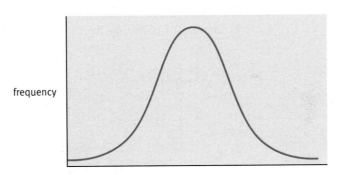

frequency

FIGURE 4.3   A normal (bell-shaped) frequency curve

Box 4.1

Research design issue

One thing which may trouble you is the issue of how precisely your data should fit this normal/bell-shaped ideal. A lot of deviation from the normal/bell-shape is possible, so you should not worry too much if the mean, median and mode do differ somewhat; for practical purposes you can disregard deviations from the ideal distribution, especially when dealing with about 30 or more scores. Unfortunately, all of this involves a degree of subjective judgement, since there are no useful ways of assessing what is an acceptable amount of deviation from the ideal when faced with the small amounts of data that student projects often involve.

Distorted curves

The main concepts which deal with distortions in the normal curve are:

- *Skewness*
- *Kurtosis*.

■ Skewness

It is always worth examining the shape of your frequency distributions. Gross skewness is the exception to our rule of thumb that non-normality of data has little influence on statistical analyses. By skewness we mean the extent to which your frequency curve is lopsided rather than symmetrical. A mid-point of a frequency curve may be skewed either to the left or to the right of the range of scores (Figures 4.4 and 4.5).

There are special terms for left-handed and right-handed skew:

- *Negative skew:*
  - More scores are to the left of the mode than to the right.
  - The mean and median are smaller than the mode.

- *Positive skew:*
  - More scores are to the right of the mode than to the left.
  - The mean and median are bigger than the mode.

There is also an index of the amount of skew shown in your set of scores. With computer analyses the ease of obtaining the index of skewness makes using complex formulae

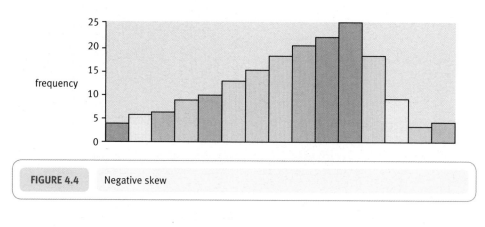

FIGURE 4.4   Negative skew

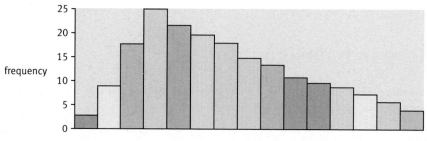

FIGURE 4.5   Positive skew

methods unnecessary. The index of skewness is positive for a positive skew and negative for a negative skew. Appendix A explains how to test for skewness in your data.

■ Kurtosis (or steepness/shallowness)

Some symmetrical curves may look rather like the normal bell-shaped curve except that they are excessively steep or excessively flat compared to the mathematically defined normal bell-shaped curve (Figures 4.6 and 4.7).

Kurtosis is the term used to identify the degree of steepness or shallowness of a distribution. There are technical words for different types of curve:

● A steep curve is called *leptokurtic*.

● A normal curve is called *mesokurtic*.

● A flat curve is called *platykurtic*.

It is possible to obtain indexes of the amount of shallowness or steepness of your distribution compared with the mathematically defined normal distribution. These are probably most useful as part of a computer analysis. For most purposes an inspection of the frequency curve of your data is sufficient in hand analyses. Knowing what the index means should help you cope with computer output; quite simply:

● A positive value of kurtosis means that the curve is steep.

● A zero value of kurtosis means that the curve is middling.

● A negative value of kurtosis means that the curve is flat.

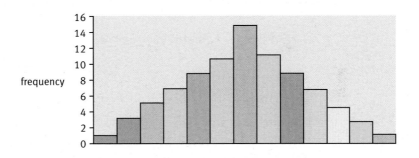

FIGURE 4.6   A shallow curve

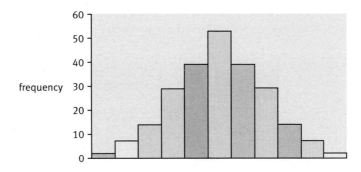

FIGURE 4.7   A steep curve

Steepness and shallowness have little or no bearing on the statistical techniques you use to analyse your data, quite unlike skewness.

4.5   Other frequency curves

■ Bimodal and multimodal frequency distributions

There is no rule that says that frequency curves have to peak in the middle and tail off to the left and right. As already explained, it is perfectly possible to have a frequency distribution with two or more peaks. Such twin-peaked distributions are called *bimodal* since they have two modes (most frequently occurring scores). Such a frequency curve might look like Figure 4.8.

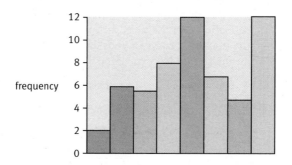

FIGURE 4.8   A bimodal frequency histogram

■ Cumulative frequency curves

There are many different ways of presenting a single set of data. Take, for example, the 50 scores in Table 4.1 for a measure of customer satisfaction from buying at online auction sites.

One way of tabulating these ratings is simply to count the number of customers scoring at each satisfaction from 1 to 5. This could be presented in several forms, for example Tables 4.2 and 4.3, and Figure 4.9.

Exactly the same distribution of scores could be represented using a *cumulative* frequency distribution. A simple frequency distribution merely indicates the number of people who achieved any particular score. A cumulative frequency distribution gives the

Table 4.1	Customer satisfaction ratings from buying at online auction sites								
3	5	5	4	4	5	5	3	5	2
1	2	5	3	2	1	2	3	3	3
4	2	5	5	4	2	4	5	1	5
5	3	3	4	1	4	2	5	1	2
3	2	5	4	2	1	2	3	4	1

Table 4.2	Frequency table based on data in Table 4.1
Number scoring 1	7
Number scoring 2	11
Number scoring 3	10
Number scoring 4	9
Number scoring 5	13

Table 4.3	Alternative layout for data in Table 4.1

Customer satisfaction scoring				
1	2	3	4	5
7	11	10	9	13

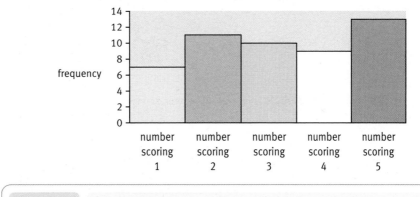

FIGURE 4.9	Histogram of Table 4.1

number scoring, say, 1, 2 or less, 3 or less, 4 or less, and 5 or less. In other words, the frequencies accumulate. Examples of cumulative frequency distributions are given in Tables 4.4 and 4.5, and Figure 4.10. Cumulative frequencies can be given also as cumulative percentage frequencies in which the frequencies are expressed as percentages and these percentages accumulated. This is shown in Table 4.4.

There is nothing difficult about cumulative frequencies – but you must label such tables and diagrams clearly or they can be very misleading.

■ Percentiles

Percentiles are merely a form of cumulative frequency distribution, but instead of being expressed in terms of accumulating scores from lowest to highest, the categorisation is in terms of whole numbers of percentages of people. In other words, the percentile is the score which a given percentage of scores equals or is less than. You do not necessarily have to report every percentage point and units of 10 might suffice for some purposes. Such a distribution would look something like Table 4.6. The table shows that 10% of

Table 4.4	Cumulative frequency distribution of customer satisfaction ratings from buying at online auction sites from Table 4.1	
Score range	**Cumulative frequency**	**Cumulative percentage frequency**
1	7	14%
2 or less	18	36%
3 or less	28	56%
4 or less	37	74%
5 or less	50	100%

Table 4.5	Alternative style of cumulative frequency distribution of customer satisfaction ratings from Table 4.1				

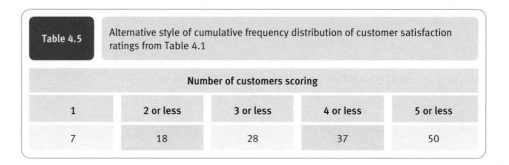

	Number of customers scoring				
1	**2 or less**	**3 or less**	**4 or less**	**5 or less**
7	18	28	37	50

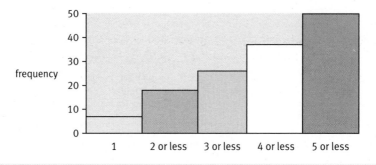

FIGURE 4.10	Cumulative histogram of the frequencies of customer satisfaction scores from Table 4.1

scores are equal to 7 or less and 80% of scores are equal to 61 or less. Note that the 50th percentile corresponds to the median score.

Percentiles are very useful to be able to describe a person's standing compared with the set of individuals on which the test or measure was initially researched. Thus if a particular person's satisfaction score with online shopping is described as being at the 90th percentile, it means that they are more satisfied with online shopping than about 90% of people. In other words, percentiles are a quick method of expressing a person's score relative to those of others.

In order to calculate the percentiles for any data it is first necessary to produce a table of cumulative percentage frequencies. This table is then examined to find the score which cuts off, for example, the bottom 10%, the bottom 20%, the bottom 30%, etc., of scores. It should be obvious that calculating percentiles in this way is actually easier if there are a large number of scores so that the cut-off points can be found precisely.

Table 4.6	Example of percentiles	
Percentile		**Score**
10th		7
20th		9
30th		14
40th		20
50th		39
60th		45
70th		50
80th		61
90th		70
100th		78

4.6   SPSS analysis

■ The data to be analysed

We will compute a frequency table and histogram of the customer satisfaction ratings from buying at online auction sites listed in Table 4.1. Please note that the SPSS procedure for generating a histogram is presented in Chapter 2, Section 2.7.

■ Entering the data

Step 1

In 'Variable View' of the 'Data Editor' name the first variable 'Satisfaction'. Remove the two decimal places.

	Name	Type	Width	Decimals
1	Satisfaction	Numeric	8	0

Step 2

In 'Data View' of the 'Data Editor' enter the customer satisfaction rating scores in the first column.

	Satisfaction
1	3
2	5
3	5
4	4
5	4
6	5
7	5
8	3
9	5
10	2

■ Frequency tables

Step 1

Select 'Analyze'
→ 'Descriptive Statistics'
→ 'Frequencies...'.

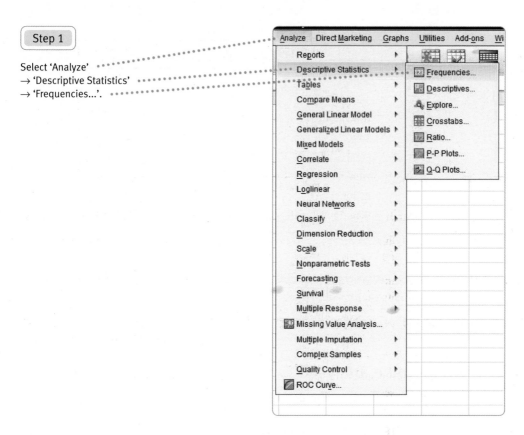

Step 2

Select 'Satisfaction'. Click the arrow
button to put it in the 'Variable(s):' box.
Select 'OK'.

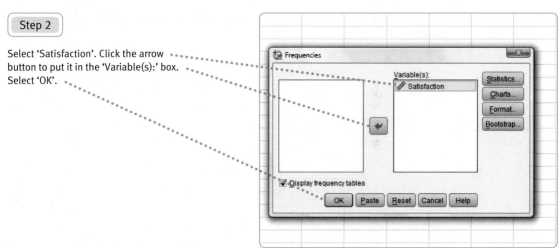

■ Interpreting the output

Satisfaction

		Frequency	Percent	Valid Percent	Cumulative Percent
Valid	1	7	14.0	14.0	14.0
	2	11	22.0	22.0	36.0
	3	10	20.0	20.0	56.0
	4	9	18.0	18.0	74.0
	5	13	26.0	26.0	100.0
	Total	50	100.0	100.0	

- The first column shows the five values of customer satisfaction ratings which are 1 to 5.
- The second column shows the frequency of these values, e.g. there are seven cases with a value of 1.
- The third column expresses these frequencies as a percentage of the total number including missing data. Of all cases, 14% have a value of 1.
- The fourth column expresses these frequencies as a percentage of the total number excluding missing data. As there are no missing cases, the percentages are the same as in the third column.
- The fifth column adds these percentages together cumulatively down the table. So 56% of the cases have a value of 3 or less.

■ Reporting the output

Notice that we omitted some of the confusion detail in Table 4.7. Tables and diagrams need to clarify the results.

Table 4.7	One style of reporting the output		
Customer satisfaction rating	**Frequency**	**Percentage frequency**	**Cumulative percentage frequency**
1	7	14.0	14.0
2	11	22.0	36.0
3	10	20.0	56.0
4	9	18.0	74.0
5	13	26.0	100.0

Key points

- The most important concept in this chapter is that of the normal curve or normal distribution. It is worth extra effort to memorise the idea that the normal curve is a bell-shaped symmetrical curve.

- Be a little wary if you find that your scores on a variable are very *skewed* since this can lose precision in certain statistical analyses.

CHAPTER 5

Standard deviation, z-scores and standard error

The standard unit of measurement in statistics

Overview

- Standard deviation is an index of how much scores deviate (differ) 'on average' from the average of the set of scores of which they are members. In other words, standard deviation is an index of the amount of variability of scores around the mean of the scores.

- Standard deviation can also be used in order to turn scores on very different variables into z-scores or 'standard scores' that are easily compared and summed since they are on the same scale of measurement. This standard scale always has a mean of zero and a standard deviation of 1.0 irrespective of the variable in question.

- Standard deviation itself always takes a positive value, *but* researchers write of a number of standard deviations above the mean (i.e. '+' relative to the mean) or a number of standard deviations below the mean (i.e. '−' relative to the mean). That is, scores above the mean of the sample will always convert to a z-score or standard score with a positive prefix. Scores below the mean will always convert to a z-score or standard score with a negative prefix.

- We never calculate the standard error directly but estimate its value from the characteristics of our sample of data.

- The standard error is simply estimated by dividing the standard deviation of scores in the population by the square root of the sample size for which we need to calculate the standard error.

● We estimate the standard deviation of the population of scores from the standard deviation of our sample of scores. There is a slight adjustment when calculating this estimated standard error – that is, the standard deviation formula involves division by $N - 1$ (i.e. the sample size minus one) rather than simply by N.

Preparation

Make sure you know the meaning of variables, scores, Σ and scales of measurement, especially nominal, interval and ratio (Chapter 1).

5.1 Introduction

Measurement ideally uses standard or universal units. It would be really stupid if, when we ask people how far it is to the nearest railway station, one person says 347 cow's lengths, another says 150 poodle jumps, and a third person says three times the distance between my doctor's house and my dentist's home. Standard units of measurement allow us to communicate easily, precisely and effectively with other people. Some variables are measured in physical ways such as metres and kilograms. Other variables can use more abstract units of measurement such as scores on an intelligence test or a personality inventory. Although it would be nice if statisticians had a standard unit of measurement, it is not intuitively obvious what this should be.

5.2 What is standard deviation?

Like a lot of statistical concepts, standard deviation was designed not to be easily comprehended by mere mortals but for its very special mathematical properties. It is actually fairly easy to *say* what the standard deviation is but much harder to *understand* what it is. Standard deviation is no more nor less than the square root of the variance of a set of scores. If you understood the concept of variance (Chapter 3) then the standard deviation is simply the square root of the value of the variance.

Unfortunately, the concept of variance is not that easy either, since it is calculated by taking each score in a set of scores and subtracting the mean from that score, squaring each of these 'deviations' or differences from the mean, summing them up to give the total, and finally dividing by the number of scores (or the number of scores – 1 to calculate the variance estimate). Easy enough computationally, but it is a bit of a struggle to fix the concept in one's head.

Notice that the standard deviation is simply the square root of the variance, i.e. the square root of something that involved squaring the deviation of each of the scores from the mean. So, since it is the square root of squares, the standard deviation gets us near to getting back to the original deviation anyway. And this is what conceptually the standard deviation is – just as the label says – it is a sort of average amount by which scores differ (deviate) from the mean. That's what it is, but most of us mortals would simply have taken the average deviation from the mean in the first place without all of this squaring and square rooting.

Standard deviation comes into its own when our data have a normal distribution (the bell-shaped distribution we discussed in Chapter 4). In these circumstances, it so happens that if one counts the number of standard deviations of a score from the mean, then one can say exactly what proportion of scores lie between the mean and that number of standard deviations from the mean. So if a score is one standard deviation from the mean then 34.13% of scores lie between this score and the mean; if a score is two standard deviations from the mean then 47.72% of scores lie between this score and the mean. How do we know this? Simply because these figures are a property of the normal curve. Most importantly, these figures apply to every normal curve. There are tables which give the percentages for every number of standard deviations from the mean.

These precise figures only apply to the normal distribution. If the data do not correspond to the normal curve then these figures are not accurate. The greater the deviation from the normal curve the more inaccurate become these figures. Perhaps now it is easier to see the importance of the normal distribution and the degree to which the normal distribution describes the frequency curve for your data.

One application of the standard deviation is something known as *z*-scores. This is simply a score re-expressed in terms of the number of standard deviations it is away from the mean score. So the *z*-score is simply the difference between the score and the mean score of the set of data, divided by the standard deviation. This is important, since no matter the precise nature of a set of scores, they can always be converted to *z*-scores which then serve as a standard unit of measurement in statistics. It also means that one can quickly convert this number of *z*-scores to the proportion of scores in which the score lies away from the mean of the set of scores.

Calculation 5.1

Converting a score into a *z*-score

To convert the age of a 32-year-old to a *z*-score, given that the mean of the set of ages is 40 years and the standard deviation of age is 6 years, just apply the following formula:

$$z\text{-score} = \frac{X - \bar{X}}{\text{SD}}$$

where X stands for a particular score, $\bar{X}$ is the mean of the set of scores and SD stands for standard deviation.

The *z*-score of any age (e.g. 32) can be obtained as follows:

$$z\text{-score}_{\text{of a 32-year-old}} = \frac{32 - 40}{6} = \frac{-8}{6} = -1.33$$

The value of −1.33 means that:

1. A 32-year-old is 1.33 standard deviations from the mean age of 40 for this set of age scores.

2. The minus sign simply means that the 32-year-old is younger (lower) than the mean age for the set of age scores. A plus sign (or no sign) would mean that the person is older (higher) than the mean age of 40 years.

→

Interpreting the results There is little to be added about interpreting the z-score, since it is defined by the formula as the number of standard deviations a score is from the mean score. Generally speaking, the larger the z-score (either positive or negative) the more atypical a score is of the typical score in the data. A z-score of 2 or more is fairly rare.

Reporting the results As z-scores are scores, they can be presented as you would any other score using tables or diagrams. Usually there is no point in reporting the mean of a set of z-scores since this will be 0.00 if calculated for all of the cases.

You may not wish to do this for a particular set of data, but you need to know that many of the statistics described in this book can involve standardised measures that are very closely related to z-scores (for example multiple regression, log-linear analysis and factor analysis).

However, it is important to know that SPSS actually does not compute standard deviation but something called the estimated standard deviation. This is slightly larger than the standard deviation. Standard deviation applies when you simply wish to describe the characteristic of a set of scores, whereas estimated standard deviation is used when one is using the characteristics of a sample to estimate the same characteristic in the population from which the sample came. It would be good to label estimated standard deviation as such despite what SPSS says in its output.

5.3   When to use standard deviation

Standard deviation is always valuable when considering any score variable. It is clearly much more informative when it is based on a normally distributed set of scores than where the distribution deviates substantially from that ideal. Variance (Chapter 3), standard deviation and standard error are all used as measures of the variation in the scores on a variable. This is because there is such a close mathematical relation between each of them. The square root of variance is standard deviation and the variance divided by the square root of the sample size is the standard error. Of course, it is important to be consistent in terms of which one is used.

Calculation 5.2

Standard deviation

The defining formula for standard deviation is as follows:

$$\text{Standard deviation} = \sqrt{\frac{\Sigma(X - \bar{X})^2}{N}}$$

The computationally quicker formula is:

$$\text{Standard deviation} = \sqrt{\frac{\Sigma X^2 - \dfrac{(\Sigma X)^2}{N}}{N}}$$

Table 5.1	Steps in the calculation of the standard deviation	
Scores (X) (age in years)		**Scores squared (X^2)**
20		400
25		625
19		361
35		1225
19		361
17		289
15		225
30		900
27		729
$\sum X = 207$		$\sum X^2 = 5115$

Table 5.1 lists the ages of nine students (N = number of scores = 9) and shows steps in calculating the standard deviation. Substituting these values in the standard deviation formula:

$$\text{Standard deviation} = \sqrt{\frac{\sum X^2 - \frac{(\sum X)^2}{N}}{N}} = \sqrt{\frac{5115 - \frac{(207)^2}{9}}{9}}$$

$$= \sqrt{\frac{5115 - 4761}{9}}$$

$$= \sqrt{\frac{354}{9}} = \sqrt{39.333} = 6.27 \text{ years}$$

(You may have spotted that the standard deviation is simply the square root of the variance.)

5.4   When not to use standard deviation

Do not use standard deviation when dealing with nominal (category variables). SPSS will do a calculation for you but the outcome is mathematically precise gibberish in this case.

5.5   Data requirements for standard deviation

Standard deviation can only be calculated on score data. Ideally, the variable in question should be normally distributed and, some would say, be measured on an equal-interval scale.

Remember that what SPSS calls standard deviation should really be labelled estimated standard deviation if one wishes to be precise.

5.6 Problems in the use of standard deviation

Getting to understand standard deviation is a bit like a child trying to play a concerto on the piano before learning to play simple scales. That is, standard deviation, because of its abstract nature, is very difficult to grasp but invariably taught early in a statistics module. Because of this, novices often stare blankly at SPSS output for standard deviation since it does not immediately tell a story to them.

5.7 SPSS analysis

■ The data to be analysed

The computation of the standard deviation and z-scores is illustrated with the nine age scores shown in the first column of Table 5.1.

■ Entering the data

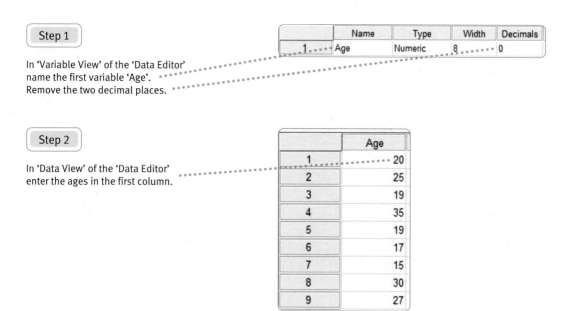

Step 1

In 'Variable View' of the 'Data Editor' name the first variable 'Age'. Remove the two decimal places.

	Name	Type	Width	Decimals
1	Age	Numeric	8	0

Step 2

In 'Data View' of the 'Data Editor' enter the ages in the first column.

	Age
1	20
2	25
3	19
4	35
5	19
6	17
7	15
8	30
9	27

■ Standard deviation

Step 1

Select 'Analyze'
→ 'Descriptive statistics'
→ 'Descriptives...'.

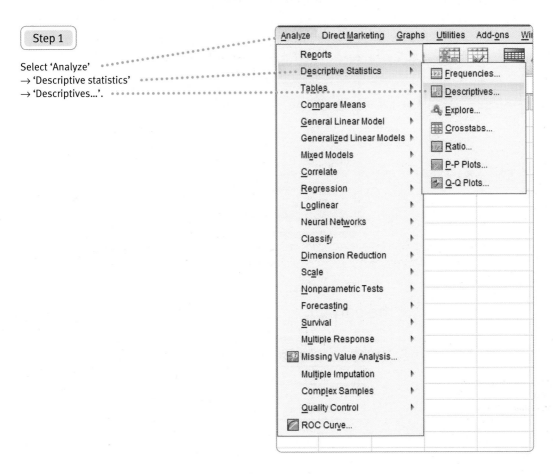

Step 2

Select 'Age'. Click the arrow button
to put it in the 'Variable(s):' box.
Select 'Options...'.

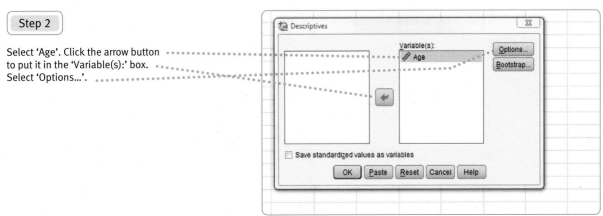

Step 3

Deselect 'Mean', 'Minimum' and 'Maximum'.
Select 'Continue'.
Select 'OK' in the previous box.

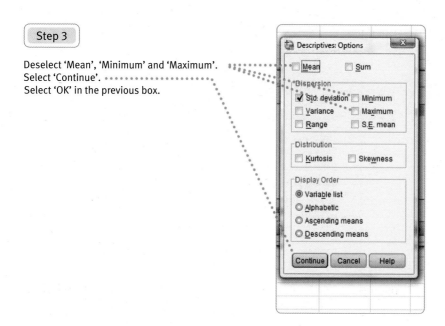

■ Interpreting the output

Descriptive Statistics

	N	Std. Deviation
Age	9	6.652
Valid N (listwise)	9	

- The number of cases is 9.
- The standard deviation of 'Age' is 6.652.

■ *Z*-scores

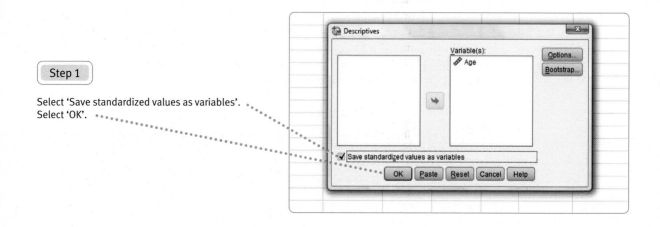

Step 1

Select 'Save standardized values as variables'.
Select 'OK'.

Step 2

The *z* or standardised scores are in the second column of 'Data View' in the 'Data Editor' and are called 'ZAge'.

	Age	ZAge
1	20	-.45099
2	25	.30066
3	19	-.60132
4	35	1.80395
5	19	-.60132
6	17	-.90198
7	15	-1.20263
8	30	1.05230
9	27	.60132

■ Other features

'Descriptives...' contains a number of statistical calculations that can easily be selected:

- Mean
- Sum
- Standard deviation (estimate)
- Range
- Minimum (score)
- Maximum (score)
- Standard error (S.E. mean)
- Kurtosis
- Skewness.

These different statistical concepts have already been explained in previous chapters.

■ Reporting the output

The standard deviation of just one variable can easily be mentioned in the text of your report: 'It was found that the standard deviation (SD) of age was SD = 6.65 years ($N = 9$).'

However, it is more likely that you would wish to record the standard deviation alongside other statistics such as the mean and range, as illustrated in Table 5.2. You would probably wish to include these statistics for other numerical score variables that you have data on.

Table 5.2	The sample size, mean, range and standard deviations of age, IQ and verbal fluency			
	N	Mean	Range	Standard deviation
Age	9	23.00	20.00	6.65
IQ	9	122.17	17.42	14.38
Verbal fluency	9	18.23	4.91	2.36

5.8   # Standard error: the standard deviation of the means of samples

Standard error is a fundamental statistical concept that needs to be understood as part of your development as a statistician. You would rarely need to compute standard error separately as its computation is part of other SPSS procedures you will probably be carrying out.

Standard error is more or less the same as standard deviation, described earlier, albeit with one big difference: standard deviation refers to a set of scores, whereas standard error refers to means of samples. In fact, the standard error is essentially the standard deviation of a set of sample means. It is even estimated (calculated) from the standard deviation of the sample of scores that the researcher has information about. This sample is used to make inferences about the characteristics of the population. Basically, but with some slight adjustments, the characteristics of the sample are assumed to be those of the population from which the sample was drawn. Conceptually, you need to imagine that you are drawing samples of a particular size (say 10) from this estimated population of scores (on some measure). Common sense suggests, and statistical theory insists, that there will be variation in the means of these different samples simply because of the vicissitudes of random selection. The standard deviation calculated on these sample means is the standard error. The standard error is simply a measure of the variation in sample means.

Usually in statistics (and definitely so in SPSS), we do not calculate the standard error but something called the estimated standard error. This is because we usually have just one sample to calculate the standard error from. The steps are that we calculate the standard deviation of the population of scores from the sample (see Figure 5.1). This

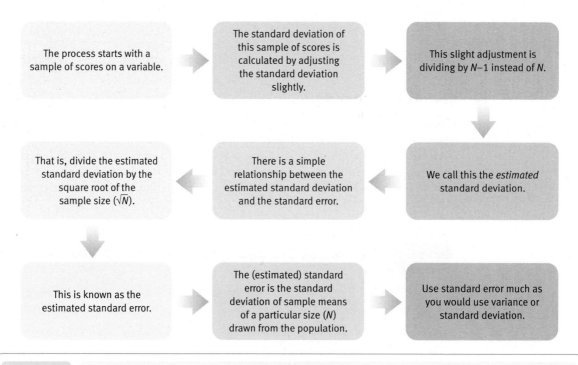

FIGURE 5.1   Estimating the population standard error from a sample of scores

entails a very small adjustment to the standard deviation formula and yields the estimated standard deviation. Then this estimated standard deviation is used to estimate the standard error of sample means using a very simple formula:

$$(\text{Estimated}) \text{ standard error} = \frac{(\text{estimated}) \text{ standard deviation of population}}{\sqrt{N}}$$

The value of N is dependent on the sample size for which you wish to obtain the standard error, which implies, of course, that there is a different standard deviation for each different size of sample. The standard error gives you an indication of the extent to which sample means can be expected to vary if drawn at random from the same population. It clearly is closely linked to the standard deviation and, often, they are used interchangeably as they are both indicative of the variation in the data. Standard error is important as a key idea in other statistics such as the *t*-test (Chapters 10 and 11).

5.9 When to use standard error

Standard error is most likely to be used as an indication of the variability or spread in the data. As such, it vies with standard deviation and variance for that task. There is a close relationship between all of these things and they can be used interchangeably by experienced researchers, though, of course, only one of the three should be used for purposes of making comparisons. Ideally the data should be on a scale with equal measurement intervals and normally distributed.

5.10 When not to use standard error

There are few if any circumstances in which it is inappropriate to use standard error if its basic data requirements are met. Standard error can be calculated on any score variable, though it is most accurate where the scores are normally distributed and the measurement approaches an equal-interval scale.

5.11 SPSS analysis for standard error

■ The data to be analysed

The computation of the estimated standard error of the mean is illustrated with the following six scores of self-esteem: 5, 7, 3, 6, 4, 5.

■ Entering the data

Enter the data in the 'Data Editor'.
Label the variable 'Esteem'.
Remove the two decimal places (see Chapter 1).

	Esteem
1	5
2	7
3	3
4	6
5	4
6	5

■ Estimated standard error of the mean

Select 'Analyze'
→ 'Descriptive Statistics'
→ 'Descriptives...'.

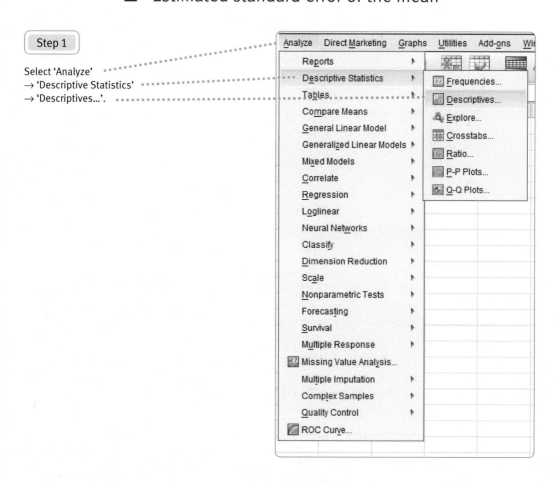

Analyze	Direct Marketing	Graphs	Utilities	Add-ons	Wir
Reports	▶				
Descriptive Statistics	▶			Frequencies...	
Tables	▶			Descriptives...	
Compare Means	▶			Explore...	
General Linear Model	▶			Crosstabs...	
Generalized Linear Models	▶			Ratio...	
Mixed Models	▶			P-P Plots...	
Correlate	▶			Q-Q Plots...	
Regression	▶				
Loglinear	▶				
Neural Networks	▶				
Classify	▶				
Dimension Reduction	▶				
Scale	▶				
Nonparametric Tests	▶				
Forecasting	▶				
Survival	▶				
Multiple Response	▶				
Missing Value Analysis...					
Multiple Imputation	▶				
Complex Samples	▶				
Quality Control	▶				
ROC Curve...					

Step 2

Select 'Esteem'.
Click on the arrow button
to put it in the 'Variable(s):' box.
Select 'Options...'.

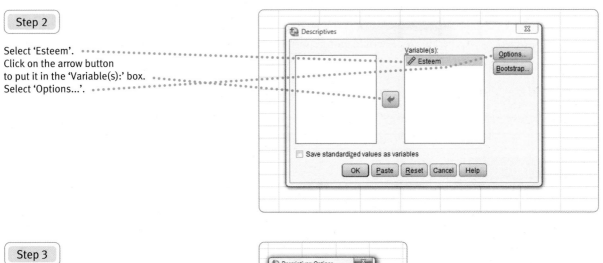

Step 3

Select 'S.E. mean'.
Select 'Continue'.
Select 'OK' in the previous box.

■ Interpreting the output

The number of cases is 9.
The standard deviation of
'Age' is 6.652.

Descriptive Statistics

	N	Minimum	Maximum	Mean		Std. Deviation
	Statistic	Statistic	Statistic	Statistic	Std. Error	Statistic
Esteem	6	3	7	5.00	.577	1.414
Valid N (listwise)	6					

- The (estimated) standard error of the mean of this sample of six scores is 0.577. It is an indication of the 'average' amount by which sample means differ from the mean of the population from which they came.

- The table shown in the screenshot gives us the value of the standard error of sample means as 0.577. It is common practice in statistics to round figures to two decimal places. Therefore, the standard error of sample means should be presented as 0.58. This is the 'average' amount by which means of samples ($N = 6$) differ from the population mean. It is an estimate based on a sample and should really be termed the estimated standard error.

- The table includes other information such as the mean (5.00), the estimated population standard deviation based on this sample, and the minimum and maximum values in the data. The final column gives the (estimated) standard deviation of the six scores, which is 1.414. However, when rounding to two decimal places, the figure will be reported as 1.41.

■ Reporting the output

Generally, one would not report the standard error of sample means on its own. It would be more usual to report it as part of certain tests of significance. However, in many circumstances it is just as informative as the variance or standard deviation of a sample, as it bears a simple relationship to both of these.

Key points

- Do not despair if you have problems in understanding standard deviation; it is one of the most abstract ideas in statistics, but so fundamental that it cannot be avoided. It can take some time to absorb completely.

- The standard error is often reported in computer output and in research publications. Very much like standard deviation, it can be used as an indicator of the variability in one's data. Variables with different standard errors essentially have different variances so long as the number of scores is the same for the two variables.

- Standard error is almost always really *estimated* standard error when working with statistics in social sciences. However, usually this estimate is referred to simply as the standard error. This is a pity, since it loses sight of the true nature of standard error.

Chapter 6

Relationships between two or more variables

Diagrams and tables

Overview

- Most research in social sciences involves relationships between two or more variables.

- Relationships between two score variables may be represented pictorially as a scattergram (or scatterplot). Alternatively, a crosstabulation table with the scores broken down into ranges (or bands) is sometimes effective.

- If both variables are nominal (category) then compound bar charts of various sorts may be used or, alternatively, crosstabulation tables.

- If there is one score variable and one nominal (category) variable then often tables of means of the score variable tabulated against the nominal (category) variable will be adequate. It is possible, alternatively, to employ a compound histogram.

Preparation

You should be aware of the meaning of variables, scores and the different scales of measurement, especially the difference between nominal (category) measurement and numerical scores.

6.1   Introduction

Although it is fundamental and important to be able to describe the characteristics of each variable in your research both diagrammatically and numerically, *interrelationships* between variables are more characteristic of research in social sciences. Public opinion polling is the most common use of single-variable statistics that most of us come across. Opinion pollsters ask a whole series of questions about political leaders and voting intentions which are generally reported separately. However, researchers often report relationships between two variables. So, for example, if one asks whether the voting intentions of men and women differ, it is really to enquire whether there is a relationship between the variable 'gender' and the variable 'voting intention'. Similarly, if one asks whether the popularity of US President Barack Obama has changed from his inauguration on 20 January 2009 to 20 January 2011 (two years in office), this really implies that there may be a relationship between the variable 'time' and the variable 'popularity of the President'. Many of these questions seem so familiar to us that we regard them almost as common sense. Given this, we should not have any great difficulty in understanding the concept of interrelationships among variables.

Interrelationships between variables form the bedrock of virtually all social science research. It is rare in social science to have research questions which require data from only one variable at a time. Much of social science concerns explanations of why things happen – what causes what – which clearly is about relationships between variables.

6.2   The principles of diagrammatic and tabular presentation

Choosing appropriate techniques to show relationships between two variables requires an understanding of the difference between nominal category data and numerical score data. If we are considering the interrelationships between *two* variables (X and Y) then the types of variable involved are as shown in Table 6.1.

Once you have decided to which category your pair of variables belongs, it is easy to suggest appropriate descriptive statistics. We have classified different situations as *Type A*, *Type B* and *Type C*. Thus *Type B* has both variables measured on the nominal category scale of measurement.

Table 6.1	Types of relationships based on nominal categories and numerical scores	
	Variable X = numerical scores	**Variable X = nominal categories**
Variable Y = numerical scores	Type A	Type C
Variable Y = nominal categories	Type C	Type B

6.3   Type A: both variables numerical scores

Where both variables take the form of numerical scores, generally the best form of graphical presentation is the *scattergram* or scatterplot. This is a sort of graph in which the values on one variable are plotted against the values on the other variable. The most familiar form of graph is one that plots a variable against time (see Figure 6.1).

One complication you sometimes come across is where several points on the scattergram overlap completely. In these circumstances you may well see a number next to a point which corresponds to the number of overlapping points at that position on the scattergram.

The horizontal axis is described as the *X*-axis and the vertical axis is called the *Y*-axis. It is helpful if you remember to label one set of scores the *X* scores since these belong on the horizontal axis, and the other set of scores the *Y* scores because these belong on the vertical axis (Figure 6.2).

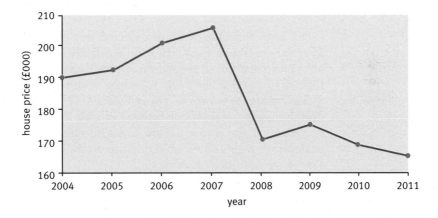

| FIGURE 6.1 | The rise and dramatic fall in UK average house prices from 2004 to 2011 (adjusted for inflation) |

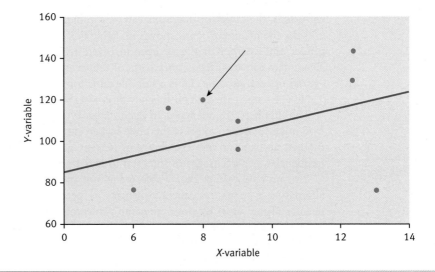

| FIGURE 6.2 | A scattergram showing the relationship between two variables |

Table 6.2	The use of bands of scores to tabulate the relationship between two numerical score variables				
Variable X	**Variable Y**				
	1–5	6–10	11–15	16–20	21–25
0–9	15	7	6	3	4
10–19	7	12	3	5	4
20–29	4	9	19	8	4
30–39	1	3	2	22	3
40–49	3	2	3	19	25

It is often difficult to think of a succinct way of presenting data from pairs of numerical scores in tabular form. The main possibility is to categorise each of your score variables into 'bands' of scores and express the data in terms of *frequencies* of occurrence in these bands; a table like Table 6.2 might be appropriate.

Such tables are known as 'crosstabulation' or 'contingency' tables. In Table 6.2 there does seem to be a relationship between variable *X* and variable *Y*. People with low scores on variable *X* also tend to get low scores on variable *Y*. High scorers on variable *X* also tend to score highly on variable *Y*. However, the trend in the table is less easily discerned than in the equivalent scattergram.

6.4   Type B: both variables nominal categories

Where both variables are in nominal categories it is necessary to report the frequencies in all of the possible groupings of the variables. If you have more than a few nominal categories, the tables or diagrams can be too big.

Take the imaginary data shown in Table 6.3 on the relationship between a person's gender and whether they have been involved in a car accident at any time in their life. These data are ideal for certain sorts of tables and diagrams because *there are few categories of each variable*. Thus a suitable table for summarising these data might look like Table 6.4 – it is called a contingency or crosstabulation table.

The numbers (frequencies) in each category are instantly obvious from this table. You might prefer to express the table in percentages rather than frequencies, but some thought needs to go into the choice of percentages. For example, you could express the frequencies as percentages of the total of males and females (Table 6.5).

You probably think that Table 6.5 is not much of an improvement in clarity. An alternative is to express the frequencies as percentages of males *and* percentages of females (Table 6.6). By presenting the percentages based on males and females separately, it is easier to see the trend for females to have had a previous car accident relatively more frequently than males.

The same data can be expressed as a *compound bar chart*. In a compound bar chart information is given about the subcategories based on a pair of variables. Figure 6.3 shows one example in which the proportions are expressed as percentages of the males and females separately.

Table 6.3	Gender and whether previously experienced a car accident for a set of 89 people	
Person	**Gender**	**Car accident**
1	male	yes
2	male	no
3	male	no
4	male	yes
5	male	no
. . .	. . .	. . .
85	female	yes
86	female	yes
87	female	no
88	female	no
89	female	yes

Table 6.4	Crosstabulation table of gender against car accident	
	Male	**Female**
Previous car accident	$f = 20$	$f = 25$
No previous car accident	$f = 30$	$f = 14$

Table 6.5	Crosstabulation table with all frequencies expressed as a percentage of the total number of frequencies	
	Male	**Female**
Previous car accident	22.5%	28.1%
No previous car accident	33.7%	15.7%

Table 6.6	Crosstabulation table with previous car accident expressed as a percentage of the male and female frequencies taken separately	
	Male	**Female**
Previous car accident	40.0%	64.1%
No previous car accident	60.0%	35.9%

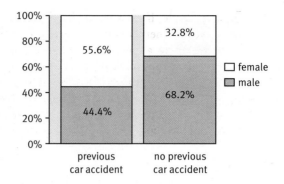

FIGURE 6.3   Compound percentage bar chart showing sex trends in previous car accidents

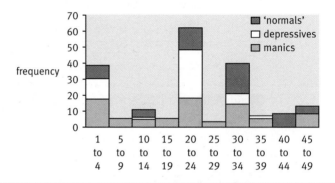

FIGURE 6.4   How *not* to do a compound bar chart

The golden rule for such data is to ensure that the number of categories is manageable. In particular, avoid having too many empty or near-empty categories. The compound bar chart shown in Figure 6.4 is a particularly bad example and is *not to be copied*. This chart fails any reasonable clarity test and is too complex to decipher quickly.

6.5 Type C: one variable nominal categories, the other numerical scores

This final type of situation offers a wide variety of ways of presenting the relationships between variables. We have examined the compound bar chart, so it is not surprising to find that there is also a *compound histogram*. To be effective, a compound histogram needs to consist of:

● a small number of categories for the nominal category variable

● a few *ranges* for the numerical scores.

So, for example, if we wish to plot the relationship between football managers' anxiety scores and whether they are managers in England's Premier League or the Championship, we might create a compound histogram like Figure 6.5 in which there are only two values of the nominal variable (Premier League and Championship) and four bands of anxiety score (low anxiety, medium anxiety, high anxiety and very high anxiety).

An alternative way of presenting such data is to use a crosstabulation table as in Table 6.7. Instead, however, it is almost as easy to draw up a table (Table 6.8) which gives the mean, median, mode, etc., for the anxiety scores of the two different groups.

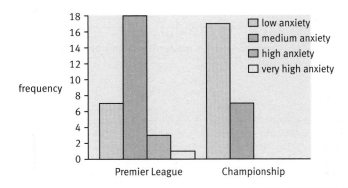

| FIGURE 6.5 | A compound histogram |

| Table 6.7 | Crosstabulation table of anxiety against type of football league |

	Frequency of anxiety score			
	0–3	4–7	8–11	12–15
Championship	7	18	3	1
Premier League	17	7	0	0

| Table 6.8 | Comparison of the statistical characteristics of anxiety in two different types of football leagues |

	Mean	Median	Mode	Interquartile range	Variance
Premier League	3.5	3.9	3	2.3–4.2	2.2
Championship	5.3	4.7	6	3.9–6.3	3.2

6.6   SPSS analysis

■ The data to be analysed

We will illustrate the drawing up of a cross-tabulation table and compound bar chart using the data shown previously in Table 6.4. This shows the number of men and women in a study who have or have not been previously involved in a car accident. If your data are already entered into SPSS then Steps 1 to 3 may be ignored.

■ Entering the data

Step 1

The quickest way to enter the data in Table 6.4 is to create the four cells as three rows.
To do this we need three variables.
In 'Variable View' of the 'Data Editor' name the first variable 'Caraccident', the second variable 'Gender', and the third variable 'Freq'.
Remove the two decimal places.

	Name	Type	Width	Decimals	Label	Values
1	Caraccident	Numeric	8	0		{1, car acci...
2	Gender	Numeric	8	0		{1, male}...
3	Freq	Numeric	8	0		None

Step 2

Label the two values of 'Caraccident' (1 = 'car accident'; 2 = 'no car accident') and 'Gender' (1 = 'Males'; 2 = 'Females').
How to do this was discussed in Chapter 1.
Select 'OK'.

Value Labels

Value Labels

Value: [   ]   Spelling...

Label: [   ]

1 = "car accident"
2 = "no car accident"

Add
Change
Remove

OK   Cancel   Help

Step 3

Enter these numbers into 'Data View' of the 'Data Editor'.
The first variable refers to 'car accident' 'males' of whom there are 20.
The second variable refers to 'car accident' 'females' of whom there are 25.
The third variable refers to 'no car accident' 'males' of whom there are 30.
The fourth variable refers to 'no car accident' 'females' of whom there are 14.

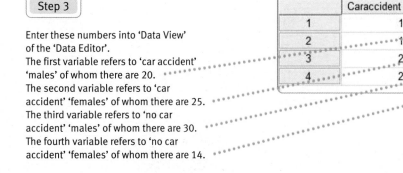

	Caraccident	Gender	Freq
1	1	1	20
2	1	2	25
3	2	1	30
4	2	2	14

■ Weighting the data

Step 1

To weight the data so that the four cells have the appropriate number of cases in them, select 'Data' → 'Weight Cases…'.

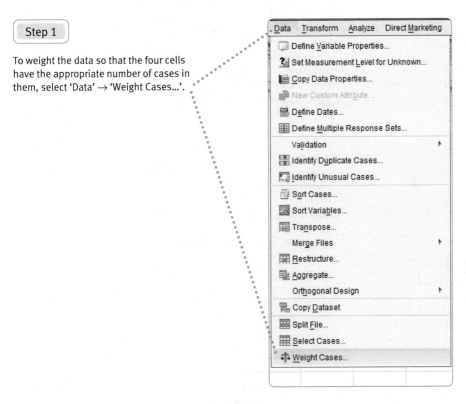

Step 2

Select 'Freq', 'Weight cases by'. Click on the arrow button to put it in the 'Frequency Variable:' box. Select 'OK'.

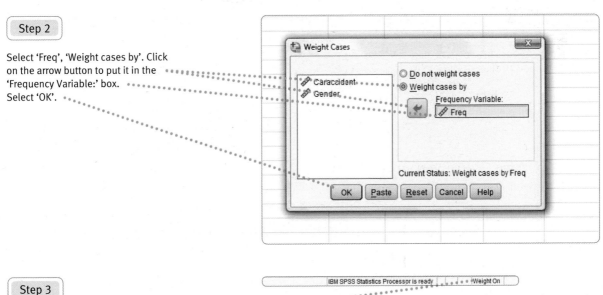

Step 3

The cases are weighted as shown by the 'Weight On' message in the lower-right corner of the 'Data Editor'.

■ Crosstabulation with frequencies

Step 1

Select 'Analyze'
→ 'Tables'
→ 'Custom Tables...'.

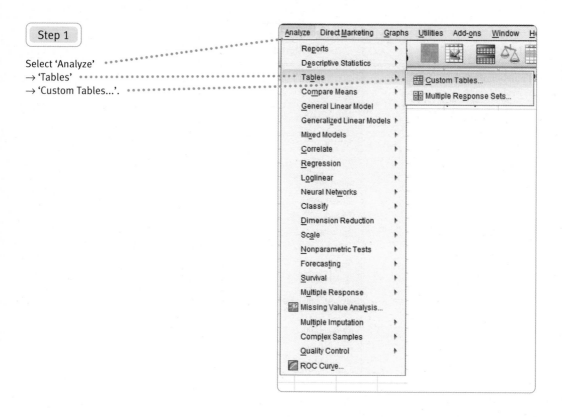

Step 2

If the variables have not been defined, then
do so (see Chapter 2). Otherwise select 'OK'.

Step 3

Select 'Caraccident' and drag it to 'Rows'.
Select 'Gender' and drag it to 'Columns'.
Ensure 'nnnn' are in the cells.
If they are not, go to the next
section to see how to select them.
Select 'OK'.

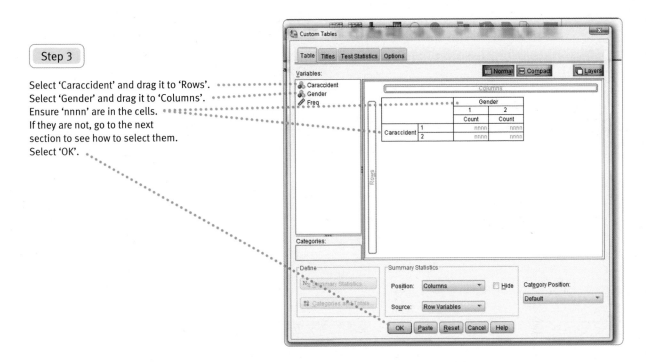

	Gender	
	1	2
	Count	Count
Caraccident 1	20	25
2	30	14

The table in the output is laid out as above
except that the two values for each variable
are not labelled. If necessary, label these
values using Steps 4 and 5 and rerun
the analysis.

Step 4

Select 'Edit' → 'Options...'.

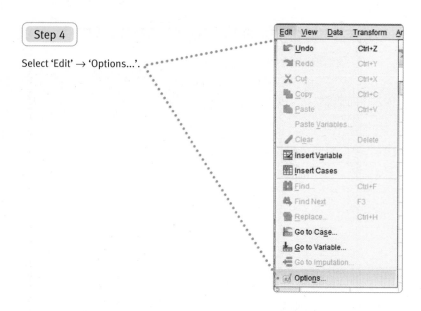

Step 5

Select 'Output Labels'.
Select the toggle down arrow below
'Variable values in labels shown as'
and 'Labels' from the drop-down menu.
Select 'OK'.

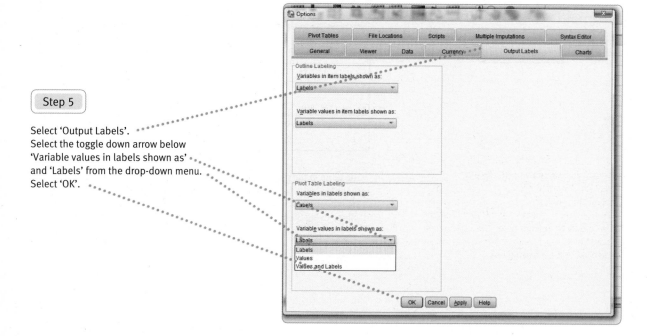

	Gender	
	male	female
	Count	Count
Caraccident car accident	20	25
no car accident	30	14

This is the table with the values labelled.

■ Displaying frequencies as a percentage of the total number

Step 1

Double click on 'car accident' in the cell of the table.

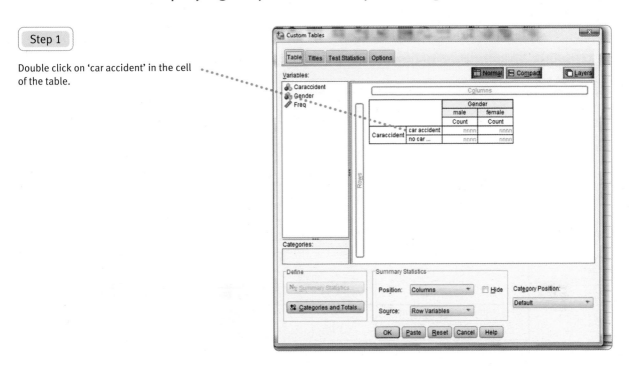

Step 2

Select 'Count' in 'Display:' and click the backward facing arrow button to put it back under 'Statistics:'.
Select 'Table N%'.
Click the arrow button to put it under 'Display:'.
Select 'Apply to Selection' to return to original dialogue box.
Select 'OK' in the previous box.

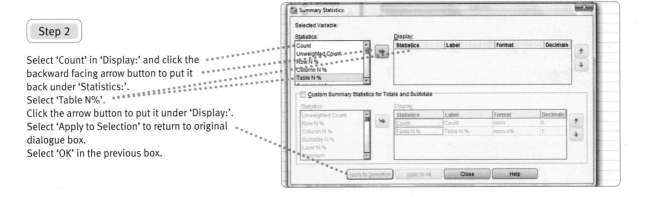

		Gender	
		male	female
		Table N %	Table N %
Caraccident	car accident	22.5%	28.1%
	no car accident	33.7%	15.7%

If you add the percentages in each of the four cells, they total 100.

■ Displaying frequencies as a percentage of the column total

Step 1

Select 'Table N%' and the arrow button
to put it back under 'Statistics:'.
Select 'Col N%' and the arrow button to
put it under 'Display:'
Select 'Apply to Selection' to
return to original dialog box.
Select 'OK'.

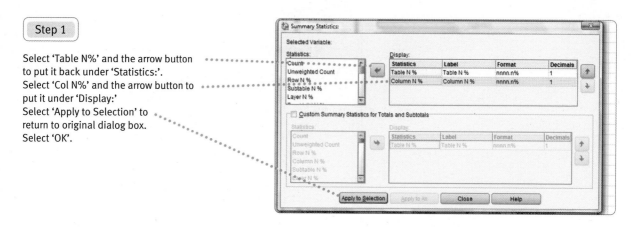

	Gender			
	male		female	
	Table N %	Column N %	Table N %	Column N %
Caraccident car accident	22.5%	40.0%	28.1%	64.1%
no car accident	33.7%	60.0%	15.7%	35.9%

If you add the percentages in each column, they total 100.

■ Compound (stacked) percentage bar chart

Step 1

To obtain a compound (stacked) percentage
bar chart in which the bars represent 100%
you need to enter the percentage figures
(called 'ColPerCent') for the two bars and
weight them.

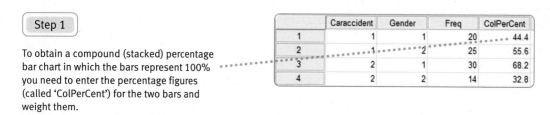

	Caraccident	Gender	Freq	ColPerCent
1	1	1	20	44.4
2	1	2	25	55.6
3	2	1	30	68.2
4	2	2	14	32.8

Step 2

Select 'Graphs'
→ 'Legacy Dialogs'
→ 'Bar...'.

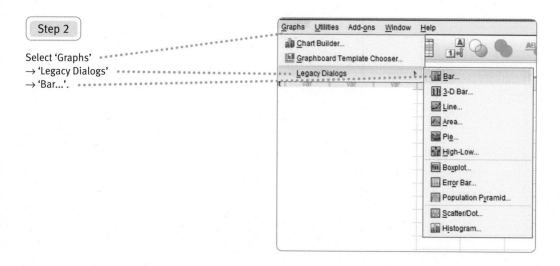

Step 3

Select 'Stacked'.
Select 'Define'.

Step 4

Select 'Caraccident'. Click the
arrow button text to 'Category Axis:'.
Select 'Gender'. Click the arrow button
next to 'Define Stacks by:'.
Select 'OK'.

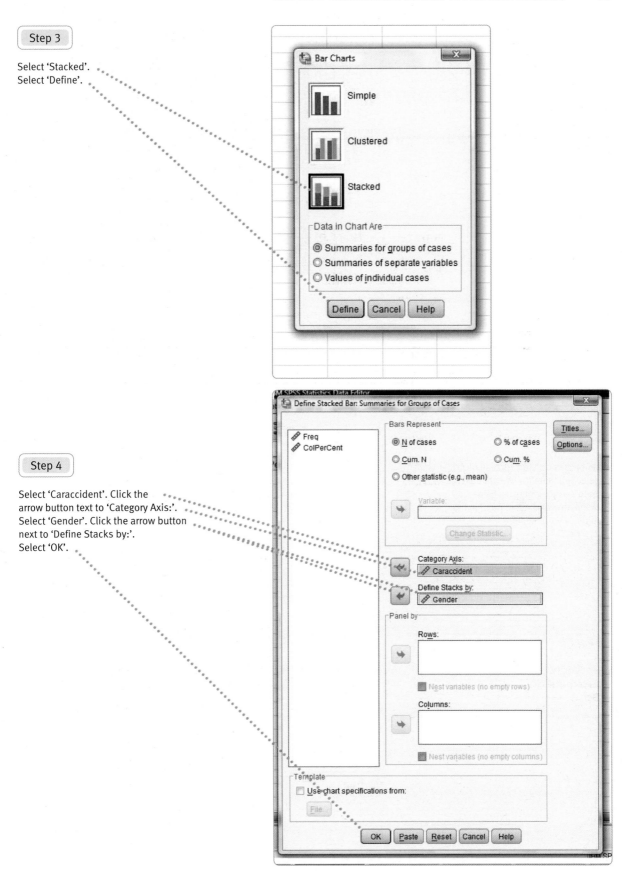

In Figure 6.6, 'count' refers to 'percent' which you could change with the chart editor (see Chapter 4 on shapes of distribution of scores).

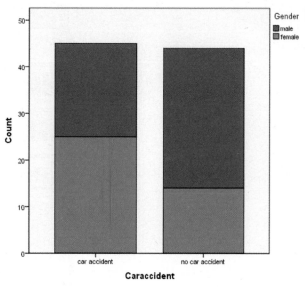

Cases weighted by Freq

FIGURE 6.6   Compound (stacked) percentage bar chart output

■ Compound histogram (clustered bar chart)

Step 1

Weight cases by 'Freq' instead of 'ColPerCent' by selecting 'Data' → 'Weight Cases…' → 'Freq' → 'Weight Cases by'.
Click the arrow button to put it in the 'Frequency Variable:' box.
Select 'OK'.

Step 2

Select 'Graphs' → 'Legacy Dialogs' → 'Bar…'.

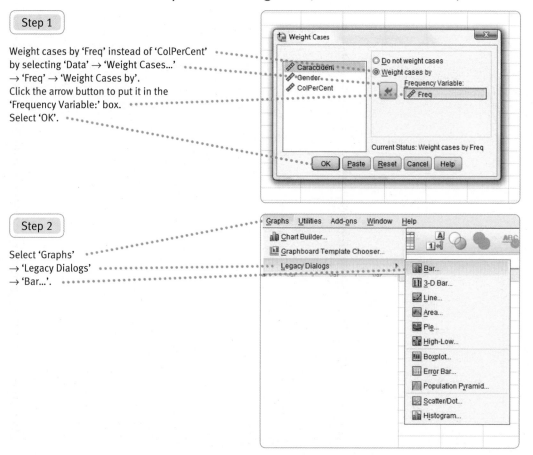

Step 3

Select 'Clustered'.
Select 'Define'.

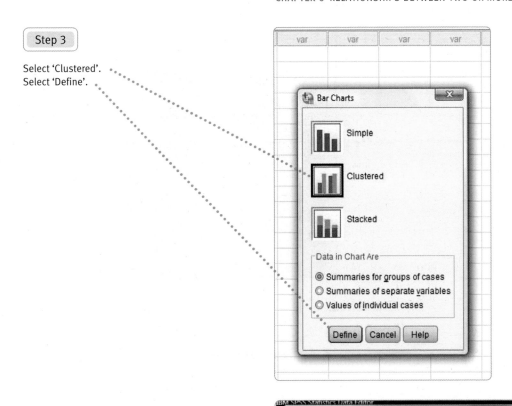

Step 4

Select 'N. of cases'.
Select 'Caraccident'.
Click the arrow button next to 'Category Axis:'.
Select 'Gender'.
Click the arrow button
next to 'Define Clusters by:'.
Select 'OK'.

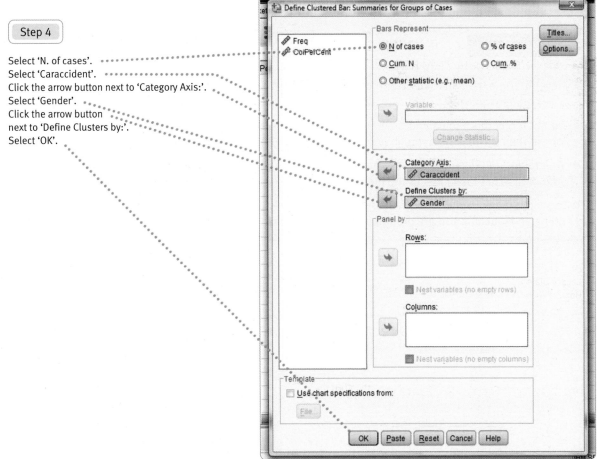

Figure 6.7 is the bar chart produced.

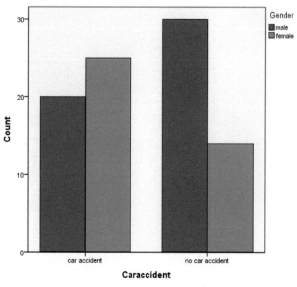

Cases weighted by Freq

FIGURE 6.7   Compound histogram (clustered bar chart) output

Key points

- Never assume that your tables and diagrams are good enough at the first attempt. They could probably be improved with a little care and adjustment.

- Do not forget that tables and diagrams are there to present clearly the major trends in your data (or lack of them). There is not much point in having tables and diagrams that do not clarify your data.

- Your tables and diagrams are not means of tabulating your unprocessed data. If you need to present your data in full then most of the methods to be found in this chapter will not help you much.

- Labelling tables and diagrams clearly and succinctly is an important part of the task – without clear titling and labelling you are probably wasting your time.

CHAPTER 7

Correlation coefficients

The Pearson correlation and Spearman's rho

Overview

- Correlation coefficients are numerical indexes of the relationship between two variables. They form the basis of many statistical procedures and are widely used in the social sciences.

- The numerical size of the *correlation coefficient* ranges from 0 (no relationship) to 1 (a perfect relationship); however, this coefficient may be either positive or negative depending on whether both sets of scores increase together (positive correlation) or whether one set increases as the other decreases (negative correlation).

- The Pearson correlation is used for score variables (though it can be used where a variable is a nominal variable with just two categories). The Spearman correlation is used when the scores are ranked from smallest to largest (i.e. non-parametric).

- Great care should be taken to inspect the scattergram between the two variables in question in order to make sure that the 'line of best fit' is straight rather than a curve. Also, small numbers of very extreme scores can substantially mask the true trend in the data – these are called outliers. The chapter explains what to do about them.

- Statistical significance is dealt with in Chapter 1.

Preparation

Revise variance (Chapter 3) and the use of the scattergram to show the relationship between two variables (Chapter 6).

7.1   Introduction

The simplest way to understand correlation coefficients is to conceive of them as a single numerical index that summarises some of the vital information in a scattergram or scatterplot. The correlation coefficient is really just an index of the spread of the data points around that best-fitting straight line. Correlation coefficients range from absolute values of 1.00 at the most to 0.00 at the least. A correlation of 1.00 means that *all* the data points fit perfectly on the straight line, whereas a correlation of 0.00 means that the data points fit the straight line very poorly. Although the scattergram is an important statistical tool for showing relationships between two variables, it is space consuming. For many purposes it is more convenient to have the main features of the scattergram expressed as a single numerical index – the *correlation coefficient* – and this is merely a numerical index which summarises some, but not all, of the key features of a scattergram. The commonest correlation coefficient is the *Pearson correlation*, also known more grandly and obscurely as the *Pearson product-moment correlation coefficient*.

The correlation coefficient thus neatly summarises a great deal of information about a scattergram. It is especially useful when you have several variables which would involve drawing numerous scattergrams, one for each pair of variables. It most certainly does not replace the scattergram entirely but merely helps you to present your findings rather more concisely than other methods. Indeed, we recommend that you draw a scattergram for every correlation coefficient you calculate even if that scattergram is not intended for inclusion in your report.

Although the correlation coefficient is a basic descriptive statistic, it is elaborated in a number of sophisticated forms such as partial correlation, multiple correlation and factor analysis. It is of paramount importance in many forms of research, especially survey, questionnaire and similar forms of research.

7.2   Principles of the correlation coefficient

The correlation coefficient basically takes the following form:

$$r_{[\text{correlation coefficient}]} = +1.00$$
$$\text{or}\quad 0.00$$
$$\text{or}\ -1.00$$
$$\text{or}\quad 0.30$$
$$\text{or}\ -0.72,\ \text{etc.}$$

So a correlation coefficient consists of two parts:

1. A positive or negative sign (although for positive values the sign is frequently omitted)

2. Any numerical value in the range of 0.00 to 1.00.

The + or – sign tells us something important about the slope of the correlation line (i.e. the best-fitting straight line through the points on the scattergram). A positive value means that the slope is *from the bottom left to the top right* of the scattergram (Figure 7.1). On the other hand, if the sign is negative (–) then the slope of the straight line goes *from upper left to lower right* on the scattergram (Figure 7.2).

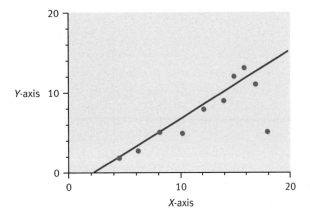

| FIGURE 7.1 | Positive correlation between two variables |

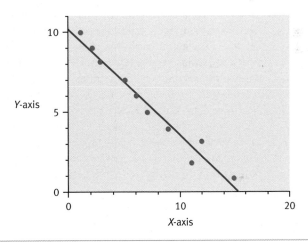

| FIGURE 7.2 | Negative correlation between two variables |

The numerical value of the correlation coefficient (0.50, 0.42, etc.) is an index of how close the points on the scattergram fit the best-fitting straight line. A value of 1.00 means that the points of the scattergram all lie exactly on the best-fitting straight line (Figure 7.3), unless that line is perfectly vertical or perfectly horizontal, in which case it means that there is no variation in the scores on one of the variables and so no correlation can be calculated.

A value of 0.00 means that the points of the scattergram are randomly scattered around the straight line. It is purely a matter of luck if any of them actually touch the straight line (Figure 7.4). In this case the best-fitting straight line for the scattergram could be virtually any line you arbitrarily decide to draw through the points. Conventionally it is drawn as a horizontal line, but any other angle of slope would do just as well, since there is no discernible trend in the relationship between the two variables on the scattergram.

A value of 0.50 would mean that although the points on the scattergram are generally close to the best-fitting straight line, there is considerable spread of these points around that straight line.

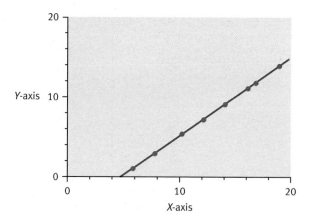

FIGURE 7.3   Perfect correlation between two variables

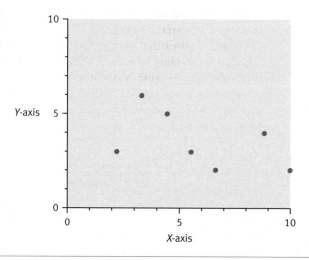

FIGURE 7.4   Near-zero correlation between two variables

The correlation coefficient is merely an index of the amount of variance of the scattergram points from the straight line. However, it is calculated in such a way that the *maximum* variance around that straight line results in a correlation of zero. In other words, the closer the relationship between the two variables, the higher is the correlation coefficient, up to a maximum value of 1.00.

To summarise, the components of the correlation coefficient are the sign (+ or −), which indicates the direction of the slope, and a numerical value which indicates how much variation there is around the best-fitting straight line through the points (i.e. the higher the numerical value the closer the fit).

■ Covariance

In the formula for the correlation coefficient we use something called the *covariance*. This is almost exactly the same as the formula for variance, but instead of multiplying scores by themselves we multiply the score on one variable (X) by the score on the second variable (Y):

$$\text{Covariance}_{\text{[of variable X with variable Y]}} = \frac{\sum(X - \bar{X})(X - \bar{Y})}{N}$$

where

X = scores on variable X
$\bar{X}$ = mean score on variable X
Y = scores on variable Y
$\bar{Y}$ = mean score on variable Y
N = number of pairs of scores.

We get a large positive value of covariance if there is a strong positive relationship between the two variables, and a big negative value if there is a strong negative relationship between the two variables. If there is no relationship between the variables then the covariance is zero. Notice that, unlike variance, the covariance can take positive or negative values.

However, the size of the covariance is affected by the size of the variances of the two separate variables involved. The larger the variances, the larger is the covariance, potentially. Obviously this would make comparisons difficult. So the covariance is adjusted by dividing by the square root of the product of the variances of the two separate variables. (Because N, the number of pairs of scores, in the variance and covariance formulae can be cancelled out in the correlation formula, the usual formula includes no division by the number of scores.) Once this adjustment is made to the covariance formula, we have the formula for the correlation coefficient:

$$r_{\text{[correlation coefficient]}} = \frac{\sum(X - \bar{X})(Y - \bar{Y})}{\sqrt{\sum(X - \bar{X})^2}\sqrt{\sum(Y - \bar{Y})^2}}$$

The lower part of the formula actually gives the largest possible value of the covariance of the two variables – that is, the theoretical covariance if the two variables lay perfectly on the straight line through the scattergram. Dividing the covariance by the maximum value it could take (if there were no spread of points away from the straight line through the scattergram) ensures that the correlation coefficient can never be greater than 1.00. The covariance formula also contains the necessary sign to indicate the slope of the relationship.

Calculation 7.1

The Pearson correlation coefficient

Our data for this calculation come from scores that measured the relationship between fear of crime and confidence in the police (Table 7.1). A worked example using SPSS can be found in Section 7.6.

It is always sound practice to draw the scattergram for any correlation coefficient you are calculating. For these data, the scattergram will be like Figure 7.5. Notice that the slope of the scattergram is negative, as one could have deduced

Table 7.1	Scores on 'Fear of Crime' and 'Confidence in Police' for 10 adults	
Individual	**Fear of Crime score**	**Confidence in Police score**
Angela	2	8
Arthur	6	3
Peter	4	9
Mike	5	7
Barbara	7	2
Jane	7	3
Jean	2	9
Ruth	3	8
Alan	5	6
Theresa	4	7

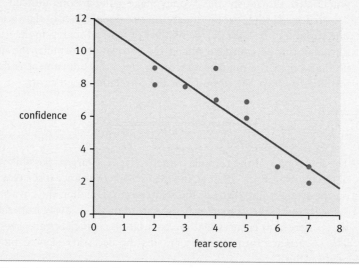

FIGURE 7.5   Scattergram for Calculation 7.1

from the tendency for those who score highly on the fear of crime questionnaire to have low scores on confidence in the police survey. You can also see not only that a straight line is a pretty good way of describing the trends in the points on the scattergram but that the points fit the straight line reasonably well. Thus we should expect a fairly high negative correlation from the correlation coefficient.

Step 1   Set the scores out in a table (Table 7.2) and follow the calculations as shown. Here N is the number of *pairs* of scores, i.e. 10.

Step 2   Substitute the values from Table 7.2 in the formula:

Table 7.2	Essential steps in the calculation of the correlation coefficient			
X score (Fear)	*Y* score (Police)	X^2	Y^2	$X \times Y$
2	8	4	64	16
6	3	36	9	18
4	9	16	81	36
5	7	25	49	35
7	2	49	4	14
7	3	49	9	21
2	9	4	81	18
3	8	9	64	24
5	6	25	36	30
4	7	16	49	28
$\sum X = 45$	$\sum Y = 62$	$\sum X^2 = 233$	$\sum Y^2 = 446$	$\sum XY = 240$

$$r_{\text{[correlation coefficient]}} = \frac{\sum XY - \dfrac{\sum X \sum Y}{N}}{\sqrt{\left(\sum X^2 - \dfrac{(\sum X^2)}{N}\right)(\sum Y^2) - \dfrac{\sum Y^2}{N}}}$$

$$= \frac{240 - \dfrac{45 \times 62}{10}}{\sqrt{\left(233 - \dfrac{45^2}{10}\right)\left(446 - \dfrac{62^2}{10}\right)}}$$

$$= \frac{240 - \dfrac{2790}{10}}{\sqrt{\left(233 - \dfrac{2025}{10}\right)\left(446 - \dfrac{3844}{10}\right)}}$$

$$= \frac{240 - 279}{\sqrt{(233 - 202.5)(446 - 384.4)}}$$

$$= \frac{-39}{\sqrt{30.5 \times 61.6}} = \frac{-39}{43.35} = -0.90$$

Interpreting the result So the value obtained for the correlation coefficient equals −0.90. This value is in line with what we suggested about the scattergram which serves as a rough check on our calculation. There is a very substantial negative relationship between fear of crime and confidence in the police. In other words, those people who were most afraid of crime had the lowest confidence in the police, and vice versa. It is not claimed that they are afraid of crime *because* they don't have confidence in the police, but merely that there is an inverse association between the two.

Reporting the results We would write something like: 'It was found that fear of crime was inversely related to confidence in the police. The Pearson correlation coefficient was −0.90 which is statistically significant at the 5% level with a sample size of 10.'

Note: Normally, when reporting a correlation coefficient it is usual to report its statistical significance. The meaning of statistical significance is explained in Chapter 1. However, the important point for now is to remember that statistical significance is invariably reported with the value of the correlation coefficient.

7.3   Some rules to check out

1. You should make sure that a straight line is the best fit to the scattergram points. If the best-fitting line is a *curve* such as in Figure 7.6 then you should not use the Pearson correlation coefficient. The reason for this is that the Pearson correlation assumes a straight line which is a gross distortion if you have a curved (curvilinear) relationship.

2. Make sure that your scattergram does not contain a few extreme cases which are unduly influencing the correlation coefficient (Figure 7.7). In this diagram you can see that the points at the top left of the scattergram are responsible for the apparent negative correlation between the two variables. Your eyes probably suggest that for virtually all the points on the scattergram there is no relationship at all. You could in these circumstances eliminate the 'outliers' (i.e. extreme, highly influential points)

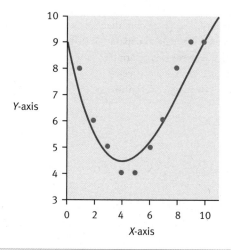

FIGURE 7.6   A curved relationship between two variables

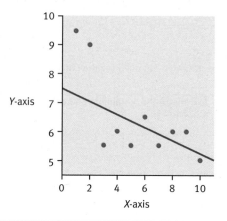

FIGURE 7.7   Influence of outliers on a correlation

and recalculate the correlation coefficient based on the remaining, more typical group of scores. If the correlation remains significant with the same sign as before then your interpretation of your data is likely to remain broadly unchanged. However, there needs to be good reason for deleting the outliers; this should not be done simply because the data as they stand do not support your ideas. It may be that something unusual had happened – perhaps an outlier arose from the responses of a slightly deaf person who could not hear the researcher's instructions, for example.

Box 7.1   Research design issue

Causality

It is typically argued that a correlation does not prove causality. The fact that two variables are related to each other is no reason to say anything other than that they are related. Statistical analysis is basically incapable of proving that one variable influenced the other variable directly. Questions such as whether one variable affected the other are addressed primarily through the nature of your research design and not through the statistical analysis as such. Conventionally, researchers have turned to experiments in which variables could be systematically manipulated by the researcher in order to be able to enhance their confidence in making causal interpretations about relationships between variables.

7.4   Coefficient of determination

The correlation coefficient is an index of how much variance two variables have in common. However, you need to square the correlation coefficient in order to know precisely how much variance is shared. The squared correlation coefficient is also known as the *coefficient of determination*.

The proportion of variance shared by two variables whose correlation coefficient is 0.5 equals 0.5^2 or 0.25. This is a proportion out of 1 so as a percentage it is $0.25 \times 100\%$ = 25%. A correlation coefficient of 0.8 means that $0.8^2 \times 100\%$ or 64% of the variance is shared. A correlation coefficient of 1.00 means that $1.00^2 \times 100\%$ = 100% of the variance is shared. Since the coefficient of determination is based on *squaring* the correlation coefficient, it should be obvious that the amount of variance shared by the two variables declines increasingly rapidly as the correlation coefficient gets smaller (Table 7.3).

Table 7.3	Variance shared by two variables	
Correlation coefficient	**Variance shared by two variables**
1.00	100%
0.90	81%
0.50	25%
0.10	1%
0.00	0%

> ## 7.5   Data requirements for correlation coefficients

The Pearson correlation coefficient requires two score variables, as does Spearman's rho (see Section 7.7). However, the scores should ideally be normally distributed for the Pearson correlation and, some would argue, on an equal-interval scale. One could consider using Spearman's rho where these requirements are not met, though the advantages of doing so may not balance the costs for anything other than the most simple of research studies because it is a far less flexible statistic.

It is possible to use the Pearson correlation coefficient when one or both variables are in the form of binary variables – that is, there are only two possible response categories. Code these binary variables as 1 for one category and 2 for the other category in SPSS. If you then run the Pearson correlation procedure on these variables, the resulting correlations are known as phi (if both variables are binary) and the point biserial (if one variable is binary and the other a score variable).

> ## 7.6   SPSS analysis

■ The data to be analysed

We will illustrate the computation of Pearson's correlation and a scatter diagram for the data in Table 7.1, which gives scores for the fear of crime and confidence in the police of 10 adults.

■ Entering the data

Step 1

In 'Variable View' of the 'Data Editor' name the first variable 'Fear' and the second variable 'Police'.
Remove the two decimal places by changing figure already here to zero.

	Name	Type	Width	Decimals
1	Fear	Numeric	8	0
2	Police	Numeric	8	0

Step 2

In 'Data View' of the 'Data Editor' enter the scores for 'Fear' in the first column and 'Police' in the second column.
Save this data file.

	Fear	Police
1	2	8
2	6	3
3	4	9
4	5	7
5	7	2
6	7	3
7	2	9
8	3	8
9	5	6
10	4	7

Pearson's correlation

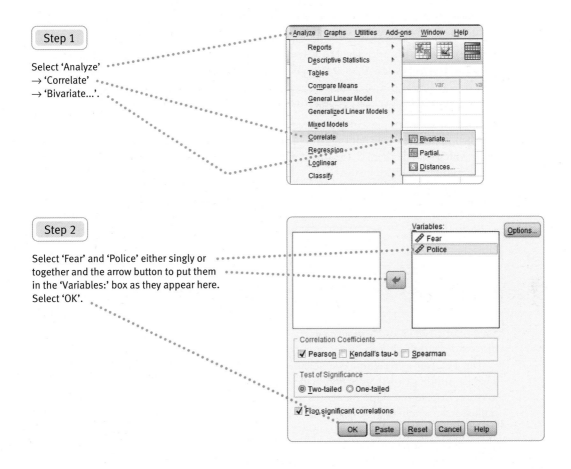

Step 1

Select 'Analyze'
→ 'Correlate'
→ 'Bivariate...'.

Step 2

Select 'Fear' and 'Police' either singly or together and the arrow button to put them in the 'Variables:' box as they appear here. Select 'OK'.

Interpreting the output

● The correlation between 'Fear' and 'Police' is −.900. The two-tailed significance or probability level is .001 or less, so the correlation is statistically significant.

● The number of cases on which this correlation is based is 10.

● This information is also given in this cell.

Correlations

		Fear	Police
Fear	Pearson Correlation	1	−.900[**]
	Sig. (2-tailed)		.000
	N	10	10
Police	Pearson Correlation	−.900[**]	1
	Sig. (2-tailed)	.000	
	N	10	10

[**]. Correlation is significant at the 0.01 level (2-tailed).

■ Reporting the output

- The correlation between fear of crime and confidence in the police is −.900. It is usual to round correlations to two decimal places, which would make it −0.90.

- The exact significance level to three decimal places is .000. This means that the significance level is less than 0.001. We would suggest that you do not use a string of zeros, as these confuse people. Always change the third zero to a 1. This means that the significance level can be reported as being $p < 0.001$.

- It is customary to present the degrees of freedom (df) rather than the number of cases when presenting correlations. The degrees of freedom are the number of cases minus 2, which makes them 8 for this correlation. There is nothing wrong with reporting the number of cases instead.

- In a report, we would write 'There is a significant negative relationship between fear of crime and confidence in the police ($r = -0.90$, $df = 8$, $p < 0.001$). Adults who are most afraid of crime also have the least confidence in the police.'

7.7   Spearman's rho – another correlation coefficient

Spearman's rho is often written as r_s. We have not used this symbol in the following discussion, although it is common in textbooks.

The Pearson correlation coefficient is the dominant correlation index in statistics. There is another called *Spearman's rho* which is not very different – practically identical, in truth. Instead of taking the scores directly from your data, the scores on a variable are ranked from smallest to largest. That is, the smallest score on variable X is given rank 1, the second smallest score on variable X is given rank 2, and so forth. The smallest score on variable Y is given rank 1, the second smallest score on variable Y is given rank 2, etc. Then Spearman's rho is calculated like the Pearson correlation coefficient between the two sets of ranks as if the ranks were scores. A special procedure is used to deal with *tied ranks*.

Sometimes certain scores on a variable are identical. There might be two or three people who scored 7 on variable X, for example. This situation is described as *tied scores* or *tied ranks*. The question is what to do about them. The conventional answer in statistics is to pretend first of all that the tied scores can be separated by fractional amounts. Then we allocate the appropriate ranks to these 'separated' scores but give each of the tied scores the average rank that they would have received if they could have been separated (Table 7.4).

The two scores of 5 are each given the rank 2.5 because if they were slightly different they would have been given ranks 2 and 3, respectively. But they cannot be separated and so we average the ranks as follows:

$$\frac{2+3}{2} = 2.5$$

Table 7.4	Ranking of a set of scores when tied (equal) scores are involved								
Scores	4	5	5	6	7	8	9	9	9	10
Ranks	1	2.5	2.5	4	5	6	8	8	8	10

This average of the two ranks corresponds to what was entered into Table 7.4. There are three scores of 9 which would have been allocated the ranks 7, 8 and 9 if the scores had been slightly different from each other. These three ranks are averaged to give an average rank of 8 which is entered as the rank for each of the three tied scores in Table 7.4.

You may wonder why we have bothered to turn the scores into ranks before calculating the correlation coefficient. The reason is that ranks are commonly used in statistics when the distributions of scores on a variable are markedly unsymmetrical and do not approximate (even poorly) a normal distribution. In the past it was quite fashionable to use rankings of scores instead of the scores themselves, but we would suggest that you avoid ranking if possible. Use ranks only when your data seem extremely distorted from a normal distribution. We realise that others may argue differently.

Calculation 7.2

Spearman's rho with or without tied ranks

We could apply the Spearman rho correlation to the data on the relationship between fear of crime and confidence in the police for a group of 10 adults which we used previously. But we must rank the two sets of scores before applying the normal Pearson correlation formula since there are tied ranks (see Table 7.5). In our calculation, N is the number of *pairs* of ranks, i.e. 10. For this calculation we have called the fear score the X score and the police score the Y score (the reverse of Calculation 7.1). This makes no difference to the calculation of the correlation coefficient.

Table 7.5	Steps in the calculation of Spearman's rho correlation coefficient						
Person	Fear score	Police score	Fear rank	Fear rank squared	Police rank	Police rank squared	Fear rank × police rank
	X score	Y score	X_r	X_r^2	Y_r	Y_r^2	$X_r \times Y_r$
1	8	2	7.5	56.25	1.5	2.25	11.25
2	3	6	2.5	6.25	8	64.00	20.00
3	9	4	9.5	90.25	4.5	20.25	42.75
4	7	5	5.5	30.25	6.5	42.25	35.75
5	2	7	1	1.00	9.5	90.25	9.50
6	3	7	2.5	6.25	9.5	90.25	23.75
7	9	2	9.5	90.25	1.5	2.25	14.25
8	8	3	7.5	56.25	3	9.00	22.50
9	6	5	4	16.00	6.5	42.25	26.00
10	7	4	5.5	30.25	4.5	20.25	24.75
			$\sum X_r = 55$	$\sum X_r^2 = 383$	$\sum Y_r = 55$	$\sum Y_r^2 = 383$	$\sum X_r Y_r = 230.50$

→

We then substitute the totals in the computational formula for the Pearson correlation coefficient, although now we call it Spearman's rho:

$$r_{[\text{correlation coefficient}]} = \frac{\sum X_r Y_r - \dfrac{\sum X_r \sum Y_r}{N}}{\sqrt{\left(\sum X_r^2 - \dfrac{(\sum X_r)^2}{N}\right)\left(\sum Y_r^2 - \dfrac{(\sum Y_r)^2}{N}\right)}}$$

$$= \frac{230.5 - \left(\dfrac{55 \times 55}{10}\right)}{\sqrt{\left(383 - \dfrac{55^2}{10}\right)\left(383 - \dfrac{55^2}{10}\right)}}$$

$$= \frac{230.5 - 302.5}{\sqrt{(383 - 302.5)(383 - 302.5)}}$$

$$= \frac{-72.00}{\sqrt{(80.5)(80.5)}}$$

$$= \frac{-72.00}{80.5}$$

$$= -0.89$$

Interpreting the results So, Spearman's rho gives a substantial negative correlation just as we would expect from these data. You can interpret the Spearman correlation coefficient more or less in the same way as the Pearson correlation coefficient so long as you remember that it is calculated using ranks.

Reporting the results We would write up the results as something like: 'It was found that fear of crime was inversely related to confidence in the police. The value of Spearman's rho correlation coefficient was −0.89 which is statistically significant at the 5% level with a sample size of 10.'

Just as with the Pearson correlation (Calculation 7.1), when reporting the Spearman's rho correlation coefficient it is normal to report the statistical significance of the coefficient (see Chapter 1).

We referred earlier to a special computational formula which could be used to calculate Spearman's rho when there are no ties. There seems little point in learning this formula, since a lack of tied ranks is not characteristic of data. You may as well simply use the method of Calculation 7.2 irrespective of whether there are ties or not. For those who want to save a little time when there are no tied ranks, the procedure of Calculation 7.3 may be used.

Calculation 7.3

Spearman's rho where there are no tied ranks

The formula used in this computation applies only when there are no tied scores. If there are any, the formula becomes increasingly inaccurate and the procedure of Calculation 7.2 should be applied. However, many researchers use the formula whether or not there are tied ranks, despite the inaccuracy problem.

Table 7.6	Steps in the calculation of Spearman's rho correlation coefficient using the speedy formula					
Person	Fear score X score	Police score Y score	Fear rank X_r	Police rank Y_r	Fear rank – police rank D (difference)	Square of previous column D^2
1	8	2	7.5	1.5	6.0	36.00
2	3	6	2.5	8	−5.5	30.25
3	9	4	9.5	4.5	5	25.00
4	7	5	5.5	6.5	−1.0	1.00
5	2	7	1	9.5	−8.5	72.25
6	3	7	2.5	9.5	−7.0	49.00
7	9	2	9.5	1.5	8.0	64.00
8	8	3	7.5	3	4.5	20.25
9	6	5	4	6.5	−2.5	6.25
10	7	4	5.5	4.5	1.0	1.00
						$\sum D^2 = 305$

For illustrative purposes we will use the same data on fear of crime and confidence in the police despite there being ties, as listed in Table 7.6. Once again, $N = 10$.

$$r_{[\text{Spearman's rho}]} = 1 - \frac{6\sum D^2}{N(N^2 - 1)}$$

$$= 1 - \frac{6 \times 305}{10(10^2 - 1)}$$

$$= 1 - \frac{1830}{10 \times (100 - 1)}$$

$$= 1 - \frac{1830}{10 \times 99}$$

$$= 1 - \frac{1830}{990}$$

$$= 1 - 1.848$$

$$= -0.848$$

$$= -0.85 \text{ to two decimal places}$$

Interpreting the results It should be noted that this value of Spearman's rho is a little different from its correct value (−0.89) as we calculated in Calculation 7.2. The reason for this difference is the inaccuracy of the speedy formula when there are tied scores. Although the difference is not major, you are strongly recommended not to incorporate this error. Otherwise the interpretation of the negative correlation is the same as we have previously discussed.

Reporting the results We would write up the results something along the lines of the following: 'It was found that fear of crime was inversely related to confidence in the police. The value of Spearman's rho correlation coefficient was −0.85 which is statistically significant at the 5% level with a sample size of 10.'

7.8   SPSS analysis for Spearman's rho

■ Calculation

Step 1

As for Pearson correlation, select 'Analyze'
→ 'Correlate' → 'Bivariate...' and the variables
you want to correlate.
Select 'Spearman'.
If you don't want Pearson, deselect it.
Select 'OK'.

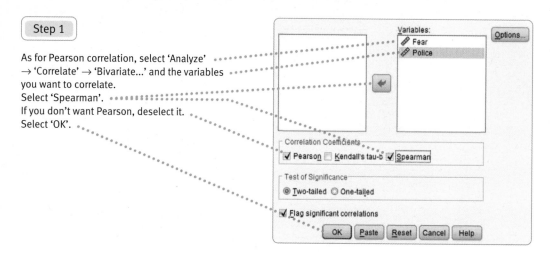

■ Interpreting the output

- Spearman's rho between 'Fear' and 'Police' is −.894. The two-tailed significance level of this correlation is .001 or less so the correlation is statistically significant.

- The number of cases is 10.

- The information is also given in this cell.

Correlations

			Fear	Police
Spearman's rho	Fear	Correlation Coefficient	1.000	-.894**
		Sig. (2-tailed)	.	.000
		N	10	10
	Police	Correlation Coefficient	-.894**	1.000
		Sig. (2-tailed)	.000	.
		N	10	10

**. Correlation is significant at the 0.01 level (2-tailed).

■ Reporting the output

- The correlation reported to two decimal places is −0.89.

- The probability of achieving this correlation by chance is less than 0.001 (i.e. $p < 0.001$).

- We would report this in the following way: 'There is a statistically significant negative correlation between fear of crime and confidence in the police (rho = −0.89, $df = 8$, $p < 0.001$). Those with the highest fear of crime tend to be those with the lowest confidence in the police and vice versa.'

7.9 Scatter diagram using SPSS

Step 1

Select 'Graphs'
→ 'Legacy Dialogs'
→ 'Scatter/Dot...'.

Step 2

Select 'Define' as 'Simple' has already been selected. It is called the default.

Step 3

To have 'Fear' as the vertical axis, select it and the arrow button next to the 'Y Axis:' box. To have 'Police' as the horizontal axis, select it and the arrow button next to the 'X Axis:' box. Select 'OK'.

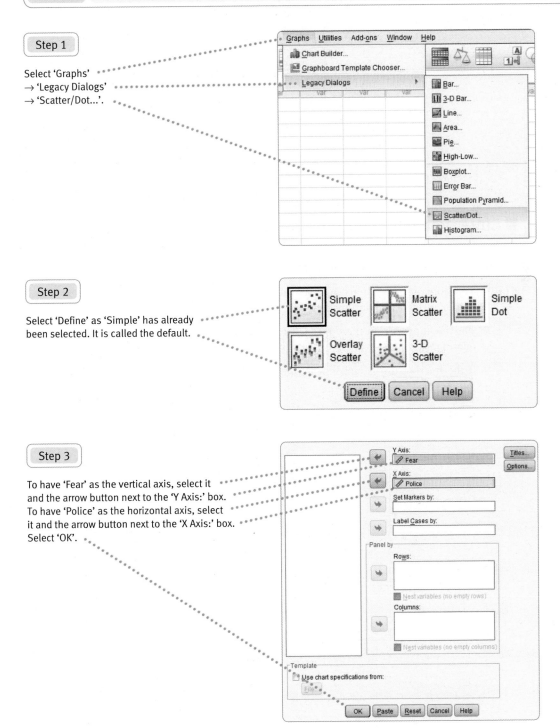

Step 4

To fit a correlation line to the scatterplot, double-click anywhere in which it opens the 'Chart Editor'.
Select 'Elements' → 'Fit Line at Total'.
Select 'Close ' in the 'Properties:' box.
A correlation line is the same as the regression line.

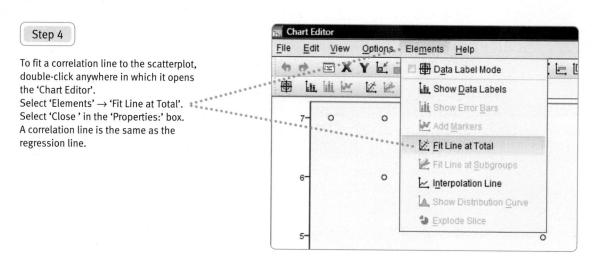

■ Interpreting the output

- In the resulting scattergram (Figure 7.8) the scatter of points is relatively narrow, indicating that the correlation is high.

- The slope of the scatter lies in a relatively straight line, indicating it is a linear rather than a curvilinear relationship.

- The line moves from the upper left to the lower right, which signifies a negative correlation.

- If the relationship is curvilinear, then Pearson's or Spearman's correlations may be misleading.

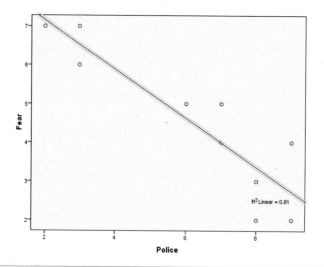

| FIGURE 7.8 | 'Fear of crime' and 'confidence in the police' scattergram |

■ Reporting the output

- You should never report a correlation coefficient without examining the scattergram for problems such as curved relationships or outliers.

- In a student project it should always be possible to include graphs of this sort. Unfortunately, journal articles and books tend to be restricted in the numbers they include because of economies of space and cost.

- We would write of the scattergram: 'A scattergram of the relationship between fear of crime and confidence in the police was examined. There was no evidence of a curvilinear relationship or the undue influence of outliers.'

7.10   Problems in the use of correlation coefficients

Most of the problems involved in using correlation can be identified by carefully looking at the scatterplots of the relationship. The problem of curvilinear relationships has already been discussed and the easiest way of identifying curvilinear relationships is simply by looking at the scatterplot. The alternative is to compare the size of the Pearson correlation on your data with the size of *eta* calculated on the same data.

Outliers are data points on the scatterplot that are at the extremes of the distribution. They are problematic because they can totally distort the correlation, such is their impact; and they can often be identified visually from the scatterplot. However, Spearman's rho is largely unaffected by outliers since they are changed into ranks along with the other scores. So one way of checking for outliers is to compare the Spearman's rho correlation with the Pearson correlation for the same data. If Spearman's rho is much smaller than the Pearson correlation, then suspect the influence of outliers which are making the Pearson correlation appear to be large.

Key points

Most of the major points have been covered already, but they bear repetition:

- Check the scattergram for your correlation coefficient for signs of a nonlinear relationship – if you find one, you should not be using the Pearson correlation coefficient.

- Check the scattergram for outliers which may spuriously be producing a correlation when overwhelmingly the scattergram says that there is a poor relationship.

- Examine the scattergram to see whether there is a positive or negative slope to the scatter and form a general impression of whether the correlation is good (the points fit the straight line well) or poor (the points are very widely scattered around the straight line). Obviously you will become more skilled at this with experience, but it is useful as a rough computational check among other things.

CHAPTER 8

Regression and standard error

Overview

- Where there is a relationship between two variables, it is then possible to estimate (or predict) a person's score on one of the variables from their score on the other variable.

- Regression basically identifies the *regression line* (that is, the best-fitting straight line) for a scatterplot between two variables. It uses a variable *X* (which is the horizontal axis of the scatterplot) and a variable *Y* (which is the vertical axis of the scatterplot). Sometimes the *X* variable is known as the *independent* or *predictor* variable and the *Y* variable is known as the *dependent* or *criterion* variable.

- To describe the regression line, one needs the slope of the line and the point at which it touches the vertical axis (the intercept). It is then possible to estimate the most likely score on the variable *Y* for any given score on variable *X*.

- *Standard error* is a term used to describe the variability of any statistical estimate including those of the regression calculation. It is similar to standard deviation (see Chapter 5) and indicates the likely spread of any of the estimates.

- Regression becomes a much more important technique when one is using several variables to predict values on another variable. These techniques are known as multiple regression (see Chapter 19).

Preparation

You should have a working knowledge of the scattergram (Chapter 6) of the relationship between two variables, and you should understand the correlation coefficient (Chapter 7).

8.1   Introduction

One of the most difficult statistical techniques for novices to understand is that of simple regression. It is actually one of the earliest statistical methods and predated historically the correlation coefficient. The first thing to understand is that regression is applied to exactly the same data as the Pearson correlation coefficient, but does something different. Look at the scatterplot in Figure 8.1. When we discussed Pearson correlation in Chapter 7, we explained how the correlation coefficient is a measure of how closely the data points fit the straight line through the data points – the bigger the correlation coefficient, the closer the data points tend to be to the straight line. Regression is different in that it describes the characteristics of the straight line itself.

The point at which the vertical axis is cut by the straight line is known as the *cut point*, *intercept* or *constant* whereas the slope is the regression *weight*. The slope is merely the amount that the line goes up (or down) for every unit that one goes along the horizontal axis. The slope can be negative, which indicates that the line goes downwards towards the right of the scatterplot. (The good news is that all of the hard work is done for you on SPSS – including the best-fitting straight line.)

However, it needs to be understood that regression is affected by which variable you put on the horizontal axis (or X-axis) and which variable you put on the vertical axis (or Y-axis). Quite different figures emerge in regression depending on your choice. Why does this matter? One of the functions of regression is to allow the user to make predictions from the value of one variable to the other variable. This is possible if it is established from a sample of data that there is a good correlation between the two variables. For example, if you measured the heights and weights of a sample of participants you would find a correlation between the two. On the basis of this information, you would assume that someone who is tall is likely to be heavier than someone who is small. The only problem is that this is not very precise.

Assume that research has shown that a simple test of verbal ability is capable of distinguishing between the better and not-so-good telephone operators in a customer service centre. Verbal ability is a *predictor* variable and number of calls taken the *criterion*

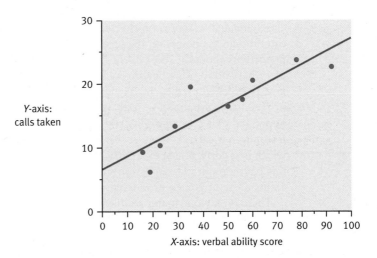

FIGURE 8.1   Scattergram of the relationship between verbal ability and number of calls taken

Table 8.1	Verbal ability and number of calls taken per hour
Verbal ability score	**Number of calls taken per hour**
56	17
19	6
78	23
92	22
16	9
23	10
29	13
60	20
50	16
35	19

variable. So it should be possible to predict which applicants are likely to be the more productive employees from scores on this easily administered test of verbal ability. Using the test might be a lot cheaper than employing people who do not make the grade. Imaginary data for such a study are shown in Table 8.1.

The scattergram (Figure 8.1) shows imaginary data on the relationship between scores on the verbal ability test and the number of calls per hour the employee takes in the customer service centre. Notice that we have made scores on the verbal ability test the horizontal dimension (*X*-axis) and the number of calls taken per hour the vertical dimension (*Y*-axis).

In order to keep the number of formulae to the minimum, the horizontal dimension (*X*-axis) should always be used to represent the variable from which the prediction is being made, and the vertical dimension (*Y*-axis) should always represent what is being predicted.

It is clear from the scattergram that the number of calls taken by workers is fairly closely related to scores on the verbal ability test. If we draw a straight line as best we can through the points on the scattergram, this line could be used as a basis for making predictions about the most likely score on work productivity from the aptitude test score of verbal ability. This line through the points on a scattergram is called the *regression line*. In order to predict the likeliest number of units per hour corresponding to a score of 70 on the verbal ability test, we simply draw a right angle from the score 70 on the horizontal axis (verbal ability test score) to the regression line, and then a right angle from the vertical axis to meet this point. In this way we can find the productivity score which best corresponds to a particular verbal ability score (Figure 8.2). Estimating from this scattergram and regression line, it appears that the best prediction from a verbal ability score of 70 is a productivity rate of about 19 or 20.

There is only one major problem with this procedure – the prediction depends on the particular line drawn through the points on the scattergram. You might draw a somewhat different line from the one we did. Subjective factors such as these are not desirable and it would be better to have a method which was not affected in this way. Mathematical ways of determining the regression line have been developed and fortunately the computations are generally straightforward.

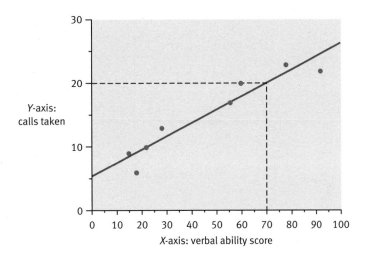

FIGURE 8.2   Using a regression line to make approximate predictions

---

8.2   Theoretical background and regression equations

The line through a set of points on a scattergram is called the regression line. In order to establish an objective criterion, the regression line is chosen which gives the closest fit to the points on the scattergram. In other words, the procedure ensures that there is a minimum sum of distances of the regression line to the points in the scattergram. So, in theory, one could keep trying different possible regression lines until one is found which has the minimum deviation of the points from it.

The sum of the deviations (Σd) of the scattergram points from the regression line should be minimal. Actually, the precise criterion is the sum of the *squared* deviations or the *least squares solution*; it would, however, be tedious to draw different regression lines, then calculate the sum of the squared deviations for each of these in order to decide which regression line has the smallest sum of squared deviations. Fortunately the formula for regression does all of that work for you.

In order to specify the regression line for any scattergram, you quantify two things:

1. The point at which the regression line cuts the vertical axis at $X = 0$. This is a number of units of measurement from the zero point of the vertical axis. It can take a positive or negative value, denoting whether the vertical axis is cut above or below its zero point. It is normally denoted in regression as point a or the *intercept*.

2. The *slope* of the regression line or, in other words, the gradient of the best-fitting line through the points on the scattergram. Just as with the correlation coefficient, this slope may be positive in the sense that it goes up from bottom left to top right, or it can be negative in that it goes downwards from top left to bottom right. The slope is normally denoted by the letter b.

The intercept and slope are both shown in Figure 8.3. To work out the slope, we have drawn a horizontal dashed line from $X = 30$ to $X = 50$ (length 20) and a vertical dashed

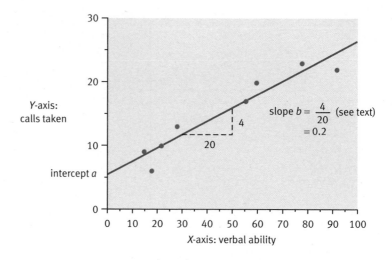

FIGURE 8.3   Slope *b* and intercept *a* of a regression line

line up to the regression line (length about 4 up the *Y*-axis). The slope *b* is the increase (+) or decrease (–) of the calls taken (in this case +4) divided by the increase in the verbal ability score (in this case 20), i.e. +0.2.

The slope is simply the number of units that the regression line moves up the vertical axis for each unit it moves along the horizontal axis. In other words, you mark a single step along the horizontal axis and work out how much increase this represents on the vertical axis. So, for example, if you read that the slope of a scattergram is 2.00, this means that for every increase of 1.00 on the horizontal axis (*X*-axis) there is an increase of 2.00 on the vertical axis (*Y*-axis). If there is a slope of –0.5 then this means that for every increase of 1 on the horizontal axis (*X*-axis) there is a decrease of 0.5 on the vertical axis (*Y*-axis).

In our example, for every increase of 1 in the verbal ability score, there is an increase of 0.2 (more accurately, 0.21) in the job performance measure (calls taken per hour). We have estimated this value from the scattergram – it may not be exactly the answer that we would have obtained had we used mathematically more precise methods. This increase defines the slope. (Note that you do not work with angles, merely distances on the vertical and horizontal axes.)

Fortunately, the application of two relatively simple formulae (see Calculation 8.1) provides all the information we need to calculate the slope and the intercept. A third formula is used to make our predictions from the horizontal axis to the vertical axis.

The major differences between correlation and regression are:

1. Regression retains the original units of measurement, so direct comparisons between regression analyses based on different variables are difficult. Correlation coefficients can readily be compared as they are essentially on a standardised measurement scale and free of the original units of measurement.

2. The correlation coefficient does *not* specify the slope of a scattergram. Correlation indicates the amount of spread or variability of the points around the regression line in the scattergram.

In other words, correlation and regression have somewhat different functions despite their close similarities.

Calculation 8.1

Regression equations

To facilitate comparison, we will take the data used in the computation of the correlation coefficient (Chapter 7). The data concern the relationship between fear of crime and confidence in the police for a group of 10 individuals. The 10 scores need to be set out in a table like Table 8.2 and the various intermediate calculations carried out. However, it is important with regression to make the X scores the predictor (independent) variable; the Y scores are the criterion (dependent) variable. N is the number of *pairs* of scores, i.e. 10. (Strictly speaking the Y^2 and $\sum Y^2$ calculations are not necessary for regression, but they are included here because they highlight the similarities between the correlation and regression calculations.)

Table 8.2	Important steps in calculating the regression equation				
Person	Fear of Crime score (X score)	Confidence in Police score (Y score)	X^2	Y^2	XY
1	8	2	64	4	16
2	3	6	9	36	18
3	9	4	81	16	36
4	7	5	49	25	35
5	2	7	4	49	14
6	3	7	9	49	21
7	9	2	81	4	18
8	8	3	64	9	24
9	6	5	36	25	30
10	7	4	49	16	28
	$\sum X = 62$	$\sum Y = 45$	$\sum X^2 = 446$	$\sum Y^2 = 233$	$\sum XY = 240$

The slope b of the regression line is given by the following formula:

$$b = \frac{\sum XY - \left(\dfrac{\sum X \sum Y}{N} \right)}{\sum X^2 - \dfrac{(\sum X)^2}{N}}$$

Thus, substituting the values from the table in the above formula:

$$b_{[slope]} = \frac{240 - \left(\dfrac{62 \times 45}{10} \right)}{446 - \dfrac{(62)^2}{10}} = \frac{240 - \dfrac{2790}{10}}{446 - \dfrac{3844}{10}}$$

$$= \frac{240 - 279}{446 - 384.4} = \frac{-39}{61.6} = -0.63$$

This tells us that the slope of the regression line is negative – it moves downwards from top left to bottom right. Furthermore, for every unit one moves along the horizontal axis, the regression line moves 0.63 units *down* the vertical axis, since in this case it is a *negative* slope.

We can now substitute in the following formula to get the cut-off point or intercept *a* of the regression line on the vertical axis:

$$a_{\text{[intercept on vertical axis]}} = \frac{\sum Y - b \sum X}{N}$$

$$= \frac{45 - (-0.63 \times 62)}{10}$$

$$= \frac{45 - (-39.06)}{10}$$

$$= \frac{84.06}{10} = 8.41$$

This value for *a* is the point on the vertical axis (confidence in the police) cut by the regression line.

If one wishes to predict the most likely score on the vertical axis from a particular score on the horizontal axis, one simply substitutes the appropriate values in the following formula:

$$Y_{\text{[predicted score]}} = a_{\text{[intercept]}} + b_{\text{[slope]}} \times X_{\text{[known score]}}$$

Thus if we wished to predict confidence in the police for a score of 8 on fear of crime, given that we know the slope *b* is –0.63 and the intercept is 8.41, we simply substitute these values in the formula:

$$\begin{aligned} Y_{\text{[predicted score]}} &= a_{\text{[intercept]}} + b_{\text{[slope]}} \times X_{\text{[known score]}} \\ &= 8.41 + (-0.63 \times 8) \\ &= 8.41 + (-5.04) \\ &= 3.37 \end{aligned}$$

This is the *best* prediction – it does not mean that people with a score of 8 on fear of crime will inevitably record a score of 3.37 on confidence in the police: it is just our most intelligent estimate.

Interpreting the results The proper interpretation of the regression equations depends on the scattergram between the two variables showing a more or less linear (i.e. straight line) trend. If it does not show this, then the interpretation of the regression calculations for the slope and intercept will be misleading since the method assumes a straight line. Curvilinear relationships (see Chapter 7) are difficult to handle mathematically.

If the scattergram reveals a linear relationship, then the interpretation of the regression equations is simple as the formulae merely describe the scattergram mathematically.

Reporting the results This regression analysis could be reported as follows: 'Because of the negative correlation between fear of crime and confidence in the police, it was possible to carry out a regression analysis to predict confidence in the police from fear of crime scores. The slope of the regression of fear of crime on police confidence *b* is –0.63 and the intercept *a* is 8.41.'

Box 8.1   Research design issue

There are always two regression lines between two variables: that from which variable *A* is predicted from variable *B*, and that from which variable *B* is predicted from variable *A*. They almost always have different slopes. However, life is made simpler if we always have the predictor on the horizontal axis and the criterion to be predicted on the vertical axis. You need to be careful what you are trying to predict and from what.

8.3   When and when not to use simple regression

Generally, simple regression of this sort would be rarely used. Usually, researchers would use the correlation coefficient in preference to regression when doing *simple* regression. Indeed, the regression weight expressed in standardised form is the same as the Pearson correlation coefficient. In terms of learning statistics, it is vital because it introduces the basic ideas of regression. Regression comes into its own when extended into what is termed multiple regression (see Chapter 19) in which there are several predictor variables involved. It is also closely related conceptually to logistic regression.

However, it can be used on any pair of score variables, especially when the data approximate equal-interval measurement, which is the assumption for most score variables in psychology.

As already mentioned, few researchers use simple regression in their analyses. It has no advantages over the Pearson correlation coefficient with which it has a lot in common. In addition, do not use simple regression where one has one or more binary variables (two-value or two-category variables) since the output may be fairly meaningless – it certainly will not look like a typical scatterplot and so may cause confusion.

8.4   Data requirements for simple regression

Two score variables are needed. It is best if these are normally distributed but some deviation from this ideal will not make much difference.

8.5   Problems in the use of simple regression

Simple regression is beset with the same problems as the Pearson correlation coefficient (see Chapter 7). So non-linear relationships are a problem as are outliers. These can be checked for using a scatterplot of the data.

From a learner's point of view, there is one extremely common mistake – putting the predictor variable in the analysis wrongly so that it is treated as the dependent variable by SPSS. Making a scatterplot should help, since it is possible to estimate the likely values from this, especially the intercept, constant or cut point on the vertical axis. This can be checked against the computed values since this may reveal such a confusion of the independent and dependent variables.

Sometimes the way in which SPSS gives the constant can cause confusion. The constant appears under the column for *B* weights or coefficients, which is not what it is. You should have no trouble if you follow the instructions in Section 8.1.

Box 8.2   Research design issue

The use of regression in prediction is a fraught issue not because of the statistical methods but because of the characteristics of the data used. In particular, note that our predictions about job performance are based on data from the people already in the job. So, for example, those with the best verbal ability might have developed these skills on the job rather than having them when they were interviewed. Thus it may not be that verbal ability determines job performance but that they are both influenced by other (unknown) factors. Similarly, if we found that age was a negative predictor of how quickly people get promoted in a banking corporation, this may simply reflect a bias against older people in the profession rather than greater ability of younger people.

8.6   SPSS analysis

■ The data to be analysed

We will illustrate the computation of simple regression and a regression plot with the data in Table 8.2 which gives a score for fear of crime and confidence in the police of 10 adults. These data are identical to those used in the chapter on correlation. In this way, you may find it easier to appreciate the differences between regression and correlation.

The confidence scores are the criterion or the dependent variable, while the fear scores are the predictor or independent variable. With regression, it is essential to make the criterion or dependent variable the vertical axis (Y-axis) of a scatterplot and the predictor or independent variable the horizontal axis (X-axis).

■ Entering the data

If you have saved the data, open it in SPSS, otherwise enter the data again (see Figure 8.2).

Step 1

In 'Variable View' of the 'Data Editor' name the first variable 'Fear' and the second variable 'Police'.
Remove the two decimal places.

	Name	Type	Width	Decimals
1	Fear	Numeric	8	0
2	Police	Numeric	8	0

Step 2

In 'Data View' of the 'Data Editor' enter 'Fear' in the first column and 'Police' in the second column.

	Fear	Police
1	2	8
2	6	3
3	4	9
4	5	7
5	7	2
6	7	3
7	2	9
8	3	8
9	5	6
10	4	7

■ Simple regression

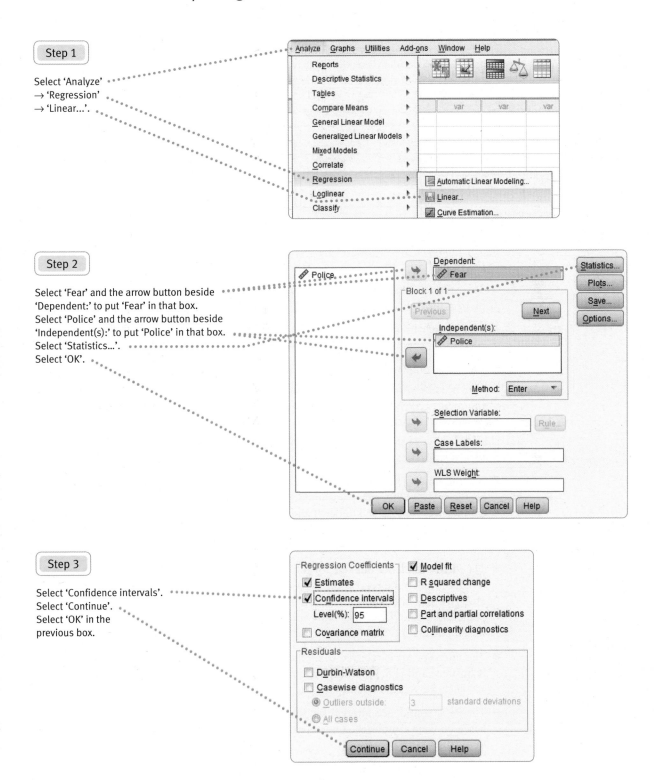

Step 1

Select 'Analyze'
→ 'Regression'
→ 'Linear...'.

Step 2

Select 'Fear' and the arrow button beside
'Dependent:' to put 'Fear' in that box.
Select 'Police' and the arrow button beside
'Independent(s):' to put 'Police' in that box.
Select 'Statistics...'.
Select 'OK'.

Step 3

Select 'Confidence intervals'.
Select 'Continue'.
Select 'OK' in the
previous box.

■ Interpreting the output

This shows the last table of the output, which has the essential details of the regression analysis. It is very easy to reverse the independent variable and dependent variable accidentally. Under the table the name of the dependent variable is given. In this case it is Police which is our dependent variable. If it read Fear then we would have made a mistake and the analysis would need to be redone as the regression values would be incorrect.

Coefficients[a]

Model		Unstandardized Coefficients		Standardized Coefficients	t	Sig.	95.0% Confidence Interval for B	
		B	Std. Error	Beta			Lower Bound	Upper Bound
1	(Constant)	8.425	.725		11.620	.000	6.753	10.097
	Police	-.633	.109	-.900	-5.832	.000	-.883	-.383

a. Dependent Variable: Fear

- The intercept or constant is 8.425. This is the point at which the regression line cuts the vertical axis.

- The unstandardised regression coefficient is –.633. This means that for every increase of 1 on the Police variable, the score on the Fear variable decreases by –.633.

- The standardised regression coefficient is –.900. This is more or less the Pearson correlation coefficient between fear of crime and confidence in the police.

- The 95% confidence interval ranges from –.833 to –.383. This means that the unstandardised coefficient is very likely to have a population between –.833 and –.383.

In simple regression involving two variables, it is conventional to report the regression equation as a slope (*b*) and an intercept (*a*). SPSS does not quite follow this terminology. Unfortunately, at this stage the SPSS output is far more complex and detailed than the statistical sophistication of most students:

- *B* is the slope. The slope of the regression line is called the unstandardised regression coefficient in SPSS. The unstandardised regression coefficient between 'fear' and 'confidence' is displayed under *B* and is –0.633, which rounded to two decimal places is –0.63. What this means is that for every increase of 1.00 on the horizontal axis, the score on the vertical axis changes by –0.633.

- The 95% confidence interval for this coefficient ranges from –0.88 (–0.883) to –0.38 (–0.383). Since the regression is based on a sample and not the population there is always a risk that the sample regression coefficient is not the same as that in the population. The 95% confidence interval gives the range of regression slopes within which you can be 95% sure that the population slope will lie.

- The intercept (*a*) is referred to as the constant in SPSS. The intercept is presented as (Constant) and is 8.425, which rounded to two decimal places is 8.43. It is the point at which the regression line cuts the vertical (*Y*) axis.

- The 95% confidence interval for the intercept is 6.753 to 10.097. This means that, based on your sample, the intercept of the population is 95% likely to lie in the range of 6.75 to 10.10.

- The column headed 'Beta' gives a value of –0.900. This is actually the Pearson correlation between the two variables. In other words, if you turn your scores into standard scores (*z*-scores) the slope of the regression and the correlation coefficient are the same thing.

8.7 Regression scatterplot

It is generally advisable to inspect a scattergram of your two variables when doing regression. This involves the steps involved in plotting a scattergram as described in Chapter 7.

Step 1

Select 'Graphs'
→ 'Legacy Dialogs'
→ 'Scatter/Dot...'.

Step 2

Select 'Define' ('Simple Scatter' is the pre-selected default).

Step 3

Select 'Fear' and the arrow button beside 'Y Axis:' to put it in this box as it is the criterion.
Select 'Police' and the arrow button beside 'X Axis:' to put it in this box as it is the predictor.
Select 'OK'.
The output is the same as that for the correlation in Section 7.6.

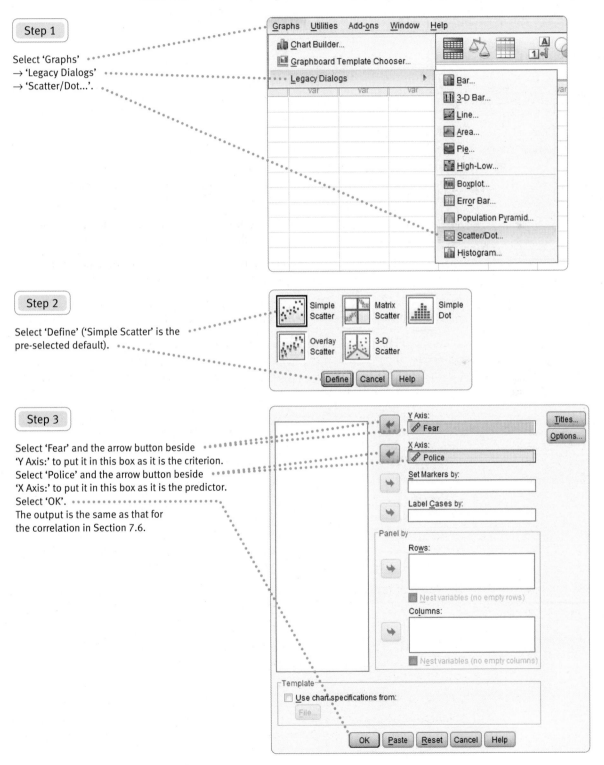

Step 4

To fit a regression line to the scatterplot,
double-click anywhere in it. This opens
the 'Chart Editor'. Select 'Elements'
and 'Fit Line at Total'.
Select 'Close' in the 'Properties:' box.

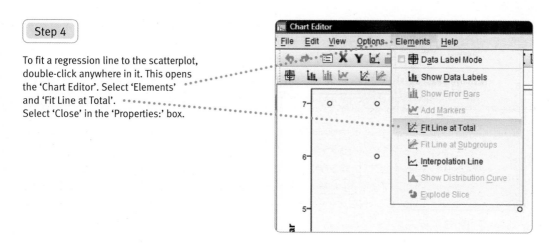

Interpreting the output

- The points on the scatterplot (Figure 8.4) are close to the regression line (i.e. the line is a good fit to the data). Furthermore, the points seem to form a straight line (i.e. the relationship is not curvilinear) and there is no sign of outliers (i.e. especially high or low points).

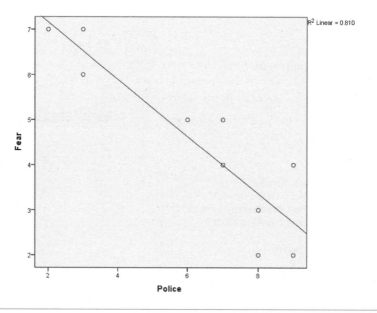

FIGURE 8.4   Regression scatterplot output

- In regression, the vertical axis is the dependent or criterion variable, in this case Police. It is a common error to mix up the axes in regression. If you have done so, then start again.

- The regression line has a negative slope in this case, i.e. it slopes from top left down to bottom right. The beta weight therefore has a negative value.

- In regression, the horizontal axis is the independent or predictor variable, in this case Fear. It is a common error to mix up the axes in regression. If you have done so, then redo the analysis by reversing the axes.

- The regression line sloping from top left down to bottom right indicates a negative relationship between the two variables. Remember that unless your axes intersect at zero on both the vertical and horizontal axes then your interpretation risks being mistaken.

- The points seem relatively close to this line, which suggests that beta (correlation) should be a large (negative) numerical value and that the confidence interval for the slope should be relatively small.

■ Reporting the output

Although all of the output from SPSS is pertinent to a sophisticated user, many users might prefer to have the bare bones at this stage.

- With this in mind, we would write about the analysis in this chapter: 'The scatterplot of the relationship between fear of crime and confidence in the police suggested a linear negative relationship between the two variables. It is possible to predict accurately a person's confidence in the police from their fear of crime score. The equation is $Y' = 8.43 + (-0.63X)$ where X is an individual's fear score and Y' is the best prediction of their police confidence score.'

- An alternative is to give the scatterplot and to write underneath $a = 8.43$ and $B = -0.63$.

- One could add the confidence intervals such as: 'The 95% confidence interval for the slope of the regression line is −0.88 to −0.38. Since this confidence interval does not include 0.00, the slope differs significantly from a horizontal straight line.' However, this would be a relatively sophisticated interpretation for novices in statistics.

8.8   # Standard error: how accurate are the predicted score and the regression equations?

We suggest you revise Chapter 5 before studying the following material.

The accuracy of the predicted score on the criterion is dependent on the closeness of the scattergram points to the regression line; if there is a strong correlation between the variables there is little error in the prediction. Examining the scattergram between two variables will give you an idea of the variability around the regression line and hence the precision of the estimated or predicted scores.

Statisticians prefer to calculate what they call the *standard error* (see Chapter 5) to indicate how certain one can be about aspects of regression such as the prediction of the intercept or cut-off points, and the slope. A standard error is much the same as the standard deviation except that it applies to the means of samples rather than individual scores. So the standard error of something is the average deviation of sample means from the mean of the sample means. *Just regard standard error of an estimate as the average amount by which an estimate is likely to be wrong.* As you might expect, since this is statistics, the average is calculated in an unexpected way, as it was for the standard deviation, which is little different.

Box 8.3   **Key concepts**

Standard error

Standard error was introduced in Chapter 5 and is discussed again in later chapters. Superficially, it may appear to be quite different from the ideas in this chapter. However, remember that whenever we use any characteristic of a sample as the basis for estimating the characteristic of a population, we are likely to be wrong to some extent. The standard error is merely the average amount by which the characteristics of *samples* from the population differ from the characteristic of the *whole* population.

Although the formulae for calculating the standard errors of the various aspects of the regression line are readily available, they add considerably to the computational labour involved in regression, so we recommend that you use a computer to relieve you of this computational chore.

The main standard errors involved in regression are:

1. The one for your predicted (or estimated) value on the criterion (this is known as the standard error of the estimate of *y*).

2. The one for the slope of the regression line *b*.

3. The one for the intercept on the vertical axis *a*.

Don't forget that the formulae for calculating these standard errors merely give you the average amount by which your estimate is wrong.

It might be more useful to estimate the likely range within which the true value of the prediction, slope or intercept is likely to fall. In other words, to be able to say that, for example, the predicted score on the criterion variable is likely to be between 2.7 and 3.3.

In statistics, this likely range of the true value is known as the *confidence interval*. Actually there are several confidence intervals depending on how confident you wish to be that you have included the true value – the interval is obviously going to be wider if you wish to be *very* confident rather than just confident. In statistics one would routinely use the 95% confidence interval. This 95% confidence interval indicates the range of values within which the true value will fall 95% of the time. That is, we are likely to be wrong only 5% of the time.

The following is a rule of thumb which is accurate enough for your purposes for now. Multiply the standard error by 2. This gives you the amount which you need to *add and subtract* from the estimated value to cut off the middle 95% of the possible values – that is the 95% confidence interval. In other words, if the estimated value of the criterion (Y-variable) is 6.00 and the standard error of this estimate is 0.26, then the 95% confidence interval is $6.00 \pm (2 \times 0.26)$ which is 6.00 ± 0.52. This gives us a 95% confidence interval of 5.48 to 6.52. Thus it is almost certain that the person's score will actually fall in the range of 5.48 to 6.52 although the most likely value is 6.00.

Exactly the same applies to the other aspects of regression. If the slope is 2.00 with a standard error of 0.10, then the 95% confidence interval is $2.00 \pm 2 \times 0.10$, which gives a confidence interval of 1.80 to 2.20.

The use of confidence intervals is not as common as it ought to be despite the fact that it gives us a realistic assessment of the precision of our estimates.

The above calculations of confidence intervals are approximate if you have fewer than about 30 pairs of scores. If you have between 16 and 29 pairs of scores the calculation will be more accurate if you multiply by 2.1 rather than 2.0. If you have between 12 and 15 pairs of scores then multiplying by 2.2 would improve the accuracy of the calculation. With fewer than 12 pairs the method gets a little more inaccurate. When you have become more knowledgeable about statistics, you could obtain precise confidence intervals by multiplying your standard error by the appropriate value of t from Significance Table 11.1 (Chapter 11). The appropriate value is in the column headed 'Degrees of freedom', corresponding to your number of pairs of scores minus 2 under the column for the 5% significance level (i.e. if you have 10 pairs of scores then you would multiply by 2.31).

Key points

- Drawing the scattergram will invariably illuminate the trends in your data and strongly hint at the broad features of the regression calculations. It will also provide a visual check on your computations.

- These regression procedures assume that the best-fitting regression line is a straight line. If it looks as if the regression line ought to be curved or curvilinear, do not apply these numerical methods. Of course, even if a relationship is curvilinear you could use the curved-line scattergram to make graphically based predictions.

- It may be that you have more than one predictor variable that you wish to use – if so, look at Chapter 19 on multiple regression.

PART 2

Inferential statistics

Chapter 9

The analysis of a questionnaire/ survey project

Overview

- One of the hardest things facing newcomers to research is the transition between the contents of statistics textbooks and collecting data. This chapter attempts to clarify how to develop an appropriate statistical analysis in circumstances in which planning has been less than perfect.

- A researcher needs clear understanding of what they are trying to achieve in the research. Hence it is important to clarify the broad research question and any hypotheses that derive from this. Hypotheses are merely statements of relationships that one wishes to explore.

- The data need to be mapped to identify the characteristics of variables. Identifying what is a score variable and what is a nominal (category) variable is important. Nominal (category) variables with just two categories can be treated as scores by giving the values 1 and 2 to the two alternative values.

- Data may need recoding to make the analysis acceptable.

- Ineffective variables are removed through a process of data cleaning.

- Data analysis consists of presenting descriptive statistics on the major variables and finding the extent of relationships among variables. This may be more or less complex.

Preparation

Review correlation (Chapter 7) and regression (Chapter 8).

9.1   Introduction

This chapter examines the analysis of questionnaire and/or survey projects. A lot of research planned by students adopts this style. The key feature is the number of variables involved; this type of research tempts researchers to write lengthy questionnaires with numerous items. It takes little effort to write a question, even less to write a poor question. Still less time is required to answer the questions if they are in a closed-ended format in which just one alternative is circled. An exploratory or pilot study will not always identify faulty questions and, more often than not, the pressures on students' time are such that pilot studies are rudimentary and based on very few individuals.

Some students, wanting to get closer to the experiences of the participants in their research, choose to ask the questions themselves rather than have a self-completion questionnaire. However, the basic problem remains very much the same – too much data. The difference is that with the open-ended interview approach the data have to be coded in a form suitable for statistical analysis. The coding process has its own problems – largely what coding categories to use and whether the categories used are easily used by the coders. Profound disagreements between the coders suggest either that the categories are inadequate or that they have been very poorly defined.

9.2   The research project

Tom Grew is a bright young sociology student who has partied for most of his time at university. So when it is time to plan a research project he has little background knowledge of sociological research and theory. Stuck for a final-year project, he designs a piece of research based on one of his interests in life – religious beliefs. His project explores the hypothesis that a strict religious upbringing leads to sexual inhibitions. Naturally, his dissertation supervisor is reluctant to let Tom loose on the public at large and so insists that the research is carried out on a consenting sample of fellow students. Pressured by deadlines for coursework essays, he hastily prepares a questionnaire which he pushes under bedroom doors in the Hall of Residence. Participants in the research are to return the completed questionnaires to him via the student mail system.

Tom's questionnaire is a simple enough affair. His questions – with spelling corrected – are as follows.

1. My gender is
    Male   Female
2. My degree course is ___
3. I am ___ years of age
4. My religion is ___
5. I would rate my religious faith as:
    Very strong   Strong   Neither   Weak   Very weak
6. I attend a place of worship ___ times per year
7. My faith in God is important to me
    Strongly agree   Agree   Neither   Disagree   Strongly disagree
8. I am a virgin
    Agree   Disagree
9. I am sexually promiscuous
    Strongly agree   Agree   Neither   Disagree   Strongly disagree

10. I fantasise about sex with several partners at the same time
    Strongly agree   Agree   Neither   Disagree   Strongly disagree
11. I feel guilty after sex with more than three people at the same time
    Strongly agree   Agree   Neither   Disagree   Strongly disagree
12. Oral sex is an abomination
    Strongly agree   Agree   Neither   Disagree   Strongly disagree
13. Sadomasochism is appealing to me
    Strongly agree   Agree   Neither   Disagree   Strongly disagree
14. I like sex
    Once a week   Twice a week   Every day   Every morning and evening   All the time
15. Pornography
    Is disgusting   Is a stimulant   Is best home-made

Suddenly Tom sees the light of day – just a few months before he finishes at university and is launched onto the job market. Despite being due for submission, the project is in a diabolical mess. No more partying for him – he has become a serious-minded student (well, sort of) and is determined to resurrect his flagging and ailing attempts at research. No longer does he burn the candle at one end – he now burns it at both ends trying to make sense of statistics and research methods books. Pretty dry stuff it all is. If only he had spent some time on statistics in his misspent youth he would not have been in this hole. Can he get out of the mess?

The short answer is no. The longer answer is that he could improve things considerably with a well-thought-out analysis of his data. Research has to be carefully planned to be at its most effective. He needed to consider his hypotheses, methods and statistical analysis in advance of even collecting the data. Tom is paying for the error of his ways. One positive aspect of all this is that Tom can at least show that he is aware of the major issues and problems with his sort of research.

9.3   The research hypothesis

Although statistics is not particularly concerned about the details of the hypotheses underlying research, a clear statement of the purposes of the research often transforms the analysis of haphazardly planned research. Of course, it is by far the best to plan meticulously before doing your research. However, this does not always happen in research – even in research by professionals.

Simply stated, Tom's research aims to find out whether there is a relationship between religious upbringing and sexual inhibitions. The trouble with this is that it is unclear quite what is meant by a religious upbringing – does it matter which sort of religion or how intensely it is part of family life? Furthermore, it is unclear what he means by sexual inhibitions – for example, not carrying out certain activities might be the result of inhibitions but it may also be that the person does not find them arousing. Given the limited range of questions which Tom included in his questionnaire, we might suggest to him that he has several measures of religiousness:

1. The first is what religion they claim to be. The range is wide and includes Roman Catholic, Protestant, Muslim and a variety of other religions. Is it possible for Tom to make suggestions as to which religions are most likely to encourage sexual repression – perhaps he thinks that Roman Catholicism and Islam are the religions most likely to inculcate sexual inhibitions? If so, he could formulate a hypothesis which relates aspects of the religion to sexual inhibition.

2. There is a question about actual attendance at church. It could be that involvement in the religious community is a key variable in the influence of religion on sexual inhibitions. This might be specified as a hypothesis.

3. There are two questions which involve the importance of religious beliefs in the lives of the respondents. Again, a hypothesis might specify religious beliefs as the important element in the possible relationship.

In terms of his measures of sexual activity, there are some very obvious things to point out. The first is that it is very difficult to relate any of the sex questions to sexual inhibition as such. Some of the questions deal with frequency of sexual activities, some deal with sexual fantasy, and others deal with somewhat 'unusual' sexual practices. Probably Tom is stuck with a fatal flaw in his research – that is, he failed to *operationalise* his concept properly; he may not have turned his *idea* of sexual inhibitions into a *measure* of that thing. Clearly Tom might have done better to include some questions which ask about sexual inhibitions. In the circumstances it might be appropriate for Tom to reformulate his hypothesis to suggest that religious upbringing influences sexual behaviours and sexual fantasy. At least this might make more sense in terms of his questionnaire.

9.4 Initial variable classification

It is useful for novice researchers to classify the variables that they have collected into category variables and numerical scores:

1. You should remember that social scientists frequently turn answers on a verbal scale into numerical scores. So questions 5, 7 and 9–14 of Tom's questionnaire all have fixed answer alternatives. Although they do not involve numbers, it is conventional in social science research to impose a numerical scale of 1 to 5 onto these answer categories. The reason for this is that the categories have verbal labels which imply increasing quantities of something. Scaling from 1 to 5 is arbitrary but has been shown to work pretty well in practice.

2. Some variables which appear at first to be just nominal categories can be turned into numerical scores simply and easily. The classic example of this in research is the variable gender which consists of just two categories: male and female. Innumerable research reports code the gender variable numerically as 1 = male and 2 = female. The logic is obvious, the numerical codings implying different quantities of the variable femaleness (or maleness). However, such variables can legitimately be treated in either way.

So, with these points in mind, we can classify each of our variables as 'category' or 'numerical score' or 'other' – meaning anything we are uncertain about (as in Table 9.1). This is quite promising in terms of statistical analysis as 12 out of the 15 variables can be classified as numerical scores. This allows some of the more powerful correlational statistical techniques to be used if required. This still leaves three variables classified as categories. These are the degree course the student is taking, their religion and their views on pornography. These are probably quite varied in terms of their answers anyway. So, Tom may find that there may be 20 or more different degree courses included in the list of replies with only a few students in each of these 20 or more categories. Similarly, the religion question could generate a multiplicity of different replies. *As they stand, these three variables are of little use in statistical analysis – they need to be recoded in some way.*

Table 9.1	Tom's 15 questions classified as category or score variables	
Nominal or category variables	**Numerical score variables**	**Other**
Question 1: Gender[a]	Question 1: Gender[a]	
Question 2: Degree course		
	Question 3: Age	
Question 4: Religion		
	Question 5: Faith	
	Question 6: Attend	
	Question 7: God	
	Question 8: Virgin	
	Question 9: Promiscuous	
	Question 10: Fantasise	
	Question 11: Guilty	
	Question 12: Oral	
	Question 13: Sadomasochism	
	Question 14: Like sex	

[a] Means that the variable may be placed in more than one column.

9.5   Further coding of data

It is difficult to know why Tom included the degree course question – it does not seem to have much to do with the issues at hand – so one approach is to discreetly ignore it. Probably a better approach is to recode the answers in a simple but appropriate way. One thing which could be done is to recode them as science or arts degree courses. In other words, the degree course could be coded as 1 if it is science and 2 if it is arts. If this is done then the variable could be classified as a numerical score much as the gender variable could be.

The religion question is more of a problem. Given that the answers will include Catholics, Mormons, Baptists, and many more, the temptation might be to classify the variable simply as *religion given* versus *no religion given*. However, this may not serve Tom's purposes too well, since it may be that the key thing is whether the religion is sexually controlling or not. One approach that Tom could take is to obtain the services of people who are knowledgeable about various religions. They could be asked to rate the religions in terms of their degree of sexual control over their members. This could be done on a short scale such as:

Very sexually controlling	Sexually controlling	Not sexually controlling

This would transform the religion variable into a numerical scale if ratings were applied from 0 to 2, for example. Those not mentioning a religion might be deemed to be in the 'not sexually controlling' category. Obviously Tom should report the degree of agreement between the raters of the religion (i.e. the interrater reliability).

Of course, Tom might decide to categorise the religions in a category form:

1. None

2. Catholic

3. Protestant

4. Muslim

5. Other.

Unfortunately, this classification retains the nominal category characteristics of the original data, although reducing the numbers of categories quite substantially.

The question about pornography seems to be a natural nominal category variable given the response alternatives. Perhaps it is best to treat it as such although it could be recoded in such a way that the 'is a stimulant' and 'is best home-made' answers are classified together as being pro-pornography while the 'is disgusting' answer is given a different score. There are no hard-and-fast rules about these decisions and at some stage you have to come to terms with the fact that some choices seem almost arbitrary. That does not mean that you should not try to base your decisions on rational arguments as far as possible.

9.6 Data cleaning

There is little point in retaining variables in your research which contain little or no variance. It is particularly important with analyses of questionnaire-type materials to systematically exclude useless variables since they can create misleading impressions at a later stage. The important steps are as follows:

1. Draw up or print out frequency counts of the values of each variable you have. This can be done as frequency tables or histograms/bar charts. It should become obvious to you if virtually every participant in the research gives much the same answer to a question. Consider deleting such non-discriminating questions.

2. In the case of variables which have a multiplicity of different values, you might consider recoding these variables into a small number of ranges. This might apply in the case of the age question in Tom's research.

3. Where you find empty or virtually empty response categories then consider combining categories. Some categories may contain just a few cases. These are probably useless for your overall analysis.

9.7 Data analysis

■ A relatively simple approach

If Tom follows our advice, all or virtually all of the variables will be coded as numerical scores. Any variables not coded in this way will have to be analysed by statistics suitable for category data – this might be the chi-square (Chapter 12) but more likely they will be treated as different values of the independent variable for the analysis of variance or a similar test. We would recommend, as far as possible within the requirements of your hypotheses, that all variables are transformed into numerical scores.

Accepting this, it would be a relatively simple matter to calculate the correlations between all of the variables in Tom's list and each other. The trouble with this is that it results in a rather large correlation matrix of 15×15 correlation coefficients – in other words a table of 225 coefficients. Although the table will be symmetrical around the diagonal of the matrix, this still leaves over 100 different correlations. It is not the purpose of statistical analysis to pour complexity on your research; statistics are there to simplify as far as is possible.

In Tom's research, the sex questions are quite numerous. He has eight different questions about sexual matters. Obviously it would be satisfactory if there were some way of combining these different answers in order that a single measure of 'sexual inhibition' could be developed. One simple thing that might be done is to add the scores on the questions together. This would require the following:

1. That the different questions are scored in the same direction. Looking at Tom's questionnaire we see that, for example, the question 'I like sex' if scored numerically from left to right would give a bigger score to those who liked sex most often. However, the answers to the question on sadomasochism if scored numerically from left to right would give a lower score to those who liked sadomasochistic sex. It is necessary to recode his answers in such a way that they are consistent. In this case all the answers which are more sexual could be rescored as necessary to make the high scores pro-sex.

2. That the standard deviations of scores on questions to be added together are similar, otherwise the questions with the biggest standard deviations will swamp the others. If they differ radically, then it is best to convert each score on a variable to a standard score and then add up answers to several questions (Chapter 6).

A similar sort of thing could be done with the three religious questions, although it might be equally appropriate, given their relatively small number, to treat them as three separate variables.

In order to test his hypotheses, Tom could correlate the sex and religion variables together. A significant relationship in the predicted direction would support Tom's hypotheses. (It would be equally appropriate to apply t-tests or analyses of variance with religion as the independent variable and sex questions as the dependent variables.)

The advantage of using correlations is that it is then possible to control for (or partial out) obvious background variables which might influence the relationships found. In this study gender and age are of particular interest since both of them might relate to our main variables of interest. Partial correlation could be used to remove the influence of gender and age from the correlation between religion and sexual inhibition.

■ A more complex approach

Given the number of questions Tom has included on his questionnaire, it is arguable that he ought to consider using factor analysis (Chapter 18) on the sex questions to explore the pattern of interrelations between the variables. He may well find that the answers to the sex questions tend to cluster together to form small groups of questions which tend to measure separate aspects of sex. For example, questions which deal with unusual sexual practices might be grouped together.

Factor analysis would identify the important clusters or factors. In addition, factor analysis will usually give factor scores which are weighted scores for each individual on each factor separately. These are expressed on the same scale and so are comparable. In other words, they have already been expressed in terms of standard scores.

It is then possible to relate scores on the religion variable(s) with scores on each of the factors just as before. Partialling out gender and age might also be appropriate.

■ An alternative complex approach

One could also employ multiple regression (Chapter 19). Probably the best approach is to use religion as the dependent (criterion) variable(s) and the separate sex variables as the independent (predictor) variables. In this way it is possible to find out which of the sex variables contribute to the prediction of the religious experiences of the participants in childhood. Tom may find that only certain of the questions are particularly and independently related to religion. Actually, Tom could control for age and gender by forcing them into the regression early in the analysis.

9.8   SPSS analysis

Refer to Part 1 for a step-by-step guide on data inputting and appropriate chapters for statistical analysis of your data.

Key points

- Although statistics can help structure poor data, it is impossible to remedy all faults though statistics. Research design and planning are always vital.

- Statistics is useful in simplifying complex data into a small number of variables. Unfortunately, for most practical purposes it is impossible to do this without resorting to computer analysis. This is because of the sheer number of variables to be analysed.

CHAPTER 10

The related *t*-test

Comparing two samples of correlated/ related scores

Overview

- The *t*-test is used to assess the statistical significance of the difference between the means of two sets of scores and whether the average score for one set of scores differs significantly from the average score for another set of scores.

- There are two versions of the *t*-test. One is used when the two sets of scores to be compared come from a single set or sample of people or when the correlation coefficient between the two sets of scores is high. This is known as the related or correlated *t*-test. The other version of the *t*-test is used when the two different sets of scores come from different groups of participants (see Chapter 11).

- The *t*-test described in this chapter is known as the related *t*-test. Basically this means that the two sets of scores are obtained from a single sample of participants. There should be a correlation between the scores on the two measures since otherwise the two sets of scores are not related. Data entry for related and unrelated variables is very different in SPSS so take care to plan your analysis before entering your data in order to avoid problems and unnecessary work.

- If you have used a matching procedure to make pairs of people similar on some other characteristics then you would also use the related *t*-test in this present chapter, especially if the two sets of scores correlate significantly.

- The related *t*-test works at its optimum if the distribution of the differences between the two sets of scores is approximately bell-shaped (that is, if there is a normal distribution).

Preparation

Review *z*-scores, standard deviation and standard error (Chapter 5).

10.1 Introduction

Many research projects in social sciences involve comparisons between two groups of scores. Each group of scores is a sample from a population of scores. There is a test called the related (correlated) *t*-test which compares the means of two *related* samples of scores to see whether the means differ significantly. The meaning of related samples can be illustrated by the following examples:

1. People's salaries are measured at two different points in time in order to see if any increase has taken place (see Table 10.1). Notice that we have mentioned individuals by name to stress that they are being measured twice – they are *not* different individuals in the two conditions. Also, some of the data have been omitted.

Table 10.1	Salaries (in £000's) measured at two different times	
	1 March	**Three years later**
Sam	17	19
Jack	14	17
...	...	...
Karl	12	19
Shahida	19	25
Mandy	10	13
Mean	$=_1 = 15.09$	$=_2 = 18.36$

2. A group of elderly people's memory test scores are measured in the morning and in the afternoon in order to see whether memory is affected by time of day (Table 10.2).

3. A group of patients' red blood cell counts are measured when they have taken an iron supplement tablet and when they have taken an inert control tablet (placebo) (see Table 10.3).

In each of the above, the researcher wishes to know whether the means of the two conditions differ from each other. The question is whether the mean scores in the two conditions are sufficiently different from each other that they fall in the extreme 5% of cases. If they

Table 10.2	Time of day and memory performance scores	
	Morning	**Afternoon**
Rebecca	9	15
Sharon	16	23
...	...	...
Neil	18	24
Mean	$=_1 = 17.3$	$=_2 = 22.1$

Table 10.3	Red blood cell counts (million cells per microlitre) for supplement and placebo conditions		
		Iron supplement	**Placebo**
	Jenny	0.27	0.25
	David	0.15	0.18
	. . .	. . .	. . .
	Mean	$\bar{=}_1 = 0.22$	$\bar{=}_2 = 0.16$

do, this allows us to generalise from the research findings. In other words, are the two means significantly different from each other?

The key characteristics of all of the previous studies are that a group of participants is measured twice on a single variable in slightly different conditions or circumstances. So in the previous studies, salary has been measured twice, memory has been measured twice and red blood cell count has been measured twice. In other words, they are *repeated measures designs* for the obvious reason that participants have been measured more than once on the same variable. Repeated measures designs are also called *related measures designs* and *correlated scores designs*.

Box 10.1   Research design issue

Repeated measures designs of the sort described in this chapter can be problematic. For example, since the participants in the research are measured under both the experimental and control conditions, it could be that their experiences in the experimental condition affect the way they behave in the control condition. Many of the problems can be overcome by *counterbalancing* conditions. By this we mean that a random selection of half of the participants in the research are put through the experimental condition first and the other half are put through the control condition first.

10.2   Dependent and independent variables

The scores in Tables 10.1–10.3 are scores on the *dependent variable*. They include the variables salary, memory and red blood cell count in the experiments.

However, there is another variable – the *independent variable*. This refers to the various conditions in which the measurements are being taken. In Table 10.1 measurements are being taken at two different points in time – on 1 March and three years later. The alternative hypothesis is that there *is* a relationship between the independent variable 'time of measurement' and the dependent variable 'salary'. Obviously, it is being assumed that salaries are *dependent* on the variable time.

10.3 Theoretical considerations

As we have seen, the most important theoretical concept with any inferential statistical test is the null hypothesis. This states that there is *no* relationship between the two variables in the research. In one of the previous examples the independent variable is time of day and the dependent variable is memory. The null hypothesis is that there is no relation between the independent variable 'time' and the dependent variable 'memory'. This implies, by definition, that the two samples, according to the null hypothesis, come from the same population. In other words, in the final analysis the overall trend is for pairs of samples drawn from this population to have identical means. However, that is the trend over many pairs of samples. The means of some pairs of samples will differ somewhat from each other simply because samples from even the same population tend to vary. Hence, little differences will be more common than big differences.

The related *t*-test gives the statistical significance of this difference between the means of two score variables. Usually, it is based on one group of participants measured on two separate occasions, which gives the two sets of scores (means). The unrelated *t*-test in Chapter 11 is different because it involves two separate *groups* of participants. Both are based on a statistical distribution known as the *t*-distribution, hence the *t*-test.

The main assumption of the related *t*-test is that the two sets of scores should correlate with each other (hence the reason it is sometimes referred to as the correlated *t*-test). This requirement of correlation is poorly understood but is vital to ensure that the related *t*-test is interpreted properly. The related *t*-test is most likely to be used when a single group of participants has been measured twice at different points in time on essentially the same variable. The resulting two sets of scores are likely to correlate with each other for the simple reason that some participants will tend to score consistently highly on the variable and others tend to score consistently low.

This type of design is illustrated in Table 10.6 (see page 152) in which a group of participants are measured at Time A and Time B. To be precise, a group of ex-smokers have been assessed after 6 months of giving up smoking and then again at 9 months in order to study whether their lung capacity has increased or not over this three-month period. While we might assume that lung capacity increases as the time since ceasing smoking increases, we would expect that some ex-smokers at Time A tend to be physiologically more 'superior' – as measured by lung capacity – to others (for example, ex-smokers who also played sport). We might also expect that the physiologically 'superior' at Time A will likewise tend to be physiologically the more able at Time B, despite the possibility that all of the participants improve to some degree over that three-month period. Do the calculations on these data and you will find that the mean lung capacity at 6 months since ceasing smoking is 5.25 litres which increases to 6.75 litres at 9 months. This is in line with the hypothesis guiding the research that lung capacity increases with the amount of time since giving up smoking. Furthermore, if you correlate the two sets of lung capacity scores you find that they do so at 0.42, which is a moderate-sized correlation though (in this case) not statistically significant.

When we measure the same thing twice for a single sample of participants, we actually gain control over more variation in the data. Basically there are two sources of variation in the scores (i.e. the dependent variable) in most research designs:

1. Variation due to the difference between the two means (the independent variable)

2. Variation due to uncontrolled factors (usually called error variance).

However, in the related *t*-test the second source of variance (that due to uncontrolled factors) can be reduced because the measures have been taken twice on a single group of participants. That is, we know that some participants will tend to score highly on both measures whereas other participants tend to get low scores. These 'individual differences' are removed from the error variance in the related *t*-test. The extent of the individual differences is reflected in the size of the correlation between the two sets of scores. The bigger the correlation, the greater reduction there is in the error variance, and the more likely is it that a significant difference will be obtained between the two means as a consequence.

Box 10.2   Research design issue

It is also possible to have a related design if you take pairs of subjects *matched* to be as similar as possible on factors which might be related to their scores on the dependent variable. So pairs of participants might be matched on sex and age so that each member of the pair in question is of the same sex and age group (or as close as possible). One member of the pair would be assigned *at random* to one experimental condition, the other member to the other experimental condition. Using the effect of time of day on the memory research question (Table 10.2), the arrangement for a matched pairs or matched subjects design might be as in Table 10.4.

The purpose of matching, like using the same person twice, is to reduce the influence of unwanted variables on the comparisons.

Table 10.4	A matched pairs design testing memory score	
Matched pairs	**Morning score**	**Afternoon score**
Both male and under 70	16	17
Both female and under 70	21	25
Both male and 70 and over	14	20
Both female and 70 and over	10	14

There is a downside, however, since by removing the variance due to individual differences the number of degrees of freedom is reduced too – and the number of degrees of freedom (*df*) affects the statistical significance of the *t*-test. The fewer degrees of freedom, the less likely is it that a significant difference will be obtained. This is fine if the reduction in the error variance due to removing the variation arising from individual differences is sufficient to compensate for the reduction in the degrees of freedom. The bigger the correlation between the two sets of scores, the more likely is this compensation to be achieved. If the correlation is zero then there is just a loss of degrees of freedom with no gains to compensate, so there is a consequent reduction in the chance of statistical significance. If there is zero correlation between the two sets of scores, it would actually be totally appropriate to analyse the data with the unrelated *t*-test (Chapter 11), although this is rarely done in practice.

Another important concept is that of the *t*-distribution. This is a theoretical statistical distribution which is similar to the *z*-distribution (discussed in Chapter 11), which in turn is similar to the *z*-score. The *t*-score is based on analogous logic to the *z*-score. The major difference is that the *t*-score involves *standard error* and not standard deviation. As we saw in the previous chapter, the standard error is nothing other than the standard deviation of a set of sample means. Using the z-distribution, it is possible to work out the standing of any score relative to the rest of the set of scores. Exactly the same applies where one has the standard error of a set of sample means. One can calculate the relative extent to which a particular sample mean differs from the average sample mean. (The average sample mean with many samples will be the same as the mean of the population, so normally the population mean is referred to rather than the average of sample means.)

The t-test can be applied to the data on the above population. Assume that for a given population, the population mean is 1.0. We have estimated the standard error by taking a known sample of 10 scores, calculating its estimated standard deviation and dividing by the square root of the sample size. All of these stages are combined in the following formula, which was discussed in Chapter 5:

$$\text{(estimated) standard error} = \frac{\sqrt{\dfrac{\sum X^2 - \dfrac{(\sum X)^2}{N}}{N-1}}}{\sqrt{N}}$$

This gives the (estimated) standard error to be 2.5. We can calculate if a sample with a mean of 8.0 ($N = 10$) is statistically unusual. We simply apply the t-test formula to the information we have:

$$t = \frac{\text{particular sample mean} - \text{population mean}}{\text{standard error of sample means}}$$

$$= \frac{8.0 - 1.0}{2.5}$$

$$= \frac{7.0}{2.5}$$

$$= 2.8$$

In other words, our sample mean is actually 2.8 standard errors *above* the average sample mean (i.e. population mean) of 1.0. Our obtained t-score was 2.8. This means that our sample mean is within the extreme 5% of sample means, i.e. that it is statistically significantly different from the average of sample means drawn from this particular population.

But what has this got to do with our research problem which we set out at the beginning of this chapter? The above is simply about a single sample compared with a multitude of samples. What we need to know is whether or not *two* sample means are sufficiently different from each other that we can say that the difference is statistically significant. There is just one remaining statistical trick that statisticians employ in these circumstances. That is, *the two samples of scores are turned into a single sample by subtracting one set of scores from the other.* We calculate the difference between a person's score in one sample and their score in the other sample. This leaves us with a sample of difference scores D which constitutes the single sample we need.

The stylised data in Table 10.5 show just what is done. The difference scores in the final column are the single sample of scores which we use in our standard error formula. For this particular sample of difference scores the mean is 4.0. According to the null hypothesis, the general trend should be zero difference between the two samples – that is, the mean of the difference scores would be zero if the sample reflected precisely the null hypothesis. Once again we are reliant on the null hypothesis to tell us what the population characteristics are. Since the null hypothesis has it that there is no difference between the *samples*, there should be zero difference in the population, that is, the average

Table 10.5	Basic rearrangement of data for the related samples *t*-test		
Person	Sample 1 (X_1)	Sample 2 (X_2)	Difference $X_1 - X_2 = D$
A	9	5	4
B	7	2	5
C	7	3	4
D	11	6	5
E	7	5	2

difference score should be 0. Since the difference between sample means – under the null hypothesis that the two samples do not differ – is zero by definition, the population mean should be zero. In other words we can delete the population mean from the formula for *t*-scores. We would of course expect some samples of difference scores to be above or below zero by varying amounts. The question is whether a mean difference of 4.0 is sufficiently different from zero to be statistically significant. If it comes in the middle 95% of the distribution of sample means then we accept the null hypothesis. If it comes in the extreme 5% then we describe it as significant and reject the null hypothesis in favour of the alternative hypothesis. We achieve this by using the *t*-test formula applied to the sample of difference scores.

Calculation 10.1

The related/correlated samples *t*-test

The data are taken from an imaginary study which looked at the relationship between the number of months a participant has not smoked and their lung capacity. The ex-smokers were tested at six months and nine months, since time of abstaining from smoking (6 or 9 months) is the independent variable. The dependent variable is lung capacity measured in litres. The null hypothesis is that there is no relation between stopping smoking and lung capacity. The data are given in Table 10.6, which includes the difference between the six-month and nine-month scores as well as the square of this difference. The number of cases, N, is the number of difference scores, i.e. 8.

We can clearly see from Table 10.6 that the nine-month measurements of lung capacity are greater, on average, than they were following six months of abstaining from smoking. The average difference in lung capacity is 1.5. The question remains, however, whether this difference is statistically significant.

Step 1   The formula for the standard error of the difference (D) scores is as follows. It is exactly as for the calculation in the main text except that we have substituted D for X.

$$\text{Standard error} = \frac{\sqrt{\dfrac{\sum D^2 - \dfrac{(\sum D)^2}{N}}{N-1}}}{\sqrt{N}}$$

Table 10.6	Steps in calculating the related/correlated samples t-test			
Subject	**6 months** X_1	**9 months** X_2	**Difference** $D = X_1 - X_2$	**Difference^2** D^2
Clara	3	7	−4	16
Martin	5	6	−1	1
Sally	5	3	2	4
Angie	4	8	−4	16
Trevor	3	5	−2	4
Sam	7	9	−2	4
Bobby	8	7	1	1
Sid	7	9	−2	4
Sums of columns	$\sum X_1 = 42$	$\sum X_2 = 54$	$\sum D = -12$	$\sum D^2 = 50$
Means of columns	$\bar{X}_1 = 5.25$	$\bar{X}_2 = 6.75$	$\bar{D} = -1.5$	

Substituting the values from Table 10.6,

$$\text{Standard error} = \frac{\sqrt{\dfrac{50 - \dfrac{(-12)^2}{8}}{8-1}}}{\sqrt{8}} = \frac{\sqrt{\dfrac{50 - \dfrac{144}{8}}{7}}}{2.828}$$

$$= \frac{\sqrt{\dfrac{50 - 18}{7}}}{2.828} = \frac{\sqrt{\dfrac{32}{7}}}{2.828} = \frac{\sqrt{4.571}}{2.828} = \frac{2.138}{2.828} = 0.756$$

Step 2 We can now enter our previously calculated values in the following formula:

$$t\text{-score} = \frac{\bar{D}}{\text{SE}}$$

where $\bar{D}$ is the average difference score and SE is the standard error, i.e.

$$t\text{-score} = \frac{-1.5}{0.756} = -1.98$$

Step 3 If we look up this t-score in Appendix D for $N - 1 = 7$ degrees of freedom, we find that we need a t-value of 2.37 or more (or −2.37 or less) to put our sample mean in the extreme 5% of sample means. In other words, our sample mean of −1.5 is in the middle 95% of sample means which are held to be statistically not significant. In these circumstances we prefer to believe that the null hypothesis is true. In other words, there is no significant difference between ex-smokers' lung capacity at six and nine months since stopping smoking.

Interpreting the results Check the mean scores for the two conditions in order to understand which group has the highest lung capacity. Although capacity was greater at nine months, the t-test is not significant, which indicates that the difference between the two groups was not sufficient to allow us to conclude that the two groups truly differ from each other.

Reporting the results We would write something along the lines of the following in our report: 'Lung capacity since the cessation of smoking was slightly higher at nine months ($\bar{X} = 6.75$) than at six months ($\bar{X} = 5.25$). However, the difference did not support the hypothesis that lung capacity differs between six months and nine months since stopping smoking, since the obtained value of t of -1.98 is not statistically significant at the 5% level.'

An alternative way of putting this is as follows: 'Lung capacity following a specified period of abstaining from smoking was slightly higher at nine months ($\bar{X} = 6.75$) than at six months ($\bar{X} = 5.25$). However, the difference did not support the hypothesis that the lung capacity differs at six months and nine months at the 5% level of significance ($t = -1.98$, $df = 7$, $p > 0.05$).'

The material in the brackets simply gives the statistic used (the *t*-test), its value (-1.98), the degrees of freedom (7) and the level of significance, which is more than that required for the 5% level ($p > 0.05$). Chapter 1 explains this in greater detail.

Warning *The distribution of the difference scores should not be markedly skewed if the t-test is to be used. Appendix A explains how to test for significant skewness.*

10.4   SPSS analysis

The computation of a related *t*-test is illustrated with the data in Table 10.6, which shows the lung capacity of the same ex-smokers at six and nine months since giving up smoking. The purpose of the analysis is to see whether stopping smoking changes lung capacity between these times.

■ Entering the data

Step 1

In 'Variable View' of the 'Data Editor' label the first variable 'Six_mths' and the second variable 'Nine_mths'. Remove the two decimal places by changing the figure for the decimals to 0.

	Name	Type	Width	Decimals
1	Six_mths	Numeric	8	0
2	Nine_mths	Numeric	8	0

Step 2

In 'Data View' of the 'Data Editor' enter the data in the first two columns.

	Six_mths	Nine_mths
1	3	7
2	5	6
3	5	3
4	4	8
5	3	5
6	7	9
7	8	7
8	7	9

■ The related *t*-test

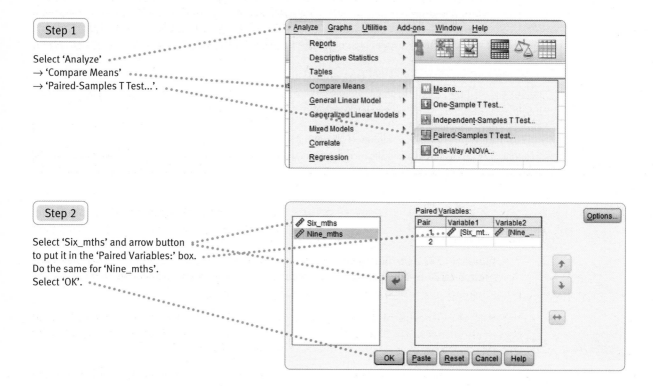

Step 1

Select 'Analyze'
→ 'Compare Means'
→ 'Paired-Samples T Test...'.

Step 2

Select 'Six_mths' and arrow button
to put it in the 'Paired Variables:' box.
Do the same for 'Nine_mths'.
Select 'OK'.

■ Interpreting the output

- The first table shows the mean, the number of cases and the standard deviation of the two groups. The mean for the 'Six_mths' is 5.25 and its standard deviation is 1.909. The two standard deviations are very similar, which is an advantage.

Paired Samples Statistics

		Mean	N	Std. Deviation	Std. Error Mean
Pair 1	Six_mths	5.25	8	1.909	.675
	Nine_mths	6.75	8	2.053	.726

- The second table shows the degree to which the two sets of scores are correlated. The correlation between them is 0.419. This is a moderate correlation, although it is not significant as the significance level is greater than 0.05. Correlated tests such as the related *t*-test should have a substantial correlation between the two sets of scores. Be careful: this table is *not* the test of significance. It is a common mistake to confuse this correlation between two variables with the significance of the difference between the two mean scores.

Paired Samples Correlations

		N	Correlation	Sig.
Pair 1	Six_mths & Nine_mths	8	.419	.301

- In the third table, the first three columns containing the figures are the basic components of the calculation of the related *t*-test. The mean of −1.500 is actually the difference between the six-month and nine-month means, so it is really the mean difference. The value of *t* is based on this mean difference (−1.500 divided by the standard error of the mean (0.756)). This calculation gives us the value of *t* (−1.984).

Paired Samples Test

| | | Paired Differences | | | | | | | |
| | | Mean | Std. Deviation | Std. Error Mean | 95% Confidence Interval of the Difference | | t | df | Sig. (2-tailed) |
					Lower	Upper			
Pair 1	Six_mths - Nine_mths	-1.500	2.138	.756	-3.287	.287	-1.984	7	.088

- The third and last table shows the *t*-value (−1.984), the degrees of freedom (7) and the two-tailed significance level (0.088). As the significance level is greater than 0.05 this difference is not significant. The one-tailed level is obtained by dividing it by 2 which is 0.044 and therefore significant. (However, unless the difference has been predicted in advance of data collection on the basis of strong theoretical and/or empirical reasons, only the two-tailed test is appropriate.)

- In the first table of the output, the mean lung capacity at six months ('Six_mths') and at nine months ('Nine_mths') is displayed under Mean. Thus the mean lung capacity is 5.25 litres at six months and 6.75 litres at nine months.

- In the second table of the output is the (Pearson) correlation coefficient between the two variables (lung capacity at six months and lung capacity at nine months). *Ideally*, the value of this should be sizeable (in fact it is 0.419) and statistically significant (which it is not, with a two-tailed significance level of 0.301). The related *t*-test assumes that the two variables are correlated, and you might consider an unrelated *t*-test (Chapter 11) to be more suitable in this case.

- In the third table of the output the difference between these two mean scores is presented under the 'Mean' of 'Paired Differences' and the standard error of this mean under 'Std. Error Mean'. The difference between the two means is −1.50 and the estimated standard error of means for this sample size is 0.76.

- The *t*-value of the difference between the sample means, its degrees of freedom and its two-tailed significance level are also shown in this third table. The *t*-value is −1.984, which has an exact two-tailed significance level of 0.088 with 7 degrees of freedom.

■ Reporting the output

- We could report these results as follows: 'The mean lung capacity of ex-smokers at six months ($M = 5.25$, SD = 1.91) and at nine months ($M = 6.75$, SD = 2.05) did not differ significantly ($t = -1.98$, $df = 7$, two-tailed $p = 0.088$).'

- In this book, to be consistent, we will report the exact probability level for non-significant results as above. However, it is equally acceptable to report them as '$p > 0.05$' or 'ns' (which is short for non-significant).

- Notice that the findings would have been statistically significant with a one-tailed test. However, this would need to have been predicted with sound reasons prior to being aware of the data. In this case one would have written to the effect: 'The two means differed significantly in the predicted direction ($t = -1.98$, $df = 7$, one-tailed $p = 0.044$).'

- A one-tailed test should only be used if prior to data collection the direction of the difference between means had been predicted on the basis of strong theoretical reasons or a strong consistent trend in the previous research. These requirements are rarely met in student research so, generally, two-tailed significance testing should be the norm.

- Once again, to be consistent throughout this book, we will report the exact probability level for significant findings where possible. Note that when SPSS displays the significance level as '.000', we need to present this as '$p < 0.001$' since the exact level is not given. It is equally acceptable to report significant probabilities as '$p < 0.05$', '$p < 0.01$' or '$p < 0.001$' as appropriate.

- If you prefer to use confidence intervals (Section 3.5), you could report your findings as: 'The mean lung capacity at six months was 5.25 (SD = 1.91) and at nine months was 6.75 (SD = 2.05). The difference was 1.50. The 95% confidence interval for this difference is −3.29 to 0.29. Since the confidence interval passes through 0.00, the difference is not statistically significant at the two-tailed 5% level.'

- Some statisticians advocate the reporting of confidence intervals rather than significance levels. However, it remains relatively uncommon to just give confidence intervals.

10.5 A cautionary note

Many researchers act as if they believe that it is the design of the research which determines whether you should use a related test. Related designs are those, after all, in which people serve in both research conditions. It is assumed that there is a correlation between subjects' scores in the two conditions. What if there is no correlation between the two samples of scores? The standard error becomes relatively large compared to the number of degrees of freedom, so your research is less likely to be statistically significant (especially if the samples are small). So while trying to control for unwanted sources of error, if there is no correlation between the scores in the two conditions of the study, the researcher may simply reduce the likelihood of achieving statistical significance. The reason is that the researcher may have obtained non-significant findings simply because (a) they have reduced the error degrees of freedom, which therefore (b) increases the error estimate, thereby (c) reducing the significance level perhaps to non-significance. Some computer programs (including SPSS) print out the correlation between the two variables as part of the correlated t-test output. If this correlation is not significant then you might be wise to think again about your test of significance. This situation is particularly likely to occur where you are using a matching procedure (as opposed to having the same people in both conditions). Unless your matching variables actually do correlate with the dependent variable, the matching can have no effect on reducing the error variance.

In the previous calculation, we found no significant change in lung capacity for ex-smokers measured at six and nine month intervals. It is worth examining the correlation between the two sets of scores to see if the assumption of correlation is fulfilled. The correlation is 0.42 but we need a correlation of 0.71 or greater to be statistically significant.

In other words the correlated scores do not really correlate – certainly not significantly. Even applying the uncorrelated version of the *t*-test described in the next chapter makes no difference. It still leaves the difference between the two age samples non-significant. We are not suggesting that if a related *t*-test fails to achieve significance you should replace it by an unrelated *t*-test, but merely that you risk ignoring trends in your data which may be important. The most practical implication is that matching variables should relate to the dependent variable, otherwise there is no point in matching in the first place.

Key points

- The related or correlated *t*-test is merely a special case of the one-way analysis of variance for related samples (Chapter 11). Although it is frequently used in research, it tells us nothing more than the equivalent analysis of variance would do. Since the analysis of variance is generally a more flexible statistic, allowing any number of groups of scores to be compared, it could also be used, particularly if you have more than two groups or conditions.

- The related *t*-test assumes that the distribution of the difference scores is not markedly skewed. If it is then the test may be unacceptably inaccurate. Appendix A explains how to test for skewness.

- If you compare many pairs of samples with each other in the same study using the *t*-test, you should consult Chapter 1 to find out about appropriate significance levels. There are better ways of making multiple comparisons, as they are called, but with appropriate adjustment to the critical values for significance, multiple *t*-tests can be justified.

- If you find that your related *t*-test is not significant, it could be that your two samples of scores are not correlated, thus not meeting the assumptions of the related *t*-test.

- Although the correlated *t*-test can be used to compare any pairs of scores, it does not always make sense to do so. For example, you could use the correlated *t*-test to compare the weights and heights of people to see if the weight mean and the height mean differ. Unfortunately, this is not the best thing to do since the numerical values involved relate to radically different things which are not comparable with each other. It is the comparison which is nonsensical in this case; the statistical test is not to blame. On the other hand, comparing a sample of people's weights at different points in time is quite meaningful.

CHAPTER 11

The unrelated *t*-test

Comparing two samples of unrelated/uncorrelated scores

Overview

- The unrelated *t*-test is used to compare the mean scores of two different samples on a single variable, so it is used primarily with score data. It tells you whether the two means are statistically significant or not.

- The *t*-value is simply the number of standard errors by which the two means are apart. The statistical significance of this *t*-value may be obtained from tables, though many prefer to use computer output which usually gives statistical significance levels.

- Data entry for related and unrelated variables is very different in SPSS, so take care to plan your analysis before entering your data in order to avoid problems and unnecessary work.

- If you have more than two sets of scores to compare, then refer to Chapter 13 on the unrelated analysis of variance.

Preparation

Review *z*-scores, standard deviation and standard error (Chapter 5).

11.1   Introduction

The *t*-test described in this chapter has various names. The unrelated *t*-test, the uncorrelated scores *t*-test and the independent samples *t*-test are the most common variants. It is also known as the Student *t*-test after its inventor who used the pen-name Student.

Often researchers compare two groups of scores from two separate groups of individuals to assess whether the average score of one group is higher than that of the other group. The possible research topics involved in such comparisons are limitless:

1. One might wish to compare an experimental group with a control group. For example, do children who are randomly assigned to a 'television' condition have more nightmares than those in the 'no television' control group? The independent variable is *t* (which has two levels – view television and no television) and the dependent variable is the number of nightmares in a month (see Table 11.1). The independent variable differentiates the two groups being compared. In the present example this is the amount of television viewing (watching or not watching television). The dependent variable is the variable which might be influenced by the independent variable. These variables correspond to the scores given in the main body of the table (i.e. number of nightmares).

2. A group of experienced probation officers may be compared with a group of inexperienced probation officers in terms of the number of hours which they take to complete their paperwork. The independent variable is experience as a probation officer (which has two levels – experienced versus inexperienced) and the dependent variable is time spent on paperwork (Table 11.2).

3. A researcher might compare the amount of bullying in two schools, one with a strict and punitive policy and the other with a policy of counselling on discipline infringements. A sample of children from each school is interviewed and the number of times they have been bullied in the previous school year obtained. The independent

Table 11.1	Number of nightmares per month in experimental and control groups	
Experimental group 'Television'		**Control group 'No television'**
17		10
14		12
16		7

Table 11.2	Monthly time spent completing paperwork (in hours) for experienced and inexperienced probation officers	
Experienced probation officers		**Inexperienced probation officers**
24		167
32		133
27		74

Table 11.3	Number of times bullied in a year in schools with different discipline policies	
Strict policy		**Counselling**
8		12
5		1
2		3

variable is policy on discipline (which has two levels – strict versus counselling); and the dependent variable is the number of times a child has been bullied in the previous school year (see Table 11.3).

The basic requirements for the unrelated/uncorrelated scores *t*-test are straightforward enough – two groups of scores coming from two distinct groups of people. The scores should be roughly similar in terms of the shapes of their distributions. Ideally both distributions should be bell-shaped and symmetrical. However, there can be marked deviance from this ideal and the test will remain sufficiently accurate.

The *t*-test is the name of a statistical technique which examines whether the two groups of scores have significantly *different* means – in other words, how likely is it that there could be a difference between the two groups as big as the one obtained if there is no difference in reality in the population?

11.2 Theoretical considerations

The basic theoretical assumption underlying the use of the *t*-test involves the characteristics of the null hypothesis. We explained the null hypothesis in Chapter 1. The following explanation uses the same format for null hypotheses as we used in that chapter.

Null hypotheses are statements that there is no relationship between two variables. The two variables in question at the moment are the independent and dependent variables. *This is another way of saying that there is no difference between the means of the two groups (i.e. columns) of scores.* The simplest null hypotheses for the above three studies are:

1. There is no relationship between television viewing and the number of dreams that children have.

2. Probation experience is not related to speed of complex decision-making.

3. The disciplinary style of a school is not related to the amount of bullying.

The alternative hypotheses to these null hypotheses can be obtained by simply deleting *no* or *not* from each of the above. Notice that the above way of writing the null hypothesis is relatively streamlined compared with what you often read in books and journals. So do not be surprised if you come across null hypotheses expressed in much more clumsy language such as:

- Children who abstain from watching television will have the same number of nightmares as children who do watch television.

- Nightmares do not occur at different frequencies in television viewing and non-television viewing children.

	Table 11.4	Possible data from the television activity and dreams experiment (dreams per seven days)	

Subject	'Television' condition	Subject	'No television' condition
Lindsay	6	Janice	2
Claudine	7	Jennifer	5
Sharon	7	Joanne	4
Natalie	8	Anne-Marie	5
Sarah	9	Helen	6
Wendy	10	Amanda	6
Ruth	8	Sophie	5
Angela	9		

These two statements tend to obscure the fact that null hypotheses are fundamentally similar irrespective of the type of research under consideration.

The television/nightmare experiment will be used to illustrate the theoretical issues. There are two different samples of scores defined by the independent variable – one for the television *abstinent* group and the other for the television *active* group. The scores in Table 11.4 are the numbers of nightmares that each child in the study has in a six-week period. We can see that, on average, the no television viewing children have fewer nightmares. Does this reflect a generalisable (significant) difference? The data might be as in Table 11.4. The table indicates that television watching leads to an increase in nightmares.

The *null hypothesis* suggests that the scores in the two samples come from the same population, since it claims that there is no relationship between the independent and dependent variables. That is, for all intents and purposes, the two samples can be construed as coming from a single population of scores; there is no difference between them due to the independent variable. Any differences between samples drawn from this null-hypothesis-defined population are due to chance factors rather than a true relationship between the independent and dependent variables. Table 11.5 is an imaginary population of scores from this null-hypothesis-defined population on the dependent variable 'number of nightmares'. The table also indicates whether the score is that of a television abstinent child or a television active one. If the two columns of scores are examined carefully, there are no differences between the two sets of scores. In other words, they have the same average scores. Statistically, all of the scores in Table 11.5 can be regarded as coming from the same population. There is no relationship between television viewing and the number of nightmares.

Given that the two samples (television active and television abstinent) come from the same population of scores on nightmares, in general we would expect no difference between pairs of samples drawn at random from this single population. Of course, sampling always introduces a chance element, so some pairs of samples would be different, but mostly the differences will cluster around zero. Overall, numerous pairs of samples will yield an *average* difference of zero. We are assuming that we consistently subtract the television active mean from the television abstinent mean (or vice versa – it does not matter so long as we always do the same thing) so that positive and negative differences cancel each other out.

Since in this case we know the population of scores under the null hypothesis, we could pick out samples of 10 scores at random from the population to represent the no television sample and, say, nine scores from the population to represent the television

Table 11.5	Imaginary population of scores for dreams study

Experimental group 'Television'		Control group 'No television'	
8	3	6	6
7	6	8	4
6	7	7	7
7	7	4	9
5	9	6	8
5	8	9	7
2	7	10	5
4	6	2	7
6	7	3	5
10	8	6	5
9	6	7	7
7	4	8	6
5		7	

sample. (Obviously the sample sizes will vary and they do not have to be equal.) Any convenient randomisation procedure could be used to select the samples (e.g. computer generated, random number tables or numbers drawn from a hat). The two samples selected at random, together with their respective means, are listed in Table 11.6.

Examining Table 11.6, we can clearly see that there is a difference between the two sample means. This difference is $7.100 - 6.556 = 0.544$. This difference between the two sample means has been obtained despite the fact that we know that there is no relationship between the independent variable and the dependent variable in the null-hypothesis-defined population. This is the nature of the random sampling process.

Table 11.6	Random samples of scores from the population in Table 11.5 to represent experimental and control conditions

Experimental group 'Television'	Control group 'No television'
4	5
5	5
10	10
7	9
7	7
5	7
7	8
9	6
9	2
	8
$\bar{X}_1 = 7.100$	$\bar{X}_2 = 6.556$

Table 11.7	Forty pairs of random samples from the population in Table 11.5

Experimental group 'Television' $N = 10$	Control group 'No television' $N = 9$	Difference (column 1 – column 2)
6.100	6.444	−0.344
6.300	5.444	0.856
6.000	6.556	−0.556
6.400	6.778	−0.378
6.600	6.111	0.489
5.700	6.111	−0.411
6.700	6.111	0.589
6.300	5.667	0.633
6.400	6.667	−0.267
5.900	5.778	0.122
6.400	6.556	−0.156
6.360	6.444	−0.084
6.400	6.778	−0.378
6.200	6.222	−0.022
5.600	5.889	−0.289
6.100	6.222	−0.122
6.800	6.667	0.133
6.100	6.222	−0.122
6.900	6.000	0.900
7.200	5.889	1.311
5.800	7.333	−1.533
6.700	6.889	−0.189
6.200	6.000	0.200
6.500	6.444	0.056
5.900	6.444	−0.544
6.000	6.333	−0.333
6.300	6.778	−0.478
6.100	5.778	0.322
6.000	6.000	0.000
6.000	6.667	−0.667
6.556	6.778	−0.222
6.700	5.778	0.922
5.600	7.000	−1.400
6.600	6.222	0.378
5.600	6.667	−1.067
5.900	7.222	−1.322
6.000	6.667	−0.667
7.000	6.556	0.444
6.400	6.556	−0.156
6.900	6.222	0.678

We can repeat this experiment by drawing more pairs of samples of these sizes from the null-hypothesis-defined population. This is shown for 40 new pairs of variables in Table 11.7.

Many of the differences between the pairs of means in Table 11.7 are very close to zero. This is just as we would expect, since the independent and dependent variables are not related. Nevertheless, the means of some pairs of samples are somewhat different. In Table 11.7, 95% of the differences between the two means come in the range 0.922 to −1.400. (Given the small number of samples we have used, it is not surprising that this range is not symmetrical. If we had taken large numbers of samples, we would have expected more symmetry. Furthermore, had we used normally distributed scores, the symmetry may have been better.) The middle 95% of the distribution of differences between pairs of sample means are held clearly to support the null hypothesis. The extreme 5% beyond this middle range are held more likely to support the alternative hypothesis.

The standard deviation of the 40 'difference' scores gives the standard error of the differences. Don't forget we are dealing with *sample* means, so the term standard error is the correct one. The value of the standard error is 0.63. This is the 'average' amount by which the differences between sample means are likely to deviate from the population mean difference of zero.

11.3   Standard deviation and standard error

The trouble with all of the above is that it is abstract theory. Normally we know nothing for certain about the populations from which our samples come. Fortunately, quite a lot can be inferred about the population given the null hypothesis and information from the samples:

1. Since the null hypothesis states that there is no relationship between the independent and dependent variables in the population, it follows that there should be no systematic difference between the scores in the pair of samples. That is, the average difference between the two means should be zero over many pairs of samples.

2. We can use the scores in a sample to estimate the standard deviation of the scores in the population. However, if we use our usual standard deviation formula the estimate tends to be somewhat too low. Consequently we have to modify our standard deviation formula (Chapter 5) when estimating the standard deviation of the population. The change is minimal – the N in the bottom half of the formula is changed to N − 1:

$$\text{Estimated standard deviation} = \sqrt{\frac{\sum X^2 - \dfrac{(\sum X)^2}{N}}{N - 1}}$$

The net effect of this adjustment is to increase the estimated standard deviation in the population – the amount of adjustment is greatest if we are working with small sample sizes for which subtracting 1 is a big adjustment.

But this only gives us the estimated standard deviation of the *scores* in the population. We really need to know about the standard deviation (i.e. standard error) of sample means taken from that population. Remember, there is a simple formula which converts the estimated standard deviation of the population to the estimated standard error of sample means drawn from that population: we simply divide the estimated standard deviation by the square root of the sample size. It so happens that the computationally most useful way of working out the standard error is as follows:

$$\text{Standard error} = \frac{\sqrt{\dfrac{\sum X^2 - \dfrac{(\sum X)^2}{N}}{N-1}}}{\sqrt{N}}$$

Still we have not finished, because this is the estimated standard error of *sample means*; we want the estimated standard error of *differences between pairs of sample means*. It makes intuitive sense that the standard error of differences between pairs of sample means is likely to be the sum of the standard errors of the two samples. After all, the standard error is merely the average amount by which a sample mean differs from the population mean of zero. So the standard error of the differences between pairs of sample means drawn from a population should be the two separate standard errors combined.

Well, that is virtually the procedure. However, the two different standard errors (SE) are added together in a funny sort of way:

$$\text{SE}_{[\text{of differences between sample means}]} = \sqrt{(\text{SE}_1^2 + \text{SE}_2^2)}$$

Finally, because the sample sizes used to estimate the two individual standard errors are not always the same, it is necessary to adjust the equation to account for this, otherwise you end up with the wrong answer. The computational formula for the estimated standard error of differences between pairs of sample means is as follows:

Standard error of differences between pairs of sample means

$$= \sqrt{\left(\frac{\left(\sum X_1^2 - \dfrac{(\sum X_1)^2}{N_1}\right) + \left(\sum X_2^2 - \dfrac{(\sum X_2)^2}{N_2}\right)}{N_1 + N_2 - 2}\right)\left(\frac{1}{N_1} + \frac{1}{N_2}\right)}$$

Although this looks appallingly complicated, the basic idea is fairly simple. It looks complex because of the adjustment for different sample sizes.

Now we simply use the *t*-test formula. The average difference between the pairs of sample means is zero assuming the null hypothesis to be true. The *t* formula is:

$$t = \frac{\text{sample 1 mean} - \text{sample 2 mean} - 0}{\text{standard error of differences between sample means}}$$

or

$$t = \frac{\text{differences between the two sample means} - 0}{\text{standard error of differences between sample means}}$$

Since in the above formula the population mean of differences between pairs of sample means is always zero, we can omit it:

$$t = \frac{\text{sample 1 mean} - \text{sample 2 mean}}{\text{standard error of differences between sample means}}$$

The formula expressed in full looks very complicated:

$$t = \frac{\bar{X}_1 - \bar{X}_2}{\sqrt{\left(\dfrac{\left(\sum X_1^2 - \dfrac{(\sum X_1)^2}{N_1}\right) + \left(\sum X_2^2 - \dfrac{(\sum X_2)^2}{N_2}\right)}{N_1 + N_2 - 2}\right)\left(\dfrac{1}{N_1} + \dfrac{1}{N_2}\right)}}$$

So t is the number of standard errors by which the difference between our two sample means differs from the population mean of zero. The distribution of t is rather like the distribution of z if you have a large sample – thus it approximates very closely the normal distribution. However, with smaller sample sizes the curve of t becomes increasingly flat and more spread out than the normal curve. Consequently we need different t-distributions for different sample sizes.

Significance Table 11.1 gives values for the t-distributions. Notice that the distribution is dependent on the degrees of freedom, which for this t-test is the total number of scores in the two samples combined minus 2.

Significance Table 11.1	5% significance values of unrelated t (two-tailed test). Appendix E gives a fuller and conventional version of this table	
Degrees of freedom (always $N - 2$ for unrelated t-test)		**Significant at 5% level: accept hypothesis**
3		±3.18 or more extreme
4		±2.78 or more extreme
5		±2.57 or more extreme
6		±2.45 or more extreme
7		±2.37 or more extreme
8		±2.31 or more extreme
9		±2.26 or more extreme
10		±2.23 or more extreme
11		±2.20 or more extreme
12		±2.18 or more extreme
13		±2.16 or more extreme
14		±2.15 or more extreme
15		±2.13 or more extreme
18		±2.10 or more extreme
20		±2.09 or more extreme
25		±2.06 or more extreme
30		±2.04 or more extreme
40		±2.02 or more extreme
60		±2.00 or more extreme
100		±1.98 or more extreme
∞		±1.96 or more extreme

Your value must be in the listed ranges for your degrees of freedom to be significant at the 5% level (i.e. to accept the hypothesis).
If your required degrees of freedom are not listed, then take the nearest *smaller* listed value. Refer to Appendix D if you need a precise value of t.
'More extreme' means that, for example, values in the ranges of +3.18 to infinity or −3.18 to minus infinity are statistically significant with three degrees of freedom.

Calculation 11.1

The unrelated/uncorrelated samples *t*-test

The calculation of the unrelated *t*-test uses the following formula:

$$t = \frac{\bar{X}_1 - \bar{X}_2}{\sqrt{\left(\dfrac{\left(\sum X_1^2 - \dfrac{(\sum X_1)^2}{N_1}\right) + \left(\sum X_2^2 - \dfrac{(\sum X_2)^2}{N_2}\right)}{N_1 + N_2 - 2}\right)\left(\dfrac{1}{N_1} + \dfrac{1}{N_2}\right)}}$$

Horrific, isn't it? Probably the worst formula that you are likely to use in statistics. However, it contains little new. It is probably best to break the formula down into its component calculations and take things step by step. However, if you prefer to try to work directly with the above formula, do not let us stand in your way.

The data are from an imaginary study involving the emotionality of children from lone-parent and two-parent families. The independent variable is family type, which has two levels – the lone-parent type and the two-parent type. The dependent variable is emotionality on a standard psychological measure – the higher the score on this test, the more emotional is the child. The data are listed in Table 11.8.

A key thing to note is that we have called the scores for the two-parent family condition X_1 and those for the lone-parent family condition X_2.

Table 11.8	Emotionality scores in two-parent and lone-parent families
Two-parent family X_1	**Lone-parent family X_2**
12	6
18	9
14	4
10	13
19	14
8	9
15	8
11	12
10	11
13	9
15	
16	

Step 1   Extend the data table by adding columns of squared scores, column totals and sample sizes as in Table 11.9. The sample size for $X_1 = N_1 = 12$; the sample size for $X_2 = N_2 = 10$.

$\sum X_1$ = sum of scores for two-parent family sample
$\sum X_1^2$ = sum of squared scores for two-parent family sample
$\sum X_2$ = sum of scores for lone-parent family sample
$\sum X_2^2$ = sum of squared scores for lone-parent family sample

→

Table 11.9	Table 11.8 extended to include steps in the calculation		
Two-parent family X_1	**Square previous column, X_1^2**	**Lone-parent family X_2**	**Square previous column, X_2^2**
12	144	6	36
18	324	9	81
14	196	4	16
10	100	13	169
19	361	14	196
8	64	9	81
15	225	8	64
11	121	12	144
10	100	11	121
13	169	9	81
15	225		
16	256		
$\sum X_1 = 161$	**$\sum X_1^2 = 2285$**	**$\sum X_2 = 95$**	**$\sum X_2^2 = 989$**

Step 2 Do each of the following calculations.

Calculation of A:

$$A = \bar{X}_1 - \bar{X}_2$$

$$= \frac{\sum X_1}{N_1} - \frac{\sum X_2}{N_2} = \frac{161}{12} - \frac{95}{10}$$

$$= 13.417 - 9.500 = 3.917$$

Calculation of B:

$$B = \sum X_1^2 - \frac{(\sum X_1)^2}{N_1} = 2285 - \frac{161^2}{12}$$

$$= 2285 - \frac{25921}{12}$$

$$= 2285 - 2160.0833 = 124.9167$$

Calculation of C:

$$C = \sum X_2^2 - \frac{(\sum X_2)^2}{N_2} = 989 - \frac{95^2}{10}$$

$$= 989 - \frac{9025}{10}$$

$$= 989 - 902.5 = 86.5$$

Calculation of D:

$$D = N_1 + N_2 - 2$$
$$= 12 + 10 - 2$$
$$= 20$$

Calculation of E:

$$E = \frac{1}{N_1} + \frac{1}{N_2} = \frac{1}{12} + \frac{1}{10}$$
$$= 0.0833 + 0.1000 = 0.1833$$

Calculation of F:

$$F = \left(\frac{B+C}{D}\right) \times E$$
$$= \left(\frac{124.9167 + 86.5000}{20}\right) \times 0.1833$$
$$= \left(\frac{211.4167}{20}\right) \times 0.1833$$
$$= 10.57083 \times 0.1833 = 1.938$$

Calculation of G:

$$G = \sqrt{F} = \sqrt{1.938} = 1.392$$

Calculation of t:

$$t = \frac{A}{G} = \frac{3.917}{1.392} = 2.81$$

Step 3 t is the t-score or the number of standard errors our sample data are away from the population mean of zero. We use Significance Table 11.1 to check the statistical significance of our value of 2.81 by checking against the row for degrees of freedom (i.e. $N_1 + N_2 - 2 = 20$ degrees of freedom). This table tells us that our value of t is in the extreme 5% of the distribution because it is larger than 2.09; so we reject the null hypothesis that family structure is unrelated to emotionality. Our study showed that emotionality is significantly greater in the two-parent family structure than in the lone-parent family structure.

Interpreting the results Remember to check carefully the mean scores for both groups in order to know which of the two groups has the higher scores on the dependent variable. In our example, this shows that the greater emotionality was found in the children from the two-parent families. The significant value of the t-test means that we are reasonably safe to conclude that the two groups do differ in terms of their emotionality.

Reporting the results The statistical analysis could be reported in the following style: 'It was found that emotionality was significantly higher ($t = 2.81$, $df = 20$, $p < 0.05$) in the two-parent families ($\bar{X} = 13.42$) than in the lone-parent families ($\bar{X} = 9.50$).'

The material in the final brackets simply reports the significance test used (the t-test), its value (2.81), the degrees of freedom ($df = 20$) and that the value of t is statistically significant ($p < 0.05$). Chapter 10 explains the approach in greater detail.

Box 11.1   Focus on

Avoiding rounding errors

When calculating by hand, you need to use rather more decimal places than when reporting your findings. If this is not done then *rounding errors* will result in your getting a different answer from that calculated by a computer. Generally speaking, you need to work to at least three decimal places on your calculator, though the actual calculated figures given by the calculator are best and easiest to use. Because of limitations of space and for clarity, the calculations reported in this book have been given to a small number of decimal places, usually three. When you report the results of the calculation, however, round the figure to no more than two decimal places. Remember to be consistent in the number of decimal places you present in your results.

11.4   A cautionary note

You should not use the *t*-test if your samples are markedly skewed, especially if they are skewed in opposite directions. Appendix A explains how to test for skewness.

11.5   Data requirements for the unrelated *t*-test

One single score variable and two distinct groups of participants are required. The unrelated *t*-test can be used where there are two separate groups of participants for which you have scores on any score variable. It is best if the scores are normally distributed and correspond to an equal-interval level of measurement, though any score data can be used with a loss of accuracy. SPSS provides two versions of the unrelated *t*-test: one where the variances of the two sets of scores are equal and the other where the two variances are significantly different.

11.6   When not to use the unrelated *t*-test

Do not use the unrelated *t*-test where you have three or more groups of participants – the mean of each group you wish to compare with the mean of each other group. Analysis of variance (ANOVA) is a more suitable statistic in these circumstances, since multiple comparisons using an unrelated *t*-test increase the likelihood of having one or more comparisons significant by chance.

11.7   Problems in the use of the unrelated *t*-test

SPSS causes users some problems. The common problem is confusing the significance of the *F*-ratio comparing the variances of the two groups of scores with the significance of the *t*-test. They are quite distinct but very close together in SPSS output.

There are two versions of the unrelated *t*-test. One is used if the two sets of scores have similar variances. This is described as 'Equal variances assumed' in SPSS. Where the *F*-ratio shows a statistically significant difference in the variances, the output for 'Equal variances not assumed' should be used.

As is often the case in statistical analysis, it is useful to be clear what the difference in the two group means indicates prior to the test of significance. The test of significance then merely confirms whether this is a big enough difference to be regarded as statistically reliable. It is very easy to get confused by SPSS output giving mean differences otherwise.

11.8   SPSS analysis

■ The data to be analysed

The computation of an unrelated *t*-test is illustrated with the data in Table 11.8, which shows the emotionality scores of 12 children from two-parent families and 10 children from single-parent families. In SPSS this sort of *t*-test is called an independent samples *t*-test. The purpose of the analysis is to assess whether emotionality scores are different in two-parent and lone-parent families.

■ Entering the data

Step 1

In 'Variable View' of the 'Data Editor' label the first variable 'Family'. This defines the two types of family. Label the second variable 'Emotion'. These are the emotionality scores. Remove the two decimal places by changing the value here to 0 if necessary.

	Name	Type	Width	Decimals
1	Family	Numeric	8	0
2	Emotion	Numeric	8	0
3				

Step 2

In 'Data View' of the 'Data Editor' enter the values of the two variables in the first two columns.

	Family	Emotion
1	2	12
2	2	18
3	2	14
4	2	10
5	2	19
6	2	8
7	2	15
8	2	11
9	2	10
10	2	13
11	2	15
12	2	16
13	1	6
14	1	9
15	1	4
16	1	13
17	1	14
18	1	9
19	1	8
20	1	12
21	1	11
22	1	9

Take a good look at step 2. Notice that there are two columns of data. The second column ('emotion') consists of the 22 emotionality scores from *both* groups of children. The data are not kept separate for the two groups. In order to identify to which group the child belongs, the first column ('family') contains lots of 1s and 2s. These indicate, in our example, children from a lone-parent family (they are the rows with 1 in 'family') and children from two-parent families (they are the rows with 2 in 'family'). Thus a single column is used for the dependent variable (in this case, emotionality, 'emotion') and another column for the independent variable (in this case, type of family, 'family'). So each row is a particular child, and their independent variable and dependent variable scores are entered in two separate columns in the Data Editor.

■ Carrying out the unrelated *t*-test

Step 1

Select 'Analyze'
→ 'Compare Means'
→ 'Independent-Samples T Test...'.

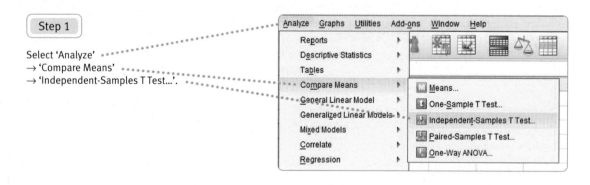

Step 2

Select 'Emotion' and the arrow button for the 'Test Variable(s):' box to put it there.
Select 'Family' and the arrow button for the 'Grouping Variable:' box to put it there.
Select 'Define Groups...' to define the two groups.

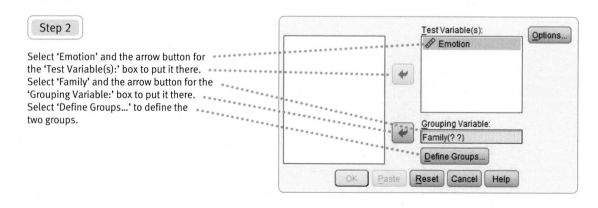

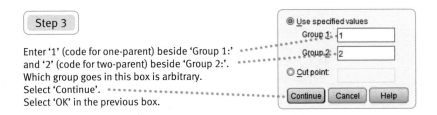

Step 3

Enter '1' (code for one-parent) beside 'Group 1:'
and '2' (code for two-parent) beside 'Group 2:'.
Which group goes in this box is arbitrary.
Select 'Continue'.
Select 'OK' in the previous box.

■ Interpreting the output

Group Statistics

	Family	N	Mean	Std. Deviation	Std. Error Mean
Emotion	1	10	9.50	3.100	.980
	2	12	13.42	3.370	.973

- The first table shows for each group the number of cases, the mean and the standard deviation. The mean of the lone parents is 9.50. There is obviously a difference, therefore, between the two types of family. The question next is whether the two means differ significantly.

- The value of *t* as shown in the second table is simply the mean difference (−3.917) divided by the standard error of the difference (1.392), which yields a value of −2.813.

- Levene's test is used when our variances are not normally distributed. See Chapters 3 and 4 for information.

- If the significance of Levene's test is greater than 0.05, which it is here at 0.650, use the information in this first row. If the significance of Levene's test is 0.05 or less, use the information in the second row. The second row gives the figures for when the variances are significantly different.

Independent Samples Test

		Levene's Test for Equality of Variances		t-test for Equality of Means					95% Confidence Interval of the Difference	
		F	Sig.	t	df	Sig. (2-tailed)	Mean Difference	Std. Error Difference	Lower	Upper
Emotion	Equal variances assumed	.212	.650	-2.813	20	.011	-3.917	1.392	-6.821	-1.013
	Equal variances not assumed			-2.836	19.768	.010	-3.917	1.381	-6.800	-1.034

- For equal variance, *t* is −2.813, which with 20 degrees of freedom is significant at 0.011 for the two-tailed level. To obtain the one-tailed level, divide this level by 2, which gives 0.006 rounded to three decimal places.

The output for the uncorrelated/unrelated *t*-test on SPSS is particularly confusing even to people with a good knowledge of statistics. The reason is that there are two versions of the uncorrelated/unrelated *t*-test. Which one to use depends on whether or not there is a significant difference between the (estimated) variances for the two groups of scores.

- Examine the first table of the output. This contains the means and standard deviations of the scores on the dependent variable (emotionality) of the two groups. Notice that an additional figure has been added by the computer to the name of the column containing the dependent variable. This additional figure indicates which of the two groups the row refers to. If you had labelled your values, these value labels would be given in the table.

- For children from two-parent families ('family 2') the mean emotionality score is 13.42 (see the first table above) and the standard deviation of the emotionality scores is 3.37. For the children of lone-parent families ('family 1') the mean emotionality score is 9.50 and the standard deviation of emotionality is 3.10.

- In the second table, look at the columns under 'Levene's Test for Equality of Variances'. If the probability value is statistically significant then your variances are *unequal*, otherwise they are regarded as equal.

- Levene's test for equality of variances in this case tells us that the variances are equal because the p value of 0.650 is not statistically significant.

- Consequently, you need the row for 'Equal variances assumed'. The t value, its degrees of freedom and its probability are displayed. The t value for equal variances is –2.813, which with 20 degrees of freedom has an exact two-tailed significance level of 0.011.

- Had Levene's test for equality of variances been statistically significant (i.e. 0.05 or less), then you should have used the second row of the output which gives the t-test values for unequal variances.

- SPSS procedures for the unrelated t-test are very useful and go beyond usual textbook treatments of the topic. That is, they include an option for calculating the t-test when the variances of the two samples of scores are significantly different from each other. Most textbooks erroneously suggest that the t-test is too inaccurate to use when the variances of the two groups are unequal. This additional version of the unrelated t-test is rarely mentioned in statistics textbooks but is extremely valuable.

■ Reporting the output

- We could report the results of this analysis as follows: 'The mean emotionality scores of children from two-parent families (M = 13.42, SD = 3.37) is significantly higher (t = –2.81, df = 20, two-tailed p = 0.011) than that of children in lone-parent families (M = 9.50, SD = 3.10).'

- It is unusual to see the t-test for unequal variances in reports, as many people are unaware of its existence. So what happens if you have to use one? In order to clarify things, we would write: 'Because the variances for the two groups were significantly unequal (F = 8.43, p < 0.05), a t-test for unequal variances was used . . .'.

- If you prefer to use the confidence intervals (see Section 3.5 in Chapter 3, and Chapter 12), you might write: 'The difference between the emotionality scores for the children from two-parent families (M = 13.42, SD = 3.37) and lone-parent families (M = 9.50, SD = 3.10) is –3.92. The 95% confidence interval for this difference is –6.82 to –1.01. Since this interval does not include 0.00, the difference is statistically significant at the two-tailed 5% level.'

Key points

- The *t*-test is commonly used in research, so it is important that you have an idea of what it does. However, it is only a special case of the analysis of variance (Chapter 13) which is a much more flexible statistic. Given the analysis of variance's ability to handle any number of samples, you might prefer to use it instead of the *t*-test in most circumstances. To complicate matters, some use the *t*-test in the analysis of variance.

- The *t*-test assumes that the variances of the two samples are similar so that they can be combined to yield an overall estimate. However, if the variances of the two samples are significantly different from each other, you should not use this version of the *t*-test. The way to see if two variances are dissimilar is to use the variance ratio test described in Chapter 13.

- If you wish to use the *t*-test but find that you fall foul of this *F*-ratio requirement, there is a version of the *t*-test which does not assume equal variances. The best way of doing such *t*-tests is to use a computer package which applies both tests to the same data. Unfortunately the calculation for the degrees of freedom is a little complex (you can have fractions involved in the values) and it goes a little beyond reasonable hand calculations. The calculation details are provided in Blalock (1972).

CHAPTER 12

Chi-square

Differences between samples of frequency data

Overview

- Chi-square is used with nominal or category data (minimum two) in the form of frequency counts.

- It tests whether the frequency counts in the various nominal categories could be expected by chance or, more specifically, whether there is a relationship.

- One-sample chi-square compares the frequencies obtained in each category with a known expected frequency distribution, whereas a two-sample chi-square uses a crosstabulation or frequency table for two variables. This gives the frequencies in the various possible combinations of categories of these two variables.

- The disparity between the actual frequencies in the data and what the frequencies would be if the null hypothesis were true is at the heart of the calculation. The bigger the disparity, the bigger the value of chi-square and the more one's findings are statistically significant.

- When the chi-square table has more than four cells (i.e. combinations of categories), interpretation becomes difficult. It is possible to subdivide a big table into a number of smaller chi-squares in order to facilitate interpretation. This is known as partitioning.

- Sometimes data may violate the mathematical foundations of chi-square too much. In these circumstances, the data may have to be modified to meet the mathematical requirements, or an alternative measure such as the Fisher exact test may be employed.

Preparation

You should be familiar with crosstabulation and contingency tables (Chapter 6).

12.1   Introduction

Often, chi-square (pronounced 'ky'-square) is written as χ^2. However, we have avoided Greek letters as far as possible.

If a researcher has several samples of data which involve *frequencies* rather than scores, a statistical test designed for frequency data must be used. The following are some examples of research of this sort:

1. Male and female schoolchildren are compared in terms of wanting to be social workers when they leave school (Table 12.1).

2. The sexual orientations of a sample of religious men are compared with those of a non-religious sample (Table 12.2).

3. Choosing to play with either a black or a white doll in black and white children (Table 12.3).

In each of these examples, both variables consist of a relatively small number of categories. The precise number of samples may vary from study to study and the number of categories of the dependent variable can be two or more. As a rule of thumb, *it is better to have just a few samples and a few categories*, since large tables can be difficult to interpret and generally require large numbers of participants or cases to be workable.

The statistical question is whether the distribution of frequencies in the different samples is so varied that it is unlikely that these all come from the same population. As

Table 12.1	Relationship between sex and wanting to be a social worker	
Intention	**Male**	**Female**
Wants to be a social worker	$f = 17$	$f = 98$
Does not want to be a social worker	$f = 67$	$f = 35$

Table 12.2	Relationship between sexual orientation and religion	
Orientation	**Religious**	**Non-religious**
Heterosexual	57	105
Gay	13	27
Bisexual	8	17

Table 12.3	Relationship between doll choice and ethnicity		
Choice	**Black child**	**White child**	**Mixed-race child**
Black doll	19	17	5
White doll	16	18	9

ever, this population is the one defined by the null hypothesis (which suggests that there is no relationship between the independent and dependent variables).

12.2 Theoretical considerations

Imagine a research study in which children are asked to choose between two video games, one violent and the other non-violent. Some of the children have been in trouble at school for fighting and the others have not been in trouble. The researcher wants to know if there is a relationship between the violence content of the preferred video game and having been in trouble for fighting at school. The data might look something like Table 12.4.

We can see from Table 12.4 that the fighters (sample 1) are more likely to prefer the violent game and the non-fighters (sample 2) are more likely to prefer the non-violent game. The frequencies obtained in the research are known as the *observed* frequencies. This merely refers to the fact that we obtain them from our empirical *observations* (that is, the data).

Assume that both of the samples come from the same population of data in which there is no relationship between the dependent and independent variables. This implies that any differences between the samples are merely due to the chance fluctuations of sampling. A useful index of how much the samples differ from each other is based on how different each sample is from the population distribution defined by the null hypothesis. As ever, since we do not know the population directly in most research, we have to estimate its characteristics from the characteristics of samples.

With the chi-square test, we simply *add* together the frequencies for whatever number of samples we have. These sums are then used as an estimate of the distribution of the different categories in the population. Since differences between the samples under the null hypothesis are solely due to chance factors, by combining samples the best possible estimate of the characteristics of the population is obtained. In other words, we simply add together the characteristics of two or more samples to give us an estimate of the population distribution of the categories. The first stage of doing this is illustrated in Table 12.5.

Table 12.4	Relationship between preferred video game and fighting	
Preference	**Sample 1 Fighters**	**Sample 2 Non-fighters**
Violent video games preferred	40	15
Non-violent video games preferred	30	70

Table 12.5	Relationship between preferred video game and fighting including the marginal frequencies (column and row frequencies)		
Preference	**Sample 1 Fighters**	**Sample 2 Non-fighters**	**Row frequencies**
Violent video games preferred	40	15	55
Non-violent video games preferred	30	70	100
Column frequencies	**70**	**85**	**Overall frequencies = 155**

So in the null-hypothesis-defined population, we would expect 55 out of every 155 to prefer the violent game and 100 out of 155 to prefer the non-violent game. But we obtained 40 out of 70 preferring the violent game in sample 1, and 15 out of 85 preferring the violent game in sample 2. How do these figures match the expectations from the population defined by the null hypothesis? We need to calculate the expected frequencies of the cells in Table 12.5. This calculation is based on the assumption that the null hypothesis population frequencies are our best information as to the relative proportions preferring the violent and non-violent games if there truly was no difference between the samples.

Sample 1 contains 70 children; if the null hypothesis is true then we would expect 55 out of every 155 of these to prefer the violent game. Thus our expected frequency of those preferring the violent game in sample 1 is:

$$70 \times \frac{55}{155} = 70 \times 0.355 = 24.84$$

Remember that these figures have been rounded for presentation and give a slightly different answer from that generated by a calculator.

Similarly, since we expect under the null hypothesis 100 out of every 155 to prefer the non-violent game, then our expected frequency of those preferring the non-violent game in sample 1, out of the 70 children in that sample, is:

$$70 \times \frac{100}{155} = 70 \times 0.645 = 45.16$$

Notice that the sum of the expected frequencies for sample 1 is the same as the number of children in that sample (24.84 + 45.16 = 70).

We can apply the same logic to sample 2 which contains 85 children. We expect that 55 out of every 155 will prefer the violent games and 100 out of every 155 will prefer the non-violent game. The expected frequency preferring the violent game in sample 2 is:

$$85 \times \frac{55}{155} = 85 \times 0.355 = 30.16$$

The expected frequency preferring the non-violent game in sample 2 is:

$$85 \times \frac{100}{155} = 85 \times 0.645 = 54.84$$

We can enter these expected frequencies (population frequencies under the null hypothesis) into our table of frequencies (Table 12.6).

The chi-square statistic is based on the differences between the observed and the expected frequencies. It should be fairly obvious that the greater the disparity between the observed frequencies and the population frequencies under the null hypothesis, the less likely is the null hypothesis to be true. Thus if the samples are very different from each other, the differences between the observed and expected frequencies will be large. Chi-square involves calculating the overall disparity between the observed and expected frequencies over all the cells in the table. To be precise, the chi-square formula involves the squared deviations over the expected frequencies, but this is merely a slight diversion to make our formula fit a convenient statistical distribution which is called chi-square. The calculated value of chi-square is then compared with a table of critical values of chi-square (Significance Table 12.1) in order to estimate the probability of obtaining our

Table 12.6	Contingency table including both observed and expected frequencies		
Preference	**Sample 1 Fighters**	**Sample 2 Non-fighters**	**Row frequencies**
Violent video games preferred	observed frequency = 4 expected frequency = 24.8	observed frequency = 15 expected frequency = 30.16	55
Non-violent video games preferred	observed frequency = 30 expected frequency = 45.16	observed frequency = 70 expected frequency = 54.84	100
Column frequencies (i.e. sum of observed frequencies in column)	70	85	**Overall frequencies = 155**

pattern of frequencies by chance (if the null hypothesis of no differences between the samples was true). This table is organised according to degrees of freedom, which is always (number of columns of data − 1) × (number of rows of data − 1). This would be (2 − 1) × (2 − 1) or 1 for Table 12.6.

Significance Table 12.1	5% and 1% significance values of chi-square (two-tailed test). Appendix E gives a fuller and conventional version of this table	
Degrees of freedom	**Significant at 5% level: accept hypothesis**	**Significant at 1% level: accept hypothesis**
1	3.8 or more	6.7 or more
2	6.0 or more	9.2 or more
3	7.8 or more	11.3 or more
4	9.5 or more	13.3 or more

Your value must be in the listed ranges for your degrees of freedom to be significant at the 5% level (column 2) or the 1% level (column 3) (i.e. to accept the hypothesis). Should you require more precise values than those listed below, these are to be found in the table in Appendix E.

Box 12.1	Focus on

Yates's correction

A slightly outmoded statistical procedure when the expected frequencies in chi-square are small is to apply Yates's correction. This is intended to make such data fit the theoretical chi-square distribution a little better. In essence all you do is subtract 0.5 from each (observed frequency − expected frequency) in the chi-square formula prior to squaring that difference. With large expected frequencies this has virtually no effect. With small tables, it obviously reduces the size of chi-square and therefore its statistical significance. We have opted for not using it in our calculations. Really it is a matter of personal choice as far as convention goes.

Calculation 12.1

Chi-square

The calculation of chi-square involves several relatively simple but repetitive calculations. For each cell in the chi-square table you calculate the following:

$$\frac{(\text{observed frequency} - \text{expected frequency})^2}{\text{expected frequency}}$$

The only complication is that this small calculation is repeated for each of the cells in your crosstabulation or contingency table. The formula in full becomes:

$$\text{chi-square} = \sum \frac{(O - E)^2}{E}$$

where O = observed frequency and E = expected frequency.

The following is an imaginary piece of research in which males and females were asked to name their preferred degree programme from a list of three: (1) business, (2) medicine and (3) neither of these. The researcher suspects that sex may be related to degree preference (Table 12.7).

We next need to calculate the expected frequencies for each of the cells in Table 12.7. One easy way of doing this is to multiply the row total and the column total for each particular cell and divide by the total number of observations (i.e. total frequencies). This is shown in Table 12.8.

Table 12.7	Relationship between degree choice and sex of respondent			
Respondents	**Business degree**	**Medicine degree**	**Neither**	**Totals**
Males	observed = 27	observed = 14	observed = 19	row 1 = 60
Females	observed = 17	observed = 33	observed = 9	row 2 = 59
Total	**Column 1 = 44**	**Column 2 = 47**	**Column 3 = 28**	**Total = 119**

Table 12.8	Calculation of expected frequencies by multiplying appropriate row and column totals and then dividing by the overall total			
Respondents	**Business degree**	**Medicine degree**	**Neither**	**Total**
Males	observed = 27	observed = 14	observed = 19	row 1 = 60
	expected = 60 × 44/119 **= 22.185**	**expected = 60 × 47/119** **= 23.697**	**expected = 60 × 28/119** **= 14.118**	
Females	observed = 17	observed = 33	Observed = 9	row 2 = 59
	expected = 59 × 44/119 **= 21.815**	**expected = 59 × 47/119** **= 23.303**	**expected = 59 × 28/119** **= 13.882**	
Total	**Column 1 = 44**	**Column 2 = 47**	**Column 3 = 28**	**Total = 119**

→

We then simply substitute the above values in the chi-square formula:

$$\text{chi-square} = \sum \frac{(O-E)^2}{E}$$

$$= \frac{(27-22.185)^2}{22.185} + \frac{(14-23.697)^2}{23.697} + \frac{(19-14.118)^2}{14.118}$$

$$+ \frac{(17-21.815)^2}{21.185} + \frac{(33-23.303)^2}{23.303} + \frac{(9-13.882)^2}{13.882}$$

$$= \frac{4.815^2}{22.185} + \frac{(-9.697)^2}{23.697} + \frac{4.882^2}{14.118} + \frac{(-4.185)^2}{21.185} + \frac{9.697^2}{23.303} + \frac{(-4.882)^2}{13.882}$$

$$= \frac{23.184}{22.185} + \frac{94.032}{23.697} + \frac{23.834}{14.118} + \frac{23.184}{21.815} + \frac{94.032}{23.303} + \frac{23.834}{13.882}$$

$$= 1.045 + 3.968 + 1.688 + 1.063 + 4.035 + 1.717$$

$$= 13.52$$

The degrees of freedom are (the number of columns − 1) × (the number of rows − 1) = (3 − 1) × (2 − 1) = 2 degrees of freedom.

We then check the table of the critical values of chi-square (Significance Table 12.1) in order to assess whether or not our samples differ amongst each other so much that they are unlikely to be produced by the population defined by the null hypothesis. The value must equal or exceed the tabulated value to be significant at the listed level of significance. Some tables will give you more degrees of freedom but you will be hard pressed to do a sensible chi-square that exceeds 12 degrees of freedom.

Interpreting the results Our value of chi-square is well in excess of the minimum value of 6.0 needed to be significant at the 5% level for 2 degrees of freedom, so we reject the hypothesis that the samples came from the population defined by the null hypothesis. Thus we accept the hypothesis that there is a relationship between television programme preferences and sex.

Only if you have a 2 × 2 chi-square is it possible to interpret the significance level of the chi-square directly in terms of the trends revealed in the data table. As we will see in Section 12.9, if we have a bigger chi-square than this (say 3 × 2 or 3 × 3) then a significant value of chi-square merely indicates that the samples are dissimilar to each other overall without stipulating which samples are different from each other.

Because the sample sizes generally differ in contingency tables, it is helpful to convert the frequencies in each cell to percentages of the relevant sample size at this stage. It is important, though, never to actually calculate chi-square itself on these percentages as you will obtain the wrong significance level if you do. It seems from Table 12.9 that males prefer business degrees more often than females do, females have a preference for medicine degrees, and males are more likely than females to say that they prefer another type of programme. Unfortunately, as things stand we are not able to say which of these trends are statistically significant unless we partition the chi-square as described in Section 12.9.

Table 12.9	Observed percentages in each sample based on the observed frequencies in Table 12.7		
Respondents	**Business degree**	**Medicine degree**	**Neither**
Males	45.0%	23.3%	31.7%
Females	28.8%	55.9%	15.3%

Reporting the results The results could be written up as follows: 'The value of chi-square was 13.52 which was significant at the 5% level with 2 degrees of freedom. Thus there is a sex difference in degree programme choice. Compared with females, males were more likely to choose a business degree and less likely to choose medicine degrees as their favourite programmes and more likely to prefer neither of these.'

However, as this table is bigger than a 2 × 2 table, it is advisable to partition the chi-square as discussed in Section 12.9 in order to say which of these trends are statistically significant.

An alternative way of writing up the results is as follows: 'There was a significant gender difference in degree programme preference (chi-square = 13.52, $df = 2$, $p < 0.05$). Compared with females, males were more likely to choose a business degree and less likely to choose a medicine degree as their favourite programmes and more likely to prefer neither of these.' Chapter 1 explains how to report statistical significance in the shorter, professional way used in this version.

12.3 When to use chi-square

There are few alternatives to the use of chi-square when dealing solely with nominal (category) variables. Chi-square can only be used with nominal (category) data. It can be used where there is just one nominal variable but also where there are two different nominal variables. There may be any *practical* number of categories (values) of each of the nominal variables, though you will probably wish to restrict yourself to just a few categories as otherwise the analysis may be very difficult to interpret. Chi-square is not used for three or more nominal variables where log-linear analysis (Chapter 22) may be the appropriate statistic.

12.4 When not to use chi-square

There are a number of limitations on the use of chi-square. The main problem is when there are too many expected frequencies which are less than five. Any more than 20–25% of the expected frequencies below five indicates that chi-square would be problematic. Sometimes a *Fisher exact test* (see below) can be used instead because low expected frequencies do not invalidate this test in the same way. An alternative is to combine categories of data together if this is appropriate, thus increasing the expected frequencies to five or above (hopefully). However, it is not always meaningful to combine categories with each other. Sometimes the alternative is simply to delete the small categories. This is all based on judgement and it is difficult to give general advice other than to be as thoughtful as possible (see Section 12.6).

12.5 Data requirements for chi-square

Each participant in the research contributes just one to the frequencies of each value of the nominal variable. It is difficult to violate this requirement using SPSS but even then it is wise to check that the number of participants you have in your analysis is the same as the total number of frequencies in the chi-square if you are inputting your own contingency or crosstabulation table into SPSS.

12.6   Problems in the use of chi-square

Chi-square is not an easy statistical test to use well. Fortunately, researchers tend to prefer score data so the problems with chi-square are not routinely experienced. The main difficulties with chi-square are as follows:

- Usually it is necessary to have a fairly substantial number of participants to use chi-square appropriately. This is because having small expected frequencies invalidates the test. Usually if you have more than about 20% or 25% expected frequencies of less than five then you should not use chi-square. You may be able to use the Fisher exact test instead in the 2 × 2 case. Otherwise it is a case of trying to rejig the contingency table in some way. But the main implication is to avoid categories of the nominal variable that attract few cases. These could be deleted or put with other categories into a combined 'other category'.

- A major problem in using chi-square is what happens when the analysis is of something larger than a 2 × 2 contingency table. The problem is that an overall significant chi-square tells you that the samples differ; it does not entirely tell you in what way the samples differ. So, for example, do women tend to prefer business degrees and men tend to prefer medicine degrees? It is possible to analyse the data as a 2 × 2 chi-square by dropping the category 'neither', for example. Indeed it is possible to form as many 2 × 2 analyses out of a bigger crosstabulation table as you wish, though it would be usual to adjust the significance level for the number of separate chi-squares carried out.

- One thing that gets students confused is that it is possible to enter a crosstabulation table directly in SPSS using a weighting procedure. This would be useful in circumstances where you have carried out a study and already have your data in the form of a simple table. However, if your data are part of a bigger SPSS spreadsheet then this weighting procedure would not be used. It all depends on what form your data are in.

12.7   SPSS analysis

■ The data to be analysed

The computation of chi-square with two or more samples is illustrated with the data in Table 12.7. This table shows which one of three types of degree programme is favoured by a sample of 119 males and females. To analyse a table of data like this one with SPSS, first we have to input the data into the Data Editor and weight the cells by the frequencies of cases in them.

- As we are working with a ready-made table, it is necessary to go through the 'Weighting Cases' procedure first (see below). Otherwise, you would enter Table 12.7 case by case, indicating which category of the row and which category of the column each case belongs to (see below). We need to identify each of the six cells in Table 12.7. The rows of the table represent the sex of the participants, while the columns represent the three types of degree programme. We will then weight each of the six cells of the table by the number of cases in them.

- The first column, called 'Sex' in the first screenshot below, contains the code for males (1) and females (2). (These values have also been labelled.)

- The second column, called 'Degree', holds the code for the three types of degree programme: business degree (1), medicine degree (2) and neither (3). (These values have also been labelled.)

■ Entering the data of Table 12.7 using the 'Weighting Cases' procedure

Step 1

In 'Variable view' of the 'Data Editor' label the first three variables 'Sex', 'Degree' and 'Freq' respectively.
Remove the two decimal places.
Label the values of 'Sex' and 'Degree'.

	Name	Type	Width	Decimals	Label	Values
1	Sex	Numeric	8	0		{1, Males}...
2	Degree	Numeric	8	0		{1, Busines...
3	Freq	Numeric	8	0		None

Step 2

In 'Data view' of the 'Data Editor' enter the appropriate values. Each row represents one of the six cells in Table 12.7.

	Sex	Degree	Freq
1	1	1	27
2	1	2	14
3	1	3	19
4	2	1	17
5	2	2	33
6	2	3	9
7			

Step 3

To weight these cells, select 'Data' → 'Weight Cases...'.

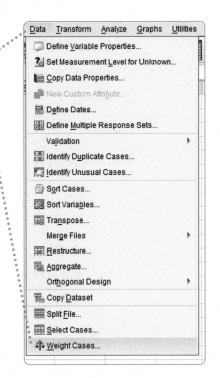

Step 4

Select 'Freq', 'Weight cases by' and the arrow button to put 'Freq' into the 'Frequency Variable:' box.
Select 'OK'.

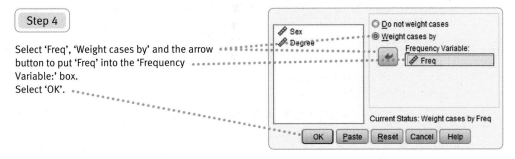

■ Entering the data of Table 12.7 case by case

	Sex	Degree
1	1	1
2	1	1
3	1	1
4	1	1
5	1	1

Enter the values for the two variables for each of the 119 cases.

■ Conducting a chi-square on Table 12.7

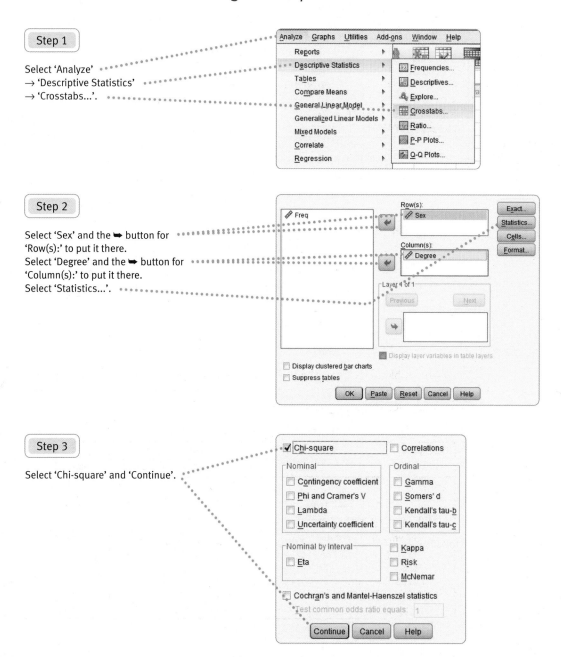

Step 1

Select 'Analyze'
→ 'Descriptive Statistics'
→ 'Crosstabs...'.

Step 2

Select 'Sex' and the ➡ button for 'Row(s):' to put it there.
Select 'Degree' and the ➡ button for 'Column(s):' to put it there.
Select 'Statistics...'.

Step 3

Select 'Chi-square' and 'Continue'.

Step 4

Select 'Cells...'.

Step 5

Select 'Expected' under 'Counts'.
Select 'Unstandardized' under 'Residuals'.
Residuals mean differences.
Select 'Continue' and then
'OK' in the previous box.

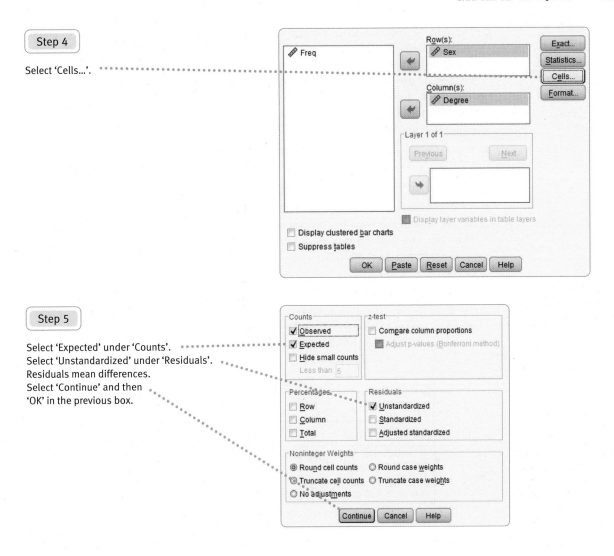

Interpreting the output

- The second table of the output (actually the first table shown here) gives the frequency (count), the expected frequency (expected count) and the difference (residual) between the two for each of the six cells of the table.

Sex * Degree Crosstabulation

			Degree			
			Business	Medicine	Neither	Total
Sex	Males	Count	27	14	19	60
		Expected Count	22.2	23.7	14.1	60.0
		Residual	4.8	-9.7	4.9	
	Females	Count	17	33	9	59
		Expected Count	21.8	23.3	13.9	59.0
		Residual	-4.8	9.7	-4.9	
Total		Count	44	47	28	119
		Expected Count	44.0	47.0	28.0	119.0

● The table shows the observed and expected frequencies of cases and the difference (residual) between them for each cell. The observed frequency (called Count) is presented first and the expected frequency (called Expected Count) second. The observed frequencies are always whole numbers, so they should be easy to spot. The expected frequencies are always expressed to one decimal place, so they are easily identified. Thus the first cell of the table (males liking business degrees) has an observed frequency of 27 and an expected frequency of 22.2.

● The final column in this table (labelled 'Total') lists the number of cases in that row followed by the expected number of cases in the table. So the first row has 60 cases, which will always be the same as the expected number of cases (i.e. 60.0).

● Similarly, the final row in this table (labelled 'Total') first presents the number of cases in that column followed by the expected number of cases in the table for that column. Thus the first column has 44 cases, which will always be equal to the expected number of cases (i.e. 44.0).

● The chi-square value, its degrees of freedom and its significance level are displayed in the third table of the output (the second table shown here) on the line starting with the word 'Pearson', the man who developed this test. The chi-square value is 13.518 which, rounded to two decimal places, is 13.52. Its degrees of freedom are 2 and its exact two-tailed probability is 0.001.

Chi-Square Tests

	Value	df	Asymp. Sig. (2-sided)
Pearson Chi-Square	13.518[a]	2	.001
Likelihood Ratio	13.841	2	.001
Linear-by-Linear Association	.000	1	.987
N of Valid Cases	119		

a. 0 cells (.0%) have expected count less than 5. The minimum expected count is 13.88.

● Also shown underneath this table is the 'minimum expected count' of any cell in the table, which is 13.88 for the last cell (females liking neither). If the minimum expected frequency is less than 5.0 then we should be wary of using chi-square. If you have a 2×2 chi-square and small expected frequencies occur, it would be better to use the Fisher exact test which SPSS prints in the output in these circumstances.

■ Reporting the output

There are two ways of describing these results. To the inexperienced eye they may seem very different but they amount to the same thing.

1. We could describe the results in the following way: 'There was a significant difference between the observed and expected frequency of males and females in their preference for a degree programme ($\chi^2 = 13.51$, $df = 2$, $p = 0.001$).'

2. Alternatively, and just as accurate: 'There was a significant association between sex and preference for different types of degree programme ($\chi^2 = 13.51$, $df = 2$, $p = 0.001$).'

In addition, we need to report the direction of the results. One way of doing this is to state that 'Females were more likely than males to prefer medicine programmes and less likely to prefer business degrees or both.'

12.8   The Fisher exact probability test

The Fisher exact probability test is not usually presented in introductory statistics books. We will only give the calculation of a 2 × 2 Fisher exact probability test, although there is a version for 2 × 3 tables. The reason for its inclusion is that much student work for practicals and projects has very small sample sizes. As a consequence, the assumptions of the chi-square test are frequently broken. The Fisher exact probability test is not subject to the same limitations as the chi-square and can be used when chi-square cannot. It is different from chi-square in that it calculates the exact probability rather than a critical value. Apart from that, a significant result is interpreted much as the equivalent chi-square would be, so we will not explain it further.

A number followed by ! is called a factorial. So 5! = 5 × 4 × 3 × 2 × 1 = 120, and 9! = 9 × 8 × 7 × 6 × 5 × 4 × 3 × 2 × 1 = 362,880. Easy enough but it can lead to rather big numbers which make the calculation awkward to handle. Table 12.10 lists factorials up to 15.

The Fisher exact probability test is applied to a 2 × 2 contingency table by extending the table to include the marginal row and column totals of frequencies as well as the overall total (see Table 12.11). The formula for the exact probability is as follows:

$$\text{Exact probability} = \frac{W!\,X!\,Y!\,Z!}{N!\,a!\,b!\,c!\,d!}$$

Imagine you have collected data on a small group of young males who are either foreign nationals or UK residents. You find that some are employed and others are not.

Table 12.10	Factorials of numbers from 0 to 15
Number	**Factorial**
0	1
1	1
2	2
3	6
4	24
5	120
6	720
7	5 040
8	40 320
9	362 880
10	3 628 800
11	39 916 800
12	479 001 600
13	6 227 020 800
14	87 178 291 200
15	1 307 674 368 000

Table 12.11	Symbols for the Fisher exact probability			
		Column 1	**Column 2**	**Row totals**
Row 1		a	b	$W (= a + b)$
Row 2		c	d	$X (= c + d)$
Column totals		$Y (= a + c)$	$Z (= b + d)$	**Overall total = N**

You wish to know if there is a relationship between residency status and having a job (Table 12.12). Substituting in the formula gives:

$$\text{Exact probability} = \frac{9! \, 5! \, 6! \, 8!}{14! \, 2! \, 7! \, 4! \, 1!}$$

The values of each of these factorials can be obtained from Table 12.10:

$$\text{Exact probability} = \frac{362\,880 \times 120 \times 720 \times 40\,320}{87\,178\,291\,200 \times 2 \times 5040 \times 24 \times 1}$$

Unfortunately you will need a scientific calculator to do this calculation.

The alternative is to cancel wherever possible numbers in the upper part of the formula with those in the lower part:

exact probability

$$= \frac{\begin{array}{c} 9 \times 8 \times 7 \times 6 \times 5 \times 4 \times 3 \times 2 \times 1 \times 5 \times 4 \times 3 \times 2 \times 1 \\ \times 6 \times 5 \times 4 \times 3 \times 2 \times 1 \times 8 \times 7 \times 6 \times 5 \times 4 \times 3 \times 2 \times 1 \end{array}}{\begin{array}{c} 14 \times 13 \times 12 \times 11 \times 10 \times 9 \times 8 \times 7 \times 6 \times 5 \times 4 \times 3 \times 2 \\ \times 1 \times 2 \times 1 \times 7 \times 6 \times 5 \times 4 \times 3 \times 2 \times 1 \times 4 \times 3 \times 2 \times 1 \times 1 \end{array}}$$

$$= \frac{5 \times 4 \times 3 \times 6 \times 5 \times 8}{14 \times 13 \times 12 \times 11 \times 10 \times 1} = \frac{14\,440}{240\,240} = 0.060$$

The value of 0.06 is the probability of getting exactly two employed males. This then is not the end of the calculation. The calculation also ought to take into account the more extreme outcomes which are relevant to the hypothesis. Basically the Fisher exact probability calculation works out (for any pattern of column and row totals) the probability of getting the obtained data or data more extreme than our obtained data. Table 12.13 gives all of the possible versions of the table if the marginal totals in Table 12.12 are retained along with the probability of each pattern calculated using the above formula.

Table 12.12	Steps in calculating the Fisher exact probability			
Respondents		**Employed**	**Unemployed**	**Row totals**
Foreign national		$a = 2$	$b = 7$	$W (= a + b) = 9$
UK resident		$c = 4$	$d = 1$	$X (= c + d) = 5$
Column totals		$Y (= a + c) + 6$	$Z (= b + d) + 8$	**Overall total = 14**

Table 12.13	All of the possible patterns of data keeping the marginal row and column totals unchanged from Table 12.15

1	8	2	7
5	0	4	1

$p = 0.003*$ $p = 0.060*$
* The sum of the probabilities of these two tables is the one-tailed significance level.

3	6	4	5
3	1	2	3

$p = 0.280$ $p = 0.420$

5	4	6	3
1	4	0	5

$p = 0.210$ $p = 0.028**$
** The two-tailed probability level is the one-tailed probability calculated above plus the probability of this table. That is, the two-tailed probability is 0.063 + 0.028 = 0.091.

Notice that some patterns are not possible with our marginal totals, for example one with 0 in the top left-hand cell. If 0 goes in that cell then we could only make the figures fit the marginal totals by using negative values, and that would be meaningless as one cannot have a negative case in a contingency table.

The calculation of significance levels is as follows:

1. One-tailed significance is simply the sum of the probability of the actual outcome (0.060) plus the probability of any possible outcome which has a more extreme outcome in the predicted direction. That is, in the present example, 0.060 + 0.003 = 0.063. The precise number of values to be added will depend on a number of factors and will sometimes vary from our example according to circumstances.

2. Two-tailed significance is not accurately estimated by doubling the one-tailed probability for the simple reason that the distribution is not symmetrical. Instead, two-tailed significance is calculated by adding to the one-tailed probability (0.063) any probabilities at the other end of the distribution from the obtained distribution which are smaller than the probability of the obtained distribution. In our example, the probability of the distribution of data in Table 12.12 is 0.060. At the other end of the distribution, only one probability is equal or less than 0.060 – the final table has a probability of 0.028. We therefore add this 0.028 to the one-tailed probability of 0.063 to give a two-tailed probability of 0.091.

Our two-tailed probability value of 0.091 is *not* statistically significant at the conventional 5% level (neither would the one-tailed test be if that were appropriate).

Interpreting the results The two-tailed significance level is 0.09 which is not statistically significant at the 0.05 (or 5%) level. Thus we cannot reject the null hypothesis that the incidence of employment is related to immigration status. It would be useful to convert the frequencies in Table 12.12 into percentages of the relevant sample size when interpreting these data as we have different numbers of foreign nationals and UK residents. Such a table would show that 80% of the UK residents were employed but only 22% of

Table 12.14	Stages in the calculation of a 2 × 3 Fisher exact probability test			
	Column 1	Column 2	Column 3	Row totals
Row 1	a	b	c	$W (= a + b + c)$
Row 2	d	e	f	$X (= d + e + f)$
Column totals	$K (= a + d)$	$L (= b + e)$	$M (= c + f)$	Overall total = N

the foreign nationals. Despite this, with such a small amount of data, the trend is not statistically significant.

Reporting the results The following would be an appropriate description: 'Although having employment was nearly four times more common in UK residents than in foreign nationals, this proved not to be statistically significant using the Fisher exact probability test. The exact probability was 0.09 which is not significant at the 0.05 level. Thus we must reject the hypothesis that employment is related to immigration status.'

Fisher exact probability test for 2 × 3 tables This is calculated in a very similar way as for the Fisher 2 × 2 test, the difference being simply the increased numbers of cells (Table 12.14). The formula for the 2 × 3 exact probability of the obtained outcome is as follows:

$$\text{Exact probability} = \frac{W!X!K!L!M!}{N!a!b!c!d!e!f!}$$

The calculation needs to be extended to cover all of the more extreme outcomes just as with the 2 × 2 version. Nevertheless, this is a very cumbersome calculation and best avoided by hand if possible.

12.9   SPSS analysis for the Fisher exact test

The chi-square procedure computes the Fisher exact test for 2 × 2 tables when one or more of the four cells has an expected frequency of less than 5. The Fisher exact test would be computed for the data in Table 12.15.

Table 12.15	Immigration status and employment	
	Employed	Unemployed
Foreign national	2	7
UK resident	4	1

Interpreting the output

Residency * Employment Crosstabulation

			Employed	Unemployed	Total
			Employment		
Residency	Foreign National	Count	2	7	9
		Expected Count	3.9	5.1	9.0
		Residual	-1.9	1.9	
	UK Resident	Count	4	1	5
		Expected Count	2.1	2.9	5.0
		Residual	1.9	-1.9	
Total		Count	6	8	14
		Expected Count	6.0	8.0	14.0

Chi-Square Tests

	Value	df	Asymp. Sig. (2-sided)	Exact Sig. (2-sided)	Exact Sig. (1-sided)
Pearson Chi-Square	4.381[a]	1	.036		
Continuity Correction[b]	2.340	1	.126		
Likelihood Ratio	4.583	1	.032		
Fisher's Exact Test				.091	.063
Linear-by-Linear Association	4.069	1	.044		
N of Valid Cases	14				

a. 3 cells (75.0%) have expected count less than 5. The minimum expected count is 2.14.
b. Computed only for a 2x2 table

Reporting the output

We would write: 'There was no significant relationship between immigration status and employment (two-tailed Fisher exact $p = 0.091$)' or 'Foreign nationals and UK residents do not differ in the frequency of possession of paid employment (two-tailed Fisher exact $p = 0.091$)'. However, with such a small sample size, the finding might best be regarded as marginally significant and a strong recommendation made that further studies should be carried out in order to establish with more certainty whether foreign nationals actually are more likely to be unemployed.

12.10 Partitioning chi-square

There is no problem when the chi-square contingency table is just two columns and two rows. The chi-square in these circumstances tells you that your two samples are different from each other. But if you have, say, a 2 × 3 chi-square (e.g. you have two samples and three categories) then there is some uncertainty as to what a significant chi-square means – does it mean that all three samples are different from each other, that sample 1 and sample 2 are different, that sample 1 and sample 3 are different, or that sample 2 and sample 3 are different? In the degree programme choice example, although we obtained a significant overall chi-square, there is some doubt as to why we obtained this. The major differences between the sexes are between the business degree and medicine degree conditions rather than between the business degree and the 'other' conditions.

Table 12.16	Three partitioned sub-tables from the 2 × 3 contingency table (Table 12.7)

Business degree versus medicine degree

Respondents	Business degree	Medicine degree	Totals
Males	27	14	row 1 = 41
Females	17	33	row 2 = 50
Totals	Column 1 = 44	Column 2 = 47	Total = 91

Business degree versus neither

Respondents	Business degree	Neither	Totals
Males	27	19	row 1 = 46
Females	17	9	row 2 = 26
Totals	Column 1 = 44	Column 3 = 28	Total = 72

Medicine degree versus neither

Respondents	Medicine degree	Neither	Totals
Males	14	19	row 1 = 33
Females	33	9	row 2 = 42
Totals	Column 2 = 47	Column 3 = 28	Total = 75

It is a perfectly respectable statistical procedure to break your large chi-square into a number of 2 × 2 chi-square tests to assess precisely where the significant differences lie. Thus in the degree programme study you could generate *three* separate chi-squares from the 2 × 3 contingency table. These are illustrated in Table 12.16.

These three separate chi-squares each have just one degree of freedom (because they are 2 × 2 tables). If you calculate chi-square for each of these tables you hopefully should be able to decide precisely where the differences are between samples and conditions.

The only difficulty is the significance levels you use. Because you are doing three separate chi-squares, the normal significance level of 5% still operates but it is *divided between the three chi-squares* you have carried out. In other words we share the 5% between three to give us the 1.667% level for each – any of the three chi-squares would have to be significant at this level to be reported as being significant at the 5% level. Significance Table 12.2 gives the adjusted values of chi-square required to be significant at the 5% level (two-tailed test). Thus if you have three comparisons to make, the

Significance Table 12.2	Chi-square 5% two-tailed significance values for 1–10 unplanned comparisons									
Degree of freedom	**Number of comparisons being made**									
	1	2	3	4	5	6	7	8	9	10
1	3.84	5.02	5.73	6.24	6.64	6.96	7.24	7.48	7.69	7.88

To use this table, simply look under the column for the number of separate comparisons you are making using chi-square. Your values of chi-square must equal or exceed the listed value to be significant at the 5% level with a two-tailed test.

minimum value of chi-square that is significant is 5.73. The degrees of freedom for these comparisons will always be 1 as they are always based on 2 × 2 contingency tables.

12.11 Important warnings

Chi-square is rather less user-friendly than is warranted by its popularity among researchers. The following are warning signs not to use chi-square or to take very great care:

1. If the expected frequencies in any cell fall lower than 5 then chi-square becomes rather inaccurate. Some authors suggest that no more than one-fifth of values should be below 5 but this is a more generous criterion. Some computers automatically print an alternative to chi-square if this assumption is breached.

2. Never do chi-square on percentages or anything other than frequencies.

3. Always check that your total of frequencies is equal to the number of participants in your research. Chi-square should not be applied where participants in the research are contributing more than one frequency each to the total of frequencies.

12.12 Alternatives to chi-square

The situation is only salvageable if your chi-square violates the expected cell frequencies rule – none should fall below 5. Even then you cannot always save the day. The alternatives are as follows:

1. If you have a 2 × 2 or a 2 × 3 chi-square table then you can use the Fisher exact probability test which is not sensitive to small expected frequencies (see Section 12.8).

2. Apart from omitting very small samples or categories, sometimes you can save the day by combining samples and/or categories in order to avoid the small expected frequencies problem; by combining in this way you should increase the expected frequencies somewhat. So, for example, take the data set out in Table 12.17. It should be apparent that by combining two samples and/or two categories you are likely to increase the expected frequencies in the resulting chi-square table.

But you cannot simply combine categories or samples at a whim – the samples or categories have to be combined meaningfully. So if the research was on the relationship between the type of degree that students take and their hobbies, you might have the following categories and samples:

Table 12.17	A 3 × 3 contingency table		
Sample	**Category 1**	**Category 2**	**Category 3**
Sample 1	10	6	14
Sample 2	3	12	4
Sample 3	4	2	5

Category 1 – socialising
Category 2 – dancing
Category 3 – stamp collecting
Sample 1 – English literature students
Sample 2 – media studies students
Sample 3 – physics students

Looking at these, it would seem reasonable to combine categories 1 and 2 and samples 1 and 2 since they seem to reflect rather similar things. No other combinations would seem appropriate. For example, it is hard to justify combining dancing and stamp collecting.

12.13   Chi-square and known populations

Sometimes but rarely in research we know the distribution in the population. If the population distribution of frequencies is known then it is possible to employ the single-sample chi-square. Usually the population frequencies are known as relative frequencies or percentages. So, for example, if you wished to know the likelihood of getting a sample of 40 university social science students in which there are 30 female and 10 male students *if* you know that the population of social science students is 90% female and 10% male, you simply use the latter proportions to calculate the expected frequencies of females and males in a sample of 40. If the sample were to reflect the population then 90% of the 40 should be female and 10% male. So the expected frequencies are $40 \times 90/100$ for females and $40 \times 10/100$ for males = 36 females and four males. These are then entered into the chi-square formula, but note that there are only two cells. The degrees of freedom for the one-sample chi-square is the number of cells minus 1 (i.e. $2 - 1 = 1$).

Key points

- Avoid as far as possible designing research with a multiplicity of categories and samples for chi-square. Large chi-squares with many cells are often difficult to interpret without numerous sub-analyses.

- Always make sure that your chi-square is carried out on frequencies and that each participant contributes only one to the total frequencies.

- Check for expected frequencies under 5; if you have any then take one of the escape routes described if possible.

Recommended further reading

Maxwell, A.E. (1961), *Analysing Qualitative Data*, London: Methuen.

PART 3

Introduction to analysis of variance

CHAPTER 13

Analysis of variance (ANOVA)

Introduction to one-way unrelated or uncorrelated ANOVA

Overview

- One-way analysis of variance compares the means of a minimum of two (unrelated) groups but is most commonly used when there are three or more mean scores to compare.

- The scores are the dependent variable; the groups are the independent variable.

- In essence, the analysis of variance calculates the variation between scores and the variation between the sample means. Both of these can be used to estimate the variation in the population. If variation between samples is much bigger, it means that the variation due to the independent variable is greater than could be expected on the basis of the variation between scores – these are compared using the F-ratio test.

- A significant finding for the analysis of variance means that, overall, some of the means differ from each other. However, *error* is variation which is not under the researcher's control.

- The interpretation of the analysis of variance can be difficult when more than two groups are used. The overall analysis of variance may be statistically significant, but it is difficult to know which of the three or more groups is significantly different from the other groups. The solution is to break the analysis into several separate comparisons to assess which sets of scores are significantly different from other sets of scores.

Preparation

It is pointless to start this chapter without a clear understanding of how to calculate the basic variance estimate formula and the computational formula for variance estimate (Chapter 3).

13.1 Introduction

Up to this point we have discussed research designs comparing the means of just *two* groups of scores. The analysis of variance (ANOVA) can also do this, but in addition can extend the comparison to three or more groups of scores. ANOVA is often used to analyse the results of experiments, but the simpler forms are routinely used in surveys and similar types of research. This chapter describes one-way analysis of variance, which can be used whenever we wish to compare two or more groups in terms of their mean scores on a dependent variable. The scores must be independent (uncorrelated or unrelated). In other words each respondent contributes just one score to the statistical analysis. Stylistically, Table 13.1 is the sort of research design for which the (uncorrelated or unrelated) one-way analysis of variance is appropriate.

The groups are the independent variable and the scores are those on the dependent variable. There are very few limitations on the research designs to which this is applicable:

1. It is possible to have any number of groups, with the minimum being two.

2. The groups consist of independent samples of scores. For example, the groups could be:
   - men versus women
   - one experimental versus one control group
   - four experimental groups and one control group
   - three different occupational types – police, prison and probation workers.

3. The scores (the dependent variable) can be for virtually any variable. The main thing is that they are numerical scores suitable for calculating the mean and variance.

4. It is *not* necessary to have equal numbers of scores in each group. With other forms of analysis of variance, not having equal numbers can cause complications.

Table 13.1	Stylised table of data for unrelated analysis of variance		
Group 1	**Group 2**	**Group 3**	**Group 4**
9	3	1	27
14	1	4	24
11	5	2	25
12	5	31	

13.2 Theoretical considerations

The analysis of variance involves very few new concepts that we have not already covered. However, some basic concepts are used in a relatively novel way. One-way ANOVA is essentially an extension of the unrelated *t*-test to cover the situation in which the researcher has three or more groups of participants. Indeed, one could use one-way ANOVA instead of the unrelated *t*-test where one has just two groups of participants, but 'convention' is against this. It is known as the one-way ANOVA since there is just one independent variable – that is, a single nominal variable forms the basis of the groups.

Essentially ANOVA works by comparing the variation in the group means with the variation within the groups using the variance or *F*-ratio. The more variation there is between the group means compared to the variation within the groups, the more likely it is that the analysis will be statistically significant. The variation between the group means is the *between groups variance*; the variation within the groups is the *within groups variance*, though it can be referred to as the *error variance* since it is the variation in scores which is unaccounted for. The bigger the error variance, the greater the possibility that we get variation between the cell means by chance. The calculation is a little more complex than this description implies but this will serve you well enough conceptually.

All measurement assumes that a score is made up of two components:

● the 'true' value of the measurement

● an 'error' component.

For example, many psychological tests tend to have a large error component compared to the true component. Error results from all sorts of factors – tiredness, distraction, unclear instructions and so forth. Normally we cannot say precisely to what extent these factors influence our scores. It is further assumed that the 'true' and 'error' components add together to give the obtained scores (i.e. the data). So, for example, an obtained score of 15 might be made up of:

$$15_{[\text{obtained score}]} = 12_{[\text{true}]} + 3_{[\text{error}]}$$

or an obtained score of 20 might be made up as follows:

$$20 = 24 + (-4)$$

The error score may take a positive or negative value.

We have no certain knowledge about anything other than the obtained scores. *The true and error scores cannot be known directly. However, in some circumstances we can infer them through intelligent guesswork.*

In the analysis of variance, each score is separated into the two components – true scores and error scores. This is easier than it sounds. Look at Table 13.2 from some fictitious research. It is a study of the effects of two different prison treatment programmes (group therapy and Cognitive Behavioural Therapy (CBT)) and an inert (no treatment) control group on sex offender risk scores in men.

Tables 13.3 and 13.4 give the best estimates possible of the 'true' scores and 'error' scores in Table 13.2. Try to work out the simple 'tricks' we have employed. All we did to produce these two new tables was the following:

Table 13.2	Stylised table of data for unrelated analysis of variance with means	
Group 1: Group therapy	Group 2: CBT	Group 3: Control
9	4	3
12	2	6
8	5	3
Mean = 9.667	Mean = 3.667	Mean = 4.000
		Overall mean = 5.778

Table 13.3	'True' scores based on the data in Table 13.2	
Group 1: **Group therapy**	**Group 2:** **CBT**	**Group 3:** **Control**
9.667	3.667	4.000
9.667	3.667	4.000
9.667	3.667	4.000
Mean = 9.667	**Mean = 3.667**	**Mean = 4.000**
		Overall mean = 5.778

Table 13.4	'Error' scores based on the data in Table 13.2	
Group 1: **Group therapy**	**Group 2:** **CBT**	**Group 3:** **Control**
−0.667	0.333	−1.000
2.333	−1.667	2.000
−1.667	1.333	−1.000
Mean = 0.000	**Mean = 0.000**	**Mean = 0.000**
		Overall mean = 0.000

1. In order to obtain a table of 'true' scores we have simply substituted the column mean for each group for the individual scores, the assumption being that the obtained scores deviate from the 'true' score because of the influence of varying amounts of error in the measurement. In statistical theory, error is assumed to be randomly distributed. Thus we have replaced all of the scores for Group 1 by the mean of 9.667. The column mean is simply the best estimate of what the 'true' score would be for the group if *we could get rid of the 'error' component*. As all of the scores are the same, there is absolutely no error component in any of the conditions of Table 13.3. The assumption in this is that the variability within a column is due to error, so the average score in a column is our best estimate of the 'true' score for that column. Notice that the column means are unchanged by this.

2. We have obtained the table of 'error' scores (Table 13.4) simply by subtracting the scores in the 'true' scores table (Table 13.3) away from the corresponding score in the original scores table (Table 13.2). What is not a 'true' score is an 'error' score by definition. Notice that the error scores show a mixture of positive and negative values, *and* that the sum of the error scores in each column (and the entire table for that matter) is zero. This is always the case with error scores and so constitutes an important check on your calculations. An alternative way of obtaining the error scores is to take the column (or group) mean away from each score in the original data table.

So what do we do now that we have the 'true' scores and 'error' scores? The two derived sets of scores – the 'true' and the 'error' scores – are used separately to estimate the variance of the population of scores from which they are samples. (That is, the calculated variance estimate for the 'true' scores is an estimate of the 'true' variation in the population, and the calculated variance estimate of the 'error' scores is an estimate of the 'error' variation in the population.) Remember, the null hypothesis for this research would suggest that differences between the three groups are due to error rather than real differences related to the influence of the independent variable. The null hypothesis suggests that both the 'true' and 'error' variance estimates are similar since they are both the result of error. *If the null hypothesis is correct*, the variance estimate derived from the 'true' scores should be no different from the variance estimate derived from the 'error' scores. After all, under the null hypothesis the variation in the 'true' scores is due to error anyway. *If the alternative hypothesis is correct*, then there should be rather more variation in the 'true' scores than is typical in the 'error' scores.

We calculate the variance estimate of the 'true' scores and then calculate the variance estimate for the 'error' scores. Next the two variance estimates are examined to see whether they are significantly different using the *F*-ratio test (the variance ratio test). This involves the following calculation:

$$F = \frac{\text{variance estimate}_{[\text{of true scores}]}}{\text{variance estimate}_{[\text{of error scores}]}}$$

(The error variance is always at the bottom in the analysis of variance. This is because we want to know if the variance estimate of the true scores is *bigger* than the variance estimate of the 'error' scores. We are not simply comparing the variance of two conditions.)

It is then a fairly straightforward matter to use Significance Table 13.1 for the *F*-distribution to decide whether or not these two variance estimates are significantly different from each other. We just need to be careful to use the appropriate numbers of degrees of freedom. If the variance estimates are similar, then the variance in 'true' scores is little different from the variance in the 'error' scores; since the estimated 'true' variance is much the same as the 'error' variance in this case, both can be regarded as 'error'. On the other hand, if the *F*-ratio is significant it means that the variation due to the 'true' scores is much greater than that due to 'error'; the 'true' scores represent reliable differences between groups rather than chance factors.

Significance Table 13.1	5% significance values of the *F*-ratio for unrelated ANOVA. Additional values are given in Significance Table 14.1					
Degrees of freedom for error or within-cells mean square (or variance estimate)	**Degrees of freedom for true or between-treatment mean square (or variance estimate)**					
	1	**2**	**3**	**4**	**5**	**∞**
1	161 or more	200	216	225	230	254
2	18.5	19.0	19.2	19.3	19.3	19.5
3	10.1	9.6	9.3	9.1	9.0	8.5
4	7.7	6.9	6.6	6.4	6.3	5.6
5	6.6	5.8	5.4	5.2	5.1	4.4
6	6.0	5.1	4.8	4.5	4.4	3.7
7	5.6	4.7	4.4	4.1	4.0	3.2
8	5.3	4.5	4.1	3.8	3.7	2.9
9	5.1	4.3	3.9	3.6	3.5	2.7
10	5.0	4.1	3.7	3.5	3.3	2.5

Your value has to equal or be larger than the tabulated value for an effect to be significant at the 5% level.

The *F*-ratio, unlike the *t*-test, is a one-tailed test. It simply determines whether the true variance estimate is bigger than the error variance estimate. The *F*-ratio cannot be smaller than zero. In other words, it is always positive. The 5% or 0.05 probability only applies to the upper or right-hand tail of the distribution. The larger the *F*-ratio is, the more likely it is to be statistically significant.

And that is just about it for the one-way analysis of variance. There is just one remaining issue: the *degrees of freedom*. If one were to work out the variance estimate of the original data in our study we would use the formula as given above:

$$\text{Variance estimate}_{[\text{original data}]} = \frac{\sum X^2 - \dfrac{(\sum X)^2}{N}}{N - 1}$$

where $N - 1$ is the number of degrees of freedom.

However, the calculation of the number of degrees of freedom varies in the analysis of variance (it is not always $N - 1$). With the 'true' and 'error' scores the degrees of freedom are a little more complex although easily calculated using formulae. But the idea of degrees of freedom can be understood at a more fundamental level with a little work.

13.3   Degrees of freedom

Degrees of freedom refer to the distinct items of information contained in your data. By information we mean something which is new and not already known. For example, if we asked you what is the combined age of your two best friends and then asked you the age of the younger of the two, you would be crazy to accept a bet that we could tell you the age of your older best friend, the reason being that if you told us that the combined ages of your best friends was 37 years and that the younger was 16 years, any fool could work out that the older best friend must be 21 years. The age of your older best friend is contained within the first two pieces of information. The age of your older friend is redundant because you already know it from your previous information.

The calculations for establishing the degrees of freedom are quite complicated. Thankfully, few of us would really need to work out the degrees of freedom from first principles. It is much easier to use simple formulae. For the one-way analysis of variance using unrelated samples, the degrees of freedom are as follows:

N = number of scores in the table
Degrees of freedom$_{[\text{original data}]}$ = $N - 1$
Degrees of freedom$_{['\text{true}'\text{ scores}]}$ = number of columns − 1
Degrees of freedom$_{['\text{error}'\text{ scores}]}$ = N − number of columns

This is not cheating – most textbooks ignore the meaning of degrees of freedom and merely give the formulae anyway.

13.4   When to use one-way ANOVA

One-way ANOVA can be used when the means of three or more groups are to be compared. These must be independent groups in the sense that a participant can only be in one group and contribute one score to the data being analysed.

Conventionally, one-way ANOVA is not used when there are just two groups to be compared. A *t*-test is usually employed in these circumstances. However, it is perfectly proper to use one-way ANOVA in these circumstances. It will give exactly the same significance level as the *t*-test on the same data when the variances do not differ. When the variances differ it may be more appropriate to use an unrelated *t*-test where the variances are pooled together more appropriately.

13.5   When not to use one-way ANOVA

The main indication that there may be problems is when the test of the homogeneity of variances is statistically significant. This means that the variances of the different groups are very different, which makes it difficult to combine them. The extent to which this is a problem is not well documented but it is probably not so important where the group sizes are equal.

13.6   Data requirements for one-way ANOVA

One-way ANOVA requires three or more independent groups of participants each of which contributes a single score to the analysis. Since one-way ANOVA essentially tests for differences between the means of the groups of participants, ideally the scores correspond to the theoretically ideal equal-interval scale of measurement. The variances of the various groups need to be approximately equal.

13.7   Problems in the use of one-way ANOVA

Confusion arises because of the traditional advice that if the one-way ANOVA is not significant, then no further analysis should be carried out comparing the different group means with each other. This may have been sound advice once but it is somewhat outmoded. It is perfectly appropriate to use the Newman–Keuls test and the Duncan's new multiple range test as multiple-comparisons tests (see Chapter 14, Section 14.11) even if the ANOVA is not significant. This begs the question whether ANOVA adds anything in these circumstances – the answer is probably no. If ANOVA is significant, then any multiple-range test is appropriate.

13.8   SPSS analysis

■ The data to be analysed

The computation of a one-way unrelated analysis of variance is illustrated with the data in Table 13.2, which shows the scores of different participants in three conditions. It is a study of the effect of therapy (group or CBT) and control (no treatment) on sex offender risk. So treatment is the independent variable and risk score the dependent variable.

■ Quick calculation methods for ANOVA

The following step-by-step procedure describes the quick way for calculating the unrelated/uncorrelated one-way ANOVA by hand. This is less error prone than the 'full' method which often suffers from accumulated rounding errors. Statistics textbooks usually describe the quick formula method. It is based on the computational formula for the variance estimate (see Chapter 3).

Calculation 13.1

One-way unrelated analysis of variance: quick method

The following calculation involves three different conditions (levels) of the independent variable. The method is easily adapted to any other number of conditions from a minimum of two.

Step 1

Draw up a data table using the format shown in Table 13.5. Calculate the totals for each column separately (i.e. T_1, T_2, T_3). (Notice that you are calculating totals rather than means with this method.) Remember that this table gives us the data on the influence of the independent variable (drug treatment, which has three levels – group therapy, CBT and control) on the dependent variable (sex offender risk).

Table 13.5	Stylised table of data for unrelated analysis of variance	
Group 1: Group therapy	**Group 2: CBT**	**Group 3: Control**
9	4	3
12	2	6
8	5	3
$N_1 = 3$	$N_2 = 3$	$N_3 = 3$
Total = $T_1 = 9 + 12 + 8 = 29$	Total = $T_2 = 4 + 2 + 5 = 11$	Total = $T_3 = 3 + 6 + 3 = 12$

1. Calculate the overall (or grand) total of the scores: $G = 9 + 12 + 8 + 4 + 2 + 5 + 3 + 6 + 3 = 52$, or simply add the column totals to obtain this value.

2. Calculate the number of scores: $N = 9$.

3. Insert the number of scores for each group (N_1, N_2 and N_3). In our example these are all 3 as the group sizes are equal, but this does not have to be so with the unrelated one-way analysis of variance.

4. Total degrees of freedom for the data table is number of scores – 1 = 9 – 1 = 8.

Step 2

Square each of the scores (X) and then sum all of these squared scores to give the sum of squared scores or $\sum X^2$:

$$\sum X^2 = 9^2 + 12^2 + 8^2 + 4^2 + 2^2 + 5^2 + 3^2 + 6^2 + 3^2 = 81 + 144 + 64 + 16 + 4 + 25 + 9 + 36 + 9 = 388.000$$

Step 3

Calculate the 'correction factor' (G^2/N) by substituting the values of G and N previously obtained in steps 1 and 2. (The correction factor is merely part of the computational formula for the variance estimate (see Chapter 3) expressed as G^2/N rather than $(\sum X)^2/N$.)

$$\text{Correction factor} = \frac{G^2}{N} = \frac{52^2}{9} = \frac{2704}{9}$$

$$= 300.444$$

Step 4

The outcome of step 2 minus the outcome of step 3 gives the total sum of squares ($SS_{[total]}$) for the data table. It is equivalent to part of the computational formula for the calculation of the variance estimate (see Chapter 3). Substituting the previously calculated values:

$$SS_{[total]} = \sum X^2 - \frac{G^2}{N}$$

$$= 388.000 - 300.444 = 87.556$$

Enter this value of the total sum of squares into an analysis of variance summary table such as Table 13.6. Enter the degrees of freedom for the total sum of squares. This is always $N - 1$ or the number of scores $- 1 = 9 - 1 = 8$.

Table 13.6	Analysis of variance summary table			
Source of variation	**Sum of squares**	**Degrees of freedom**	**Mean square (variance estimate)**	**F-ratio**
Between groups	68.222	2	34.111	$\frac{34.111}{3.222} = 10.59^{a}$
Error (within groups)	19.334	6	3.222	
Total	**87.556**	**8**		

[a] Significant at the 5% level.

Step 5

The sum of squares between groups ($SS_{[between]}$) can be calculated as follows using the correction factor (from step 3) and the column totals (T_1, etc.) and cell sizes (n_1, etc.) from Table 13.5:

$$SS_{[between]} = \frac{T_1^2}{N_1} + \frac{T_2^2}{N_2} + \frac{T_3^2}{N_3} - \frac{G^2}{N} = \frac{29^2}{3} + \frac{11^2}{3} + \frac{12^2}{3} - 300.444$$

$$= \frac{841}{3} + \frac{121}{3} + \frac{144}{3} - 300.444$$

$$= 280.333 + 40.333 + 48.000 - 300.444$$

$$= 368.666 - 300.444$$

$$= 68.222$$

The degrees of freedom between subjects are the number of columns $- 1 = c - 1 = 3 - 1 = 2$. The mean square between groups is $SS_{[between]}$/degrees of freedom$_{[between]} = 68.222/2 = 34.111$. These values are entered in Table 13.6.

Step 6

Calculate the error (i.e. error or 'within') sum of squares ($SS_{[error]}$) by subtracting the 'between' sum of squares from the total sum of squares:

$$SS_{[error]} = SS_{[total]} - SS_{[between]} = 87.566 - 68.222 = 19.344$$

The degrees of freedom for error are the number of scores minus the number of columns: $N - c = 9 - 3 = 6$. The mean square for error is $SS_{[error]}/$degrees of freedom$_{[error]} = 19.334/6 = 3.222$. These values are entered in Table 13.6.

Step 7   The F-ratio is the between-groups mean square divided by the error mean square. This is $34.111/3.222 = 10.6$. This value can be checked against Significance Table 13.1. We need a value of F of 5.1 or more to be significant at the 5% level of significance with two degrees of freedom for the between-groups mean square and with six degrees of freedom for the error mean square. Thus our obtained F-ratio of 10.6 is statistically significant at the 5% level.

Interpreting the results   The most important step in interpreting your data is simple. You need a table of the means for each of the conditions such as Table 13.7. It is obvious from this table that two of the cell means are fairly similar whereas the mean of Group 1 is relatively high. This would suggest to an experienced researcher that *if* the one-way analysis of variance is statistically significant, then a multiple-comparisons test (Section 14.11) is needed in order to test for significant differences between pairs of group means.

Table 13.7	Table of cell means		
Group 1: Group therapy		**Group 2: CBT**	**Group 3: Control**
Mean = M_1 = 9.67		Mean = M_2 = 3.67	Mean = M_3 = 4.00

Reporting the results   The results of this analysis could be written up as follows: 'The data were analysed using an unrelated one-way analysis of variance. It was found that there was a significant effect of the independent variable therapy type on the dependent variable sex offender risk ($F = 10.59$, $df = 2, 6$, $p < 0.05$). The mean for the group therapy ($M = 9.67$) appears to indicate greater risk scores than for the CBT group ($M = 3.67$) and the placebo control ($M = 4.00$).' Of course, you can use Appendix I to test for significance at other levels.

In order to test whether the mean for group 1 is significantly greater than for the other two groups, it is necessary to apply a multiple-comparisons test such as the Scheffé test (Section 14.11) if the differences had not been predicted. The outcome of this should also be reported.

We have given intermediate calculations for the F-ratio; these are not usually reported but may be helpful for calculation purposes.

13.9   Computer analysis for one-way unrelated ANOVA

Step 1

Enter the data from Table 13.5. Code the three conditions '1', '2' and '3' respectively. Label them 'Group Therapy', 'CBT' and 'Control'. Save this file to use in Chapter 15.

	Condition	Risk
1	1	9
2	1	12
3	1	8
4	2	4
5	2	2
6	2	5
7	3	3
8	3	6
9	3	3
10		

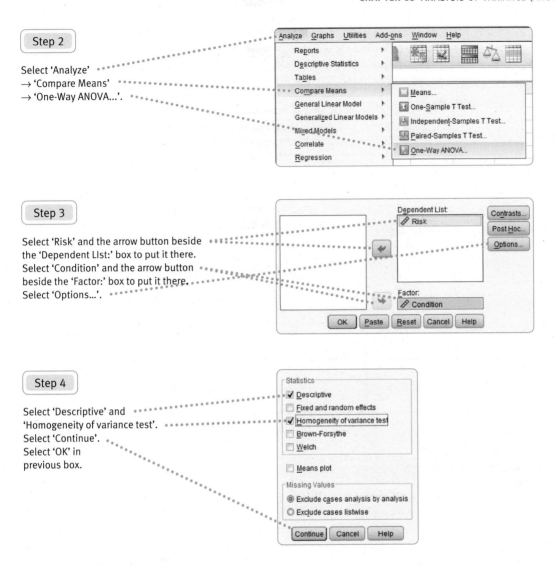

Step 2

Select 'Analyze'
→ 'Compare Means'
→ 'One-Way ANOVA...'.

Step 3

Select 'Risk' and the arrow button beside
the 'Dependent List:' box to put it there.
Select 'Condition' and the arrow button
beside the 'Factor:' box to put it there.
Select 'Options...'.

Step 4

Select 'Descriptive' and
'Homogeneity of variance test'.
Select 'Continue'.
Select 'OK' in
previous box.

■ Interpreting the output

- The first table provides various descriptive statistics such as the number (N) of cases, the mean and the standard deviation for the three conditions and the total sample.

Descriptives

Risk

	N	Mean	Std. Deviation	Std. Error	95% Confidence Interval for Mean		Minimum	Maximum
					Lower Bound	Upper Bound		
Group Therapy	3	9.67	2.082	1.202	4.50	14.84	8	12
CBT	3	3.67	1.528	.882	-.13	7.46	2	5
Placebo Control	3	4.00	1.732	1.000	-.30	8.30	3	6
Total	9	5.78	3.308	1.103	3.23	8.32	2	12

- The second table gives Levene's test of how similar the variances are. As this test is not significant (with a significance of 0.756), the variances are similar or homogeneous. If the variances were not similar, we should try to transform the scores to make them so, otherwise there may be problems interpreting the analysis of variance.

Test of Homogeneity of Variances

Risk

Levene Statistic	df1	df2	Sig.
.293	2	6	.756

- The third table shows the results of the analysis of variance. The F-ratio is significant at 0.011 as it is less than 0.05.

ANOVA

Risk

	Sum of Squares	df	Mean Square	F	Sig.
Between Groups	68.222	2	34.111	10.586	.011
Within Groups	19.333	6	3.222		
Total	87.556	8			

- The F-ratio is the between-groups mean square divided by the within-group mean square, which gives an F-ratio of 10.586 (34.111/3.222 = 10.5869).

- This indicates that there is a significant difference between the three groups. However, it does not necessarily imply that all the means are significantly different from each other. In this case, one suspects that the means 3.67 and 4.00 are not significantly different.

- Which of the means differs from the others can be further determined by the use of multiple comparison tests such as the unrelated t-test. To do this, follow the procedure for the unrelated t-test described in Chapter 11. You do not have to re-enter your data. However, do an unrelated t-test defining the groups as 1 and 2, then redefine the groups as 1 and 3, and finally redefine the groups as 2 and 3. For our example, group 1 is significantly different from groups 2 and 3, which do not differ significantly from each other.

- Because we are doing three comparisons, the exact significance level of each t-test should be multiplied by 3 to obtain the Bonferroni significance level (see Section 14.11).

- It is useful to know how much variance the independent variable accounts for or explains. This is given by a statistic called eta squared (η^2). This statistic is not available with the one-way ANOVA SPSS procedure. It is available with the general linear model SPSS procedure described in Chapters 14–16. If you use the univariate option of the general linear model you will see that eta squared for this analysis is about 0.78. This means that the three conditions account for about 80% of the variance in male sex offender risk scores. Researchers are encouraged to report this statistic as it gives an indication of the size of an effect.

■ Reporting the output

We could report the results of the output as follows: 'The effect of the treatment was significant overall ($F_{2,6} = 10.58$, $p = 0.011$, $\eta^2 = 0.78$). When a Bonferroni adjustment was made for the number of comparisons (see Section 14.11), the only significant difference was between the means of group therapy and CBT conditions ($t = 4.02$, $df = 4$, two-tailed $p < 0.05$). The mean of group therapy ($M = 9.67$, SD = 2.08) was significantly greater than that for CBT ($M = 3.67$, SD = 1.53). There was no significant difference between the mean of the control and the mean of either the group therapy or the CBT group.'

Key points

- The *t*-test is simply a special case of one-way ANOVA, so these tests can be used interchangeably when you have two groups of scores. They give identical significance levels. The square of the two-tailed *t* value equals the one-tailed *F* value (e.g. $1.96^2 = 3.8416$) and the square root of the one-tailed *F* value equals the two-tailed *t* value (e.g. $3.8416 = 1.96^2$).

- Do not be too deterred by some of the strange terminology used in the analysis of variance. Words like treatments and levels of treatment merely reveal the agricultural origins of these statistical procedures; be warned that it gets worse. Levels of treatment simply refers to the number of different conditions for each independent variable. Thus if the independent variable has three different values it is said to have three different levels of the treatment.

- The analysis of variance with just two conditions or sets of scores is relatively easy to interpret. You merely have to examine the difference between the means of the two conditions. It is not so easy where you have three or more groups. Your analysis may not be complete until you have employed a multiple-comparisons procedure as in Section 14.11. Which multiple comparisons test you use may be limited by whether your ANOVA is significant or not.

- We have used computational procedures which are not identical to those in most textbooks. We have tried to explain the analysis of variance by referring to the basic notion of variance estimate. Virtually every textbook we have seen merely gives computational procedures alone. More typical calculation methods are also included in this book.

- When the *F*-ratio is statistically significant for a one-way analysis of variance with more than two groups, you need to determine which groups differ significantly from each other. If you had good grounds for predicting which groups differed, you could use an unrelated *t*-test to see if the difference was significant (see Chapter 11). If you did not have a sound basis for predicting which groups differed, you would use a multiple comparison test such as the Scheffé test (Section 14.11).

CHAPTER 14

Two-way analysis of variance for unrelated/ uncorrelated scores

Two studies for the price of one?

Overview

- The two-way analysis of variance involves two independent variables and a single dependent (score) variable. It has the potential to indicate the extent to which the two independent variables may combine to influence scores on this dependent (score) variable.

- The main effects are the influence of the independent variables acting separately; the interaction is the influence of the independent variables acting in combination with each other.

- Much of the two-way analysis of variance proceeds like two separate one-way analyses. However, there is the interaction which is really a measure of the multiplicative (rather than additive) influence of the two independent variables acting in combination.

- The two-way analysis of variance can be extended to any number of independent variables, though the process rapidly becomes very cumbersome with each additional independent variable. As with most statistical analyses, it is important to concentrate as much on the patterns of means in the data as the statistical probabilities.

- Although the two-way ANOVA can be regarded as an efficient design insofar as it allows two different independent variables to be incorporated into the study, its ability to identify interactions may be more important. An interaction is simply a situation in which the combined effect of two variables is greater than the sum of the effects of each of the two variables acting separately.

Preparation

Chapter 13 on the one-way analysis of variance contains material essential to the full understanding of this chapter.

14.1 Introduction

Often researchers wish to assess the influence of more than a single independent variable at a time. The one-way analysis of variance deals with a single independent variable which can have two or more levels. However, analysis of variance copes with several *independent* variables in a research design. These are known as multifactorial ANOVAs. The number of 'ways' is the number of independent variables. Thus a two-way analysis of variance allows two independent variables to be included, three-way analysis of variance allows three independent variables and so on. *There is only one dependent variable no matter how many 'ways' in each analysis of variance.* If you have two or more *dependent* variables, each of these will entail a separate analysis of variance. Although things can get very complicated conceptually, two-way analysis of variance is relatively straightforward and introduces just one major new concept – *interaction*.

In this chapter we will be concentrating on examples in which all of the scores are independent (uncorrelated). Each person therefore contributes just one score to the analysis. In other words, it is an *uncorrelated* design.

Generally speaking, the 'multivariate' analysis of variance is best suited to experimental research in which it is possible to allocate participants at random into the various conditions. Although this does not apply to the one-way analysis of variance, there are problems in using two-way and multi-way analyses of variance in survey and other non-experimental research. The difficulty is that calculations become more complex if you do not have equal numbers of scores in each of the cells or conditions.

Imagine you are interested in the effects of nutrition *and* physical activity on the mental functioning of school children. A typical research design for a two-way analysis of variance could study the effect of the *independent variables* exercise *and* food withdrawal on the *dependent variable* of the number of mistakes made on a test of comprehension. The research design and data might look like that shown in Table 14.1.

In a sense one could regard this experiment conceptually as two separate experiments, one studying the effects of food withdrawal and the other studying the effects of exercise. The effects of each of the two independent variables are called the *main* effects. Additionally the analysis normally looks for *interactions*, which are basically findings which cannot be explained on the basis of the distinctive effects of exercise and food withdrawal acting separately. For example, it could be that people do especially badly if they have been deprived of food *and* have been made to exercise. They do more badly than the additive

Table 14.1	Data for typical two-way analysis of variance: number of mistakes on comprehension test		
	Food withdrawal		
	4 hours	**12 hours**	**24 hours**
Exercise	16	18	22
	12	16	24
	17	25	32
No exercise	11	13	12
	9	8	14
	12	11	12

effects of exercise and food deprivation would predict. Interactions are about the effects of specific combinations of variables.

In the analysis of variance we sometimes talk of the *levels of a treatment* – this is simply the number of values that any independent variable can take. In the above example, the exercise variable has two different values – that is, there are two levels of the treatment or variable 'exercise'. There are three levels of the treatment or variable 'food withdrawal'. Sometimes, a two-way ANOVA is identified in terms of the numbers of levels of treatment for each of the independent variables. So a 2 × 3 ANOVA has two different levels of the first variable and three for the second variable. This corresponds to the above example.

14.2 Theoretical considerations

Much of the two-way analysis of variance is easy if it is remembered that it largely involves two separate 'one-way' analyses of variance as if there were two separate experiments. To continue on our topic of nutrition and academic performance, for example, a UK county council recently (and controversially) trialled the use of Omega-3 dietary supplements on children's exam performance. Imagine you are assigned to assess the scientific credibility of this policy, so you run an experiment in which one group of school children are given Omega-3 supplements in their diet to see if it has any effect on their exam performance. In the belief that girls generally do better educationally than boys and hence have a lesser need for Omega-3 than boys, the researchers included sex as their other independent variable. The data are given in Table 14.2.

Table 14.2 represents a 2 × 2 ANOVA. Comparing the four condition means (cell means), the exam scores for females not receiving the supplement seem rather higher than those of any other groups. In other words, it would appear that the lack of the Omega-3 supplement has more effect on women. Certain gender and Omega-3 supplement conditions in combination have a great effect on exam scores. This suggests an interaction. That is, particular cells in the analysis have much higher or lower scores than can be explained simply in terms of the gender trends or dietary supplement trends acting separately.

Table 14.2	Data table for study of dietary supplements		
	Omega-3 supplement	**No Omega-3 supplement**	
Males	3	9	
	7	5	
	4	6	
	6	8	
	Cell mean = 5.00	Cell mean = 7.00	Row mean = 6.00
Females	11	19	
	7	16	
	10	18	
	8	15	
	Cell mean = 9.00	Cell mean = 17.00	Row mean = 13.00
	Column mean = 7.00	**Column mean = 12.00**	**Overall mean = 9.50**

The assumption in the two-way analysis of variance is that the variation in Table 14.2 comes from four sources:

- 'Error'

- The main effect of gender

- The main effect of Omega-3 supplement

- The interaction of sex and Omega-3 supplement.

The first three components above are dealt with exactly as they were in the one-way unrelated analysis of variance. The slight difference is that instead of calculating the variance estimate for one independent variable we now calculate two variance estimates – one for each independent variable. However, the term 'main effect' should not cause any confusion. It is merely the effect of an independent variable acting alone as it would if the two-way design were turned into two separate one-way designs.

The interaction consists of any variation in the scores which is left after we have taken away the 'error' and main effects for the sex and Omega-3 supplements sub-experiments. That is, priority is given to finding main effects at the expense of interactions.

14.3   Steps in the analysis

■ Step 1

To produce an 'error' table we simply take our original data and subtract the cell mean from every score in the cell. Thus, for instance, we need to subtract 5.00 from each score in the cell for males receiving the Omega-3 supplement, 17.00 from each cell for the females not receiving the Omega-3 supplement, etc. In the present example the 'error' table is as in Table 14.3.

We calculate the 'error' variance estimate for this in the usual way. The formula, as ever, is:

$$\text{Variance estimate}_{['error']} = \frac{\sum X^2 - \dfrac{(\sum X)^2}{N}}{df}$$

The degrees of freedom (df), analogously to the one-way analysis of variance, is the number of scores minus the number of conditions or cells. This leaves 12 degrees of freedom (16 scores minus four conditions or cells).

■ Step 2

To produce a table of the main effects for the Omega-3 supplement treatment, simply substitute the column means from the original data for each of the scores in the columns. The Omega-3-supplement mean was 7.00, so each Omega-3 supplement score is changed to 7.00, thus eliminating any other source of variation. Similarly, the no-Omega-3-supplement mean was 12.00, so each score is changed to 12.00 (see Table 14.4).

The variance estimate of the above scores can be calculated using the usual variance estimate formula. The degrees of freedom are calculated in the familiar way – the number of columns minus one (i.e. $df = 1$).

Table 14.3	'Error' scores for study of dietary supplements		
	Omega-3 supplement	**No Omega-3 supplement**	
Males	$3 - 5 = -2$	$9 - 7 = 2$	
	$7 - 5 = 2$	$5 - 7 = -2$	
	$4 - 5 = -1$	$6 - 7 = -1$	
	$6 - 5 = 1$	$8 - 7 = 1$	
	Cell mean = 0.00	Cell mean = 0.00	Row mean = 0.00
Females	$11 - 9 = 2$	$19 - 17 = 2$	
	$7 - 9 = -2$	$16 - 17 = -1$	
	$10 - 9 = 1$	$18 - 17 = 1$	
	$8 - 9 = -1$	$15 - 17 = -2$	
	Cell mean = 0.00	Cell mean = 0.00	Row mean = 0.00
	Column mean = 0.00	**Column mean = 0.00**	**Overall mean = 0.00**

Table 14.4	Main effect scores for study of dietary supplements		
	Omega-3 supplement	**No Omega-3 supplement**	
Males	7.00	12.00	
	7.00	12.00	
	7.00	12.00	
	7.00	12.00	Row mean = 9.50
Females	7.00	12.00	
	7.00	12.00	
	7.00	12.00	
	7.00	12.00	Row mean = 9.50
	Column mean = 7.00	**Column mean = 12.00**	**Overall mean = 9.50**

■ Step 3

To produce a table of the main effect of sex, remember that the independent variable sex is tabulated as the rows (not the columns). In other words, we substitute the row mean for the males and the row mean for the females for the respective scores (Table 14.5).

The variance estimate of the above scores can be calculated with the usual variance estimate formula. Even the degrees of freedom are calculated in the usual way. However, *as the table is on its side* compared to our usual method, the degrees of freedom are the number of *rows* minus one in this case (2 – 1, or one degree of freedom).

The calculation of the main effects (variance estimates) for sex and the Omega-3 supplement follows exactly the same procedures as in the one-way analysis of variance.

■ Step 4

The remaining stage is to calculate the interaction. This is simply anything which is left over after we have eliminated 'error' and the main effects. So for any score, the interaction

Table 14.5	Main effect scores for study of dietary supplements with row means substituted								
Males	6.00	6.00	6.00	6.00	6.00	6.00	6.00	6.00	Row mean = 6.00
Females	13.00	13.00	13.00	13.00	13.00	13.00	13.00	13.00	Row mean = 13.00

score is found by taking the score in your data and subtracting the 'error' score and the sex score and the Omega-3 supplement score.

Table 14.6 is our data table less the 'error' variance, in other words a table which replaces each score by its cell mean.

It is obvious that the row means for the males and females are not the same. The row mean for males is 6.00 and the row mean for females is 13.00. To get rid of the sex effect we can subtract 6.00 from each male score and 13.00 from each female score in the previous table. The results of this simple subtraction are found in Table 14.7.

Table 14.6	Data table with 'error' removed		
	Omega-3 supplement	**No Omega-3 supplement**	
Males	5.00	7.00	
	5.00	7.00	
	5.00	7.00	
	5.00	7.00	Row mean = 6.00
Females	9.00	17.00	
	9.00	17.00	
	9.00	17.00	
	9.00	17.00	Row mean = 13.00
	Column mean = 7.00	**Column mean = 12.00**	**Overall mean = 9.50**

Table 14.7	Data table with 'error' and sex removed		
	Omega-3 supplement	**No Omega-3 supplement**	
Males	−1.00	1.00	
	−1.00	1.00	
	−1.00	1.00	
	−1.00	1.00	Row mean = 0.00
Females	−4.00	4.00	
	−4.00	4.00	
	−4.00	4.00	
	−4.00	4.00	Row mean = 0.00
	Column mean = −2.50	**Column mean = 2.50**	**Overall mean = 0.00**

Table 14.8	Interaction table, i.e. data table with 'error', sex and Omega-3 supplement all removed		
	Omega-3 supplement	**No Omega-3 supplement**	
Males	1.5	−1.5	
	1.5	−1.5	
	1.5	−1.5	
	1.5	−1.5	Row mean = 0.00
Females	−1.5	1.5	
	−1.5	1.5	
	−1.5	1.5	
	−1.5	1.5	Row mean = 0.00
	Column mean = 0.00	**Column mean = 0.00**	**Overall mean = 0.00**

You can see that the male and female main effect has been taken into account, since now both row means are zero. That is, there remains no variation due to sex. But you can see that there remains variation due to Omega-3 treatment. Those getting the supplement now score −2.50 on average and those not getting the Omega-3 treatment score +2.50. To remove the variation due to the Omega-3 treatment, subtract −2.50 from the Omega-3 supplement column and 2.50 from the non-Omega-3 supplement column (Table 14.8). Do not forget that *subtracting a negative number is like adding a positive number*.

Looking at Table 14.8, although the column and row means are zero throughout, the scores in the cells are not. This shows that there still remains a certain amount of variation in the scores even after 'error' and the two main effects have been taken away. That is, there is an interaction, which may or may not be significant. We have to check this using the *F*-ratio test.

What the interaction table implies is that women *without* the Omega-3 supplement and men *with* the Omega-3 supplement are getting the higher scores on the dependent variable.

We can calculate the variance estimate for the interaction by using the usual formula. Degrees of freedom need to be considered. The degrees of freedom for the above table of the interaction are limited by:

● all scores in the cells having to be equal (i.e. no 'error' variance)

● all marginal means (i.e. row and column means) having to equal zero.

In other words, there can be only one degree of freedom in this case.

There is a general formula for the degrees of freedom of the interaction:

Degrees of freedom$_{[interaction]}$ = (number of rows − 1) × (number of columns − 1)

Since there are two rows and two columns in this case, the degrees of freedom are:

$(2 − 1) \times (2 − 1) = 1 \times 1 = 1$

■ Step 5

All of the stages in the calculation are entered into an analysis of variance summary table (Table 14.9). Notice that there are several *F*-ratios because you need to know whether there is a significant effect of sex, a significant effect of the Omega-3 supplement and a

Table 14.9	Analysis of variance summary table			
Source of variation	Sums of squares	Degrees of freedom	Mean square	F-ratio
Main effects				
Sex	196.00	1	196.00	58.96[a]
Omega-3 supplement	100.00	1	100.00	30.00[a]
Interaction				
Sex with Omega-3 supplement	36.00	1	36.00	10.81[a]
'Error'	40.00	12	3.33	–
Total (data)	372.00	15	–	–

[a] Significant at the 5% level.

Table 14.10	Alternative data table showing different trends		
	Omega-3 supplement	No Omega-3 supplement	
Males	Cell mean = 5.00	Cell mean = 5.00	Row mean = 5.00
Females	Cell mean = 5.00	Cell mean = 17.00	Row mean = 11.00
	Column mean = 5.00	Column mean = 11.00	

significant interaction of the sex and Omega-3 supplement variables. In each case you divide the appropriate mean square by the 'error' mean square. If you wish to check your understanding of the processes involved, see if you can obtain the above table by going through the individual calculations.

The significant interaction indicates that some of the cells or conditions are getting exceptionally high or low scores which cannot be accounted for on the basis of the two main effects acting independently of each other. In this case, it would appear that females getting the Omega-3 supplement and males not getting the Omega-3 supplement are actually getting higher scores than sex or supplement acting separately and independently of each other would produce. In order to interpret an interaction you have to remember that the effects of the independent variables are separately removed from the table (i.e. the main effects are removed first). It is only after this has been done that the interaction is calculated. In other words, ANOVA gives priority to main effects, and sometimes it can confuse interactions for main effects. Table 14.10 presents data from the present experiment in which the cell means have been altered to emphasise the lack of main effects.

In this example, it is absolutely clear that all the variation in the cell means is to do with the female/no-supplement condition. All the other three cell means are identical at 5.00. Quite clearly the males and females in the Omega-3 supplement condition have exactly the same average score. Similarly, males in the Omega-3 supplement and no-supplement conditions are obtaining identical means. In other words, there seem to be no main effects at all. The females in the no-supplement condition are the only group getting exceptionally high scores.

This would suggest that there is an interaction but no main effects. However, if you do the analysis of variance on these data you will find that there are two main effects and an interaction! The reason for this is that the main effects are estimated before the interaction, so the exceptionally high row mean for females and the exceptionally high column mean for the no-supplement condition will lead to the interaction being mistaken for main effects as your ANOVA summary table might show significant main effects. So you need to examine your data with great care as you carry out your analysis of variance, otherwise you will observe main effects which are an artefact of the method and ignore interactions which are actually there! The analysis of variance may be tricky to execute but it can be even trickier for the novice to interpret properly.

It is yet another example of the importance of close examination of the data alongside the statistical analysis itself.

14.4 When to use two-way ANOVA

Two-way ANOVA, like other forms of ANOVA, is ideally suited to randomised experimental studies. ANOVA was initially developed to analyse the data from agricultural experiments. Of course, ANOVA can be used in other contexts, but care has to be taken to avoid making the analysis too cumbersome. Survey data are usually too complex to use ANOVA on, though not in every case.

It should be noted that ANOVA is very closely related to multiple regression (Chapter 19) which may be preferred for survey-type data.

14.5 When not to use two-way ANOVA

While two-way ANOVA does have fairly restricted data requirements, it is actually difficult to avoid using it when interactions may be an important aspect of the analysis. This is because SPSS has no non-parametric alternatives to two-way ANOVA.

14.6 Data requirements for two-way ANOVA

The independent (grouping) variables should consist of relatively small numbers of categories, otherwise the data analysis will be exceedingly cumbersome. This is not usually a problem for researchers designing randomised experiments as the practicalities of the research will place limits on what can be done.

It is best if the scores in each condition have more or less similar variances, which SPSS can test is the case. There does not have to be the same number of participants in each condition of the study, though it is generally better if there are when the requirements of ANOVA are violated, such as when the variances of scores in each condition are different.

14.7 Problems in the use of two-way ANOVA

The major problem is the interpretation of two-way ANOVA. It has to be appreciated that the calculation gives priority to finding main effects to such an extent that it can attribute to main effect influences that really are due to the interaction. Take Figure 14.1.

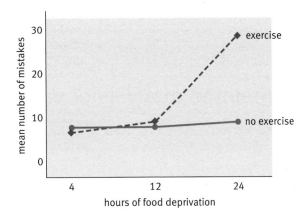

FIGURE 14.1   ANOVA graph of mistakes made by school children in a comprehension test, where an interaction may be confused with a main effect

If you look at the 'no exercise' line you will see that there are no differences in terms of mistakes between any of the three food deprivation conditions. This would seem to indicate that there is no main effect for the variable 'food deprivation' simply because all of the means are the same. If we look at the line for the 'exercise' condition, there is no difference between the four-hour and the 12-hour period of food deprivation, which again would indicate no main effect for food deprivation. The number of mistakes is the same for both conditions. This would suggest that there is no main effect of food deprivation. It is only when we consider the 24-hour food deprivation group given exercise that we find that the number of mistakes changes. We would say much the same of the exercise variable. If we consider the four-hour and the 12-hour periods of food deprivation, there is virtually no difference between the exercise groups and the no-exercise groups. This would be indicative of no main effect for exercise. Only when we consider the 24-hour food deprivation groups do we get a big difference due to exercise.

If the ANOVA tells us that there is a significant main effect for either or both exercise and food deprivation, we need to be very cautious since this is at odds with what the pattern of the data in Figure 14.1 tells us. We suspect an interaction. However, it is possible that the interaction is not significant according to the SPSS output.

The message is that the ANOVA may be confusing things and we need to be very cautious when interpreting the output. This is a case where simple descriptive statistics are vital to the interpretation of our data.

Anyone contemplating more complex ANOVAs than this should be wary that three-way, four-way, and so on ANOVAs generate massive numbers of interactions that are extremely difficult to interpret. We would suggest that very complex ANOVAs should be avoided unless you have a very good reason for using them and until your level of statistical skill is well developed.

14.8   SPSS analysis

The following step-by-step procedure describes the quick way for calculating the two-way unrelated ANOVA by hand.

Calculation 14.1

Two-way unrelated analysis of variance: quick method

Step 1 Enter your data into a table such as Table 14.11. These are the data given in Table 14.1 for the study into the effects of food deprivation and exercise on errors on a video test with a few additions. These additions are:

- The totals of scores in each cell (i.e. the cell totals or T_1, etc.)
- The totals of scores in each row (i.e. the row totals or R_1, etc.)
- The totals of scores in each column (i.e. the column totals or C_1, etc.)
- The overall total of all of the scores (i.e. the grand total or G).

These additions are analogous to the calculations in Table 14.2 of the previous computational method. With the quick method we do not calculate the means, merely the totals.

Table 14.11	Data for the two-way analysis of variance with added totals			
	Food withdrawal			
	4 hours	**12 hours**	**24 hours**	
Exercise	16	18	22	
	12	16	24	
	17	25	32	
	T_1 = cell total = 45	T_2 = cell total = 59	T_3 = cell total = 78	R_1 = row total = 182
No exercise	11	13	12	
	9	8	14	
	12	11	12	
	T_4 = cell total = 32	T_5 = cell total = 32	T_6 = cell total = 38	R_2 = row total = 102
	$C1$ = column total = 77	$C2$ = column total = 91	$C3$ = column total = 116	G = grand total = 284

Step 2 Square each of the scores and calculate the total of squared scores ($\sum X^2$):

Sum of squared scores = $\sum X^2$

$$= 16^2 + 12^2 + 17^2 + 18^2 + 16^2 + 25^2 + 22^2 + 24^2 + 32^2 + 11^2 + 9^2 + 12^2$$
$$+ 13^2 + 8^2 + 11^2 + 12^2 + 14^2 + 12^2$$

$$= 256 + 144 + 289 + 324 + 256 + 625 + 484 + 576 + 1024 + 121 + 81$$
$$+ 144 + 169 + 64 + 121 + 144 + 196 + 144$$

$$= 5162$$

Step 3 Carry out the following essential intermediate calculations to be used in later steps. They are R, C, T and something called the correction factor.

$$C = \frac{C_1^2 + C_2^2 + C_3^2}{\text{number of scores per food deprivation condition}} = \frac{77^2 + 91^2 + 116^2}{6}$$

$$= \frac{5929 + 8281 + 13\,456}{6}$$

$$= \frac{27\,666}{6} = 4611.000$$

$$R = \frac{R_1^2 + R_2^2}{\text{number of scores per exercise condition}} = \frac{182^2 + 102^2}{9}$$

$$= \frac{33\,124 + 10\,404}{9}$$

$$= \frac{43\,528}{9} = 4836.444$$

$$T = \frac{T_1^2 + T_2^2 + T_3^2 + T_4^2 + T_5^2 + T_6^2}{\text{number of scores per cell}} = \frac{45^2 + 59^2 + 78^2 + 32^2 + 32^2 + 38^2}{3}$$

$$= \frac{2025 + 3481 + 6084 + 1024 + 1024 + 1444}{3}$$

$$= \frac{15\,082}{3} = 5027.333$$

$$\text{Correction factor} = \frac{\text{grand total}^2}{\text{number of scores}} = \frac{G^2}{N} = \frac{284^2}{18} = \frac{80\,656}{18} = 4480.889$$

Thus

$C = 4611.000$

$R = 4836.444$

$T = 5027.333$

$\dfrac{G^2}{N} = 4480.889$ (i.e. correction factor)

Also $\sum X^2 = 5162$ (from step 2).

Enter the following calculations into the analysis of variance summary table (Table 14.12).

Table 14.12	Analysis of variance summary table			
Source of variation	**Sum of squares**	**Degrees of freedom**	**Mean square**	**F-ratio**
Main effects				
Exercise	355.555	1	355.555	31.67[a]
Food deprivation	130.111	2	65.555	5.84[a]
Interaction				
Food deprivation with exercise	60.778	2	30.389	2.71
'Error'	134.667	12	11.222	–
Total	681.111	17	–	–

[a] Significant at the 5% level.

Step 4

Calculate the sum of squares for the independent variable 'exercise' (i.e. $SS_{[exercise]}$). (The elements of the calculation have already been calculated in step 3.)

$$SS_{[exercise]} = R - \frac{G^2}{N}$$
$$= 4836.444 - 4480.889$$
$$= 355.555$$

The degrees of freedom for $SS_{[exercise]}$ are the number of conditions (or levels) of the exercise variable minus one (i.e. $2 - 1 = 1$).

Step 5

Calculate the sum of squares for the food deprivation variable. (The elements of this calculation have already been calculated in step 3.)

$$SS_{[food\ deprivation]} = C - \frac{G^2}{N}$$
$$= 4611.000 - 4480.889$$
$$= 130.111$$

The degrees of freedom are the number of conditions (or levels) of the food deprivation variable minus one (i.e. $3 - 1 = 2$).

Step 6

Calculate the interaction sum of squares (i.e. $SS_{[interaction]}$). (All of the elements of this calculation have already been calculated in step 3.) Insert these values:

$$SS_{[interaction]} = T - C - R + \frac{G^2}{N}$$
$$= 5027.333 - 4611.000 - 4836.444 + 4480.889$$
$$= 60.778$$

The degrees of freedom $SS_{[interaction]}$ are (number of conditions (or levels) of the food deprivation variable $- 1) \times$ (number of conditions (or levels) of the exercise variable $- 1) = (3 - 1) \times (2 - 1) = 2 \times 1 = 2$ degrees of freedom.

Step 7

Calculate the error sum of squares. (This is based on the total sum of squares calculated in step 2 and T calculated in step 3.) Enter these values.

$$SS_{[error]} = \sum X^2 - T = 5162 - 5027.333 = 134.667$$

The degrees of freedom for $SS_{[error]}$ are the number of scores $-$ (number of rows) $\times$ (number of columns). Thus the degrees of freedom for error are $18 - (2 \times 3) = 18 - 6 = 12$. This value should be entered in the analysis of variance summary table.

Step 8

The main parts of the computation have now been completed and you should have entered the sums of squares and the degrees of freedom into the analysis of variance summary table. You also need to calculate the three F-ratios in Table 14.12 by dividing the main effect and interaction mean squares by the error mean squares.

Your value has to equal or be larger than the tabulated value for an effect to be significant at the 5% level for a two-tailed test (i.e. to accept the hypothesis).

Step 9

The statistical significance of each of these F-ratios is obtained by consulting Significance Table 14.1. If your value is larger than the listed value for the appropriate degrees of freedom then the F-ratio is statistically significant at the 5% level of significance. The column entry is the degrees of freedom for the particular main effect or interaction in question, and the rows are always the degrees of freedom for error. As you can see, the two main effects in Table 14.12 are statistically significant whereas the interaction is not.

Significance Table 14.1	5% significance values of the F-ratio for unrelated ANOVA. Additional values are given in Significance Table 13.1					
Degrees of freedom for error or mean square (or variance estimate)	**Degrees of freedom for between-treatments mean square (or variance estimate)**					
	1	**2**	**3**	**4**	**5**	**∞**
1	161 or more	200	216	225	230	254
2	18.5	19.0	19.2	19.3	19.3	19.5
3	10.1	9.6	9.3	9.1	9.0	8.5
4	7.7	6.9	6.6	6.4	6.3	5.6
5	6.6	5.8	5.4	5.2	5.1	4.4
6	6.0	5.1	4.8	4.5	4.4	3.7
7	5.6	4.7	4.4	4.1	4.0	3.2
8	5.3	4.5	4.1	3.8	3.7	2.9
9	5.1	4.3	3.9	3.6	3.5	2.7
10	5.0	4.1	3.7	3.5	3.3	2.5
13	4.7	3.8	3.4	3.2	3.0	2.2
15	4.5	3.7	3.3	3.1	2.9	2.1
20	4.4	3.5	3.1	2.9	2.7	1.8
30	4.2	3.3	2.9	2.7	2.5	1.6
60	4.0	3.2	2.8	2.5	2.4	1.4
∞	3.8	3.0	2.6	2.4	2.2	1.0

Interpreting the results Remember that the interpretation of any data should be based first of all on an examination of cell means and variances (or standard deviations) as in Table 14.13. The tests of significance merely confirm whether or not your interpretations can be generalised. It would appear from Table 14.13 that the cell means for the no-exercise condition are relatively unaffected by the amount of food deprivation. However, in the exercise conditions increasing levels of food deprivation produce a greater number of mistakes. There also appears to be a tendency for there to be more mistakes when the participants have taken exercise than when they have not.

Reporting the results The results of this analysis may be written up as follows: 'A two-way ANOVA was carried out on variance on the data. The two main effects of food deprivation ($F = 31.67$, $df = 2, 12$, $p < 0.05$) and exercise ($F = 5.84$, $df = 1, 12$, $p < 0.05$) were statistically significant. The number of errors

Table 14.13	Table of means for the two-way ANOVA			
	Food deprivation			
	4 hours	**12 hours**	**24 hours**	
Exercise	15.000	19.667	26.000	Row mean = 20.22
No exercise	10.667	10.667	12.667	Row mean = 11.333
	Column mean = 12.833	**Column mean = 15.167**	**Column mean = 19.333**	**Overall mean = 15.777**

related to the number of hours of food deprivation. Four hours of food deprivation resulted in an average of 12.83 errors, 12 hours of food deprivation resulted in an average of 15.17 errors, and 24 hours of food deprivation resulted in 19.33 errors on average. Taking exercise before the test resulted on average in 20.22 errors and the no-exercise condition resulted in substantially fewer errors ($M = 15.78$). The interaction between food deprivation was not significant despite the tendency of the scores in the exercise condition with 24 hours of food deprivation to be much higher than those in the other conditions ($F = 2.71$, $df = 2, 12$, ns). Inspection of the graph (Figure 14.2) suggests that there is an interaction since the exercise and no-exercise lines are not parallel. It would appear that the interaction is being hidden by the main effects in the ANOVA.'

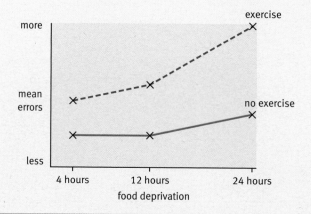

FIGURE 14.2	ANOVA graph of mistakes made in a comprehension test, showing possible interaction of food deprivation with exercise consumption

The significant F-ratio for the main effect of food deprivation needs to be explored further by the use of multiple-comparisons tests (Section 14.11). Because there are only two exercise conditions, this is unnecessary for independent variables having only two levels: there is no doubt where the differences lie in circumstances where there are only two values of an independent variable. Given the implications of the graph for the question of an interaction, it would be sensible to carry out multiple comparisons comparing all of the six cell means of the 2×3 ANOVA with each other (Section 14.11).

14.9   Computer analysis for two-way unrelated ANOVA

The computation of a two-way unrelated analysis of variance is illustrated with the data in Table 14.1. The table shows the scores of different participants in six conditions, reflecting the two factors of food deprivation and exercise. The purpose of the analysis is to evaluate whether the different combinations of exercise and food deprivation differentially affect the mean number of mistakes made.

Step 1

Enter the data. The two codes for 'Exercise' (1 = exercise and 2 = no exercise) are in the first column. The three codes for 'FoodDep' are in the second column (1 = 4 hours, 2 = 12 hours, and 3 = 24 hours). The errors are in the third column. Label these codes in this way. Remove the decimal places in 'Variable View'.

	Exercise	FoodDep	Errors
1	1	1	16
2	1	1	12
3	1	1	17
4	1	2	18
5	1	2	16
6	1	2	25
7	1	3	22
8	1	3	24
9	1	3	32
10	2	1	11
11	2	1	9
12	2	1	12
13	2	2	13
14	2	2	8
15	2	2	11
16	2	3	12
17	2	3	14
18	2	3	12

Step 2

Select 'Analyze'
→ 'General Linear Model'
→ 'Univariate...'.

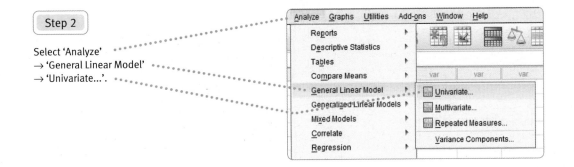

Step 3

Select 'Errors' and the arrow button beside the 'Dependent Variable:' box to put it there.
Select 'Exercise' and 'Food Dep' either singly or together and the arrow button beside 'Fixed Factor(s):' to put them there.
Select 'Options...'.

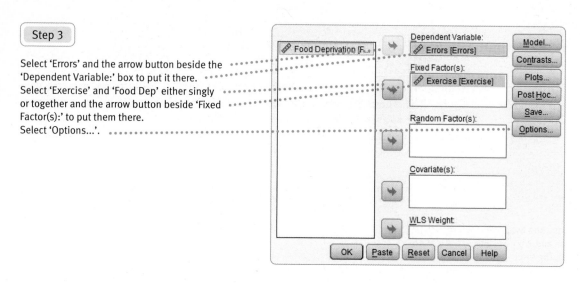

Step 4

Select 'Descriptive statistics', 'Estimates of effect size' and 'Homogeneity tests'.
Select 'Continue'.
Select 'Plots...' from the previous screen, which reappears.

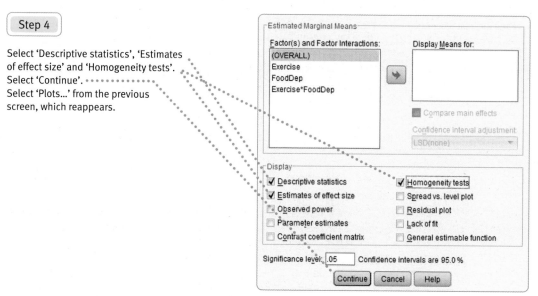

Step 5

Select 'Exercise' and the arrow button beside the 'Horizontal Axis:' box to put it there.
Select 'FoodDep' and the arrow button beside the 'Separate Lines:' box to put it there.
Select 'Add'.
Select 'Continue'.
Select 'OK' in the box from Step 3.

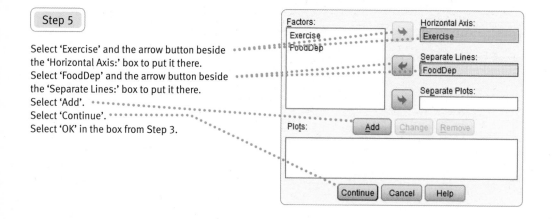

Interpreting the output

- The second table of the output (the first table here) provides the means, standard deviations, and number (N) of cases for the two variables of 'Exercise' and 'Food Deprivation' separately and together. So the mean for the 'Exercise' condition is given against the 'Total' (i.e. 20.22). The mean for the '4 hrs' 'Food Deprivation' is given against the 'Total' (i.e. 12.83).

Descriptive Statistics

Dependent Variable:Errors

Exercise	Food Deprivation	Mean	Std. Deviation	N
Exercise	4 hrs	15.00	2.646	3
	12 hrs	19.67	4.726	3
	24 hrs	26.00	5.292	3
	Total	20.22	6.099	9
No exercise	4 hrs	10.67	1.528	3
	12 hrs	10.67	2.517	3
	24 hrs	12.67	1.155	3
	Total	11.33	1.871	9
Total	4 hrs	12.83	3.061	6
	12 hrs	15.17	5.981	6
	24 hrs	19.33	8.066	6
	Total	15.78	6.330	18

- The third table of the output gives Levene's test to see if the variances are similar. As the significance of this test is 0.068 (which is above 0.05), the variances are similar. If this test was significant, the scores should be transformed say by using a logarithmic scale to make the variances similar. This is a matter of trial and error – try different transformations until the variances are the same.

Levene's Test of Equality of Error Variances[a]

Dependent Variable:Errors

F	df1	df2	Sig.
2.786	5	12	.068

Tests the null hypothesis that the error variance of the dependent variable is equal across groups.

a. Design: Intercept + Exercise + FoodDep + Exercise * FoodDep

● The fourth table of the output gives the significance levels for the two variables of 'Exercise' and 'FoodDep' and their interaction as well as their partial etas squared. Partial eta squared is the sum of squares for an effect (e.g. 355.556 for exercise) divided by the sum of squares for that effect added to the sum of squares for the error (355.556 + 134.667). In other words, it does not take account of the variance explained by the other effects.

Tests of Between-Subjects Effects

Dependent Variable:Errors

Source	Type III Sum of Squares	df	Mean Square	F	Sig.	Partial Eta Squared
Corrected Model	546.444ª	5	109.289	9.739	.001	.802
Intercept	4480.889	1	4480.889	399.287	.000	.971
Exercise	355.556	1	355.556	31.683	.000	.725
FoodDep	130.111	2	65.056	5.797	.017	.491
Exercise * FoodDep	60.778	2	30.389	2.708	.107	.311
Error	134.667	12	11.222			
Total	5162.000	18				
Corrected Total	681.111	17				

a. R Squared = .802 (Adjusted R Squared = .720)

● In the analysis of variance table the *F*-ratio for the two main effects ('Exercise' and 'FoodDep') is presented first.

● For the first variable of exercise the *F*-ratio is 31.683, which is significant at less than the 0.0005 level. Since there are only two conditions for this effect, we can conclude that the mean score for one condition is significantly higher than that for the other condition.

● For the second variable of food deprivation the *F*-ratio is 5.797, which has an exact significance level of 0.017. In other words, this *F*-ratio is statistically significant at the 0.05 level, which means that the means of the three food conditions are dissimilar.

● Which of the means differ from the others can be further determined by the use of multiple-comparison tests such as the unrelated *t*-test.

● The *F*-ratio for the two-way interaction between the two variables (Exercise * FoodDep) is 2.708. As the exact significance level of this ratio is 0.107 we would conclude that there was no significant interaction.

Figure 14.3 shows the plot for the means of the six conditions. It may be edited with the 'Chart Editor'. The style of the different coloured lines may be changed so that they can be more readily distinguished.

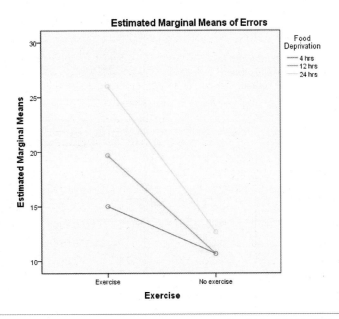

| FIGURE 14.3 | Means of the six conditions from two-way unrelated ANOVA |

■ Editing the graph

Step 1

To change the style of the line to that shown
in Figure 14.4, double-click on the plot to select
the 'Chart Editor'. Select the line in the legend
to be changed.

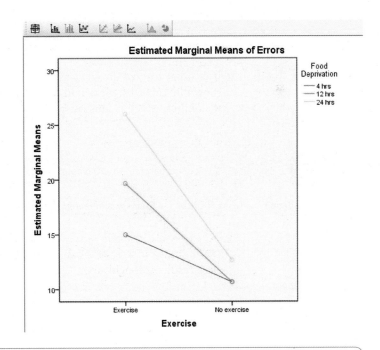

| FIGURE 14.4 | Using the 'Chart Editor' |

Step 2

Select the downward arrow button next to 'Style' and select the style of line desired.
Change the size of the line if desired.
Change the colour if desired.
Select 'Apply' and then 'Close'.
Select the next line to be edited and repeat these steps.

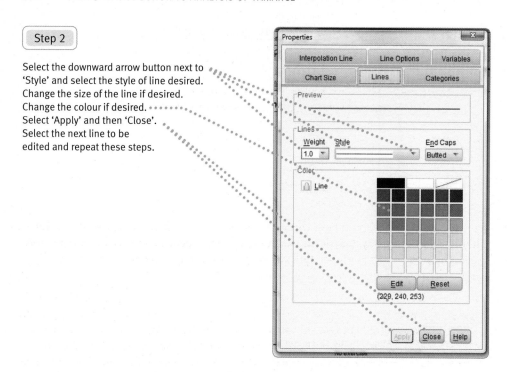

Reporting the output

- We could report the results of the output as follows: 'A two-way unrelated ANOVA showed that significant effects were obtained for exercise ($F_{2,12} = 31.68$, $p < 0.001$, partial $\eta^2 = 0.73$) and food deprivation ($F_{2,12} = 5.80$, $p = 0.017$, partial $\eta^2 = 0.49$) but not for their interaction ($F_{2,12} = 2.70$, $p = 0.107$, partial $\eta^2 = 0.31$).'

- It is usual to give an analysis of variance summary table. A simple one, like that shown in Table 14.14, would leave out some of the information in the third table in the output, which is unnecessary.

Table 14.14	Analysis of variance summary table from computer analysis				
Source of variation	**Sums of squares**	**Degrees of freedom**	**Mean square**	**F-ratio**	**Probability**
Exercise	355.56	1	355.56	31.68	< .001
Food deprivation	130.11	2	65.06	5.80	< .05
Exercise with food deprivation	60.78	2	30.39	2.71	Not significant
Error	134.67	12	11.22		

- Because the 'FoodDep' factor has more than two conditions, we need to use an appropriate multiple-comparison test to determine the means of which groups differ significantly (see Section 14.11).

- We also need to report the means and standard deviations of the groups which differ significantly. These descriptive statistics are given in the second table of the output.

14.10 Three or more independent variables

The two-way ANOVA can be extended to include three or more independent variables, although you are always restricted to analysing a single dependent variable. Despite this, it should be noted that the complexity of experimental research is constrained by a number of factors, including the following:

1. Having a lot of different conditions in an experiment may involve a lot of research and planning time. Preparing complex sets of instructions for participants in the different experimental conditions, randomly assigning individuals to these groups and many other methodological considerations usually limit our level of ambition in research designs. In some disciplines, the logistics of experiments are different since the units may not be people but, for example, seedlings in pots containing one of several different composts, with different amounts of fertiliser, and one of several different growing temperatures. These are far less time consuming.

2. Interpreting ANOVA is more skilful than many researchers realise. Care is needed to interpret even a two-way analysis properly because main effects are prioritised in the calculation, which results in main effects being credited with variation which is really due to interaction.

Since theoretically but not practically there is no limit to the number of independent variables possible in the analysis of variance, the potential for complexity is enormous. However, caution is recommended when planning research. The problems of interpretation get somewhat more difficult the more independent variables there are. The complexity is largely the result of the number of possible *interactions*. Although there is just one interaction with a two-way analysis of variance, there are four with a three-way analysis of variance. The numbers accelerate rapidly with greater numbers of independent variables. As far as possible, we would recommend any researcher to be wary of going far beyond a two-way analysis of variance without very careful planning and without some experience with these less complex designs.

It is possible to disregard the interactions and simply to analyse the different variables in the experiment as if they were several one-way experiments carried out at the same time. The interpretations would be simpler by doing this. However, this is rarely if ever done in social sciences research and it is conventional always to consider interactions.

14.11 Multiple-comparisons testing in ANOVA

ANOVA brings problems of interpretation when the independent variable (the grouping variable) has three or more categories. The problem arises because if the ANOVA is significant, this does not indicate that all of the means are significantly different from each other – it merely implies that the pattern of means is unlikely to have occurred by chance as a consequence of random sampling from a population in which the groups do not differ. If the independent variable has just two categories, then a significant ANOVA indicates that the two means involved do differ significantly from each other.

We will illustrate this using some data (Table 14.15) looking at aggression levels amongst offenders undertaking a hormone treatment programme. What is obvious is that the mean aggression score is higher in the Hormone 1 condition than in the other two conditions. Indeed, there seems to be little difference between the Hormone 2 group and the Placebo control group. If any comparison is statistically significant, it is likely to be the comparison between the Hormone 1 group and the Hormone 2 group. The comparison between the Hormone 1 group and the Placebo control group is the next most likely significant difference. It is very unlikely that the comparison between the Hormone 2 group and the Placebo control group will be statistically significant.

It would seem to be obvious to compare the pairs of means using the t-test in these circumstances. There is just one problem with what is otherwise a good idea – that is, the more statistical analyses one carries out on any data the more likely is one to get at least one statistically significant finding by chance. So if that method is to be used, then some adjustment should be made to deal with this problem. One way of doing this is the Bonferroni procedure, which basically involves adjusting the significance level for the number of t-tests used. However, there is little point in doing this as SPSS has far better multiple-comparisons tests available.

The problem is generally to decide which one(s) to use. It has to be said that there is little clarity in the literature on this matter. One way of dealing with this would be to use all of the available multiple-comparisons tests in SPSS on the grounds that if they all lead to the same conclusion there is no problem – a problem only arises if they give different conclusions. However, we would recommend instead that you consider using the Newman–Keuls test (S-N-K in SPSS) or Duncan's new multiple range test, which are both available in SPSS. There are two reasons as follows:

1. These are among the more powerful multiple range tests and are not prone to problems.

Table 14.15	Data for a study of the effects of hormones		
Group 1	**Group 2**	**Group 3**
Hormone 1	**Hormone 2**	**Placebo control**
9	4	3
12	2	6
8	5	3
Mean = 9.667	Mean = 3.667	Mean = 4.000

2. They can be used when the ANOVA is not statistically significant overall. This is important because in the past it used to be claimed that ANOVA had to be significant before any paired comparisons could be tested for. This produced obvious anomalous situations in which certain means were clearly very different but had to be disregarded because of this unfortunate 'rule'. It should be added that some of the multiple-comparisons tests were developed as alternatives to ANOVA anyway, so it is legitimate to use them on their own.

These two tests assume that each condition has the same number of cases in them. A test that does not assume this is the Scheffé test. However, it is a more conservative test, which means that differences are less likely to be significant.

Of course, the issue of multiple comparisons disappears when the independent variables in the ANOVA have only two different values. With a one-way ANOVA, it is easy to obtain multiple comparisons. However, with the two-way ANOVA and more complex versions, one has to resort to breaking the analysis up into individual one-way ANOVAs in order to employ multiple-comparisons. It is probably sound advice, wherever possible, then to plan the two-way ANOVA in a way in which each independent variable has only two values, which circumvents the problem. However, this is not always desirable, of course. SPSS will calculate the multiple-comparisons tests for two-way (and more complex) ANOVAs simply by doing two (or more) separate one-way ANOVAs.

It is appropriate to carry out the Newman–Keuls test (S-N-K in SPSS) or Duncan's new multiple range test whenever one is doing an unrelated samples one-way ANOVA irrespective of the outcome of the ANOVA. If the variances of your groups depart markedly from being equal, it is possible to select a multiple-comparisons test which does not assume equal variances. The Games–Howell would be a good choice in these circumstances. SPSS will calculate a homogeneity of variance test as one of the procedure's options.

Multiple-comparisons testing is available for two-way and more complex ANOVAs. However, be aware that SPSS will not attempt to calculate these where there are only two conditions of the independent (grouping) variable.

Knowing precisely where significant differences lie between different conditions of your study is important. The overall trend in the ANOVA may tell you only part of the story. SPSS has a number of post-hoc procedures which are, of course, applied after the data are collected and not planned initially. They all do slightly different things and the discussion of them is beyond the scope of this book.

■ Multiple-comparisons tests using SPSS

Step 1

Open the data file if you have access to it, or enter the data manually.

	Condition	Aggression
1	1	9
2	1	12
3	1	8
4	2	4
5	2	2
6	2	5
7	3	3
8	3	6
9	3	3

Step 2

Select 'Analyze'
→ 'Compare Means'
→ 'One-Way ANOVA...'.

Step 3

Select 'Aggression' and the arrow button beside
the 'Dependent List:' box to put it there.
Select 'Condition' and the arrow button
beside the 'Factor:' box to put it there.
Select 'Post Hoc...'.

Step 4

Select 'S-N-K', 'Duncan' and 'Scheffé'.
Select 'Continue'.
Select 'OK' in the previous box.

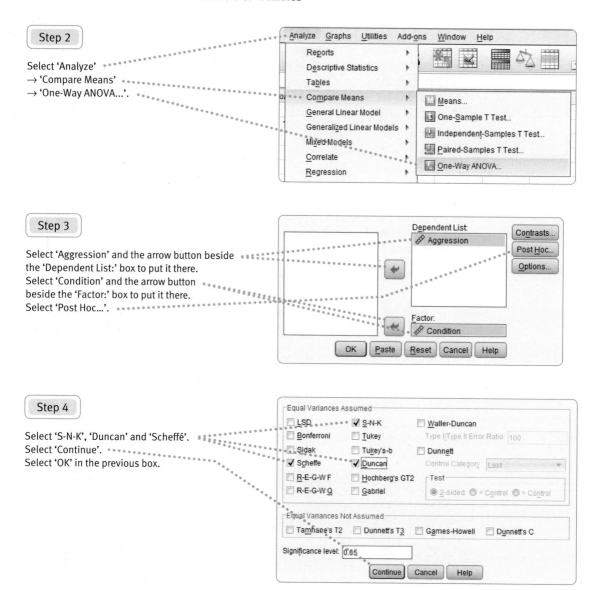

■ Interpreting the output

- The first table shows the results for the analysis of variance. The F-ratio for the between-groups effect (i.e. the effects of hormones) is 10.586, which has an exact significance level of 0.011. In other words, the between-groups effect is significant. Overall the means for the three groups differ.

ANOVA

Aggression

	Sum of Squares	df	Mean Square	F	Sig.
Between Groups	68.222	2	34.111	10.586	.011
Within Groups	19.333	6	3.222		
Total	87.556	8			

- The second and last table gives the results for the three multiple-comparison tests. For example, using the Scheffé test, the Hormone 1 mean is significantly different from the Hormone 2 mean (sig. = 0.018) and the Placebo control mean (sig. = 0.023).

Multiple Comparisons

Dependent Variable:Aggression

	(I) Condition	(J) Condition	Mean Difference (I-J)	Std. Error	Sig.	95% Confidence Interval	
						Lower Bound	Upper Bound
Scheffe	Hormone 1	Hormone 2	6.000[*]	1.466	.018	1.30	10.70
		Placebo	5.667[*]	1.466	.023	.97	10.37
	Hormone 2	Hormone 1	-6.000[*]	1.466	.018	-10.70	-1.30
		Placebo	-.333	1.466	.975	-5.03	4.37
	Placebo	Hormone 1	-5.667[*]	1.466	.023	-10.37	-.97
		Hormone 2	.333	1.466	.975	-4.37	5.03

*. The mean difference is significant at the 0.05 level.

- For homogeneous subsets, Hormone 2 and Placebo control are in the same subset – i.e. not significantly different. Hormone 1 is the only group in this subset. Consequently, it is significantly different from the other two group means.

Homogeneous Subsets

Aggression

	Condition	N	Subset for alpha = 0.05	
			1	2
Student-Newman-Keuls[a]	Hormone 2	3	3.67	
	Placebo	3	4.00	
	Hormone 1	3		9.67
	Sig.		.828	1.000
Duncan[a]	Hormone 2	3	3.67	
	Placebo	3	4.00	
	Hormone 1	3		9.67
	Sig.		.828	1.000
Scheffe[a]	Hormone 2	3	3.67	
	Placebo	3	4.00	
	Hormone 1	3		9.67
	Sig.		.975	1.000

Means for groups in homogeneous subsets are displayed.

a. Uses Harmonic Mean Sample Size = 3.000.

- The last table, entitled 'Homogeneous Subsets', lists the sets of means which do *not* differ significantly from each other. So taking the section for the Student–Newman–Keuls test, there are two subsets of means. Subset 1 indicates that the Hormone 2 and Placebo control means of 3.67 and 4.00 do not differ significantly. Subset 2 contains just the Hormone 1 mean of 9.67. Thus the mean of Hormone 1 differs significantly from the means of both Hormone 2 and the Placebo control. However, the means of Hormone 2 and the Placebo control do not differ significantly. The pattern is identical for the Duncan and Scheffé tests in this case – but it is not always so.

- Therefore the three multiple-comparison tests all suggest the same thing: that there are significant differences between Hormone 1 and Hormone 2, and between Hormone 1 and the Placebo control. There are no other differences. So, for example, it is not possible to say that Hormone 2 and the Placebo control are significantly different.

■ Reporting the output

We could report the results of the output as follows: 'A one-way unrelated analysis of variance showed an overall significant effect for the type of drug treatment ($F_{2,6} = 10.59$, $p = 0.011$). Scheffé's range test found that the Hormone 1 group differed from the Hormone 2 group ($p = 0.018$) and the Placebo control ($p = 0.023$) but no other significant differences were found.'

Key points

- Only when you have a 2×2 unrelated analysis of variance is the interpretation of the data relatively straightforward. For 2×3 or larger analyses of variance you need to read Chapter 16 as well.

- Although at heart simple enough, the two-way analysis of variance is cumbersome to calculate by hand and is probably best done on a computer if you have anything other than small amounts of data.

- Analysis of variance always requires a degree of careful interpretation of the findings and cannot always be interpreted in a hard-and-fast way. This is a little disconcerting given its apparent mathematical sophistication.

- Before calculating the analysis of variance proper, spend a good deal of effort trying to make sense of the pattern of column, row and cell means in your data table. This should alert you to the major trends in your data. You can use your interpretation in combination with the analysis of variance summary table to obtain as refined an interpretation of your data as possible.

CHAPTER 15

Analysis of covariance (ANCOVA)

Controlling for additional variables

Overview

- The analysis of covariance (ANCOVA) involves procedures by which it is possible to control for additional variables which may be influencing the apparent trends in the data.

- Analysis of covariance designs often include a pre-test measure of the dependent variable. The analysis adjusts for these pre-test differences. It adjusts or controls the data so that the pre-test scores are equal. This is especially useful when participants cannot be randomly allocated to different conditions of the design.

- Remember that in properly randomised experimental designs, extraneous influences are controlled partly by this process of randomly assigning participants to conditions. Of course, this may not always have the desired outcome, which is why some researchers will use a pre-test to check that the participants are similar on the dependent variable prior to actually running the experiment. If the pre-test data suggest that the participants are not equated on the dependent variable then ANCOVA may be employed to help correct this.

Preparation

Chapters 13 and 14 are essential as this chapter utilises many of the ideas from different types of ANOVA.

15.1   Introduction

The analysis of covariance (ANCOVA) is very much like the analysis of variance (ANOVA). The big difference is that it allows you to take account of any variable(s) which might correlate with the dependent variable (apart, of course, from any independent variables in your analysis of variance design). In other words, it is possible to adjust the analysis of variance for differences between your groups that might affect the outcome. For example, you might find that social class correlates with your dependent variable, and that social class differs for the groups in your ANOVA. Using ANCOVA you can adjust the scores on your dependent variable for these social class differences. This is in essence to equate all of the groups so that their mean social class is the same. ANCOVA can be calculated by hand, but it is easier to use SPSS since you are likely to want to equate for several variables, not just one. Furthermore, you should check to see that your covariate does, in fact, correlate with the dependent variable, otherwise your analysis becomes less sensitive, not more so.

15.2   Example of the analysis of covariance

Table 15.1 gives data that might be suitable for the analysis of covariance. The study is of the effects of different types of treatment given to prisoners at Belmarsh Prison suffering from stress. The dependent variable is stress. For each participant, a pre-test measure of stress given prior to therapy is also given. Notice that the pre-test scores of group 3, the no-treatment control group, tend to be larger on this pre-measure. Therefore, it could be that the apparent effects of therapy are to do with pre-existing differences between the three groups. Analysis of covariance could be used to allow for these pre-existing differences.

Table 15.1   Example of analysis of covariance data

Group 1 Counsellor		Group 2 Medication		Group 3 No-treatment control	
Dependent variable Stress	Covariate Pre-test	Dependent variable Stress	Covariate Pre-test	Dependent variable Stress	Covariate Pre-test
27	38	30	40	40	60
15	32	27	34	29	52
2	35	24	32	35	57

> ## Calculation 15.1

One-way analysis of covariance

The data are found in Table 15.1. The analysis of covariance involves a number of steps which remove the influence of the covariate on the dependent variable prior to calculating the analysis of variance on these adjusted scores. It is unnecessary to calculate the adjusted scores directly and adjusted sums of squares are used instead. The one-way analysis of covariance (ANCOVA) involves three major steps. Finally, in order to judge what the data say after the influence has been removed, we also need a table of the adjusted cell means for the dependent variable, that is, what is left when the covariate is removed from the dependent variable.

Step 1 (one-way unrelated ANOVA on the dependent variable) For clarity we have given the data on the dependent variable in Table 15.2.

Table 15.2	Scores on the dependent variable		
Group 1		**Group 2**	**Group 3**
27		30	40
15		27	29
22		24	35

1. Calculate the sum of the squared scores by squaring each score on the dependent variable and adding to give the total:

$$\sum X^2 = 27^2 + 15^2 + 22^2 + 30^2 + 27^2 + 24^2 + 40^2 + 29^2 + 35^2 = 7309$$

2. Sum the scores to give:

$$G = 27 + 15 + 22 + 30 + 27 + 24 + 40 + 29 + 35 = 249$$

3. Calculate the total number of scores on the dependent variable, $N = 9$.

4. Calculate the correction factor using the following formula:

$$\frac{G^2}{N} = \frac{249^2}{9} = 6889.000$$

5. Obtain the total sum of squares for the dependent variable by taking the sum of the squared scores minus the correction factor. This is $7309 - 6889.000 = 420.000$. This is entered into the ANOVA summary table for the dependent variable (Table 15.3).

6. Enter the degrees of freedom for the total sum of squares for the dependent variable. This is always $N - 1$ or the number of scores $- 1 = 9 - 1 = 8$.

7. The sum of squares between groups ($SS_{[between]}$) can be calculated as follows using the correction factor calculated above, the totals of each column and the number of scores in each column (e.g. N_1):

Table 15.3	ANOVA summary table for scores on the dependent variable			
Source of variation	**Sum of squares**	**Degrees of freedom**	**Mean square (variance estimate)**	**F-ratio**
Between groups[dependent]	268.667	2	134.333	5.33[a]
Error[dependent]	151.333	6	25.222	
Total[dependent]	420.000	8		

[a] Significant at the 5% level.

$$SS_{[between]} = \frac{T_1^2}{N_1} + \frac{T_2^2}{N_2} + \frac{T_3^2}{N_3} - \frac{G^2}{N}$$

$$= \frac{64^2}{3} + \frac{81^2}{3} + \frac{104^2}{3} - 6889.000$$

$$= 268.667$$

This value of the between-groups sum of squares for the dependent variable is entered into the ANOVA summary table (Table 15.3).

8. Enter the degrees of freedom for the between-groups sum of squares = columns − 1 = c − 1 = 3 − 1 = 2.

9. Calculate the error (i.e. error or within) sum of squares ($SS_{[error]}$) by subtracting the between-groups sum of squares from the total sum of squares:

$$SS_{[error]} = SS_{[total]} - SS_{[between]}$$

$$= 420.000 - 268.667$$

$$= 151.333$$

10. The degrees of freedom for error are the number of scores minus the number of columns = N − c = 9 − 3 = 6.

Step 2 (unrelated ANOVA on the covariate) Again we can create a table of the covariate scores (Table 15.4) and carry out an unrelated ANOVA in exactly the same way as above for the dependent variable.

Table 15.4	Scores on the covariate	
Group 1	**Group 2**	**Group 3**
38	40	60
32	34	52
35	32	57

1. Calculate the sum of the squared scores by squaring each score on the covariate and adding to give the total:

$$\Sigma X^2 = 38^2 + 32^2 + 35^2 + 40^2 + 34^2 + 32^2 + 60^2 + 52^2 + 57^2 = 17\,026$$

2. Sum the scores to give:

$$G = 38 + 32 + 35 + 40 + 34 + 32 + 60 + 52 + 57 = 380$$

3. Calculate the total number of scores for the covariate, $N = 9$.

4. Calculate the correction factor using the following formula:

$$\frac{G^2}{N} = \frac{380^2}{9} = 16\,044.444$$

5. Obtain the sum of squared scores for the covariate by taking the sum of the squared scores minus the correction factor. This is $17\,026 - 16\,044.444 = 981.556$. This is entered into the ANOVA summary table for the covariate (Table 15.5).

6. Enter the degrees of freedom for the total sum of squares for the dependent variable. This is always $N - 1$ or the number of scores $- 1 = 9 - 1 = 8$.

7. The sum of squares between groups ($SS_{[between]}$) can be calculated as follows using the correction factor which has already been calculated, the totals of each column and the number of scores in each column for the covariate (e.g. N_1):

$$SS_{[between]} = \frac{T_1^2}{N_1} + \frac{T_2^2}{N_2} + \frac{T_3^2}{N_3} - \frac{G^2}{N} = \frac{105^2}{3} + \frac{106^2}{3} + \frac{169^2}{3} - 16\,044.444 = 896.222$$

This value of the between-groups sum of squares for the covariate is entered into the ANOVA summary table (Table 15.5).

8. Also, enter the degrees of freedom for the between-groups sum of squares for the covariate = columns $- 1 = c - 1 = 3 - 1 = 2$.

9. Calculate the error (i.e. error or within) sum of squares ($SS_{[error]}$) by subtracting the between-groups sum of squares from the total sum of squares:

$$SS_{[error]} = SS_{[total]} - SS_{[between]} = 981.556 - 896.223 = 85.333$$

The degrees of freedom for error are the number of scores minus the number of columns = $N - c = 9 - 3 = 6$.

Table 15.5	ANOVA summary table for scores on the covariate			
Source of variation	Sum of squares	Degrees of freedom	Mean square (variance estimate)	F-ratio
Between groups[covariate]	896.223	2	448.112	31.51[a]
Error[covariate]	85.333	6	14.222	
Total[covariate]	981.556	8		

[a] Significant at the 0.1% level.

Step 3 (calculating the covariation summary table) This is very similar to the calculation of the unrelated ANOVA but is based on the cross-products of the dependent variable and covariate scores (Table 15.6). Basically it involves multiplying each dependent variable score by the equivalent covariate score. In this way it is similar to the calculation of the Pearson correlation coefficient which involves the calculation of the covariance. Table 15.6 can be used to calculate a summary table for the cross-products (Table 15.7). The calculation is analogous to that for ANOVA in steps 1 and 2 above. The only substantial difference is that it involves calculation of the cross-products of $X \times Y$ instead of X^2.

1. Calculate the overall (or grand) total of the X scores:

   $$G_X = 27 + 15 + 22 + 30 + 27 + 24 + 40 + 29 + 35 = 249$$

2. Calculate the overall (or grand) total of the Y scores:

   $$G_Y = 38 + 32 + 35 + 40 + 34 + 32 + 60 + 52 + 57 = 380$$

3. Calculate the number of scores for the dependent variable, $N = 9$.

Table 15.6   Data and cross-products table

	Group 1			Group 2			Group 3	
X Dependent	Y Covariate	$X \times Y$	X Dependent	Y Covariate	$X \times Y$	X Dependent	Y Covariate	$X \times Y$
27	38	1026	30	40	1200	40	60	2400
15	32	480	27	34	918	29	52	1508
22	35	770	24	32	768	35	57	1995
$\Sigma X = 64$	$\Sigma Y = 105$	$\Sigma XY = 2276$	$\Sigma X = 81$	$\Sigma Y = 106$	$\Sigma XY = 2886$	$\Sigma X = 104$	$\Sigma Y = 169$	$\Sigma XY = 5903$
$\Sigma X \Sigma Y = 64 \times 105 = 6720$			$\Sigma X \Sigma Y = 81 \times 106 = 8586$			$\Sigma X \Sigma Y = 104 \times 169 = 17576$		
$N_1 = 3$			$N_2 = 3$			$N_3 = 3$		

Grand total of all X scores $= \Sigma X = G_X = 64 + 81 + 104 = 249$

Grand total of all Y scores $= \Sigma Y = G_Y = 105 + 106 + 169 = 380$

Table 15.7   Summary table for the covariation

Source of variation	Sum of squares	Degrees of freedom	Mean square (variance estimate)	F-ratio
Between groups[covariation]	447.334	2		
Error[covariation]	104.333	6		
Total[covariation]	551.667	8		

➜

4. Calculate the correction factor by substituting the already calculated values:

$$\text{Correction factor} = \frac{G_X \times G_Y}{N} = \frac{249 \times 380}{9} = \frac{94\,620}{9} = 10\,513.333$$

5. Calculate the number of scores for each group (N_1, N_2, N_3). In our example these are all 3 as the group sizes are equal, but this does not have to be so.

6. Total degrees of freedom for the data table = the number of scores $- 1 = 9 - 1 = 8$.

7. Multiply each X score by the equivalent Y score to give the cross-products and sum these cross-products to give $\sum XY$ which is the sum of cross-products:

$$\sum XY = (27 \times 38) + (15 \times 32) + (22 \times 35) + (30 \times 40) + (27 \times 34)$$
$$+ (24 \times 32) + (40 \times 60) + (29 \times 52) + (35 \times 57)$$
$$= 1026 + 480 + 770 + 1200 + 918 + 768 + 2400 + 1508 + 1995$$
$$= 11\,065$$

8. Obtain the total sum of covariation by subtracting the correction factor from the sum of cross-products:

$$\text{Total sum of covariation} = \sum XY - \frac{G_X \times G_Y}{N} = 11\,065 - 10\,513.333 = 551.667$$

9. These values give the total sum of covariation (551.667) and the degrees of freedom (8).

10. Sum the scores on the dependent variable and independent variables separately for each of the groups separately. This gives us $\sum X_1$, $\sum X_2$, $\sum X_3$, $\sum Y_1$, $\sum Y_2$, $\sum Y_3$, since we have three groups in our instance.

11. The sum of the covariation between groups is calculated as follows:

$$\text{Sum of covariation between groups} = \frac{\sum X_1 \sum Y_1}{N_1} + \frac{\sum X_2 \sum Y_2}{N_2} + \frac{\sum X_3 \sum Y_3}{N_3} - \frac{G_X G_Y}{N}$$
$$= \frac{64 \times 105}{3} + \frac{81 \times 106}{3} + \frac{104 \times 169}{3} - 10\,513.333$$
$$= \frac{6720}{3} + \frac{8586}{3} + \frac{17\,576}{3} - 10\,513.333$$
$$= 2240.000 + 2862.000 + 5858.667 - 10\,513.333$$
$$= 447.334$$

12. The degrees of freedom for the covariation between groups is the number of groups $- 1 = 3 - 1 = 2$.

13. These values of the sum of covariation between groups and degrees of freedom between groups can be entered in Table 15.7.

14. The sum of the covariation of error can be obtained now by subtracting the sum of the between-groups covariation from the total of covariation:

$$\text{Sum of the covariation of error} = \text{total of covariation} - \text{covariation between groups}$$
$$= 551.667 - 447.334$$
$$= 104.333$$

15. This value of the covariation for error can now be entered into Table 15.7.

16. The degrees of freedom for error are calculated in a way which removes one degree of freedom for the covariation. This is simply the total number of scores $-$ the number of groups $- 1 = 9 - 3 - 1 = 5$. This can be entered in Table 15.7.

The above calculation steps for covariation are only superficially different from those for the analysis of variance in steps 1 and 2.

Step 4 | **(calculating the ANCOVA summary table, i.e. the dependent table with the covariate partialled out)** This is achieved by taking away the variation in the scores due to the covariate from the variation in the dependent variable. Once we have the three summary tables (dependent variable, covariate and cross-products), it is a fairly simple matter to calculate the adjusted dependent variable sums of squares and enter them into Table 15.8, the summary table for a one-way ANCOVA.

The formulae are:

$$SSError_{[adjusted]} = SSError_{[dependent]} - \frac{(Error_{[covariation]})^2}{SSError_{[covariate]}}$$

$$SSTotal_{[adjusted]} = SSTotal_{[dependent]} - \frac{(Total_{[covariation]})^2}{SSTotal_{[covariate]}}$$

Be very careful to distinguish between the covariation and the covariate.

These calculations are as follows:

$$SSError_{[adjusted]} = SSError_{[dependent]} - \frac{(Error_{[covariation]})^2}{SSError_{[covariate]}}$$

$$= 151.333 - \frac{104.333^2}{85.333}$$

$$= 151.333 - \frac{10\,885.375}{85.333}$$

$$= 151.333 - 127.563 = 23.77$$

$$SSTotal_{[adjusted]} = SSTotal_{[dependent]} - \frac{(Total_{[covariation]})^2}{SSTotal_{[covariate]}}$$

$$= 420.000 - \frac{551.667^2}{981.556}$$

$$= 420.000 - \frac{304\,336.479}{981.556}$$

$$= 420.000 - 310.055 = 109.945$$

Table 15.8	ANCOVA summary table			
Source of variation	**Sum of squares**	**Degrees of freedom**	**Mean square (variance estimate)**	**F-ratio**
Between groups$_{[adjusted]}$	86.175	2	43.088	$\frac{43.088}{4.754} = \mathbf{9.06}^a$
Error$_{[adjusted]}$	23.770	5	4.754	
Total$_{[adjusted]}$	109.945	8		

^{a} Significant at the 5% level.

Enter these values into the ANCOVA summary table (Table 15.8) and the between sum of squares obtained by subtracting the error sum of squares from the total sum of squares.

Note that the degrees of freedom for the error term in the ANCOVA summary table are listed as 5. This is because we have constrained the degrees of freedom by partialling out the covariate. The formula for the degrees of freedom for the adjusted error is number of scores – number of groups – 1 = 9 – 3 – 1 = 5.

Step 5   The *F*-ratio in the ANCOVA summary table is calculated in the usual way. It is the between mean square divided by the error mean square. This is 9.06. The significance of this is obtained from the Significance Table in Appendix I. We look under the column for two degrees of freedom and the row for five degrees of freedom. This indicates that our *F*-ratio is above the minimum value for statistical significance and is therefore statistically significant.

Step 6   (**adjusting group means**) No analysis of variance can be properly interpreted without reference to the means of the data table. This is not simple with ANCOVA as the means in the data are the means unadjusted for the covariate. Consequently it is necessary to adjust the means to indicate what the mean would be when the effect of the covariate is removed. The formula for this is as follows:

Adjusted group mean = Unadjusted group mean

$$- \frac{(\text{Error}_{[\text{covariance}]})}{\text{SSError}_{[\text{covariate}]}} \times (\text{Group mean}_{[\text{covariate}]} - \text{Grand mean}_{[\text{covariate}]})$$

The unadjusted group means are merely the means of the scores on the dependent variable for each of the three groups in our example. These can be calculated from Table 15.2. The three group means are group 1 = 21.333, group 2 = 27.000 and group 3 = 34.667.

The group means for the covariate can be calculated from Table 15.4. They are group 1 = 35.000, group 2 = 35.333 and group 3 = 56.333.

The grand mean of the covariate is simply the mean of all of the scores on the covariate in Table 15.4 which equals 42.222 for our example.

The sums of squares for error have already been calculated. The sum of squares for error for the cross-products is 104.333 and is found in Table 15.7. The sum of squares for error for the covariate is 85.333 and is found in Table 15.5.

We can now substitute all of these values into the formula and enter these values into Table 15.9.

Group 1: Adjusted mean = 30.27 obtained as follows:

$$21.333 - \left(\frac{104.333}{84.333} \times (35.000 - 42.222) \right) = 21.333 - (1.237 \times (-7.222))$$

$$= 21.333 - (-8.934)$$

$$= 30.267$$

Table 15.9	Unadjusted and adjusted means for stress		
Means	**Group 1 Counsellor**	**Group 2 Medication**	**Group 3 Control**
Unadjusted	21.33	27.00	34.67
Adjusted	30.27	35.52	17.21

Group 2: Adjusted mean = 35.52 obtained as follows

$$27.000 - \left(\frac{104.333}{84.333} \times (35.333 - 42.222) \right) = 27.000 - (1.237 \times (6.889))$$

$$= 27.000 - (-8.522)$$
$$= 35.522$$

Group 3: Adjusted mean = 17.21 obtained as follows

$$34.667 - \left(\frac{104.333}{84.333} \times (56.333 - 42.222) \right) = 34.667 - (1.237 \times 14.111)$$

$$= 34.667 - 17.455$$
$$= 17.21$$

Notice how the adjusted means in Table 15.9 show a completely different pattern from the unadjusted means in this case.

Interpreting the results The analysis of covariance makes it clear that the post-test measures of stress differ overall once the pre-test differences are controlled. However, by considering the means of the adjusted levels of stress it seems clear that the stress scores of the control group were actually lower than those of either of the treatment groups.

Reporting the results This analysis may be written up as follows: 'An analysis of covariance (ANCOVA) was applied to the three groups (counsellor, medication, and no-treatment control) in order to see whether the different treatments had an effect on post-test levels of stress controlling for pre-test stress. There was found to be a significant effect of the type of treatment (ANCOVA, $F = 9.06$, $df = 2, 5$; significant at the 5% level). The unadjusted means indicated that stress was higher in the control group ($M = 34.67$) than with a counsellor ($M = 21.33$) or with medication treatment ($M = 35.52$). However, this seems to be the result of the influence of the covariate (pre-therapy levels of stress as measured at the pre-test), since the adjusted means for the groups indicate that the least stress is found in the untreated control group ($M = 17.21$), compared with the counsellor group ($M = 30.27$) and the medication group ($M = 35.52$). Thus, the two treatment conditions increased stress relative to the control group.

Conceptually, be very wary when speaking of causality in relation to the analysis of covariance. Controlling for a covariate has no strong implication in relation to the issue of causality. In general, it is fairly difficult to meet in full the requirements of data for ANCOVA, which should encourage extra caution when the results of an ANCOVA are marginal in terms of significance.

15.3   When to use ANCOVA

The analysis of covariance needs to be used with restraint. It is not good practice to have more than a few covariates, for example. These covariates should be selected because it is known that they correlate with the dependent variable – if not, there is no point in using it. Covariates should correlate poorly with each other for ANCOVA to be effective to avoid multicollinearity (two or more independent or predictor variables which are highly correlated).

15.4   When not to use ANCOVA

There is a requirement that the relationship between the covariate and the dependent variable should be similar throughout the data. It should not be the case that the regression slope is different in the different conditions of the study, because ANCOVA works with the average slope, which may not be appropriate within a particular condition if the regression is not consistent. SPSS offers a test of homogeneity of regression. This simply means that the regression slope is constant for each condition of the independent variable.

Covariates that are unreliable can cause difficulty because ANCOVA assumes that all covariates are reliable. In social sciences, few variables are reliable in the same sense that, say, a measure of age is. Estimates of the adjusted mean may be overinflated if covariates are unreliable and it is likely that the test of significance is reduced in power (error of measurement). It is also important to recognise that ANCOVA should not be used as a substitute for proper random allocation of participants (where random allocation is feasible).

15.5   Data requirements for ANCOVA

Generally, any ANOVA model can be used as an ANCOVA. The covariates in ANCOVA should have a clear *linear* relationship with the dependent variable, otherwise ANCOVA will not be helpful. Curvilinear relationships are inappropriate because of the way in which ANCOVA works. Avoid the use of non-continuous variables such as gender as covariates in ANCOVA. These could, however, potentially be used as an additional independent variable.

15.6   SPSS analysis

■ The data to be analysed

The analysis of covariance is much the same as the analysis of variance dealt with elsewhere but with one major difference. This is that the effects of additional variables (covariates) are taken away as part of the analysis. It is a bit like using partial correlation to get rid of the effects of a third variable on a correlation. We will illustrate the computation of ANCOVA with the data shown in Table 15.10.

Table 15.10	Data for a study of the effects of stress (analysis of covariance)					
Group 1 Drug X		Group 2 Drug Y		Group 3 Placebo (control)		
Pre	Post	Pre	Post	Pre	Post	
5	9	3	4	2	3	
4	12	2	2	3	6	
6	8	1	5	2	3	

The study is the one we used earlier in this chapter but it has been extended. We have three groups of prisoners from Belmarsh Prison who are participating in a drug trial on stress. The three groups of participants have been given one of three drug treatments (drug X; drug Y; or a placebo control). The dependent variable is a measure of stress. The study has been changed so that it now includes a pre-test measure of stress as well as a post-treatment measure. Ideally, the pre-test measures should have the same mean irrespective of the condition. But you will notice that the mean pre-test score for the Drug X group is higher than for the other two groups. It is possible that the higher post-test scores of Drug X group is simply a consequence of them starting with higher levels of stress and not an effect of the drug treatment.

It could be that differences in stress prior to the treatment affect the outcome of the analysis. Essentially, by adjusting the scores on the dependent variable to 'get rid' of these pre-existing differences, it is possible to disregard the possibility that these pre-existing differences are affecting the analysis. So, if (a) the pre-treatment or test scores are correlated with the post-treatment or test scores, and (b) the pre-test scores or test scores differ between the three treatments, then these pre-test differences can be statistically controlled by partialling them out of the analysis.

It is possible to compute an ANOVA for these data but by using ANCOVA we can treat the pre-test measure of stress as a covariate. Two important things can be achieved:

1. The ANCOVA on SPSS will give you the means on the dependent variable adjusted for the covariate. In other words, it will equate all the participants on the covariate and make adjustments to the scores of the dependent variable to reflect this equally.

2. ANCOVA adjusts the error variance to take into account the tendency for individual differences to affect the dependent variable. This gives a new significance level which can be more statistically significant, though, of course, this does not have to be so.

■ One-way ANCOVA

Step 1

Enter the data (the data is the same as in Table 15.10).

	Condition	Posttest	Pretest
1	1	9	5
2	1	12	4
3	1	8	6
4	2	4	3
5	2	2	2
6	2	5	1
7	3	3	2
8	3	6	3
9	3	3	2

Step 2

Select 'Analyze'
→ 'General Linear Model'
→ 'Univariate...'.

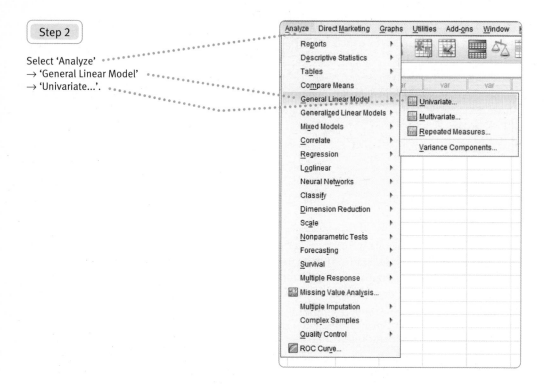

■ Testing that the slope of the regression line within the cells is similar

Step 1

Select 'Posttest' and click the arrow button
beside the 'Dependent Variable:' box
to put it there.
Select 'Condition' and click the arrow
button beside the 'Fixed Factor(s):' box
to put it there.
Select 'Pretest' and click the arrow
button beside the 'Covariate(s):' box
to put it there.
Select 'Model...'.

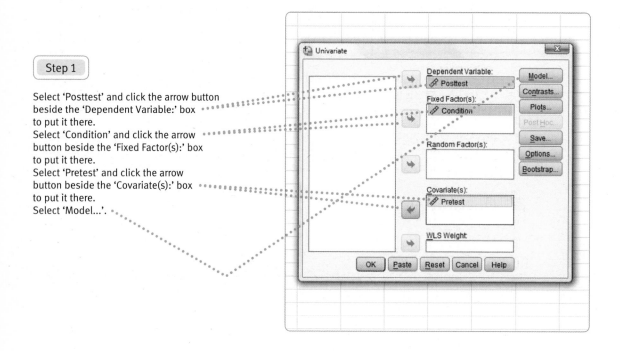

Step 2

Select 'Custom'.
Select 'Condition' and click the arrow
button to put it in the 'Model:' box.
Do the same for 'Pretest'.
Select both variables (ctrl+A) and click
the arrow button to put the interaction
between them in the 'Model:' box.
Select 'Continue'.
Select 'OK' in the previous box.

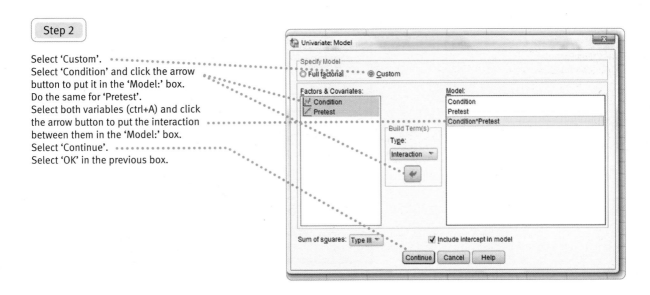

■ Interpreting the output

Tests of Between-Subjects Effects

Dependent Variable:Posttest

Source	Type III Sum of Squares	df	Mean Square	F	Sig.
Corrected Model	82.722[a]	5	16.544	10.269	.042
Intercept	19.230	1	19.230	11.936	.041
Condition	24.333	2	12.167	7.552	.067
Pretest	.100	1	.100	.062	.819
Condition * Pretest	12.571	2	6.286	3.901	.146
Error	4.833	3	1.611		
Total	388.000	9			
Corrected Total	87.556	8			

a. R Squared = .945 (Adjusted R Squared = .853)

The interaction between the conditions and the covariate is not significant, which means that the prerequisite that the slope of the regression line within the three conditions is similar is met.

■ Running ANCOVA

Step 1

To get to this pop-up box, enter the data from Table 15.10 and follow Steps 1 and 2 above for testing that the slope of the regression line within the cells is similar.

Step 2

Select 'Full Factorial'.
Select 'Continue'.

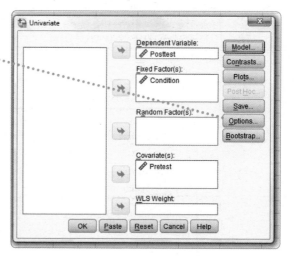

Step 3

Select 'Options...' when the univariate
dialog box reappears.

Step 4

Select 'Condition' and click the arrow button
to put it in the 'Display Means for:' box.
Select 'Descriptive statistics' and
'Estimates of effect size'.
Select 'Continue'.
Select 'OK' in the previous box.

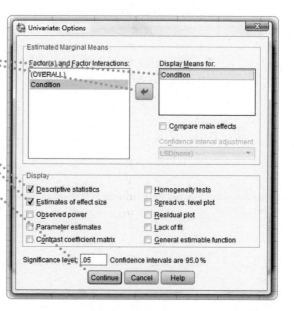

■ Interpreting the output from running ANCOVA

- The second table of the output (the first table here) shows the unadjusted means for the three conditions. This table simply gives the means for the three conditions at the post-test. Total is the average post-test score in the original data.

Descriptive Statistics

Dependent Variable:Posttest

Condition	Mean	Std. Deviation	N
drug x	9.67	2.082	3
drug y	3.67	1.528	3
placebo control	4.00	1.732	3
Total	5.78	3.308	9

- The fourth and last table (the second table here) shows the adjusted means for these three conditions. The adjusted means of the three treatments are the estimated means when all groups are adjusted to be identical on the covariate (in this case pre-treatment stress scores).

Condition

Dependent Variable:Posttest

Condition	Mean	Std. Error	95% Confidence Interval	
			Lower Bound	Upper Bound
drug x	10.881[a]	1.955	5.856	15.906
drug y	2.952[a]	1.443	-.756	6.661
placebo control	3.500[a]	1.269	.237	6.763

a. Covariates appearing in the model are evaluated at the following values: Pretest = 3.11.

- The means for the post-test given in this output table have been adjusted for the effect of the covariate on the three conditions. The effect of the covariate has effectively been removed from the data.
  - The adjusted mean is 10.881 for Drug X, 2.952 for Drug Y and 3.500 for the placebo control.
  - We can see that these adjusted means seem to differ from the unadjusted means shown in the second table of the output. For the first treatment, the adjusted mean is 10.88 and the unadjusted mean is 9.67; for the second treatment, the adjusted mean is 2.95 and the unadjusted mean is 3.67; while for the third treatment, the adjusted mean is 3.50 and the unadjusted mean is 4.00.

- The third table shows the F-ratio for the analysis of covariance. Following removal of the effects of covariate, there is not a significant difference between the means of the three conditions as the p value (significance) is 0.099 which is not statistically significant. Partial eta squared is 0.603.
  - The F-ratio for the effect is 3.796 (13.213/3.481 = 3.796).
  - The probability of this F-ratio is 0.099. In other words, it is greater than the 0.05 critical value and so is not statistically significant.

Tests of Between-Subjects Effects

Dependent Variable:Posttest

Source	Type III Sum of Squares	df	Mean Square	F	Sig.	Partial Eta Squared
Corrected Model	70.151[a]	3	23.384	6.718	.033	.801
Intercept	27.684	1	27.684	7.953	.037	.614
Pretest	1.929	1	1.929	.554	.490	.100
Condition	26.425	2	13.213	3.796	.099	.603
Error	17.405	5	3.481			
Total	388.000	9				
Corrected Total	87.556	8				

a. R Squared = .801 (Adjusted R Squared = .682)

■ Reporting the output

We could report the results of the output as follows: 'A one-way ANCOVA showed that when pre-test stress was controlled for, the main effect of treatment on post-test stress was not significant ($F2$, $5 = 3.80$, $p = 0.099$, partial $\eta^2 = 0.60$)'. In addition, we would normally give an ANCOVA summary table as in Table 15.11.

Table 15.11	ANCOVA summary table for effects of treatments on stress controlling for pre-treatment stress			
Source of variance	**Sums of squares**	**Degrees of freedom**	**Mean square**	**F-ratio**
Covariate (pre-treatment stress scores)	1.93	1	1.93	0.55[a]
Main effect (treatment)	26.43	2	13.21	3.80
Residual error	17.41	5	3.48	

[a] Significant at 5% level.

Key points

- Relying on ANCOVA to deal with the problems due to employing non-randomised allocation to the cells of the ANOVA ignores the basic reason for doing randomised experiments in the first place – that the researcher does not know what unknown factors influence the outcome of the research. Random allocation to conditions is the only practical and sound way of fully controlling for variables not included in the design.

- It is not wise to use ANCOVA to try to correct for the sloppiness of your original design or procedures. Although, especially when using computers, you can include many covariates, it is best to be careful when planning your research to reduce the need for this. In randomised experiments, probably the control of the pre-test measure is the only circumstance requiring ANCOVA. Of course, there are circumstances in which pre-tests are undesirable, especially as they risk sensitising participants as to the purpose of the study or otherwise influencing the post-test measures.

Recommended further reading

Cramer, D. (2003), *Advanced Quantitative Data Analysis*, Buckingham: Open University Press, Chapter 11.

Glantz, S.A. and Slinker, B.K. (2001), *Primer of Applied Regression and Analysis of Variance*, 2nd edition, New York: McGraw-Hill.

CHAPTER 16

Multivariate analysis of variance (MANOVA)

Overview

- MANOVA is very much like ANOVA. The big difference is that it has several different dependent variables. These dependent variables are all score variables. The independent variable is a category variable (or variables).

- There are versions of MANOVA which are equivalent to the various ANOVA designs covered in Chapters 13 and 14. Thus it is possible to have one-way MANOVAs, two-way and more (factorial) MANOVAs, and MANCOVAs in which the effects of one or more covariates can be removed from the data. Related designs are possible but beyond the scope of this book, as is MANCOVA.

- Essentially MANOVA combines the dependent variables to see whether the different groups (conditions) differ in terms of their 'means' on this combined set of dependent variables.

- A MANOVA summary table is produced which includes a multivariate test of significance. Commonly these include Pillai's trace, Wilks' lambda, Hotelling's trace and Roy's largest root. SPSS gives all of these.

- Consideration has to be given to what is to be gained by using MANOVA. For example, where the dependent variables are highly correlated and have a single underlying dimension, the scores on the dependent variables could be totalled and used as the score variable in ANOVA instead. This may yield a slightly more powerful test but only in these circumstances.

- If MANOVA is significant, then this indicates that the groups in the experiment (say) differ in terms of a combination(s) of the dependent variables. This leaves the researcher to examine the data in more detail by doing ANOVAs on the individual dependent variables.

- If MANOVA fails to reach statistical significance, then no further analyses are needed or are appropriate. The hypothesis that the groups are distinguishable on the basis of the set of dependent variables has been rejected because of this lack of significance.

- If you are planning to use MANOVA before collecting your data, problems may be avoided by making sure that each of your groups (or cells) has the same number of participants. If you do this then violating the assumptions of MANOVA is less of a problem.

Preparation

Revise Chapters 13 and 14 on the analysis of variance (ANOVA). MANOVA adds little to this in terms of conceptual difficulty and so cannot be adequately carried out without understanding ANOVA, which is also part of the MANOVA procedures.

16.1   Introduction

MANOVA is similar to ANOVA but instead of looking for differences in group means on a single dependent variable, MANOVA examines the influence of the group participants on a set of several dependent variables simultaneously. Again, similar to ANOVA, each dependent variable is a score variable. As a very simple example, the research question may be whether a new energy drink, 'Re-Energise', affects athleticism in athletes (see Table 16.1). Thus, at random, some athletes are given 'Re-Energise', others are given a placebo (coloured water) drink and others are given nothing at all. Now there are many different athletic skills that the researcher might wish to assess in this study – for example, reaction time, stamina, physical strength and running speed. All of these skills seem related conceptually, at least, to the research question and it would seem

| Table 16.1 | Data table for a study of the effects of 'Re-Energise' on athleticism |

Group (independent variable)											
Re-Energise condition				Placebo condition				No-treatment condition			
RT*	St	Ps	Rs	RT	St	Ps	Rs	RT	St	Ps	Rs
8**	5	7	7	1	3	2	2	4	3	5	4
7	7	6	5	4	5	3	3	1	2	3	6
9	8	5	9	7	2	1	2	3	5	2	6
7	5	8	8	2	5	6	1	1	4	6	2

* RT = reaction time, St = stamina, Ps = physical strength, Rs = running speed. Scores are from four cases in each column.
** The scores are for the four dependent variables.

somewhat short-sighted simply to select one. MANOVA allows the researcher to include a number of variables which may be affected by the energy drink. Better and clearer outcomes will be achieved if your research avoids the trap of throwing variables into the MANOVA simply because you have these data available. Carefully selecting the dependent variables because they have a strong conceptual or theoretical bearing on the research question will yield dividends. For example, as the energy drink research is about athleticism, adding in a variable about social networking to the list of dependent variables would add nothing to the analysis.

So, MANOVA is simply an extension of the analysis of variance to cover circumstances where there are multiple dependent variables measured in the form of scores. In previous chapters based on the analysis of variance we have seen that it is possible to analyse research designs with any of the following:

- Just one independent variable. This is known as a one-way analysis of variance. The independent variable is that which forms the different groups.

- Two or more independent variables. It would be possible to extend our energy drink study to include more than one independent variable. A simple example would be to have a second independent variable. We previously referred to this design as a two-way ANOVA design. If we added a third grouping variable (independent variable) then this would be termed a three-way ANOVA design, and so forth. These two-way, three-way, and so forth designs are sometimes referred to as factorial designs.

- Any of the above designs with additional covariates controlled for. So, for example, age of participants might be added as a covariate in the above designs. This is known as the analysis of covariance (ANCOVA) (Chapter 15).

MANOVA can deal with all three of the above types of design and more.

Box 16.1   Focus on

The Hotelling two-sample t^2

You may have a very simple study with just two groups (e.g. experimental and control conditions) yet have several dependent variables which relate to your hypothesis. Such designs are usually analysed using the t-test (Chapter 11). There is a multivariate version of the t-test for research designs in which there are just two groups of participants but several dependent variables. This is known as the Hotelling two-sample t^2. (If you want to do this analysis, just remember it is the same as MANOVA, which reduces effectively to the Hotelling two-sample t^2 if you have just two groups in your study. So simply follow the MANOVA procedures.)

16.2   Questions for MANOVA

There are two obvious questions to ask about MANOVA at this stage:

1. Why would one want to analyse several different dependent variables at the same time rather than do a number of separate ANOVAs?

2. How does one combine several dependent variables?

The answers to these questions are not simple.

■ Why not do several ANOVAs?

The answer to this question partly lies in the common comment in statistics that the more tests of significance one carries out then the more likely that significant findings emerge *by chance*. These do not represent real differences and, consequently, are not meaningful. So the more ANOVAs one does on one's data the more likely it is that a statistically significant finding will emerge. The purpose of research is not primarily to obtain significant findings but to provide an account or narrative or theoretical explanation which links together the findings of the researcher. For example, if the findings are not reliable then one may be trying to explain chance findings as meaningful findings which represent something which is happening in the real world.

■ How to combine dependent variables?

Initially, you might think that the easiest option would be to simply add up the scores for each participant to give a total score. This will generate a single dependent variable which can be entered into a regular ANOVA and there would be no reason to bother with MANOVA. However, the drawback is that you risk losing some of the information contained in your data. If this is not clear then imagine you ask your participants six questions the answers to which are scored on a 5-point Likert scale from strongly disagree to strongly agree. Then you give a score from 1 to 5 for each of the different points on the rating scales. Finally you add up each individual's scores to give a total score. Usually, information is lost from the data by doing so. So if someone scores 17 on the scale you simply do not know from that total what answers they gave. There are many possible ways of scoring 17 on the six questions. The total score does represent something but it has lost some of the detail of the original replies. Hence, ANOVA carried out on the total scores also loses information from the original data.

This is not always a problem. It is a problem when more than one dimension underlies scores on the various dependent variables. If the correlations between our dependent variables show some high correlations but also some low correlations then it is likely that more than one dimension underlies our scores. However, if the variables are highly correlated and constitute a single underlying dimension, totalling the scores to then subject these total scores to ANOVA may be extremely effective. It also has the advantage that there is no loss of degrees of freedom in the analysis – loss of degrees of freedom can be a problem in MANOVA but this is dependent on the total picture of the analysis and there is no simple way of balancing the different advantages and different disadvantages of the different approaches.

16.3   MANOVA's two stages

■ Stage 1: MANOVA

MANOVA and ANOVA follow a similar process except that in MANOVA we have several dependent variables to examine at the same time. So the question is whether the different groups are different in terms of the means that they have on several dependent variables. Once again, these differences in means are turned into sums of squares. But there is a big problem in doing this for a MANOVA design. It is not merely that there are several dependent variables but also that the several dependent variables may well be correlated with each other – that is, they measure, in part, the same thing. The analysis needs to make allowance for the extent to which the dependent variables are correlated. If it did not do so then the analysis would be claiming the same variance several times over. The extent of this depends on the size of the correlation between variables and the number of variables which correlate. Once the sums of squares associated with the different groups in the research design have been calculated, then multivariate tests of significance are computed and a significance level(s) provided. If the analysis is significant, then this shows that the groups of participants differ in terms of their scores over the set of dependent variables combined. It does not tell us which dependent variables are responsible for the differences. That is the job of the second stage.

Things are more complicated than this, of course. Like all tests of significance, MANOVA was subject to a set of assumptions by the person who developed the procedures. Parts of the computer output for MANOVA simply tell the user whether these assumptions have been met.

■ Stage 2: The relative importance of each dependent variable

From the MANOVA procedure, we know whether the groups in our research are different overall on the several dependent variables combined. That is the basic test of the hypothesis. If the multivariate test of significance in MANOVA is not significant, then the null hypothesis is preferred over the hypothesis. Even if we get a significant result from the multivariate test of significance, we remain at something of a loss since this tells us nothing as such about which groups vary and on what variables. We really need to understand something more about the pattern of variables on which the groups differ – that is, what combinations of variables tend to produce differences in group means?

A reasonable approach to this is to do a number of ANOVAs – one for each dependent variable. Hold on a minute, you may be thinking, didn't we decide at the start of the chapter that it was not a good idea to do this? The problem was the multitude of tests of significance being employed and this was part of the reason for opting for MANOVA in the first place. But MANOVA gives us protection from Type 1 errors. A Type 1 error occurs when the statistical test rejects a true null hypothesis. If the MANOVA is not significant then the analysis is protected from the risk of Type 1 error simply because no further analyses are carried out on the individual dependent variables.

If the MANOVA is statistically significant, then this supposedly 'protects' the analysis from Type 1 errors and indicates that it is legitimate to do ANOVAs on each of the various dependent variables. In other words, a significant MANOVA puts a cap on the risk of finding a significant result by chance – that is, committing the Type 1 error. Unfortunately, this is just not adequate for a number of reasons. The main one is that often there is one dependent variable which is affected by the independent variable and the rest of the dependent variables are not affected. In these circumstances, the significant MANOVA protects the affected dependent variable from Type 1 errors but the other variables are not protected. So one of the ANOVAs would be protected but the rest not. Quite what will happen depends on the details of the data and analysis.

Another problem with it is that even if you test each dependent variable separately, in the end you do not quite know what was affected by the independent variable(s). Although you could name the various significant dependent variables, this does not tell you what it is about the dependent variable which is affected. That is, what do the dependent variables have in common which produces the differences between the groups of participants?

16.4 Doing MANOVA

If you have mastered the basics of ANOVA then you may regard MANOVA as just a small step further. The major problem in implementing MANOVA lies in seeing the wood

Table 16.2	Data for the MANOVA analysis: effects of different types of team building

Group (independent variable)								
Team building with motivational speaker Dependent variables			Team building at a retreat Dependent variables			No team building controls Dependent variables		
Like*	Productivity	Overtime	Like*	Productivity	Overtime	Like*	Productivity	Overtime
9**	12	14	4	6	15	9	6	10
5	9	14	5	4	12	1	2	5
8	11	12	4	9	15	6	10	12
4	6	5	3	8	8	2	5	6
9	12	3	4	9	9	3	6	7
9	11	14	5	3	8	4	7	8
6	13	14	2	8	12	1	6	13
6	11	18	6	9	11	4	9	12
8	11	22	4	7	15	3	8	15
8	13	22	4	8	28	3	2	14
9	15	18	5	7	10	2	8	11
7	12	18	4	9	9	6	9	10
8	10	13	5	18	18	3	8	13
6	11	22	7	12	24	6	14	22

* Like = job satisfaction ratings; Productivity = number of reports produced over a month; Overtime = number of hours over a month.
** The scores are the scores on the three dependent variables.

for the trees in terms of the computer output. But by this stage, this is probably a familiar difficulty. The reason why MANOVA is essentially easy is that the only new thing that you really need to know is that there are things known as multivariate tests. These are analogous to the *F*-ratios (or Levene's test which is used by SPSS) which we are familiar with from ANOVA. Actually there are several multivariate tests which, despite being differently calculated, do much the same sort of thing – tell you if your group 'means' are different on the set of dependent variables as a whole. These multivariate tests include Pillai's trace, Wilks' lambda, Hotelling's trace and Roy's largest root.

The research summarised in Table 16.2 is a one-way MANOVA design in which we have a single independent variable – the group – but several dependent variables. The study investigates efficiency of team-building sessions with a motivational speaker, team-building sessions at a retreat, or no team building. Participants were randomly assigned to these three different conditions. Gender is regarded as a second independent variable. There are equal numbers of male and female participants. If you can, it is best to have equal group sizes for MANOVA as it helps you to avoid problems (see later). Three dependent measures were used: (1) the difference between the liking ratings for their job (job satisfaction), (2) the number of reports produced over a month, and (3) the number of hours of overtime each participant does over a month.

Accordingly, Table 16.3 shows that all three measures (dependent variables) intercorrelate positively, although there is some considerable variation in the size of the correlations. This suggests that more than one dimension underlies these variables. The variables cannot

Table 16.3	Correlations between the three dependent variables		
	Difference between job satisfaction ratings	Number of reports produced	Number of hours overtime
Job satisfaction ratings	–	0.60	0.30
Number of reports produced		–	0.51
Number of hours			–

Table 16.4	Result of multivariate tests				
Effect	Value	*F*	Hypothesis df	Error df	Significance
Intercept Pillai's trace	0.94	184.71	3.00	37.00	0.00
Groups Pillai's trace	0.490	4.11	6.00	76.00	0.00

convincingly be totalled in this case, given the wide range in the size of the correlations. So a MANOVA analysis seems appropriate.

The MANOVA analysis of the data produces primarily a MANOVA summary table which is similar to the ANOVA summary table in Chapter 13. There are even values of the *F*-ratio much as in ANOVA. However, this is based on different calculations from ANOVA since it is applied to the multivariate test (for example, Pillai's trace, Wilks' lambda, Hotelling's trace and Roy's largest root). Pillai's trace is probably the one to rely on because it is more robust and less affected by the data not meeting its requirements. To keep the tables as simple as possible, we have confined our analysis to Pillai's trace only. In MANOVA you do not calculate the sums of squares but the value of Pillai's trace (and possibly the others). The MANOVA summary table (Table 16.4) gives the results of this analysis. Apart from that, you will find much the same statistics as for analysis of variance.

So it should be self-evident from Table 16.4 that we have a significant effect of group (type of team building). Generally speaking, Pillai's trace gives much the same outcome as Wilks' lambda, Hotelling's trace and Roy's largest root. It does not much matter which you choose – and, of course, you can use all four if you so wish, though this will clutter your report. If you do not get any significant findings then this is the end of MANOVA – you do not go any further since your hypothesis has been rejected.

If you have significant findings, then you need to know what they indicate. There are several steps in order to do this.

■ Step 1

The simplest interpretation would be to conclude that there are differences on the composite of the three dependent variables related to the independent variables (groups). This may in any research study be sufficient to confirm the hypothesis. In our particular example, there are differences in the 'means' of the composite of the three dependent variables due to the independent variable group (condition).

■ Step 2

In order to have a better understanding of what is going on in the data, you need the corresponding univariate ANOVAs to the MANOVA. SPSS gives you these as part of the basic output from MANOVA. An example is given in Table 16.5. As you can see, there is an ANOVA for each dependent variable. It may look confusing at first, but taken one dependent variable at a time a basic understanding of one-way ANOVA will be sufficient. What seems clear from Table 16.5 is that two of the three dependent variables show virtually identical significant patterns. That is, the summary table shows that the two main effects for (1) job satisfaction and (2) number of reports produced are significant. The third dependent variable, number of hours, does not reach significance. This would suggest that the significant MANOVA is largely the result of the first two variables rather than the third variable. But it should be noted that you may obtain a significant MANOVA yet none of the ANOVAs are statistically significant. This means exactly what it says but you also need to realise that a linear combination of the dependent variables is related to group membership, despite the fact that individually the dependent variables may fail to be related to group membership.

Table 16.5	Part of a table of the individual ANOVAs for the three dependent variables				
Dependent variable	Sum of squares	Degrees of freedom	Mean square	*F*-ratio	Significance
Number of hours overtime	98.14	2	49.07	1.67	0.20
Job satisfaction ratings	97.19	2	48.60	15.71	0.000
Number of reports produced	122.33	2	61.17	6.87	0.03

■ Step 3

A table of estimated marginal means is helpful at this stage. SPSS generates separate tables for each of the main effects and each interaction. In the present case, we have reproduced only the estimated marginal means for the significant main effect (the team building variable). This can be seen in Table 16.6. It is clear from this that scores on each of the first two dependent variables are highest for the control, second highest for team building at a retreat, and lowest for team building by the motivational speaker. Furthermore, the groups seem to be best differentiated on the job satisfaction and the number of reports produced over a month. The number of hours carried out over a month does not seem to show such a clear trend.

Table 16.6	Estimated marginal means for groups on each dependent variable		
	Job satisfaction ratings	Number of reports produced	Number of hours overtime
Teamwork training by motivational speaker	7.29	11.21	14.93
Teamwork training at a retreat	4.43	8.36	13.86
Control – no teamwork training	3.79	7.14	11.29

Table 16.7	The Box's *M* test for covariance homogeneity (equality)
Box's *M*	18.70
F	1.38
df_1	12
df_2	7371
Significance	0.17

Remember that this is a down-to-basics account of MANOVA. We do not pretend that it offers the most sophisticated approach. You might wish, especially, to check whether your data actually meet the requirements of MANOVA in terms of the characteristics of the data. One quite important thing is the Box's *M* test of equality of the covariance matrix. We do not need to know too much about this test but we do need to know what to do if the test is statistically significant. The Box's *M* test is illustrated in Table 16.7. If it yields a significant value (as it does in our case), this means that the covariances are not similar, which violates one of the assumptions on which MANOVA was built. This can affect the probability levels obtained in the MANOVA. However, this is crucial only if the MANOVA significance levels just reach the 0.05 level of significance. If your MANOVA findings are very significant then there is not a great problem. You should not worry if the different cells (groupings) of your MANOVA have unequal sample sizes, as violating the requirements of the MANOVA makes no practical difference to the significance level in this case. If you have very different sample sizes and your findings are close to the boundary between statistical significance and statistical non-significance, then you should worry more – one solution is to equate the sample sizes by randomly dropping cases from cells as necessary. But this could have as much effect on your findings as violating the equal covariances principle anyway. So bear this in mind when designing your MANOVA.

16.5 When to use MANOVA

MANOVA can be used when the researcher has employed a randomised experimental design in which there are several groups of participants but where several different variables have been measured to reflect different aspects of the dependent variable described in the hypothesis. There is no point (and a great deal to be lost) in simply trying to combine different dependent variables together in MANOVA that have no *conceptual* relationship to each other and the hypothesis. MANOVA will indicate whether the means for the groups on the combined dependent variables differ significantly. Of course, it is possible to use MANOVA even in circumstances where participants were not randomly allocated to the different groups formed by the independent variable. In such a study, researchers would be less likely to refer to the causal influence of the independent variable on the dependent variable.

MANOVA is used when there are three or more different groups (just like one-way ANOVA). If there are just two groups (as in the unrelated *t*-test), then the analysis becomes Hotelling's *t*-test, which is just the same as any other unrelated *t*-test conceptually but uses a combination of several different dependent variables.

16.6   When not to use MANOVA

If the dependent variables are very highly correlated with each other then there may be simpler ways of combining the variables (for example, by simply adding up the scores of each participant over the several dependent variables and then carrying out an ANOVA on these summated scores). What is the advantage of this? One of the problems of using MANOVA is that degrees of freedom are lost due to the number of dependent variables in the analysis. This, effectively, reduces the statistical significance of MANOVA, which is not desirable if it can be avoided. So if there is an alternative but unproblematic way of combining the separate dependent variables then this can be employed to good effect. This will not work where some dependent variables correlate with each other highly while others do not, since it is unclear how the dependent variables should be combined to give a combined score on the dependent variable. But these are the circumstances in which MANOVA is likely to be at its most effective and so would be the preferred approach.

We would not recommend the use of MANOVA if you have many dependent variables to combine. For example, if one has a lengthy questionnaire (say, 10 or more questions) then it would not be helpful to treat answers to each question as a separate dependent variable as parts of MANOVA, as there are more informative ways of combining items to yield a small number of combined variables. It would be better, for example, to factor analyse (Chapter 18) the set of dependent variables. In this way, the structure of the items will be clarified.

16.7   Data requirements for MANOVA

- The independent variable (grouping variable) consists of three or more different categories for MANOVA (do not use score variables as the independent variable unless they have been recoded into a small number of categories).

- Always try to ensure that the sample size of each group in the MANOVA is the same. This helps avoids problems in the analysis if assumptions related to the equality of the covariance matrices are not met.

- The two-sample equivalent to the *t*-test is known as the Hotelling's *t*-test but it would be calculated on SPSS using the MANOVA procedure.

- There need to be several dependent variables which take the form of numerical scores.

16.8 Problems in the use of MANOVA

It is possible to run before you can walk with MANOVA. Many of the features of SPSS MANOVA output require understanding of ANOVA – post-hoc multiple comparison tests and the like are discussed in the chapters on ANOVA and are not dealt with in this chapter for reasons of clarity. So it is best to have a grounding in ANOVA before moving on to MANOVA.

16.9 SPSS analysis

■ The data to be analysed

The data in Table 16.2 will be used as an the example for SPSS analysis for MANOVA.

■ Applying MANOVA

Please note that the screenshot does not show all the cases, only 1–25.

	Group	Jobsatisfaction	Reports	Overtime
1	1	9	12	14
2	2	4	6	15
3	3	9	6	10
4	1	5	9	14
5	2	5	4	12
6	3	1	2	5
7	1	8	11	12
8	2	4	9	15
9	3	6	10	12
10	1	4	6	5
11	2	3	8	8
12	3	2	5	6
13	1	9	12	3
14	2	4	9	9
15	3	3	6	7
16	1	9	11	14
17	2	5	3	8
18	3	4	7	8
19	1	6	13	14
20	2	2	8	12
21	3	1	6	13
22	1	6	11	18
23	2	6	9	11
24	3	4	9	12
25	1	8	11	22

Step 1

Enter the data. 'Group' is the independent variable. The rest are the dependent variables (instructions for coding and labelling group conditions have already been discussed in Chapter 1).

Step 2

Select 'Analyze'
→ 'General Linear Model'
→ 'Multivariate...'.

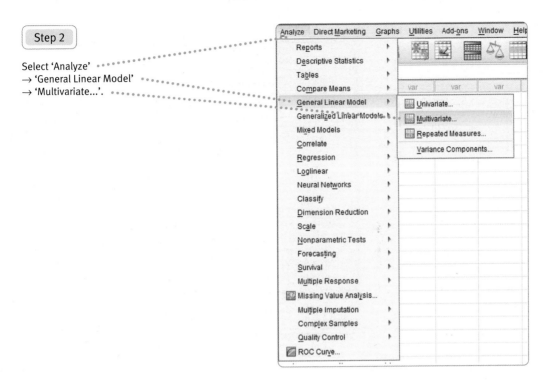

Step 3

In the 'Multivariate' dialog box, using the arrow button, move the dependent variables from the large left-hand panel to the small 'Dependent Variables:' box.
Move the grouping variable from the left to the 'Fixed Factor(s):' box.
Select 'Options...'.

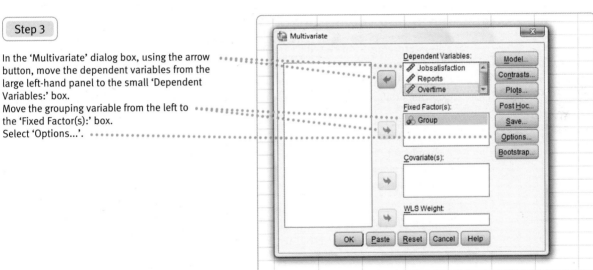

Step 4

In the 'Multivariate: Options' dialog box, using the arrow button, move 'Group' over to the right-hand 'Display Means for:' panel. Select 'Descriptive statistics' and 'Estimates of effect size'. Select 'Continue'. Select 'OK' in the previous box.

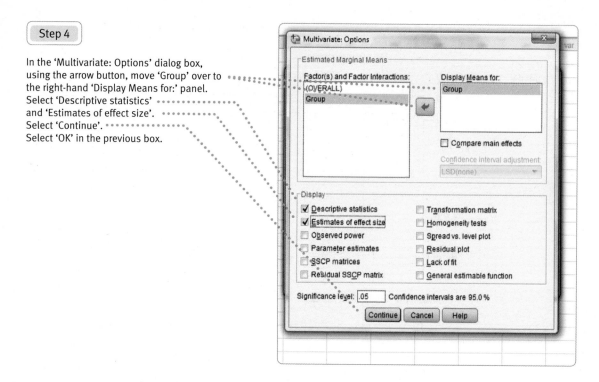

■ Interpreting the output

- The interpretation of the SPSS output from MANOVA is complicated when options are selected, but there is only a small core of the SPSS output that contains the results of the MANOVA analysis. If this is significant then one would normally go on to examine other aspects of the output that deal with the individual dependent variables.

- The SPSS output for MANOVA contains the results of separate ANOVA analyses for each separate dependent variable. These are considered when the overall MANOVA is significant. However, the individual ANOVAs actually do not tell us about the combined dependent variable, since we need to know the contribution of each dependent variable to the combined scores before we can know this.

- The table 'Between-Subjects Factors' merely identifies the groups based on the independent variable and gives the sample size involved. It is good that equal sample sizes were used, as this helps avoid technical problems.

Between-Subjects Factors

		Value Label	N
Group	1	motivation	14
	2	retreat	14
	3	control	14

● The table 'Descriptive Statistics' gives the mean scores on the three dependent variables for each grouping variable.

Descriptive Statistics

	Group	Mean	Std. Deviation	N
Jobsatisfaction	motivation	7.29	1.637	14
	retreat	4.43	1.222	14
	control	3.79	2.259	14
	Total	5.17	2.305	42
Reports	motivation	11.21	2.082	14
	retreat	8.36	3.565	14
	control	7.14	3.110	14
	Total	8.90	3.384	42
Overtime	motivation	14.93	5.784	14
	retreat	13.86	6.011	14
	control	11.29	4.322	14
	Total	13.36	5.512	42

● The table 'Multivariate Tests' contains the MANOVA analysis. There are several multivariate tests that are very similar. Use the Pillai's trace as using all four is cumbersome. The MANOVA is significant at the 0.001 level. Thus the group means on the composite dependent variable differ significantly at the 0.001 level. Therefore the hypothesis is supported.

Multivariate Tests[c]

Effect		Value	F	Hypothesis df	Error df	Sig.	Partial Eta Squared
Intercept	Pillai's Trace	.937	184.710[a]	3.000	37.000	.000	.937
	Wilks' Lambda	.063	184.710[a]	3.000	37.000	.000	.937
	Hotelling's Trace	14.976	184.710[a]	3.000	37.000	.000	.937
	Roy's Largest Root	14.976	184.710[a]	3.000	37.000	.000	.937
Group	Pillai's Trace	.490	4.109	6.000	76.000	.001	.245
	Wilks' Lambda	.522	4.733[a]	6.000	74.000	.000	.277
	Hotelling's Trace	.892	5.349	6.000	72.000	.000	.308
	Roy's Largest Root	.865	10.953[b]	3.000	38.000	.000	.464

a. Exact statistic
b. The statistic is an upper bound on F that yields a lower bound on the significance level.
c. Design: Intercept + Group

● The table 'Tests of Between-Subjects Effects' gives the significance of the individual ANOVAs applied to the three dependent variables separately. As can be seen, two of the dependent variables differ significantly according to the group. However, the dependent variable 'overtime' does not produce significant results.

Tests of Between-Subjects Effects

Source	Dependent Variable	Type III Sum of Squares	df	Mean Square	F	Sig.	Partial Eta Squared
Corrected Model	Jobsatisfaction	97.190[a]	2	48.595	15.709	.000	.446
	Reports	122.333[b]	2	61.167	6.869	.003	.260
	Overtime	98.143[c]	2	49.071	1.668	.202	.079
Intercept	Jobsatisfaction	1121.167	1	1121.167	362.438	.000	.903
	Reports	3330.381	1	3330.381	374.000	.000	.906
	Overtime	7493.357	1	7493.357	254.676	.000	.867
Group	Jobsatisfaction	97.190	2	48.595	15.709	.000	.446
	Reports	122.333	2	61.167	6.869	.003	.260
	Overtime	98.143	2	49.071	1.668	.202	.079
Error	Jobsatisfaction	120.643	39	3.093			
	Reports	347.286	39	8.905			
	Overtime	1147.500	39	29.423			
Total	Jobsatisfaction	1339.000	42				
	Reports	3800.000	42				
	Overtime	8739.000	42				
Corrected Total	Jobsatisfaction	217.833	41				
	Reports	469.619	41				
	Overtime	1245.643	41				

a. R Squared = .446 (Adjusted R Squared = .418)
b. R Squared = .260 (Adjusted R Squared = .223)
c. R Squared = .079 (Adjusted R Squared = .032)

● The table of 'Estimated Marginal Means' headed 'Group' shows the means of the three dependent variables for the three groups. Which means differ for each dependent variable needs to be determined with further SPSS analysis.

Group

Dependent Variable	Group	Mean	Std. Error	95% Confidence Interval	
				Lower Bound	Upper Bound
Jobsatisfaction	motivation	7.286	.470	6.335	8.237
	retreat	4.429	.470	3.478	5.379
	control	3.786	.470	2.835	4.737
Reports	motivation	11.214	.798	9.601	12.827
	retreat	8.357	.798	6.744	9.970
	control	7.143	.798	5.530	8.756
Overtime	motivation	14.929	1.450	11.996	17.861
	retreat	13.857	1.450	10.925	16.789
	control	11.286	1.450	8.353	14.218

■ Reporting the output

In the example, the findings were significant and we might report: 'MANOVA showed there was a significant multivariate effect of team building on the three dependent variables (Pillai's $F_{6,76} = 4.11$, $p < 0.01$, partial $\eta^2 = 0.25$). Each dependent variable was subjected to a further ANOVA in order to show whether this trend is the same for each of the separate dependent variables. For the measure of the job satisfaction ratings, an ANOVA showed there was an overall significant difference between the means ($F_{2,39} = 15.71$, $p = 0.0001$, partial $\eta^2 = 0.45$). The mean number of reports produced was different according to group ($F_{2,39} = 61.17$, $p = 0.03$, partial $\eta^2 = 0.26$). However, the number of hours of overtime failed to reach statistical significance ($F_{2,39} = 49.07$, *ns*, partial $\eta^2 = 0.08$).'

Key points

- MANOVA basically deals with a very simple problem – the risk of falsely accepting a hypothesis because you have carried out multiple tests of significance.

- Try to avoid an unfocused approach to MANOVA. It is *not* a particularly useful technique for sorting out what to do with numerous dependent variables that you have measured merely because you could.

- MANOVA is not appropriate if all of your dependent variables are highly intercorrelated. It may be better in these circumstances to combine the dependent variables to give a total score which is then analysed using ANOVA, for example.

Recommended further reading

Diekhoff, G. (1992), *Statistics for the Social and Behavioral Sciences*, Dubuque, IL: Wm. C. Brown, Chapter 15.

Hair, J.F., Jr., Black, W.C., Babin, B.J. and Anderson, R.E. (2009), *Multivariate Data Analysis*, 7th edition, Upper Saddle River, NJ: Pearson Prentice Hall, Chapter 6.

Tabachnick, B.G. and Fidell, L.S. (2007), *Using Multivariate Statistics*, 5th edition, Boston, MA: Allyn & Bacon, Chapter 7.

PART 4

More advanced statistics and techniques

CHAPTER 17

Partial correlation

Spurious correlation, third or confounding variables (control variables), suppressor variables

Overview

- Partial correlation is used to statistically adjust a correlation to take into account the possible influence of a third (or confounding) variable or variables. These are sometimes known as control variables.

- That is, partial correlation deals with the third-variable problem in which additional variables may be the cause of spurious correlations or may hide (suppress) the relationship between two variables.

- If one control variable is used then we have a first-order partial correlation. If two control variables are used then the result is a second-order partial correlation.

- Partial correlation may be helpful in trying to assess the possibility that a relationship is a causal relationship.

Preparation

Revise the Pearson correlation coefficient (Chapter 7) if necessary. Make sure you know what is meant by a causal relationship.

17.1 Introduction

The partial correlation coefficient is particularly useful when trying to make causal statements from field research. It is not useful in experimental research. This is because different methods are used in experimental research to establish causal relationships. Look at the following research outlines taking as critical a viewpoint as possible:

- **Project 1** Researchers examine the published suicide rates in different geographical locations in the country. They find that there is a significant relationship between unemployment rates in these areas and suicide rates. They conclude that unemployment causes suicide.

- **Project 2** Researchers examine the relationship between clothes size and liking shopping. They find a relationship between the two but claim that it would be nonsense to suggest that liking shopping makes your clothes size bigger.

The researchers draw rather different conclusions. In the first case it is suggested that unemployment *causes* suicide whereas in the second case the researchers are reluctant to claim that liking shopping makes your clothes size bigger. The researchers in both cases may be correct in their interpretation of the correlations, but should we take their interpretations at face value? The short answer is no, since correlations do not prove causality in themselves.

In both cases, it is possible that the relationships obtained are spurious (or artificial) ones which occur because of the influence of other variables which the researcher has not considered. The relationship between unemployment and suicide could be due to the influence of a third variable. In this case the variable might be social class. If we found, for example, that being from a lower social class was associated with a greater likelihood of unemployment *and* with being more prone to suicide, this would suggest that the relationship between unemployment and suicide was due to social class differences, not because unemployment leads directly to suicide.

Box 17.1 Research design issue

Partial correlation can never prove that causal relationships exist between two variables. The reason is that partialling out a third, fourth or fifth variable does not rule out the possibility that there is an additional variable which has not been considered which is the cause of the correlation. However, partial correlation may be useful in examining the validity of claims about specified variables which might be causing the relationship. Considerations of causality are a minor aspect of partial correlation.

17.2 Theoretical considerations

Partial correlation is a statistically precise way of calculating what the relationship between two variables would be if one could take away the influence of one (or more) additional variables. In essence, you are controlling for a third variable or partialling out a third variable. This revises the value of your correlation coefficient to take into account third variables.

Table 17.1	A correlation matrix involving three variables		
	Variable X Numerical score	Variable Y Verbal score	Variable C Age in years
Variable X Numerical score	1.00	0.97	0.80
Variable Y Verbal score	0.97	1.00	0.85
Variable C Age in years	0.80	0.85	1.00

Partial correlation can be applied to your own data if you have the necessary correlations available. However, partial correlation can also be applied to published research without necessarily obtaining the original data itself – so long as the appropriate correlation coefficients are available. All it requires is that the values of the correlations between your two main variables and the possible third variable are known.

A table of correlations between several variables is known as a correlation matrix. Table 17.1 is an example featuring the following three variables: numerical intelligence test score (which we have labelled X in the table), verbal intelligence test score (which we have labelled Y in the table) and age (which we have labelled C in the table) in a sample of 30 teenagers.

Notice that the diagonal from top left to bottom right consists of 1.00 repeated three times. This is because the correlation of numerical score with itself, of verbal score with itself, and of age with itself will always be a perfect relationship ($r = 1.00$) – it has to be, since you are correlating exactly the same numbers together. Also notice that the matrix is symmetrical around the diagonal. This is fairly obvious, since the correlation of the numerical score with the verbal score has to be exactly the same as the correlation of the verbal score with the numerical score.

Remember that we have used the letters X, Y and C for the different columns and rows of the matrix. The C column and C row are the column and row, respectively, for the *control* variable (age in this case).

Box 17.2   Key concepts

Mediator and moderator variables

There is a crucial conceptual distinction in research which has a bearing on our discussion of partialling or controlling for third variables. This is the difference between moderator and mediator variables. This is not a statistical issue, as such, but a key issue in relation to research design and methodology.

A *mediator* variable explains the relationship between two other variables (usually best expressed as the independent and dependent variables). For example, imagine that there is a correlation between using online social

networking sites (independent variable) and happiness (dependent variable) such that those using online social networking sites are happier. Although this relationship would be interesting, we do not know the processes which create the relationship. So we might imagine another variable, extensiveness of social network, which might be influenced by using social networking sites and might lead to greater happiness. The variable, extensiveness of social network, can be described as a mediator variable, since it mediates the relationship between using online social networking sites and happiness. The way that we have described this implies a causal relationship. That is, basically, greater use of social networking sites (independent variable) influences social networking (the mediator variable) which then influences happiness (the dependent variable).

A *moderator* variable is something quite different. It is a variable which reveals that the relationship between the independent and dependent variables is not consistent throughout the data. Imagine that the researcher is investigating the relationship between income (independent variable) and happiness (the dependent variable). However, this time the researcher is interested in whether the genders differ in terms of the size of the relationship. Imagine that for men the correlation between income and happiness is 0.6 but that for women the correlation is only 0.0. This implies quite different conclusions for men and

for women. In one case there is quite a substantial correlation and in the other case no correlation. In other words, gender moderates the relationship between income and happiness. A moderator variable does not explain the relationship. We would have to consider further the explanation of why the relationship is different in women and men. It could be, for example, that women's social networks are more influenced by having children and so mixing with other women with children than men's. Perhaps men's social networks are more affected by having the money to go to the pub, the golf club or the yacht club, for instance. This, of course, is to begin to ask why gender moderates the relationship between income and happiness – notice that we are hinting at possible mediating variables. Moderator variables, in themselves, are not directly about establishing causal relationships, so randomisation is not an issue for the research design.

17.3 The calculation

The calculation of the partial correlation coefficient is fairly speedy so long as you have a correlation matrix ready-made. Assuming this, the calculation should cause no problems. Computer programs for the partial correlation will normally be capable of calculating the correlation matrix for you, if necessary. Calculation 17.1 works out the relationship between verbal and numerical scores in Table 17.1 controlling for age ($r_{XY.C}$), and Calculation 17.2 examines its statistical significance.

Calculation 17.1

Partial correlation coefficient

The calculation is based on the correlations found in Table 17.1. The formula is as follows:

$$r_{XY.C} = \frac{r_{XY} - (r_{XC} \times r_{YC})}{\sqrt{1 - r_{XC}^2}\sqrt{1 - r_{YC}^2}}$$

where

$r_{XY.C}$ = correlation of verbal and numerical scores with age controlled as denoted by C
r_{XY} = correlation of numerical and verbal scores (= 0.97)
r_{XC} = correlation of numerical scores and age (the control variable) (= 0.80)
r_{YC} = correlation of verbal scores and age (the control variable) (= 0.85).

Using the values taken from the correlation matrix in Table 17.1 we find that

$$r_{XY.C} = \frac{0.97 - (0.80 \times 0.85)}{\sqrt{1 - 0.80^2}\sqrt{1 - 0.85^2}}$$

$$= \frac{0.97 - 0.68}{\sqrt{1 - 0.64}\sqrt{1 - 0.72}}$$

$$= \frac{0.29}{\sqrt{0.36}\sqrt{0.28}} = \frac{0.29}{0.6 \times 0.53} = \frac{0.29}{0.32} = 0.91$$

Thus controlling for age has hardly changed the correlation coefficient – it decreases only very slightly from 0.97 to 0.91.

Interpreting the results A section on interpretation follows. However, when interpreting a partial correlation you need to consider what the unpartialled correlation is. This is the baseline against which the partial correlation is understood. Although usually we would look to see if partialling reduces the size of the correlation, it can increase it.

Reporting the results The following is one way of reporting this analysis: 'Since age was a correlate of both verbal and numerical ability, it was decided to investigate the effect of controlling for age on the correlation. After partialling, the correlation of 0.97 declined slightly to 0.91. However, this change is very small and the correlation remains very significant, so age had little or no effect on the correlation between verbal and numerical abilities.'

Calculation 17.2

Statistical significance of the partial correlation

The calculation of statistical significance for the partial correlation can be carried out simply using tables of the significance of the Pearson correlation coefficient (see Appendix B). However, in order to do this you will need to adjust the sample size by subtracting 3. Thus if the sample size is 10 for the Pearson correlation, it is $10 - 3 = 7$ for the partial correlation coefficient with one variable controlled. So in our example in Table 17.1, which was based on a sample of 30 teenagers, we obtain the 5% significance level from the table in Appendix B by finding the 5% value for a sample size of $30 - 3 = 27$. The minimum value for statistical significance at the 5% level is 0.367 (two-tailed).

Interpreting the results The statistical significance of the partial correlation coefficient is much the same as for the Pearson correlation coefficient on which it is based. A statistically significant finding means that the partial correlation coefficient is unlikely to have been drawn from a population in which the partial correlation is zero.

Reporting the results The statistical significance of the partial correlation may be reported in exactly the same way as for any correlation coefficient. The degrees of freedom are different since they have to be adjusted for the number of control variables. If the sample size for the correlation is 10, then subtract 3 to give seven degrees of freedom if just one variable is being controlled for. In other words, subtract the total number of variables including the two original variables plus all of the control variables. So if there were four control variables in this example, the degrees of freedom become $10 - 2 - 4 = 4$.

17.4   Multiple control variables

It may have struck you that there might be several variables that a researcher might wish to control for at the same time. For example, a researcher might wish to control for age and social class at the same time, or even age, social class and sex. This can be done relatively easily by SPSS.

There are a number of terms that are used which are relatively simple if you know what they mean:

1. *Zero-order correlation* The correlation between your main variables (e.g. r_{XY}).

2. *First-order partial correlation* The correlation between your main variables controlling for just *one* variable (e.g. $r_{XY.C}$).

3. *Second-order partial correlation* The correlation between your main variables controlling for *two* variables at the same time (the symbol for this might be $r_{XY.CD}$).

Not surprisingly, we can extend this quite considerably; for example, a *fifth*-order partial correlation involves *five* control variables at the same time (e.g. $r_{XY.CDEFG}$). The principles remain the same no matter what order of partial correlation you are examining.

17.5   Suppressor variables

Sometimes you might find that you actually obtain a low correlation between two variables which you had expected to correlate quite substantially. In some instances this is because a third variable actually has the effect of reducing or suppressing the correlation between the two main variables. Partial correlation is useful in removing the inhibitory effect of this third variable. In other words, it can sometimes happen that controlling the influence of a third variable results in a *larger* correlation. Indeed, it is possible to find that an initially negative correlation becomes a positive correlation when the influence of a third variable is controlled.

17.6   An example from the research literature

Baron and Straus (1989) took the officially reported crime rates for rapes from most US states and compared these with the circulation figures for soft-core pornography in these areas. The correlation between rape rates and the amounts of pornography over these states was 0.53. (If this confuses you, the correlations are calculated 'pretending' that each state is like a person in calculating the correlation coefficient.) The temptation is to interpret this correlation as suggesting that pornography leads to rape. However, Howitt and Cumberbatch (1990) took issue with this. They pointed out that the proportions of divorced men in these areas also correlated substantially with both pornography circulation rates and rape rates. The data are listed in Table 17.2.

Table 17.2	Correlation between rape, pornography and divorce		
	Variable X **Rape rates**	**Variable Y** **Pornography** **circulation**	**Variable C** **Proportion of** **divorced men**
Variable X: Rape rates	1.00	0.53	0.67
Variable Y: Pornography circulation		1.00	0.59
Variable C: Proportion of divorced men			1.00

It might be the case that rather than pornography causing rape, the apparent relationship between these two variables is merely due to the fact that divorced men are more likely to engage in these 'alternative sexual activities'. It is a simple matter to control for this third variable, as set out in Calculation 17.3.

Calculation 17.3

Partial correlation coefficient for rape and pornography controlling for proportion of divorced men

The formula is

$$r_{XY.C} = \frac{r_{XY} - (r_{XC} \times r_{YC})}{\sqrt{1 - r_{XC}^2}\sqrt{1 - r_{YC}^2}}$$

where

$r_{XY.C}$ = correlation of rape rates with pornography controlling for proportion of divorced men

r_{XY} = correlation of rape and pornography (= 0.53)

r_{XC} = correlation of rape and proportion of divorced men (= 0.67)

r_{YC} = correlation of pornography and proportion of divorced men (= 0.59).

Using the values taken from the correlation matrix in Table 17.2 we find that:

$$r_{XY.C} = \frac{0.53 - (0.67 \times 0.59)}{\sqrt{1 - 0.67^2}\sqrt{1 - 0.59^2}} = 0.22$$

In this case, the correlation when the third variable is taken into account has changed substantially to become much nearer zero. It would be reasonable to suggest that the partial correlation coefficient indicates that there is *no* causal relationship between pornography and rape – quite a dramatic change in interpretation from the claim that pornography causes rape. The argument is not necessarily that the proportion of divorced men directly causes rape and the purchase of pornography. However, since it is an unlikely hypothesis that rape and pornography *cause* divorce, the fact that partialling out divorce reduces greatly the correlation between rape and pornography means that our faith in the original 'causal' link is reduced.

17.7 When to use partial correlation

Partial correlation is built on the assumption that the relationships between the variables in question are linear. That is, if plotted on a scattergram the points are best represented by a straight line. Where the relationships depart from linearity then partial correlation may be misleading. This aside, the partial correlation can be a useful technique for estimating the influence of a third variable on any correlation coefficient.

17.8 When not to use partial correlation

Many techniques in statistics can do a similar job to partial correlation – that is, control for the influences of third variables: for example, analysis of covariance and multiple regression. If you are using these, then it is sensible to partial out influences of third variables using these techniques rather than carry out an additional partial correlation analysis.

17.9 Data requirements for partial correlation

At a minimum, partial correlation requires three score variables, each of which should ideally be normally distributed. There can be any number of third variables partialled at the same time, though it is recommended that the ones to include are carefully planned to be the minimum needed.

17.10 Problems in the use of partial correlation

The main problem when using partial correlation is that some researchers try to make too strong claims about what they can achieve. In particular, it should be understood that partial correlation is not about establishing causality by removing the spurious influence of third variables. They may take away the influence of a variable which may be influencing the relationship between the two key variables, but that does not mean that the remaining partialled correlation is a causal one. There may be any number of other third variables that need to be removed before any confidence can be gained about the relationship being a causal one. It is the research design that enables causality to be assessed (such as randomised experiments) and not the statistical analysis.

17.11 SPSS analysis

■ The data to be analysed

Table 17.3 is the data to be analysed. The basic data consist of two variables – one is scores on a measure of numerical intelligence and the other variable is scores on a measure of verbal intelligence. Partial correlation tells us what the correlation between verbal intelligence and numerical intelligence would be *if* their associations with age were removed.

Table 17.3	Numerical and verbal intelligence test scores and age		
Numerical scores	**Verbal scores**	**Age**	
90	90	13	
100	95	15	
95	95	15	
105	105	16	
100	100	17	

■ Partial correlation

Step 1

In 'Variable View' of the 'Data Editor' name the three variables 'Num_IQ', 'Verb_IQ' and 'Age'.
Remove the two decimal places by setting the number to 0.

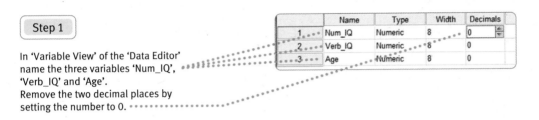

Step 2

In 'Data View' of the 'Data Editor' enter the numerical IQ scores in the first column, the verbal scores in the second column and age in the third column.

Step 3

Select 'Analyze'
→ 'Correlate'
→ 'Partial...'.

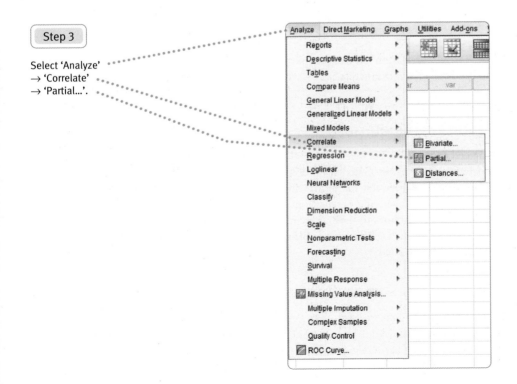

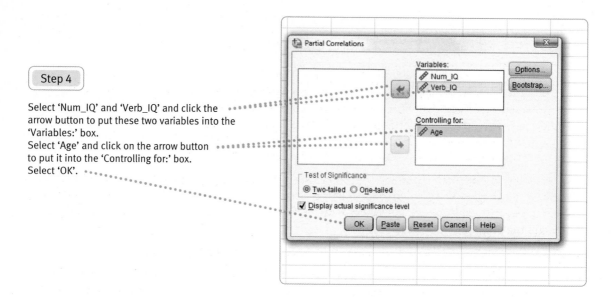

Step 4

Select 'Num_IQ' and 'Verb_IQ' and click the arrow button to put these two variables into the 'Variables:' box.
Select 'Age' and click on the arrow button to put it into the 'Controlling for:' box.
Select 'OK'.

■ Interpreting the output

Correlations

Control Variables			Num_IQ	Verb_IQ
Age	Num_IQ	Correlation	1.000	.776
		Significance (2-tailed)	.	.224
		df	0	2
	Verb_IQ	Correlation	.776	1.000
		Significance (2-tailed)	.224	.
		df	2	0

The partial correlation between numerical and verbal IQ controlling for age is 0.776. The two-tailed significance is 0.224 which is not significant. There are two degrees of freedom.

■ Reporting the output

We need to mention the original correlation between numerical and verbal intelligence, which is 0.912 (from Calculation 17.1). So we could report the results as follows: 'The correlation between numerical and verbal intelligence is 0.92 ($df = 3$, two-tailed $p = 0.025$). However, the correlation between numerical and verbal intelligence controlling for age declines to 0.78, which is not significant (two-tailed $p = 0.224$). In other words, there is no significant relationship between numerical and verbal intelligence when age is controlled.'

Key points

- If you are doing a *field* rather than a laboratory project, check your research hypotheses. If they appear to suggest that one variable *causes* another then consider using partial correlation. It can potentially enhance one's confidence about making causal interpretations if a significant correlation remains after partialling. However, caution should still be applied, since there always remains a risk that an additional variable suppresses the relationship between your two main variables.

- Do not forget that even after partialling out third variables, any causal interpretation of the correlation coefficient remaining has to be tentative. No correlation coefficient (including partial correlation coefficients) can establish causality in itself. You establish causality largely through your research design, not the statistics you apply.

- Do not overlook the possibility that you may need to control more than one variable.

- Do not assume that partial correlation has no role except in seeking causal relationships. Sometimes, for example, the researcher might wish to control for male–female influences on a correlation without wishing to establish causality. Partial correlation will reveal the strength of a non-causal relationship having controlled for a third variable. Causality is something the researcher considers; it is not something built into a correlation coefficient as such.

- Do not forget to test the statistical significance of the partial correlation – as shown above, it is very easy.

CHAPTER 18

Factor analysis

Simplifying complex data

Overview

- Factor analysis is used largely when the researcher has substantial numbers of variables seemingly measuring similar things. It has proven particularly useful with questionnaires.

- Factor analysis reduces data involving a number of variables (factors) down to a smaller number of factors which encompass the original variables.

- Factors are simply variables.

- The correlations of factors with the original variables are known as factor loadings, although they are merely correlation coefficients. Hence they range from −1.0 through 0.0 to +1.0. It is usual to identify the nature of each factor by examining the original variables which correlate highly with it. Normally each factor is identified by a meaningful name.

- Because the process is one of reducing the original variables down to the smallest number of factors, it is important not to have too many factors. The scree plot may be used to identify those factors which are likely to be significantly different from a chance factor.

- Factors are mathematically defined to have the maximum sum of squared factor loadings at every stage. They may be more easily interpreted if they are rotated. This maximises the numbers of large factor loadings and small factor loadings while minimising the number of moderate factor loadings, making interpretation easier.

- Factor scores provide a way of treating factors like any other variable. They are similar to standard or z-scores in that they have symmetrical numbers of positive and negative values and their mean is 0.00. They can be used to compare groups in terms of their mean factor scores.

Preparation

Review variance (Chapter 3), correlation coefficient (Chapter 7) and correlation matrix (Chapter 17).

18.1   Introduction

Researchers frequently collect large amounts of data. With data on so many variables, it becomes difficult to make sense of the complexity of the data. With questionnaires, one naturally seeks patterns in the correlations between questions. However, the sheer number of interrelationships makes this hard. Take the following brief questionnaire:

Item 1: Mediums can talk to the dead.

| Agree strongly | Agree | Neither | Disagree | Disagree strongly |

Item 2: I have had 'out of body' experiences.

| Agree strongly | Agree | Neither | Disagree | Disagree strongly |

Item 3: Satanism is a true religion.

| Agree strongly | Agree | Neither | Disagree | Disagree strongly |

Item 4: I believe in ghosts.

| Agree strongly | Agree | Neither | Disagree | Disagree strongly |

Item 5: Speaking in tongues is a peak religious experience.

| Agree strongly | Agree | Neither | Disagree | Disagree strongly |

Item 6: Karma is a real phenomenon.

| Agree strongly | Agree | Neither | Disagree | Disagree strongly |

Item 7: Most people are reincarnated.

| Agree strongly | Agree | Neither | Disagree | Disagree strongly |

Item 8: Astrology is a science, not an art.

| Agree strongly | Agree | Neither | Disagree | Disagree strongly |

Item 9: Animals have souls.

| Agree strongly | Agree | Neither | Disagree | Disagree strongly |

Item 10: I believe in miracles.

| Agree strongly | Agree | Neither | Disagree | Disagree strongly |

Agree strongly could be scored as 1, agree scored as 2, neither as 3, disagree as 4 and disagree strongly as 5. This turns the words into numerical scores. Correlating the answers to each of these 10 questions with each of the others for 300 respondents generates a large correlation matrix (a table of all possible correlations between all of the possible pairs of questions). Ten questions will produce 10^2 or 100 correlations. Although the correlation matrix is symmetrical about the diagonal from top left to bottom right, there remain 45 *different* correlations to examine. Such a matrix might be much like the one in Table 18.1.

Factor analysis can be beneficial. It is a technique which helps you overcome the complexity of correlation matrices. In essence, it takes a matrix of correlations and generates a much smaller set of 'supervariables' which characterise the main trends in

Table 18.1	Correlation matrix of 10 Items								
	Item 1	**Item 2**	**Item 3**	**Item 4**	**Item 5**	**Item 6**	**Item 7**	**Item 8**	**Item 9**	**Item 10**
Item 1	1.00`	0.50	0.72	0.30	0.32	0.20	0.70	0.30	0.30	0.10
Item 2	0.50	1.00	0.40	0.51	0.60	0.14	0.17	0.55	0.23	0.55
Item 3	0.72	0.40	1.00	0.55	0.64	0.23	0.12	0.17	0.22	0.67
Item 4	0.30	0.51	0.55	1.00	0.84	0.69	0.47	0.44	0.56	0.35
Item 5	0.32	0.60	0.64	0.84	1.00	0.14	0.77	0.65	0.48	0.34
Item 6	0.20	0.14	0.23	0.69	0.14	1.00	0.58	0.72	0.33	0.17
Item 7	0.70	0.17	0.12	0.47	0.77	0.58	1.00	0.64	0.43	0.76
Item 8	0.30	0.55	0.17	0.44	0.65	0.72	0.64	1.00	0.27	0.43
Item 9	0.30	0.23	0.22	0.56	0.48	0.33	0.43	0.27	1.00	0.12
Item 10	0.10	0.55	0.67	0.35	0.34	0.17	0.76	0.43	0.12	1.00

the correlation matrix. These supervariables or factors are generally much easier to understand than the original matrix.

18.2 Data issues in factor analysis

One crucial question is what sample size is appropriate for a factor analysis? There is no simple answer to this. Recommendations can vary from 100 to 1000 participants. However, students rarely have the opportunity to collect data from this sort of number of participants. Does this mean that they should never carry out a factor analysis?

The simple advice is to have as big a sample size as possible – the more variables, the bigger the sample size should be. Your work is almost certain to be acceptable to most researchers if it is based on 300 or more participants. The smaller your sample size is below this, the more your work is likely to be criticised by someone.

So what should one do in circumstances where this conventional criterion cannot be met? One thing to remember is that none of the sample size criteria has a real empirical justification. So, there are circumstances in which one might be justified carrying out a factor analysis on a smaller sample size – for example, the more exploratory your study is the more you are likely to be simply trying to find interesting aspects of your data for future further exploration. Of course, one should acknowledge the limitations of your factor analysis because of the small sample size. But we would also suggest that you consider the following:

1. It is bad practice to simply throw a bunch of variables into a factor analysis. The axiom 'junk in, junk out' applies here. Be selective about which variables you put into a factor analysis. Probably you could do a factor analysis on most of your data in the sense that a computer will perform a calculation. But what is the point of this? It is better to confine yourself to variables which you feel are likely to measure a particular concept which you think important as well. As soon as you begin to be selective, the smaller the number of variables you put into the factor analysis, the less will small sample size be a problem.

2. If you have a small sample size, then be especially vigilant when you carry out your basic examination of your data using descriptive statistics. For example, consider discarding from the factor analysis variables that have little variability; variables that produce the same response from the vast majority of participants because, for example, they are rarely agreed with; variables for which many of your participants fail to give an answer; and variables that participants have difficulty understanding. In other words, get rid of variables which are in some way problematic as they contribute junk (error) to your data. You would be well advised to do this anyway for any data.

3. The bigger the typical correlation there is between your variables, the more likely is it that your factor analysis will be reliable (stable across studies) so the more acceptable would be a smaller sample size. Similarly, the bigger the communality estimates, the smaller the sample size can be.

4. The more variables you have for each factor you extract, the more stable your analysis is likely to be. In other words, if you have only one or two factors rather than 10 factors then the more reliable your factor analysis will be.

The minimum sample size issue tends to be most strongly expressed in relation to factor analysis. Other statistical techniques tend not to be subject to the same stringency. It is important to bear in mind the sample size issue, since you need to be able to estimate roughly the confidence you can place in your analysis.

18.3 Concepts in factor analysis

In order to understand factor analysis, it is useful to start with a simple and highly stylised correlation matrix such as the one in Table 18.2.

You can probably detect that there are *two* distinct clusters of variables. Variables *A*, *C* and *E* all tend to correlate with each other pretty well. Similarly, variables *B*, *D* and *F* all tend to correlate with each other. Notice that the members of the first cluster (*A*, *C*, *E*) do not correlate well with members of the second cluster (*B*, *D*, *F*) – they would not be very distinct clusters if they did. In order to make the clusters more meaningful, we need to decide what variables contributing to the first cluster (*A*, *C*, *E*) have in common; next we need to explore the similarities of the variables in the second cluster (*B*, *D*, *F*). Calling the variables by arbitrary letters does not help us very much. But what if we add a little detail by identifying the variables more clearly and relabelling the matrix of correlations as in Table 18.3?

Table 18.2	Stylised correlation matrix between variables A to F					
	Variable A	**Variable B**	**Variable C**	**Variable D**	**Variable E**	**Variable F**
Variable A	1.00	0.00	0.91	−0.05	0.96	0.10
Variable B	0.00	1.00	0.08	0.88	0.02	0.80
Variable C	0.91	0.08	1.00	−0.01	0.90	0.29
Variable D	−0.05	0.88	−0.01	1.00	−0.08	0.79
Variable E	0.96	0.02	0.90	−0.08	1.00	0.11
Variable F	0.10	0.80	0.29	0.79	0.11	1.00

Table 18.3	Stylised correlation matrix with variable names added					
	Chess	**Crosswords**	**Darts**	**Scrabble**	**Juggling**	**Sudoku**
Chess	1.00	0.00	0.91	−0.05	0.96	0.10
Crosswords	0.00	1.00	0.08	0.88	0.02	0.80
Darts	0.91	0.08	1.00	−0.01	0.90	0.29
Scrabble	−0.05	0.88	−0.01	1.00	−0.08	0.79
Juggling	0.96	0.02	0.90	−0.08	1.00	0.11
Sudoku	0.10	0.80	0.29	0.79	0.11	1.00

Interpretation of the clusters is now possible. Drawing the clusters from the table we find:

First cluster
variable A = skill at chess
variable C = skill at throwing darts
variable E = skill at juggling

Second cluster
variable B = skill at doing crosswords
variable D = skill at doing the word game Scrabble
variable F = skill at Sudoku

Once this 'fleshing out of the bones' has been done, the meaning of each cluster is somewhat more apparent. The first cluster seems to involve a general skill in the area of spatial awareness; the second cluster seems to involve verbal skill.

This sort of interpretation is easy enough in clear-cut cases like this and with small correlation matrices. Life and statistics, however, are rarely that simple. Remember that in Chapter 17 on partial correlation we found that a zero correlation between two variables may become a large positive or negative correlation when we take away the influence of a third variable or a suppressor variable which is hiding the true relationship between two main variables. Factor analysis enables us to handle such complexities which would be next to impossible by just inspecting a correlation matrix. The *output* from a factor analysis based on the correlation matrix presented above might look rather like the one in Table 18.4.

Table 18.4	Factor loading matrix	
Variable	**Factor 1**	**Factor 2**
Skill at chess	0.98	−0.01
Skill at crosswords	0.01	0.93
Skill at darts	0.94	0.10
Skill at Scrabble	−0.07	0.94
Skill at juggling	0.97	−0.01
Skill at Sudoku	0.15	0.86

What does this table mean? There are two things to understand:

1. Factor 1 and Factor 2 are like the clusters of variables we have seen above. They are really variables but we are calling them supervariables because they take a large number of other variables into account. Ideally there should only be a small number of factors to consider.

2. The numbers under the columns for factor 1 and factor 2 are called *factor loadings*. Really they are nothing other than correlation coefficients recycled with a different name. So the variable 'skill at chess' correlates 0.98 with the supervariable which is factor 1. 'Skill at chess' does not correlate at all well with the supervariable which is factor 2 (the correlation is nearly zero at −0.01). Factor loadings follow all of the rules for correlation coefficients so they vary from −1.00 through 0.00 to +1.00.

We interpret the meaning of factor 1 in much the same way as we interpreted the clusters above. We find the variables which correlate best with the supervariable or factor in question by looking at the factor loadings for each of the factors in turn. Usually you will hear phrases like 'chess, darts and juggling load highly on factor 1'. All this means is that they correlate highly with the supervariable, factor 1. Since we find that chess, darts and juggling all correlate well with factor 1, they must define the factor. We try to see what chess, darts and juggling have in common – once again we would suggest that spatial awareness is the common element. We might call the factor spatial awareness. Obviously there is a subjective element in this, since not everyone would interpret the factors identically.

In order to interpret the meaning of a factor we need to decide which items are the most useful in identifying what the factor is about. While every variable may have something to contribute, those with the highest loadings on a factor probably have the most to contribute to its interpretation. So where does one draw the line between useful and not so useful factor loadings? Generally speaking, you will not go far wrong if you take factor loadings with an absolute value of 0.50 and above as being important in assessing the meaning of the factor. Now this is a rule of thumb and with a very big sample size smaller factor loadings may be taken into account. With a very small sample size, the critical size of the loading might be increased to 0.60.

When you have identified the highly loading items on the factor, write them out as a group on a piece of paper. Then peruse these items over and over again until you are able to suggest what these items seem to have in common or what it is they represent. There are no rules for doing this and, of course, different researchers may well come up with different interpretations of exactly the same list of items. This is not a problem any more than it is whenever we try to label any sort of concept.

18.4   Decisions, decisions, decisions

However, there are five issues that should be raised as they underlie the choices to be made.

■ 1. Rotated or unrotated factors?

The most basic sort of factor analysis is the principal components method. It is a mathematically based technique which has the following characteristics:

1. The factors are extracted in order of magnitude from the largest to the smallest in terms of the amount of variance explained by the factor. Since factors are variables they will have a certain amount of variance associated with them.

2. Each of the factors explains the *maximum amount* of variance that it possibly can.

The amount of variance 'explained' by a factor is related to something called the *eigenvalue*. This is easy to calculate since it is merely the *sum* of the *squared* factor loadings of a particular factor. Thus the eigenvalue of a factor for which the factor loadings are 0.86, 0.00, 0.93, 0.00, 0.91 and 0.00 is $0.86^2 + 0.00^2 + 0.93^2 + 0.00^2 + 0.91^2 + 0.00^2$ which equals 2.4.

But maximising each successive eigenvalue or amount of variance is a purely mathematical choice which may not offer the best factors for the purposes of understanding the conceptual underlying structure of a correlation matrix. For this reason, a number of different criteria have been suggested to determine the 'best' factors. Usually these involve maximising the number of high factor loadings on a factor and minimising the number of low loadings (much as in our stylised example). This is not a simple process because a factor analysis generates several factors – adjustments to one factor can adversely affect the satisfactoriness of the other factors. This process is called *rotation* because in pre-computer days it involved rotating the axes on a series of scattergrams until a satisfactory factor structure was obtained. Nowadays we do not use graphs to obtain this simple structure but procedures such as Varimax do this for us. Principal components are the unadjusted factors which explain the greatest amounts of variance but are not always particularly easy to interpret.

These are quite abstract ideas and you may still feel a little confused as to which to use. Experimentation by statisticians suggests that the rotated factors tend to reveal underlying structures a little better than unrotated ones. We would recommend that you use rotated factors until you find a good reason not to.

■ 2. Orthogonal or oblique rotation?

Routinely researchers will use *orthogonal rotations* rather than *oblique rotations*.

1. Orthogonal rotation simply means that none of the factors or supervariables are actually allowed to correlate with each other. This mathematical requirement is built into the computational procedures.

2. Oblique rotation means that the factors or supervariables are allowed to correlate with each other (although they can end up uncorrelated) if this helps to simplify the interpretation of the factors. Computer procedures such as Promax and Oblimin produce correlated or oblique factors.

Since the oblique factors are supervariables which correlate with each other, it is possible to produce a correlation matrix of the correlations between factors. This matrix can then be factor-analysed to produce new factors. Since second-order factors are 'factors of factors' they are very general indeed. You cannot get second-order factors from uncorrelated factors since the correlation matrix would contain only zeros. Some of the controversy among factor analysts is related to the use of such second-order factors.

■ 3. How many factors?

We may have misled you into thinking that factor analysis reduces the number of variables that you have to consider. It can, but not automatically so, because in fact without some intervention on your part you could have as many factors as variables you started off with. This would not be very useful as it means that your factor matrix is as complex as your correlation matrix. Furthermore, it is difficult to interpret all of the factors, since the later ones tend to be junk and consist of nothing other than error variance.

You need to limit the number of factors to those which are 'statistically significant'. There are no commonly available and universally accepted tests of the significance of a factor. However, one commonly accepted procedure is to ignore any factor for which the eigenvalue is less than 1.00. The reason for this is that a factor with an eigenvalue of less than 1.00 is not receiving its 'fair share' of variance by chance. What this means is that a factor with an eigenvalue under 1.00 cannot possibly be statistically significant – although this does not mean that those with an eigenvalue greater than 1.00 are actually statistically significant. For most purposes it is a good enough criterion, although skilled statisticians might have other views.

Another procedure is the *scree test*. This is simply a graph of the amount of variance explained by successive factors in the factor analysis. The point at which the curve flattens out indicates the start of the non-significant factors. Getting the number of factors right matters most of all when one is going to rotate the factors to a simpler structure. If you have too many factors the variance tends to be shared very thinly.

■ 4. Communality

Although up to this point we have said that the diagonal of a correlation matrix from top left to bottom right will consist of ones, an exception is usually made in factor analysis. The reason for this is quite simple if you compare the two correlation matrices in Tables 18.5 and 18.6.

You will notice that matrix 1 contains substantially higher correlation coefficients than matrix 2. Consequently the ones in the diagonal of matrix 2 contribute a disproportionately large amount of variance to the matrix compared to the equivalent ones in matrix 1 (where the rest of the correlations are quite large anyway). The factors obtained from matrix 2 would largely be devoted to variance coming from the diagonal. In other words, the factors would have to correspond more or less to variables *A*, *B* and *C*–hardly a satisfactory simplification of the correlation matrix. Since most data in the social sciences tend to produce low correlations, we need to do something about the problem. The difficulty is obviously greatest when the intercorrelations between the variables tend to be small than where the intercorrelations tend to be large. This is simply because the value in the diagonal is disproportionately larger than the correlations.

The solution usually adopted is to substitute different values in the diagonal of the correlation matrix in place of the ones seen in Tables 18.5 and 18.6. These replacement

Table 18.5	Correlation matrix 1		
	Variable *A*	Variable *B*	Variable *C*
Variable *A*	1.00	0.50	0.40
Variable *B*	0.50	1.00	0.70
Variable *C*	0.40	0.70	1.00

Table 18.6	Correlation matrix 2		
	Variable *A*	Variable *B*	Variable *C*
Variable *A*	1.00	0.12	0.20
Variable *B*	0.12	1.00	0.30
Variable *C*	0.20	0.30	1.00

values are called the *communalities*. Theoretically, a variable can be thought of as being made of three different types of variance:

1. *Specific variance* Variance which can only be measured by that variable and is specific to that variable.

2. *Common variance* Variance which a particular variable has in common with other variables.

3. *Error variance* Just completely random variance which is not systematically related to any other source of variance.

A correlation of any variable with itself is exceptional in that it consists of all of these types of variance (that is why the correlation of a variable with itself is 1.00), whereas a correlation between two different variables consists only of variance that is common to the two variables (common variance).

Communality is in essence the correlation that a variable would have with itself based solely on common variance. Of course, this is a curious abstract concept. Obviously it is not possible to know the value of this correlation directly, since variables do not come readily broken down into the three different types of variance. All that we can do is estimate the communality as best we can. The highest correlation that a variable has with any other variable in a correlation matrix is used as the communality. This is shown in Table 18.7.

So if we want to know the communality of variable *A* we look to see what its highest correlation with anything else is (in this case it is the 0.50 correlation with variable *B*). Similarly we estimate the communality of variable *B* as 0.70 since this is its highest correlation with any other variable in the matrix. Likewise the communality of variable *C* is also 0.70 since this is its highest correlation in the matrix with another variable. We then substitute these communalities in the diagonal of the matrix as shown in Table 18.8.

These first estimates can be a little rough and ready. Normally in factor analysis, following an initial stab using methods like this, better approximations are made by using the 'significant' factor loading matrix in order to 'reconstruct' the correlation

Table 18.7	Correlation matrix 1 (communality italicised in each column)		
	Variable A	**Variable B**	**Variable C**
Variable A	1.00	0.50	0.40
Variable B	*0.50*	1.00	*0.70*
Variable C	0.40	*0.70*	1.00

Table 18.8	Correlation matrix 1 but using communality estimates in the diagonal		
	Variable A	**Variable B**	**Variable C**
Variable A	0.50	0.50	0.40
Variable B	0.50	0.70	0.70
Variable C	0.40	0.70	0.70

Table 18.9	Part of a factor loading matrix	
	Factor 1	**Factor 2**
Variable *A*	0.50	0.70
Variable *B*	0.40	0.30

matrix. For any pair of variables, the computer multiplies their two loadings on each factor, then sums the total. Thus if part of the factor loading matrix was as shown in Table 18.9, the correlation between variables *A* and *B* is $(0.50 \times 0.40) + (0.70 \times 0.30) = 0.20 + 0.21 = 0.41$. This is not normally the correlation between variables *A* and *B* found in the original data but one based on the previously estimated communality and the significant factors. However, following such a procedure for the entire correlation matrix does provide a slightly different value for each communality compared with our original estimate. These new communality estimates can be used as part of the factor analysis. The whole process can be repeated over and over again until the best possible estimate is achieved. This is usually referred to as a process of *iteration* – successive approximations to give the best estimate.

Actually, as a beginner to factor analysis you should not worry too much about most of these things for the simple reason that you could adopt an off-the-peg package for factor analysis which, while not satisfying every researcher, will do the job pretty well until you get a little experience and greater sophistication.

■ 5. Factor scores

We often carry out a factor analysis to determine whether we can group a larger number of variables such as questionnaire items into a smaller set of 'supervariables' or factors. For example, we may have made up 10 questions to measure the way in which people express anxiety and a further 10 questions to assess how they exhibit depression. Suppose that the results of our factor analysis show that all or almost all of the 10 questions on anxiety load most highly on one of these factors and all or almost all of the 10 questions on depression load most highly on the other factor. This result would suggest that rather than analyse each of the 20 questions separately we could combine the answers to the 10 questions on anxiety to form one measure of anxiety and combine the answers to the 10 questions on depression to form a measure of depression. In other words, rather than have 20 different measures to analyse, we now have two measures. This simplifies our analysis.

The most common way of combining variables which are measured on the same scale is to simply add together the numbers which represent that scale. This is sometimes referred to as a summative scale. For example, if respondents only had to answer 'Yes' or 'No' to each of our 20 questions, then we could assign an answer which indicated the presence of either anxiety or depression a higher number than an answer which reflected the absence of either anxiety or depression. We could assign the number 2 to show the presence of either anxiety or depression and the number 1 to show the absence of either anxiety or depression. Alternatively, we could assign the number 1 to indicate the presence of either anxiety or depression and the number 0 to the absence of either. We would then add together the numbers for the anxiety items to form a total or overall anxiety score and do the same for the depression items. If we had assigned the number 2 to indicate the presence of either anxiety or depression, then the total score for these two variables would vary between a minimum score of 10 and a maximum score of 20. Alternatively, if we had assigned the number 1 to reflect the presence of either anxiety or depression, then the total score for these two variables would vary between a minimum score of 0 and a maximum score of 10.

Another way of assigning numbers to each of the variables or items that go to make up a factor is to use the factor score for each factor. There are various ways of producing factor scores and this is generally done with the computer program which carries out the factor analysis. A factor score may be based on all the items in the factor analysis. The items which load or correlate most highly on a factor are generally weighted the most heavily. So, for example, anxiety items which load or correlate most highly with the anxiety factor will make a larger contribution to the factor score for that factor. Factor scores may be positive or negative but will have a mean of zero. The main advantage of factor scores is that they are more closely related to the results of the factor analysis. In other words, scores represent these factors more accurately. Their disadvantage is that the results of a factor analysis of the same variables are likely to vary according to the method used and from sample to sample so that the way that the factor scores are derived is likely to vary. Unless we have access to the data, we will not know how the factor scores were calculated.

One key thing to remember about factor scores is that they allow you to use the factors as if they were like any other variable. So they can be correlated with other variables, for example, or they might be used as the dependent variable in ANOVA.

18.5 When to use factor analysis

Factor analysis can be used whenever you have a set of score variables (or it can be used with binary (yes–no) variables). It identifies patterns in the correlations between these variables. However, it is not desirable to put every variable that meets these criteria into your factor analysis, since the output will be somewhat meaningless. It is better to confine your factor analysis to a set of variables that is relatively coherent in the first place. So if you have a number of items intended to measure 'strength of religious feeling', say, then do not throw into the analysis other variables such as gender, age and number of marathons run in a year, as what you get may not make too much sense at all. But this would be advice that should generally be applied to statistical analysis: aim to have a coherent set of data that addresses the questions that you are interested in; avoid simply collecting data because you can; and avoid statistically analysing data simply because it is there.

18.6 When not to use factor analysis

Factor analysis merely identifies patterns in data and is not, for example, a test of significance. Neither does it have independent and dependent variables. So if either of these is in your mind then you do not need factor analysis. Also it makes little sense to carry out a factor analysis if one has less than a handful of variables. So it is unlikely that you would wish to do a factor analysis where you had say five or fewer variables.

18.7   Data requirements for factor analysis

There is some controversy about the number of participants required for a study using factor analysis. The suggestions vary widely according to different sources. Generally speaking, you would not carry out a factor analysis with fewer than about 50 participants. For student work a smaller sample than this would be common and in this context probably acceptable as part of learning and assessment. However, one also finds suggestions that for a factor analysis to be stable one should have a minimum of about 10 participants per variable. Sometimes the figure given is greater than this. Basically, the more participants the better, though factor analysis may be illuminating even if one is at the lower end of acceptable numbers of participants.

18.8   Problems in the use of factor analysis

Our experience is that beginners have the greatest difficult with the least statistical of the aspects of factor analysis – that is, the interpretation of factors. Partly this is because many statistical techniques seem to require little special input from the user but factor analysis requires some inductive reasoning and is not merely a rule-following task. However, the task is really relatively straightforward since it merely involves explaining why a number of variables should be closely related. Usually, and this is a rule-of-thumb, we recommend that the variables that have a factor loading of about 0.5 on a particular factor should be considered when trying to name the factor. Of course, –0.5 and bigger negative values also count.

Factor analysis is a somewhat abstract procedure, so it can take a little while to grasp the core ideas. But persevere, since it is the first step towards a variety of procedures that help you explore complex data rather than simply test significance.

18.9   SPSS analysis

■ The data to be analysed

The computation of a principal components analysis is illustrated with the data in Table 18.10, which consist of scores on six variables for nine individuals. This is only for illustrative purposes; it would be considered a ludicrously small number of cases to perform a factor analysis on. Normally, you should think of having at least two or three times as many cases as you have variables.

■ Principal component analysis with orthogonal rotation

Step 1

In 'Variable View' of the 'Data Editor' name the six variables 'Chess', 'Crosswords' and so on. Remove the two decimal places by setting number to 0.

	Name	Type	Width	Decimals
1	Chess	Numeric	8	0
2	Crosswords	Numeric	8	0
3	Darts	Numeric	8	0
4	Scrabble	Numeric	8	0
5	Juggling	Numeric	8	0
6	Sudoku	Numeric	8	0

Table 18.10	Scores of nine individuals on six variables					
Individual	Chess	Crosswords	Darts	Scrabble	Juggling	Sudoku
1	10	15	8	26	15	8
2	6	16	5	25	12	9
3	2	11	1	22	7	6
4	5	16	3	28	11	9
5	7	15	4	24	12	7
6	8	13	4	23	14	6
7	6	17	3	29	10	9
8	2	18	1	28	8	8
9	5	14	2	25	10	6

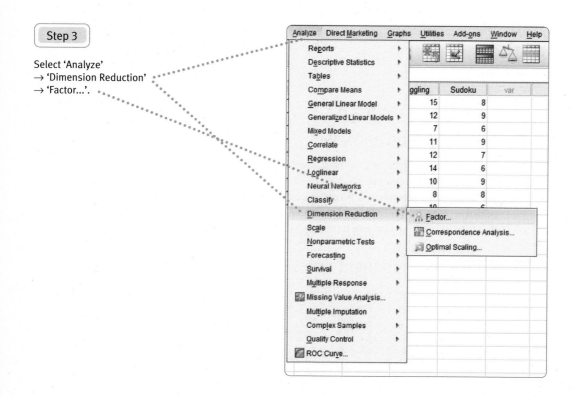

Step 2

In 'Data View' of the 'Data Editor' enter the values.

	Chess	Crosswords	Darts	Scrabble	Juggling	Sudoku
1	10	15	8	26	15	8
2	6	16	5	25	12	9
3	2	11	1	22	7	6
4	5	16	3	28	11	9
5	7	15	4	24	12	7
6	8	13	4	23	14	6
7	6	17	3	29	10	9
8	2	18	1	28	8	8
9	5	14	2	25	10	6

Step 3

Select 'Analyze'
→ 'Dimension Reduction'
→ 'Factor...'.

Analyze   Direct Marketing   Graphs   Utilities   Add-ons   Window   Help

- Reports ▸
- Descriptive Statistics ▸
- Tables ▸
- Compare Means ▸
- General Linear Model ▸
- Generalized Linear Models ▸
- Mixed Models ▸
- Correlate ▸
- Regression ▸
- Loglinear ▸
- Neural Networks ▸
- Classify ▸
- Dimension Reduction ▸
- Scale ▸
- Nonparametric Tests ▸
- Forecasting ▸
- Survival ▸
- Multiple Response ▸
- Missing Value Analysis...
- Multiple Imputation ▸
- Complex Samples ▸
- Quality Control ▸
- ROC Curve...

Dimension Reduction ▸
- Factor...
- Correspondence Analysis...
- Optimal Scaling...

ggling	Sudoku	var
15	8	
12	9	
7	6	
11	9	
12	7	
14	6	
10	9	
8	8	

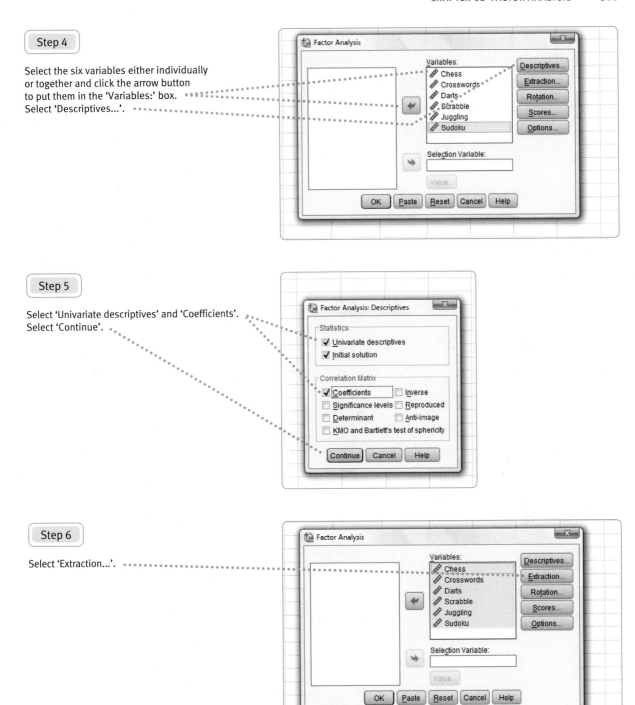

Step 4

Select the six variables either individually or together and click the arrow button to put them in the 'Variables:' box. Select 'Descriptives...'.

Step 5

Select 'Univariate descriptives' and 'Coefficients'. Select 'Continue'.

Step 6

Select 'Extraction...'.

Step 7

Select 'Scree Plot'.
Select 'Continue'.

Step 8

Select 'Rotation...'.

Step 9

Select 'Varimax'.
Select 'Continue'.

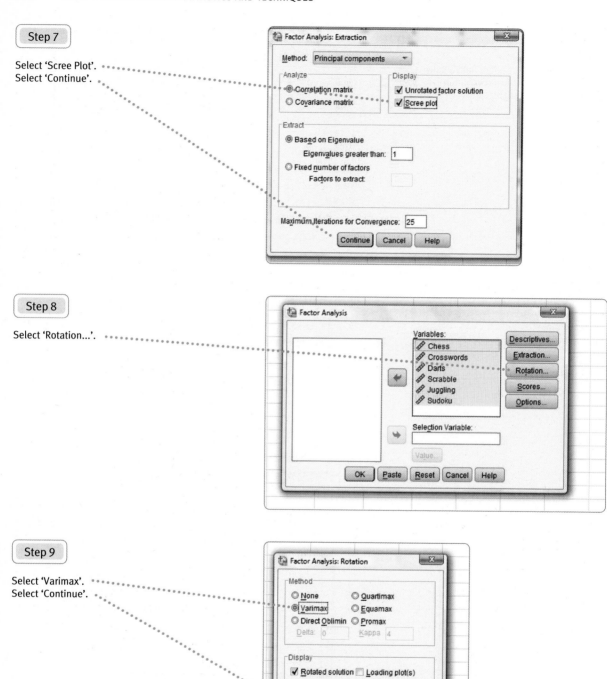

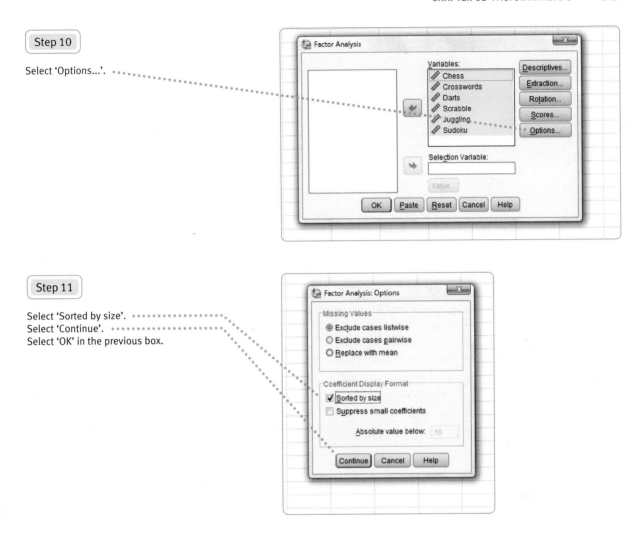

Step 10

Select 'Options...'.

Step 11

Select 'Sorted by size'.
Select 'Continue'.
Select 'OK' in the previous box.

■ Interpreting the output

- The first table gives the mean, standard deviation and number of cases for each variable. N shows the number of cases on which your analysis is based. This information is essential, particularly if you have missing data.

Descriptive Statistics

	Mean	Std. Deviation	Analysis N
Chess	5.67	2.598	9
Crosswords	15.00	2.121	9
Darts	3.44	2.186	9
Scrabble	25.56	2.404	9
Juggling	11.00	2.598	9
Sudoku	7.56	1.333	9

- The second table presents the correlation matrix. From this it appears that there are two groups of variables that are strongly intercorrelated. One consists of chess, juggling and darts, and the other of crosswords, Scrabble and Sudoku. These have been indicated – but remember that as a correlation matrix is symmetrical only the lower half below the diagonal has been marked. Normally in factor analysis the correlation matrix is much more difficult to decipher than this. Our data are highly stylised.

Correlation Matrix

		Chess	Crosswords	Darts	Scrabble	Juggling	Sudoku
Correlation	Chess	1.000	.000	.910	-.047	.963	.096
	Crosswords	.000	1.000	.081	.883	.023	.795
	Darts	.910	.081	1.000	-.005	.902	.291
	Scrabble	-.047	.883	-.005	1.000	-.080	.789
	Juggling	.963	.023	.902	-.080	1.000	.108
	Sudoku	.096	.795	.291	.789	.108	1.000

- The largest correlations are presented in green for the first group of variables and in yellow for the second group. Because factor analysis usually involves a lot of variables and there is a limit to what can be got onto a computer screen, normally the correlation matrix is difficult to see in its entirety.

- The third table shows that two principal components were initially extracted in this case. The computer ignores factors with an eigenvalue of less than 1.00. This is because such factors consist of uninterpretable error variation. Of course, your analysis may have even more (or fewer) factors.

Total Variance Explained

Component	Initial Eigenvalues			Extraction Sums of Squared Loadings			Rotation Sums of Squared Loadings		
	Total	% of Variance	Cumulative %	Total	% of Variance	Cumulative %	Total	% of Variance	Cumulative %
1	2.951	49.186	49.186	2.951	49.186	49.186	2.876	47.931	47.931
2	2.579	42.981	92.167	2.579	42.981	92.167	2.654	44.236	92.167
3	.264	4.401	96.567						
4	.124	2.062	98.630						
5	.058	.974	99.604						
6	.024	.396	100.000						

Extraction Method: Principal Component Analysis.

- The first two factors (components – highlighted in yellow) will be analysed further by SPSS as their eigenvalues are larger than 1.00.

- The scree plot (Figure 18.1) also shows that a break in the size of eigenvalues for the factors occurs after the second factor: the curve is fairly flat after the second factor. Since it is important in factor analysis to ensure that you do not have too many factors, you may wish to do your factor analysis and rotation stipulating the number of factors once you have the results of the scree test. (This can be done by inserting the number in the 'Number of factors:' in the 'Factor Analysis: Extraction' subdialog box.) In the case of our data this does not need to be done since the computer has used the first two factors and ignored the others because of the minimum eigenvalue requirement of 1.00. It is not unusual for a component analysis to be recomputed in the light of the pattern that emerges.

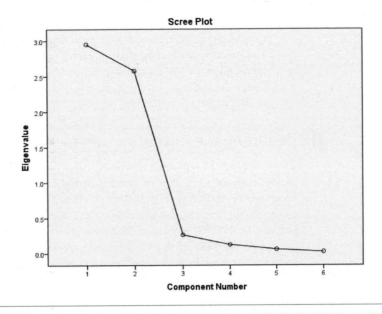

FIGURE 18.1 Scree plot

- These two components are then orthogonally rotated and the loadings of the six variables on these two factors are shown in the fourth table entitled 'Rotated Component Matrix'. The numbers are called factor loadings and are essentially correlation coefficients.

Rotated Component Matrix[a]

	Component	
	1	2
Chess	.980	-.012
Juggling	.979	-.011
Darts	.962	.104
Crosswords	.006	.951
Scrabble	-.078	.951
Sudoku	.153	.914

Extraction Method: Principal Component Analysis.
Rotation Method: Varimax with Kaiser Normalization.

a. Rotation converged in 3 iterations.

- The variables are ordered or sorted according to their loading on the first factor from those with the highest loadings to those with the lowest loadings. This helps interpretation of the factor, since the high loading items are the ones that primarily help you decide what the factor is.
  - On the first factor, 'Chess' and 'Scrabble' have the highest loading (0.980) followed by 'Juggling' (0.979) and 'Darts' (0.962).
  - On the second factor, 'Crosswords' and 'Scrabble' have the highest loading (0.951) followed by 'Sudoku' (0.914). The apparent lack of difference in size of loading of 'Crosswords' and 'Scrabble' is due to rounding. This can be seen if you double-click on the rotated component matrix table and then double-click on these two loadings in turn.

– We would interpret the meaning of these factors in terms of the content of the variables that loaded most highly on them.

– The percentage of variance that each of the orthogonally rotated factors accounts for is given in the third table under '% of Variance' in the 'Rotation Sums of Squared Loadings' columns. It is 47.931 for the first factor and 44.236 for the second factor.

■ Reporting the output

The exact way of reporting the results of a factor analysis will depend on the purpose of the analysis. One way of describing the results would be as follows: 'A principal components analysis was conducted on the correlations of the six variables. Two factors were initially extracted with eigenvalues equal to or greater than 1.00. Orthogonal rotation of the factors yielded the factor structure given in Table 18.11. The first factor accounted for 48% of the variance and the second factor 44%. The first factor seems to be spatial awareness and the second factor seems to be verbal flexibility.' With factor analysis, since the factors have to be interpreted, differences in interpretation may occur.

Table 18.11	Orthogonal factor loading matrix for six skills		
Variable	**Factor 1**	**Factor 2**
Skill at chess	0.98	−0.01
Skill at crosswords	0.01	0.95
Skill at darts	0.96	0.10
Skill at Scrabble	−0.08	0.95
Skill at juggling	0.98	−0.01
Skill at Sudoku	0.15	0.91

Key points

● Do not be afraid to try out factor analysis on your data. It is not difficult to do if you are familiar with using simpler techniques on a computer.

● Do not panic when faced with output from a factor analysis. It can be very lengthy and confusing because it contains things that mere mortals simply do not want to know. Usually the crucial aspects of the factor analysis are to be found towards the end of the output. If in doubt, do not hesitate to contact your local expert – computer output is not always user friendly.

● Take the factor analysis slowly – it takes a while to build your skills sufficiently to be totally confident.

● Do not forget that interpreting the factors can be fairly subjective – you might not always see things as other people do and it might not be you who is wrong.

● Factor analysis can be applied only to correlations calculated using the Pearson correlation formula.

Recommended further reading

Bryman, A. and Cramer, D. (2011), *Quantitative Data Analysis with IBM SPSS Statistics 17, 18 and 19: A Guide for Social Scientists*, Hove: Routledge. Chapter 11.

Child, D. (2006), *The Essentials of Factor Analysis*, 3rd edition, London; New York: Continuum.

Kline, P. (1994), *An Easy Guide to Factor Analysis*, London: Routledge.

Tabachnick, B.G. and Fidell, L.S. (2007), *Using Multivariate Statistics*, 5th edition, New York: Allyn and Bacon, Chapter 13.

CHAPTER 19

Multiple regression and multiple correlation

Overview

- So far we have studied regression and correlation in which just two variables are used – variable X and variable Y. Multiple regression and correlation are extensions of these which include several different X variables ($X_1, X_2, X_3, \ldots$), but only one Y variable is involved. If we wish to relate how well a student does in an examination, we may wish to correlate examination performance with intelligence. This would be simple or bivariate correlation (or regression). If we considered an additional variable to intelligence – amount of preparation – then we might expect higher correlations with examination performance.

- Multiple regression and correlation basically indicate the best predictor of the Y variable, then the next best predictor (correlate), and so forth. They indicate how much weight to give to each predictor to yield the best prediction or correlation.

- Stepwise multiple regression is a way of choosing predictors of a particular dependent variable on the basis of statistical criteria. Essentially the statistical procedure decides which independent variable is the best predictor, the second best predictor, etc. The emphasis is on finding the best predictors at each stage.

- Hierarchical multiple regression allows the researcher to decide which order to use for a list of predictors by putting the predictors or groups of predictors into blocks of variables. The computer will carry out the regression taking each block in the order that it was entered and provides a way of forcing the variables to be considered in the sequence chosen by the researcher.

Preparation

Revise Chapter 8 on simple regression and the standard error in relation to regression. You should also be aware of standard scores from Chapter 5 and the coefficient of determination for the correlation coefficient in Chapter 7. Optimal understanding of this chapter is aided if you understand the concepts of partial correlation and zero-order correlation described in Chapter 17.

19.1 Introduction

Traditionally, researchers often aim to isolate the influence of one variable on another. For example, they might examine whether poor nutrition in childhood leads to lower socio-economic status (SES) in later life. The fundamental difficulty with this is that other variables which might influence a SES are ignored. In real life, variables rarely act independently of each other. An alternative approach is to explore the complex pattern of variables which may relate to SES. Numerous factors may be involved in SES including parental educational level, the quality of teaching at school, the child's general level of intelligence or IQ, whether or not the child went to nursery school, the sex of the child and so forth. We rarely know all the factors which might be related to important variables such as SES before we begin research; so we will tend to include variables which turn out to be poor predictors of the criterion. Multiple regression quite simply helps us choose empirically the most effective set of predictors for any criterion.

Multiple regression can be carried out with scores or standardised scores (z-scores). Standardised multiple regression has the advantage of making the regression values directly analogous to correlation coefficients. The consequence of this is that it is easy to make direct comparisons between the influence of different variables. In unstandardised multiple regression the variables are left in their original form. Standardised and unstandardised multiple regression are usually done simultaneously by computer programs.

19.2 Theoretical considerations

The techniques described in this chapter concern linear multiple regression which assumes that the relationships between variables fall approximately on a straight line.

Multiple regression is an extension of simple (or bivariate) regression (Chapter 8). In simple regression, a single dependent variable (or criterion variable) is related to a single independent variable (or predictor variable). For example, job satisfaction may be regressed against years of experience. In other words, can job satisfaction be predicted from the number of years employed in an industry? In multiple regression, on the other hand, the criterion is regressed against several potential predictors. For example, to what extent is job satisfaction related to various factors such as salary, size of organisation, economic prosperity, years in current role, age, and so on? Of course, years of experience might be included in the list of predictors studied.

Multiple regression serves two main functions:

1. To determine the minimum number of predictors needed to predict a criterion. Some of the predictors which are significantly related to the criterion may also be correlated with each other and so may not all be necessary to predict the criterion. Say, for example, that the two predictors of years of experience and salary both correlate highly with each other and that both these variables were positively related to the criterion of job satisfaction (although salary is more strongly related to job satisfaction than is years of experience). If most of the variation between job satisfaction and years of experience was also shared with salary, then years of experience alone may be sufficient to predict job satisfaction. Another related example of this would be the recruitment consultant who wished to use aptitude tests to select the best applicants for a job. Obviously a lot of time and money could be saved if redundant or overlapping tests could be weeded out, leaving just a minimum number

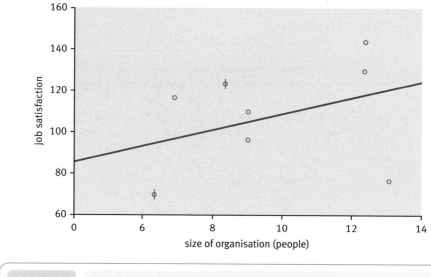

FIGURE 19.1   A simple scatterplot

of tests which predict worker quality. A regression analysis would indicate the similarity between the tests.

2. To explore whether certain predictors remain significantly related to the criterion when other variables are controlled or held constant. For example, work experience might be partly a function of age so that those who are older may be more satisfied with their jobs. We may be interested in determining whether years of experience is still significantly related to job satisfaction when age is controlled.

To explain multiple regression, it is useful to remember the main features of simple regression:

1. Simple regression can be represented by the scatterplot in Figure 19.1 in which values of the criterion are arranged along the vertical axis and values of the predictor are arranged along the horizontal axis. For example, job satisfaction may be the criterion and size of organisation the predictor. Each point on the scatterplot indicates the position of the criterion and predictor scores for a particular individual in the sample. The relationship between the criterion and the predictor is shown by the slope of the straight line through the points on the scattergram. This best-fitting straight line is the one which minimises the (squared) distances between the points and their position on the line. This slope is known as the regression coefficient.

2. The intercept constant is the point at which the regression line intersects or cuts the vertical axis, in other words, the value on the vertical axis when the value on the horizontal axis is zero.

3. To determine the predicted score of the criterion from a particular score of the predictor, we draw a line parallel to the vertical axis from the score on the horizontal axis to the regression line. From here we draw a second line parallel to the horizontal axis to the vertical axis, which gives us the predicted score of the criterion.

4. Unless there is a perfect relationship between the predictor and the criterion, the predicted score of the criterion will usually differ from the actual score for a particular case.

5. Unlike the correlation coefficient, regression is dependent on the variability of the units of measurement involved. This makes regressions on different samples and different variables very difficult to compare. However, we can standardise the scores on the predictor and the criterion variables. By expressing them as standard scores (i.e. z-scores), each variable will have a mean of 0 and a standard deviation of 1. Furthermore, the intercept or intercept constant will always be 0 in these circumstances.

Regression equations

Simple regression is usually expressed in terms of the following regression equation:

$$Y \quad = \quad a \quad + \quad bX$$

predicted score on criterion variable   intercept constant   regression coefficient × predictor score

In other words, to predict a particular criterion score, we multiply the particular score of the predictor by the regression coefficient and add to it the intercept constant. Note that the values of the intercept constant and the regression coefficient remain the same for the equation, so the equation can be seen as describing the relationship between the criterion and the predictor.

When the scores of the criterion and the predictor are standardised to z-scores, the regression coefficient is the same as Pearson's correlation coefficient (Chapter 7) and ranges from +1.00 through 0.00 to −1.00. Regression weights standardised in this way are known as beta weights.

In multiple regression, the regression equation is the same except that there are several predictors and each predictor has its own (partial) regression coefficient:

$$Y = a + b_1X_1 + b_2X_2 + b_3X_3 + \ldots$$

A partial regression coefficient expresses the relationship between a particular predictor and the criterion controlling for, or partialling out, the relationship between that predictor and all the other predictors in the equation. This ensures that each predictor variable provides an independent contribution to the prediction.

The relationship between the criterion and the predictors is often described in terms of the percentage of variance of the criterion that is *explained* or *accounted for* by the predictors. (This is much like the coefficient of determination for the correlation coefficient.) One way of illustrating what the partial regression coefficient means is through a Venn diagram (Figure 19.2) involving the criterion Y and the two predictors X_1 and X_2. Each of the circles signifies the amount of variance of one of the three variables. The area shaded in Figure 19.2(a) is common only to X_1 and Y, and represents the variance of Y that it shares with variable X_1. The shaded area in Figure 19.2(b) is shared only by X_2 and Y, and signifies the amount of variance of Y that it shares with variable X_2. Often a phrase such as 'the amount of variance explained by variable X' is used instead of 'the amount of variance shared by variable X'. Both terms signify the amount of overlapping variance.

The number of regression equations that can be compared in a multiple regression increases exponentially with the number of predictors. With only *two* predictors, the maximum number of regression equations that can be examined is three – the two predictors on their own and the two combined:

1. $Y = a + b_2X_2$

2. $Y = a + b_1X_1 + b_2X_2$

3. $Y = a + b_1X_1$

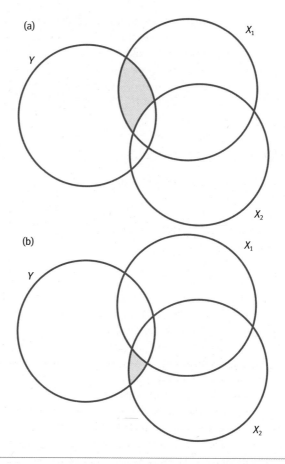

FIGURE 19.2 Venn diagrams illustrating partial regression coefficients

With *three* predictors (X_1, X_2 and X_3) the number of regression equations that can be looked at is seven – three with only one predictor, three with two predictors and one with all three predictors:

1. $Y = a + b_1X_1$

2. $Y = a + b_2X_2$

3. $Y = a + b_3X_3$

4. $Y = a + b_1X_1 + b_2X_2$

5. $Y = a + b_1X_1 + b_3X_3$

6. $Y = a + b_2X_2 + b_3X_3$

7. $Y = a + b_1X_1 + b_2X_2 + b_3X_3$

To work out the number of regression equations that can be compared with any number of predictors, we raise 2 to the power of the number of predictors and subtract 1 from the result. In the case of three predictors this is 7 ($2^3 - 1 = 8 - 1 = 7$).

> ### Box 19.1 Research design issue
>
> Regression can involve the raw scores or standard scores. Computers will usually print out both sorts.
>
> 1. Regression involving 'standard scores' gives regression coefficients which can more readily be compared in terms of their size since they range between +1.0 and −1.0 like simple correlation coefficients (i.e. Pearson correlation). In other words, the predictor variables are comparable irrespective of the units of measurement on which they were originally based. This is just like any other standard scores (Chapter 5).
>
> 2. Regression involving 'non-standard scores' or raw scores is about the 'nuts and bolts' of prediction. Like our account of simple regression, it provides predicted numerical values for the criterion variable based on an individual's scores on the various predictor variables. However, the size of the regression coefficient is no indication of the importance of the unstandardised predictor, since the size is dependent on the units of measurement involved.

■ Selection

Since multiple regression is particularly useful with a large number of predictors, such an analysis involves many regression equations. Obviously the complexity of the analysis could be awesome. In order not to have to look at every potential equation, a number of different approaches have been suggested for selecting and testing predictors. These approaches include *hierarchical* (or *blockwise*) *selection* and *stepwise selection*. Hierarchical selection enters predictors into the regression equation on some practical or theoretical consideration. Stepwise selection employs statistical criteria to choose the smallest set of predictors which best predict the variation in the criterion. In contrast to these methods, entering all predictors into the regression equation is known as *standard* multiple regression. Finally, *setwise* regression compares all possible sets of predictors such as all predictors singly, in pairs, in trios and so on until the best set of predictors is identified.

1. In *hierarchical selection* predictors are entered singly or in blocks according to some practical or theoretical rationale. For example, potentially confounding variables such as socio-demographic factors may be statistically controlled by entering them first into the regression equation. Alternatively, similar variables may be grouped (or 'blocked') together and entered as a block, such as a block of personality variables, a block of attitude variables and so on. The computer tells us the net influence of each block in turn.

2. In *stepwise selection* the predictor with the highest zero-order correlation is entered first into the regression equation if it explains a significant proportion of the variance of the criterion. The second predictor to be considered for entry is that which has the highest partial correlation with the criterion. If it explains a significant proportion of the variance of the criterion it is entered into the equation. At this point the predictor which was entered first is examined to see if it still explains a significant proportion of the variance of the criterion. If it no longer does so, it is dropped from the equation. The analysis continues with the predictor which has the next highest partial correlation with the criterion. The process stops when no more predictors are entered into or removed from the equation.

Box 19.2 gives further possibilities for multiple regression analyses.

| Box 19.2 | Focus on |

Some approaches to multiple regression

Among the choices of methods for multiple regression are:

- Single-stage entry of all predictors, and all predictors are employed whether or not they are likely to be good predictors (i.e. irrespective of their potential predictive power).

- Blocks. There are circumstances in which the researcher does not wish to enter all of the variables at the same time. Instead, it is possible to enter the predictors in sets, one set at a time. These are sets specified by the researcher and are usually called blocks. There can be any number of variables in a block from a minimum of one. There are a number of advantages to this. Putting variables into blocks allows the variables in the block to be analysed together, either before or after other variables. One might put variables into blocks because they are similar in some way. For instance, they may be a particular type of variable (e.g. health variables, education variables and social-class variables could all form separate blocks). Another use is to 'control' for certain variables first – that is, age and social class may be entered as the first block. This is often done as a way of controlling for the influence of demographic variables. If the first block included demographic variables such as gender, age and social class, this is the equivalent of partialling them out of the analysis (see Chapter 17). Once this is done, one can compare the outcome of this block with what happens when other predictors are introduced.

- Finding best predictors. The analysis may proceed on a stepwise basis by finding the best predictors in a set of predictors and eliminating the poor predictors. This is particularly appropriate where the main objective of the researcher is to find explanatory models of influences

on the dependent variable, rather than to predict with the highest possible accuracy.

- Reverse (backwards) elimination of predictors. In this the first model is initially employed. That is, the model in our earlier example is calculated. All of the predictor variables are included. Having done that, the worst predictor is dropped. Usually this is the least significant predictor. Essentially the model is recalculated on the basis of the remaining predictors. Then the remaining worst predictor is dropped and again the model is recalculated. The researcher is looking to see whether dropping a variable or variables actually substantially worsens the model. This is not simply a matter of the goodness-of-fit of the model to the data; some models may be better at predicting one value of the dependent variable rather than the other. If one is trying to avoid letting men out of prison early if they are likely to re-offend, the model which maximises the number of recidivists (re-offenders) correctly identified may be preferred over the model which misclassifies recidivists as likely to be non-recidivists. This is obviously a complex judgement based on a wide variety of considerations.

- There are models which mix blocks and stepwise approaches.

Except for the simple case where the maximum possible accuracy of prediction is required and all variables may be entered *en masse*, the choice of approach is a matter of judgement that partly comes with experience and practice. It does no harm to try out a variety of approaches on one's data, especially if one is inexperienced with the techniques, though, of course, one has to be able to justify the final choice of model.

19.3 Stepwise multiple regression example

Our example asks whether a person's socio-economic status (SES) (the criterion variable) can be predicted from their parental SES, their IQ and their age (the predictor variables). The minimum information we need to carry out a multiple regression is the number of people in the sample and the correlations between all the variables, though you would normally work with the actual scores when carrying out a multiple

Table 19.1	Data for stepwise multiple regression		
SES	**Parental SES**	**IQ**	**Age**
1	2	1	2
2	2	3	1
2	2	3	3
3	4	3	2
3	3	4	3
4	3	2	2

Table 19.2	Correlation matrix for a criterion and three predictors		
	SES	**Parental SES**	**IQ**
Parental SES	0.70		
IQ	0.37	0.32	
Age	0.13	0.11	0.34

regression. Table 19.1 shows the scores of six people on the four variables of SES, Parental SES, IQ and Age. It has been suggested that with stepwise regression it is desirable to have 40 times more cases than predictors. Since we have three predictors, we will say that we have a sample of 120 cases. (However, much reported research fails to follow this rule of thumb.) In order to interpret the results of multiple regression, it is usually necessary to have more information than this, but for our purposes the fictitious correlation matrix presented in Table 19.2 should be sufficient.

The calculation of multiple regression with more than two predictors is complicated and so will not be shown. However, the basic results of a stepwise multiple regression analysis are given in Table 19.3. What this simple example shows is that only two of the three 'predictors' actually explain a significant percentage of variance in socio-economic status (SES). That they are significant is assessed using a t-test. The values of t are given in Table 19.3 along with their two-tailed significance levels. A significance level of 0.05 or less is regarded as statistically significant.

The two significant predictor variables are Parental SES and IQ. The first variable to be considered for entry into the regression equation is the one with the highest zero-order correlation with SES. This variable is Parental SES. The *proportion* of variance in SES explained or predicted by Parental SES is the square of its correlation with SES,

Table 19.3	Some regression results				
Predictor variables	**r**	**B**	**Beta**	**t**	**Significance**
Parental SES	0.70	0.83	0.65	9.56	0.001
IQ	0.37	0.17	0.16	2.42	0.02
Constant = −0.17, R^2 = 0.52, Adjusted R^2 = 0.51, R = 0.72					

which is 0.49 ($0.7^2 = 0.49$). The next predictor to be considered for entry into the regression equation is the variable which has the highest partial correlation with the criterion (after the variance due to the first predictor variable has been removed). These partial correlations have not been presented; however, IQ is the predictor variable with the highest partial correlation with the criterion variable SES.

The two predictors together explain 0.52 of the variance of SES. The figure for the total proportion of variance explained is arrived at by squaring the overall R (the multiple correlation), which is 0.72^2 or 0.52. The multiple correlation is likely to be bigger the smaller the sample and for more predictors. Consequently, this figure is usually adjusted for the size of the sample and the number of predictors, which reduces it in size somewhat. Finally, the partial regression or beta coefficients for the regression equation containing the two predictors are also shown in Table 19.3 and are 0.65 for Parental SES and 0.16 for IQ. There is also a constant (usually denoted as a) which is –0.17 in this instance. The constant is the equivalent to the intercept (or cut-point) described in Chapter 8. We can write this regression equation as follows:

$$SES = a + (0.83 \times \text{Parental SES}) + (0.17 \times \text{IQ})$$

According to our fictitious example, Parental SES is more important than IQ in predicting SES.

Box 19.3   Research design issue

There is a concept, *multicollinearity*, which needs consideration when planning a multiple regression analysis. This merely refers to a situation in which several of the predictor variables correlate with each other very highly. This results in difficulties because small sampling fluctuations may result in a particular variable appearing to be a powerful predictor while other variables may appear to be relatively weak predictors. So variables A and B, both of which predict the criterion, may correlate with each other at, say, 0.9. However, because variable A, say, has a *minutely* better correlation with the criterion, it is selected first by the computer. Variable B then appears to be a far less good predictor. When the intercorrelations of your predictor variables are very high, perhaps above 0.8 or so, then the dangers of multicollinearity are also high. In terms of research design, it is a well-known phenomenon that if you measure several different variables using the same type of method then there is a tendency for the variables to intercorrelate simply because of that fact. So, if all of your measures are based on self-completion questionnaires or on ratings by observers, you may find strong intercorrelations simply because of this. Quite clearly, care should be exercised to ensure that your predictor measures do not intercorrelate highly. If multicollinearity is apparent then be very careful about claiming that one of the predictors is far better than another.

Box 19.4   Focus on

Prediction and multiple regression

Prediction in regression is often not prediction at all. This can cause some confusion. In everyday language prediction is indicating what will happen in the future on the basis of some sign in the present. Researchers, however, often use regression analysis with no intention of predicting future events. Instead, they collect data on the relation between a set of variables (let's call them X_1, X_2 and X_3) and another variable (called Y). They think that the X variables may be correlated with Y. The data on all of these variables are available to the researcher. The analysis proceeds essentially by calculating the overall correlation of the several X variables with the Y variable. The overall correlation of a set of variables with another single variable is called multiple correlation. If there is a multiple correlation between the variables, we can use the value of this correlation together with other information to estimate the value of the Y variable from a pattern of X variables. Since the multiple correlation is rarely a perfect correlation, our estimate of Y is bound to be a little inaccurate. Explained this way, we have not used the concept of prediction. If we know the multiple correlation between variables based on a particular sample of participants, we can use the size of the correlation to estimate the value of Y for other individuals based on knowing their pattern of scores on the X variables. That is the task of multiple regression. Prediction in multiple regression, then, is really estimating the unknown value of Y for an individual who was not part of the original research sample from that individual's known pattern of scores on the X variables.

19.4 Reporting the results

Multiple regression can be performed in a variety of ways for a variety of purposes. Consequently, there is no standard way of presenting results from a multiple regression analysis. However, there are some things which are best routinely mentioned. In particular, the reader needs to know the variables on which the analysis was conducted, the particular form of the multiple regression used, regression weights and the main pattern of predictors. Other information may be added as appropriate. By all means consult journal articles in your field of study for other indications as to style. We would say the following when reporting the simple example in Section 19.3: 'A stepwise multiple regression was carried out in order to investigate the best pattern of variables for predicting SES. Parental SES was selected for entry into the analysis first and explained 49% of the variance in SES. IQ was entered second and together with Parental SES explained 52% of the variance in SES. Greater educational attainment was associated with greater Parental SES and IQ. A third variable, Age, was not included in the analysis as it was not a significant, independent predictor of SES.'

19.5 What is stepwise multiple regression?

Multiple regression is like simple or bivariate regression (Chapter 8) except that there is more than one predictor variable. Multiple regression is used when the variables are generally normally distributed. In other words, it is used when the criterion is a quantitative or score variable. In stepwise multiple regression the predictor variables are entered one variable at a time or step according to particular statistical criteria.

The first predictor to be considered for entry on the first step is the predictor that has the highest correlation with the criterion (Chapter 6). This predictor on its own will explain the most variance in the criterion. This correlation has to be statistically significant for it to be entered. If it is not significant, the analysis stops here with no predictors being entered.

The second predictor to be considered for entry on the second step is the one that explains the second highest proportion of the variance after its relation with the first predictor and the criterion is taken into account. In other words it is the predictor that has the highest part correlation with the criterion after the first predictor has been removed. Once again, this first-order part correlation has to be statistically significant for it to be entered. If it is not significant, the analysis stops after the first predictor has been entered.

The third predictor to be considered for entry on the third step is the predictor that has the highest part correlation after its association with the first two predictors and the criterion is taken into account. This second-order part correlation has to be statistically significant for it to be entered. If it is not significant, the analysis stops after the second step and does not proceed any further. If it is significant, then it is entered. At this stage, the second-order part correlations of the first two predictors with the criterion are examined. It is possible that one or both of these second-order part correlations are not significant. If this is the case, then the predictor with the non-significant second-order part correlation will be dropped from the analysis. The process continues until no other predictor explains a significant proportion of the variance in the criterion.

We will illustrate a stepwise multiple regression with the data in Table 19.1, which shows the scores of six people on the four variables of SES, Parental SES, IQ and Age. We would not normally use such a small sample to carry out a stepwise multiple correlation as it is unlikely that any of the correlations would be significant. So what we have done to make the correlations significant is to weight or multiply these six cases by 20 times so that we have a sample of 120, which is a reasonable number for a multiple regression.

The correlations between these four variables are shown in Table 19.2 (see also Chapter 6). We can see that the predictor with the highest correlation is Parental SES which is 0.70 and which is statistically significant. So Parental SES is the first predictor to be entered into the stepwise multiple regression.

The two first-order part correlations of SES with IQ and Age controlling for Parental SES are 0.16 and 0.05 respectively. As the first-order part correlation for IQ is higher than that for Age and is statistically significant, it is entered in the second step. The second-order part correlation for Age is 0.00 and is not significant. Consequently the analysis stops after the second step.

19.6 When to use stepwise multiple regression

Stepwise multiple regression should be used when you want to find out what are the smallest number of predictors that you need which make a significant contribution in explaining the maximum amount of variance in the criterion variable, what these predictors are and how much of the variance of the criterion variable they explain. It may be helpful to use stepwise multiple regression when you have a large number of predictor variables and you want to get a quick impression of which of these explain most of the variance in the criterion variable.

19.7 When not to use stepwise multiple regression

Ideally it is better to use theoretical criteria rather than purely statistical ones in determining how you think your predictor variables are related to your criterion variable. This may be done by looking at particular variables or groups of variables at a time as is done in simple path analysis or by putting the variables in a multiple regression in a particular order. Hierarchical regression (see Section 19.11) is the procedure used for entering predictor variables in a particular sequence. Stepwise multiple regression would not generally be used when one or more of the predictor variables are nominal (category) variables involving three or more categories as these have to be converted into dummy variables. The dummy variables are best entered in a single step as a block to see what contribution this predictor variable makes to the criterion. This is done using hierarchical multiple regression.

19.8   Data requirements for stepwise multiple regression

Although multiple regression can handle categorical variables when they have been turned into dummy variables, a basic requirement for any form of simple or multiple regression is that the scatterplot of the relation between a predictor variable and the criterion should show homoscedasticity, which means that the plot of the data points around the points of the line of best fit should be similar. This can be roughly assessed by plotting the line of best fit in a scatterplot and seeing if this assumption seems to have been met for each of the predictor variables (Chapter 8). It is important that the criterion or dependent variable should be a continuous score which is normally distributed. If the criterion is a binomial variable, then it is far better to use binomial logistic regression (Chapter 21). If it is a multinomial variable, then multinomial logistic regression should be used (Chapter 20).

19.9   Problems in the use of stepwise multiple regression

Care needs to be taken in interpreting the results of a stepwise multiple regression. If two predictor variables show multicollinearity in that they are highly correlated, then the predictor variable which has the higher relation with the criterion variable will be entered first even if this relation is minutely bigger than that with the other predictor variable. As both variables are strongly related to each other, it is likely that the other variable may not be entered as a significant predictor in the multiple regression even though it may be an equally strong candidate. As the relation between each predictor and the criterion is similar, the results for this analysis may not be very reliable in the sense that the other predictor may have the higher relation with the criterion in a second sample. Consequently it is important to look at the zero-order and the partial correlations of these variables to see whether the difference in the size of their relation can be considered small.

19.10   SPSS analysis

■ The data to be analysed

We will illustrate the computation of a stepwise multiple regression analysis with the data shown in Table 19.1, which consist of scores for six individuals on the four variables of SES, Parental SES, IQ and Age respectively.

Because this is for illustrative purposes and to save space, we are going to enter these data 20 times to give us a respectable amount of data to work with. Obviously you would *not* do this if your data were real. It is important to use quite a lot of research participants or cases for multiple regression. Ten or 15 times your number of variables would be reasonably generous. Of course, you can use less for data exploration purposes.

■ Stepwise multiple regression analysis

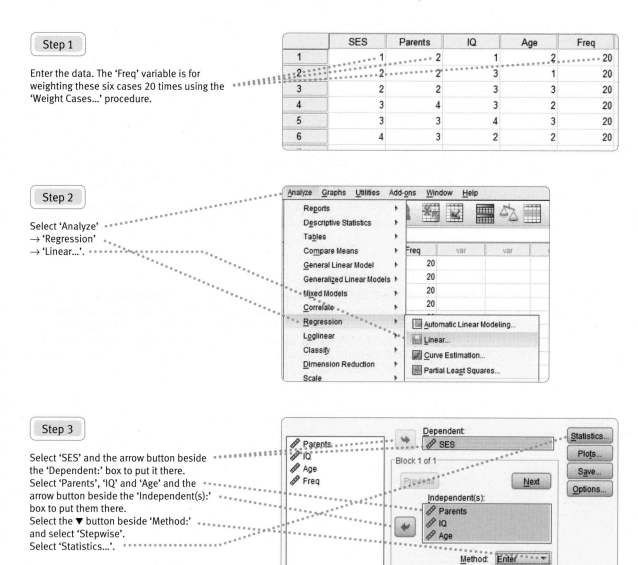

Step 1

Enter the data. The 'Freq' variable is for weighting these six cases 20 times using the 'Weight Cases...' procedure.

Step 2

Select 'Analyze'
→ 'Regression'
→ 'Linear...'.

Step 3

Select 'SES' and the arrow button beside the 'Dependent:' box to put it there.
Select 'Parents', 'IQ' and 'Age' and the arrow button beside the 'Independent(s):' box to put them there.
Select the ▼ button beside 'Method:' and select 'Stepwise'.
Select 'Statistics...'.

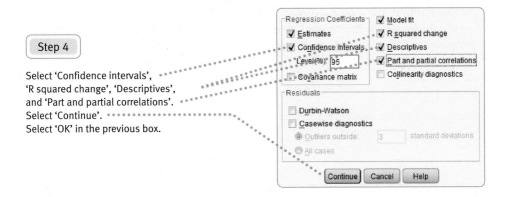

Step 4

Select 'Confidence intervals', 'R squared change', 'Descriptives', and 'Part and partial correlations'. Select 'Continue'. Select 'OK' in the previous box.

■ Interpreting the output

- There is a great deal of information in the output. Multiple regression is a complex area and needs further study in order to understand all of its ramifications. In interpreting the results of this analysis we shall restrict ourselves to commenting on the following statistics: multiple R, R square, adjusted R square, B, beta, R square change and part correlations. Most of these are dealt with in a simple fashion in Chapter 20.

- In stepwise multiple regression, each new step is discussed as a model. In this example, two significant steps were involved. The first step (Model 1) uses the predictor Parents (= Parental SES). The second step (Model 2) is built on this predictor with the addition of a second predictor IQ. Generally, it is reasonable to concentrate on the highest numbered model.

- Notice how badly the first table in particular is laid out. If you double-click on a table it will be enclosed in a rectangle. To move any but the first line, move the cursor to that line. When it changes to a double arrow ($\leftrightarrow$), click the left button of the mouse and, holding the left button down, move the line to the position you want before releasing the button. By dragging the column dividers in this way you should be able to obtain a better and more easily read table.

Variables Entered/Removed[a]

Model	Variables Entered	Variables Removed	Method
1	Parents	.	Stepwise (Criteria: Probability-of-F-to-enter <= .050, Probability-of-F-to-remove >= .100).
2	IQ	.	Stepwise (Criteria: Probability-of-F-to-enter <= .050, Probability-of-F-to-remove >= .100).

a. Dependent Variable: SES

- The second table of the output, 'Model Summary', gives the values of multiple R, R square and adjusted R square for the two steps (models). This is really a table of the multiple correlation coefficients between the models and the criterion. It also includes statistics indicating the improvement of fit of the models with the data. Each model in this example gives an improvement in fit. This can be seen from the final figures where the change in fit is significant for both Model 1 and Model 2. (The regression weights (*B* and beta) are to be found in the third table of the output entitled 'Coefficients' – see below.)

Model Summary

Model	R	R Square	Adjusted R Square	Std. Error of the Estimate	Change Statistics				
					R Square Change	F Change	df1	df2	Sig. F Change
1	.701ᵃ	.491	.487	.689	.491	113.786	1	118	.000
2	.718ᵇ	.515	.507	.675	.024	5.850	1	117	.017

a. Predictors: (Constant), Parents
b. Predictors: (Constant), Parents, IQ

- The predictor that is entered on the first step of the stepwise analysis (Model 1) is the predictor that has the highest correlation with the criterion. In this example this predictor is 'Parents'. (Note 'a' immediately underneath the Model Summary table indicates this.)

- As there is only one predictor in the regression equation on the first step, multiple *R* is the same as the correlation between Parents and SES (the dependent or criterion variable). In this case it is 0.701, or 0.70 to two decimal places.

- *R* square is simply the multiple correlation coefficient squared, which in this instance is 0.491, or 0.49 to two decimal places. This indicates that 49% of the variance in the criterion is shared with or 'explained by' the first predictor.

- Adjusted *R* square is *R* square which has been adjusted for the size of the sample and the number of predictors in the equation. The effect of this adjustment is to reduce the size of *R* square, so adjusted *R* square is 0.487, or 0.49 to two decimal places.

- The variable that is entered second in the regression equation is the predictor which generally explains the second greatest significant proportion of the variance in the criterion. In this example, this variable is 'IQ'.

- The multiple *R*, *R* square and adjusted *R* square for Model 2 are 0.718, 0.515 and 0.507 respectively which, rounded to two decimal places, are 0.72, 0.52 and 0.51. As might be expected, these values are bigger than the corresponding figures for Model 1. This is to be expected because there is an additional predictor contributing to a better prediction.

- In Model 2, then, two variables ('Parental SES' and 'IQ') explain or account for 51% of the variance in the criterion.

- *R* square change presented under 'Change Statistics' in the second table shows the increase in the proportion of the variance in the criterion variable ('SES') by predictors that have been entered after the first predictor ('Parental SES'). In this case there is only one other predictor ('IQ'). This predictor explains a further 2.4% of the variance in the criterion.

- Examine the table headed 'Coefficients'. Find the column headed Beta in the table. The first entry is 0.701 for Model 1. This is exactly the same as the value of the multiple correlation above for Model 1. That is because beta is the standardised regression coefficient, which is the same as the correlation when there is only one predictor. It is as if all your scores had been transformed to *z*-scores before the analysis began.

Coefficients[a]

Model		Unstandardized Coefficients		Standardized Coefficients	t	Sig.	95.0% Confidence Interval for B		Correlations		
		B	Std. Error	Beta			Lower Bound	Upper Bound	Zero-order	Partial	Part
1	(Constant)	.100	.234		.428	.669	-.363	.563			
	Parents	.900	.084	.701	10.667	.000	.733	1.067	.701	.701	.701
2	(Constant)	-.167	.254		-.656	.513	-.670	.337			
	Parents	.833	.087	.649	9.561	.000	.661	1.006	.701	.662	.615
	IQ	.167	.069	.164	2.419	.017	.030	.303	.369	.218	.156

a. Dependent Variable: SES

● For Model 2 Beta is 0.649 for the first predictor ('Parental SES') and 0.164 for the second predictor ('IQ').

● The analysis stops at this point, as the third predictor ('Age') does not explain a further significant proportion of the criterion variance. Notice that in the final table of the output entitled 'Excluded Variables', 'Age' has a t value of 0.000 and a significance level of 1.000. This tells us that 'Age' is a non-significant predictor of the criterion ('SES').

Excluded Variables[c]

Model		Beta In	t	Sig.	Partial Correlation	Collinearity Statistics Tolerance
1	IQ	.164[a]	2.419	.017	.218	.900
	Age	.051[a]	.775	.440	.071	.988
2	Age	.000[b]	.000	1.000	.000	.882

a. Predictors in the Model: (Constant), Parents

b. Predictors in the Model: (Constant), Parents, IQ

c. Dependent Variable: SES

● The part correlations for Parental SES and IQ are 0.615 and 0.156 respectively, which when squared means that they explain about 37.8% and 2.4% of the variance in SES when not taking account of the variance they share together. As the total percentage of variance these two variables explain is about 51.5%, the percentage of variance they share is about 11.3% (51.5 – 40.2).

■ Reporting the output

There are various ways of reporting the results of a stepwise multiple regression analysis. In such a report we should include the following kind of statement: 'In the stepwise multiple regression, Parental SES was entered first and explained 49% of the variance in SES ($F_{1,118} = 113.76$, $p < 0.001$). IQ was entered second and explained a further 2% ($F_{1,117} = 5.85$, $p = 0.017$). Higher SES was associated with higher Parental SES and IQ.'

A table is sometimes presented. There is no standard way of doing this but Table 19.4 is probably as clear as most.

Table 19.4	Stepwise multiple regression of predictors of SES (only significant predictors are included)					
Variable	**Multiple R**	**B**	**Standard error b**	**Beta**	**t**	**Significance of t**
Parental SES	0.70	0.83	0.09	0.65	9.56	0.001
IQ	0.72	0.17	0.07	0.16	2.42	0.05

19.11 What is hierarchical multiple regression?

Hierarchical multiple regression is used to determine how much variance in the criterion, dependent or outcome variable is explained by predictors (independent variables) when they are entered in a particular sequence. The more variance that a predictor explains, the potentially more important that variable may be. The variables may be entered in a particular sequence on practical or theoretical grounds. An example of a practical situation is where we are interested in trying to predict how good someone might be at their job. We could collect a number of variables that we think might be related to how good they might be. This might include how well they did at school, how many outside interests they have, how many positions of responsibility they hold, how well they performed in interview and so on. Now some of these variables might be easy to obtain, such as finding out how well they did at school or how many outside interests they have, while other variables might be more difficult to obtain, such as how well they performed at interview. We may be interested in whether using these variables enables us to make much better predictions about how likely someone is to be good at their job than the easier ones. If they do not add much to how well we are able to predict job competence, then it might be better not to use them. So we could add the other variables in the first step of our hierarchical multiple regression and see how much of the variance in job competence is generally explained. We could then add the more difficult variables in the second step to see how much more of the variance in job competence these variables explain.

Turning to a more theoretical situation, we may be interested in trying to explain how much different variables or types of variables explain some criterion such as SES. We may arrange the variables in a particular sequence. We may be interested first in how much basic demographic variables explain, such as social class and age. Next we may wish to consider whether going to pre-school made any difference to explaining SES beyond social class and age. Third, we may wish to look at the effects of Parental SES on SES. And finally, we may want to examine the effects of other variables such as motivation and number of children in the family, for example. Entering these variables in a sequence like this will enable us to see how much each group or block of variables adds to how well we can predict SES.

Hierarchical multiple regression will be illustrated with the same data as we used earlier in this chapter except that we will add another variable, that of 'Motivation'. These data are shown in Table 19.5. We will enter Motivation in the first step of the analysis, Parental SES in the second step and IQ and Age in the third step.

Table 19.5	Data for hierarchical multiple regression			
SES	**Parental SES**	**IQ**	**Age**	**Motivation**
1	2	1	2	2
2	2	3	1	1
2	2	3	3	5
3	4	3	2	4
3	3	4	3	3
4	3	2	2	2

To work out the proportion of variance in SES that is explained at each step, we calculate the squared multiple correlation (R^2), which is derived by multiplying the standardised (partial) beta regression coefficient by the correlation coefficient for each predictor and the criterion in that step and summing their products. The correlations between SES and Parental SES, IQ, Age and Motivation are about 0.70, 0.37, 0.13 and 0.07 respectively. The standardised regression coefficient for motivation in the first step is its correlation which is 0.07. Consequently motivation explains about 0.5% (0.07 × 0.07 × 100) of the variance in SES, which is effectively none. The standardised regression coefficients for class and ability in the second step are about −0.14 and 0.74 respectively. So the variance explained by both motivation and Parental SES is about 51% {[(0.07 × −0.14) + (0.70 × 0.74)] × 100}. If we subtract the per cent of variance in the first step from that in the second step, we see that Parental SES explains about a further 50.5%. Finally, the standardised regression coefficients for Motivation, Parental SES, IQ and Age are about −0.439, 0.730, 0.185 and 0.314 respectively. Thus the variance explained by all four of these predictors in the third step is about 59% {[(0.07 × −0.439) + (0.70 × 0.730) + (0.37 × 0.185) + (0.13 × 0.314)] × 100}. If we subtract the per cent of variance in the second step from that in the third step, we see that IQ and Age explain about a further 8.5%. We can see that Parental SES explains the most variance in SES even when motivation is taken into account. There is no reason to calculate these yourself as they can be found under Model Summary in 'Interpreting the output' later in this chapter.

19.12   When to use hierarchical multiple regression

Hierarchical multiple regression should be used when you want to enter the predictor variables in a particular sequence as described above. It is also used to determine whether there is a significant interaction between your predictor variables and the criterion. The interaction term is created by multiplying the predictor variables together and entering this term in a subsequent step in the multiple regression after the predictor variables have been entered. If the interaction term explains a significant proportion of the variance in the criterion, this implies that there is an interaction between these predictor variables. The nature of this interaction needs to be determined.

19.13   When not to use hierarchical multiple regression

Hierarchical multiple regression should not be used when there is no reason why the predictor variables should be entered in a particular order. If there are no good grounds for prioritising the variables, then it is better to enter them in a single block or step. This is known as a standard multiple regression.

19.14   Data requirements for hierarchical multiple regression

The data requirements for hierarchical multiple regression are the same as those for stepwise multiple regression outlined earlier in this chapter. The criterion variable should be a quantitative variable which is normally distributed. The relation between each predictor and the criterion should show homoscedasticity in the sense that the plot of the data points around the best-fitting regression line should be similar at each point along the regression line. A rough idea of whether this is the case can be obtained by producing a scatterplot with a line of best fit between each predictor and the criterion as shown at the beginning of this chapter.

19.15   Problems in the use of hierarchical multiple regression

As in all regression and correlation analyses, it is important to look at the mean and standard deviation of the variables. If the mean is very low or high then this suggests that the variation in the variable may not be well spread. A variable that has a smaller standard deviation indicates that it has a smaller variance, which means that the relation between this variable and the criterion may be smaller than a predictor that has a larger variance when all other things are equal.

19.16   SPSS analysis

■ The data to be analysed

We will illustrate the computation of a hierarchical multiple regression analysis with the data shown in Table 19.5, which consist of scores for six individuals on the five variables of SES, Parental SES, IQ, Age and Motivation, which is on a scale of 1 to 5, with 5 being the most motivated and 1 the least. Hierarchical analysis is used when variables are entered in an order predetermined by the researcher on a 'rational' basis rather than in terms of statistical criteria. This is done by ordering the independent variables in terms of blocks of the independent variables, called Block 1, Block 2, etc. A block may consist of just one independent variable or several. In this particular analysis, we will make Block 1 Motivation ('Motivation'), which is essentially a personality variable we would like to control for. Block 2 will be Parental SES ('Parents'). Block 3 will be IQ ('IQ') and Age ('Age'). The dependent variable or criterion to be explained is SES ('SES').

In our example, the model essentially is that SES is affected by Parental SES and motivational factors such as IQ and Age. Motivation is being controlled for in this model, since we are not regarding it as a fixed entity like the other variables.

When doing a path analysis, it is necessary to do several hierarchical multiple regressions. One redoes the hierarchical multiple regression using different blocks and in different orders so that various models of the interrelationships can be explored.

■ Hierarchical multiple regression analysis

Step 1

Enter the data. The 'Freq' variable is for weighting these six cases 20 times using the 'Weight Cases...' procedure.

	SES	Parents	IQ	Age	Freq	Motivation
1	1	2	1	2	20	2
2	2	2	3	1	20	1
3	2	2	3	3	20	5
4	3	4	3	2	20	4
5	3	3	4	3	20	3
6	4	3	2	2	20	2

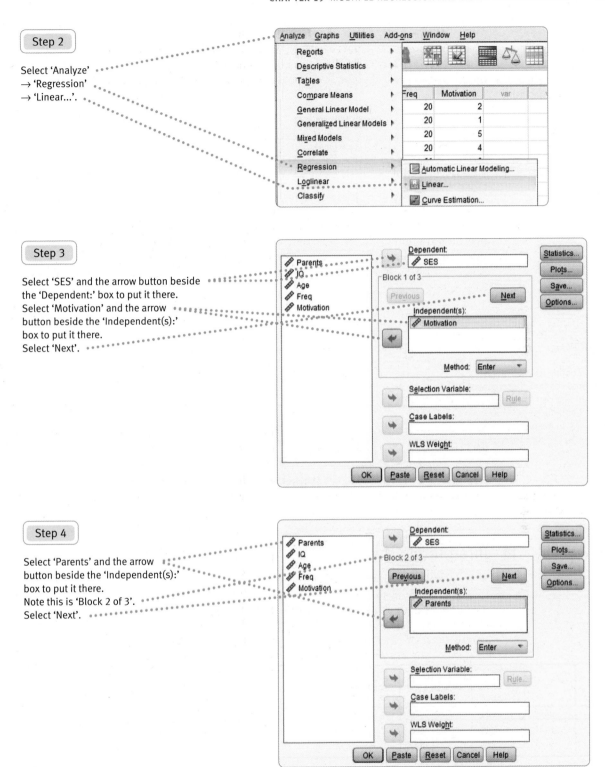

Step 2

Select 'Analyze'
→ 'Regression'
→ 'Linear...'.

Step 3

Select 'SES' and the arrow button beside
the 'Dependent:' box to put it there.
Select 'Motivation' and the arrow
button beside the 'Independent(s):'
box to put it there.
Select 'Next'.

Step 4

Select 'Parents' and the arrow
button beside the 'Independent(s):'
box to put it there.
Note this is 'Block 2 of 3'.
Select 'Next'.

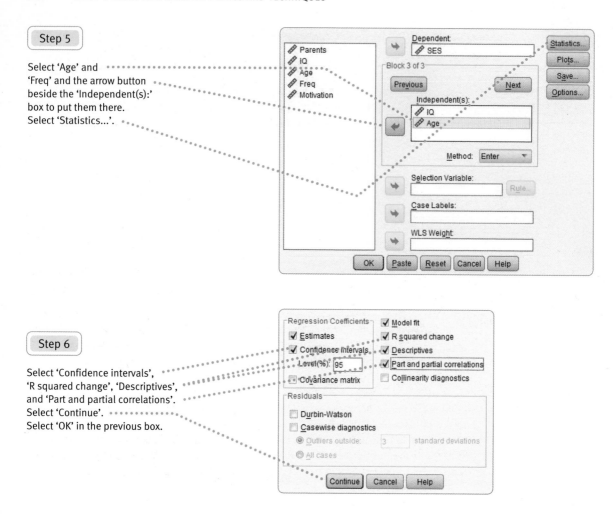

Step 5

Select 'Age' and
'Freq' and the arrow button
beside the 'Independent(s):'
box to put them there.
Select 'Statistics...'.

Step 6

Select 'Confidence intervals',
'R squared change', 'Descriptives',
and 'Part and partial correlations'.
Select 'Continue'.
Select 'OK' in the previous box.

■ Interpreting the output

- As summarised in the second table of the output entitled 'Model Summary', the variable entered on the first block is 'Motivation'. The R square for this block is effectively 0.0 (0.004), which means that motivation explains 0% of the variance of SES.

Model Summary

Model	R	R Square	Adjusted R Square	Std. Error of the Estimate	Change Statistics				
					R Square Change	F Change	df1	df2	Sig. F Change
1	.065ᵃ	.004	-.004	.963	.004	.497	1	118	.482
2	.714ᵇ	.509	.501	.679	.505	120.333	1	117	.000
3	.769ᶜ	.591	.577	.626	.082	11.500	2	115	.000

a. Predictors: (Constant), Motivation
b. Predictors: (Constant), Motivation, Parents
c. Predictors: (Constant), Motivation, Parents, IQ, Age

- The statistical significance of the *F*-ratio of 0.497 for this block or model is 0.482. As this value is above the critical value of 0.05, this means that the regression equation at this first stage does not explain a significant proportion of the variance in SES.

- The variable entered on the second block is 'Parents' (Parental SES). The adjusted *R* square for this block or model is 0.501, which means that Parental SES together with motivation explain 50.1% of the variance of SES.

- The statistical significance of the *F*-ratio for this block is 0.000 which means that it is less than 0.001. As this value is much lower than the critical value of 0.05, the first two steps of the regression equation explain a significant proportion of the variance in SES.

- The variables entered on the third and final block are IQ and Age. The adjusted *R* square for this block is 0.577, which means that all four variables explain 57.7% of the variance of SES.

- The *F*-ratio for this block is 0.000. As this value is much lower than the critical value of 0.05, the first three steps in the regression equation explain a significant proportion of the variance in SES.

- The simplest interpretation of the output comes from examining the fourth table entitled 'Coefficients' of the output. Especially useful are the Beta column and the Sig. (of *t*) column. These tell us that the correlation (beta) between Motivation and SES is −0.439 when the other predictors are taken into account. This correlation is significant at the 0.000 level which means that it is less than 0.001. This coefficient is now significant because the two variables of Parental SES and Age suppress the zero-order coefficient between Motivation and SES. Having controlled for Motivation in Block 1, the correlation between Parental SES and SES is 0.730. This is also significant at the 0.000 level. Finally, having controlled for Motivation and Parental SES, the correlations for each of the variables in Block 3 (IQ and Age) with SES are given separately.

Coefficients[a]

Model		Unstandardized Coefficients		Standardized Coefficients	t	Sig.	95.0% Confidence Interval for B		Correlations		
		B	Std. Error	Beta			Lower Bound	Upper Bound	Zero-order	Partial	Part
1	(Constant)	2.369	.205		11.543	.000	1.963	2.776			
	Motivation	.046	.065	.065	.705	.482	-.083	.176	.065	.065	.065
2	(Constant)	.250	.241		1.036	.302	-.228	.728			
	Motivation	-.100	.048	-.140	-2.082	.040	-.195	-.005	.065	-.189	-.135
	Parents	.950	.087	.740	10.970	.000	.778	1.122	.701	.712	.711
3	(Constant)	-.563	.284		-1.984	.050	-1.124	-.001			
	Motivation	-.313	.068	-.439	-4.615	.000	-.447	-.178	.065	-.395	-.275
	Parents	.938	.084	.730	11.180	.000	.771	1.104	.701	.722	.667
	IQ	.188	.068	.185	2.769	.007	.053	.322	.369	.250	.165
	Age	.438	.130	.314	3.374	.001	.181	.694	.127	.300	.201

a. Dependent Variable: SES

- The part correlations for Motivation, IQ, Parental SES and Age were −0.275, 0.667, 0.165 and 0.201 respectively, which when squared means that they account for about 7.6%, 44.5%, 2.7% and 4.0% of the variance in SES, not taking into account the variance that they share between them. As the total percentage of variance these four variables explain is about 59.1%, the percentage of variance they share together is 0.3% (59.1 − 58.8).

■ Reporting the output

- There are various ways of reporting the results of a hierarchical multiple regression analysis. In such a report we would normally describe the percentage of variance explained by each set or block of predictors (from the value of the R square).

- One way of reporting these results is to state that: 'In a hierarchical multiple regression, potential predictors of SES were entered in blocks. Motivation was entered first, then Parental SES was added in the second block, and IQ and Age were added in the final block. The final model indicated that motivation was a negative predictor ($B = 0.31$), Parental SES was a positive predictor $B = 0.94$), and IQ and Age were also positive predictors ($B = 0.19$ and 0.44). All predictors were significant at the 1% level.'

- One would also need to summarise the regression equation as in Table 19.6.

Table 19.6	Hierarchical multiple regression of predictors of SES		
Blocks	**B**	**Standard error B**	**Beta**
Block 1:			
Motivation	−0.31	0.07	−0.44*
Block 2:			
Parental SES	0.94	0.08	0.73*
Block 3:			
IQ	0.19	0.07	0.19*
Age	0.44	0.13	0.31*

* Significant at 0.01.

Key points

- Multiple regression is only practicable in most cases using a computer, since the computations are numerous.

- Normally one does not have to compute the correlation matrix independently between variables. The computer program usually does this on the raw scores. There may be a facility for entering correlation matrices, which might be useful once in a while when you are re-analysing someone else's correlation matrix.

- Choose hierarchical selection for your multiple regression if you are trying to test out theoretical predictions or if you have some other rationale. One advantage of this is that you can first of all control for any social or demographic variables (sex, social class, etc.) which might influence your results. Then you can choose your remaining predictors in any order which you think best meets your needs.

- Choose stepwise selection methods in circumstances in which you simply wish to choose the best and smallest set of predictors. This would be ideal in circumstances in which you wish to dispense with time-consuming (and expensive) tests, say in an industrial setting involving personnel selection. The main considerations here are entirely practical.

- Avoid construing the results of multiple regression in cause and effect terms.

Recommended further reading

Cramer, D. (2003), *Advanced Quantitative Data Analysis*, Buckingham: Open University Press, Chapters 5 and 6.

Glantz, S.A. and Slinker, B.K. (2001), *Primer of Applied Regression and Analysis of Variance*, 2nd edition, New York: McGraw-Hill.

Pedhazur, E.J. (1982), *Multiple Regression in Behavioral Research: Explanation and Prediction*, 2nd edition, New York: Holt, Rinehart & Winston, Chapter 6

Tabachnick, B.G. and Fidell, L.S. (2007), *Using Multivariate Statistics*, 5th edition, Boston, MA: Allyn & Bacon, Chapter 5.

CHAPTER 20

Multinomial logistic regression

Distinguishing between several different categories or groups

Overview

- Multinomial logistic regression is a form of multiple regression in which a number of predictors are used to calculate values of a single nominal dependent or criterion variable.

- There may be any number of values (categories) of the dependent variable, with a minimum of three. It can be used with just two categories but binomial multiple regression (Chapter 21) would be more appropriate in these circumstances.

- It is used to assess the most likely group (category) to which a case belongs on the basis of a number of predictor variables. That is, the objective is to find the pattern of predictor variables that identify of which category an individual is most likely to be a member.

- Multinomial logistic regression uses nominal or category variables as the criterion or dependent variable. The independent or predictor variables may be score variables or nominal (dichotomised) variables. In this chapter we concentrate on nominal variables as predictors.

- The concept of the dummy variable is crucial in multinomial logistic regression. A dummy variable is a way of dichotomising a nominal category variable with three or more different values. A new variable is computed for each category (just one!) and participants coded as having that characteristic or not. The code for belonging to the category is normally 1 and the code for belonging to any of the other categories is normally 0.

- Multinomial logistic regression produces *B*-weights and constants just as in the case of other forms of regression. However, the complication is that these are applied to the logit. This is the natural (or Napierian) logarithm of the odds ratio (a close relative of probability). This allows the computation of the likelihood that an individual is in a particular category of the dependent or criterion variable given his or her pattern on the predictor variables.

● A classification table is produced which basically describes the accuracy of the predictors in placing participants correctly in the category or group to which they belong.

Preparation

Make sure you are familiar with Chapter 12 on chi-square and Chapters 8 and 19 on regression.

20.1 Introduction

A simple example should clarify the purpose of multinomial logistic regression. Healthcare professionals who work with patients would find it helpful to identify the 'lifestyle' characteristics which differentiate between three types – heart disease, diabetes and cancer patients. The key variable would be type of patients, and *heart disease*, *diabetes* and *cancer* would be the three different values (categories) of this nominal (category) variable. In a regression, type of patient would be called the dependent variable or the criterion or the predicted variable. Just what is different between the three groups of patients – that is, what differentiates the groups defined by the different values of the dependent variable? The researcher would collect a number of measures (variables) from each of the participants in the study in addition to their patient type. These measures are really predictor variables, since we want to know whether it is possible to assess which sort of patient an individual is on the basis of information about aspects of their background. Such predictors are also known as independent variables in regression.

Imagine the researcher has information on the following independent variables (predictor variables):

● Age of patient (younger versus older; i.e. 30 plus)

● Body Mass Index (BMI)

● Smoker

● Socio-economic status (SES)

● Alcohol use

● General nutrition

● Physical exercise.

These data could be analysed in a number of ways. One very obvious choice would be to carry out a succession of chi-square tests. The type of patient could be one of the variables and any of the variables in the above list could be the predictor variable. An example of this is shown in Table 20.1. Examining the table, these data seem to suggest that if the patient is a smoker then they are unlikely to suffer from heart disease, more likely to be a diabetes patient, but most likely to have cancer. Similar analyses could be carried out for each of the predictor variables in the list.

Table 20.1	An example of how the patient groups could be compared on the predictors		
	Heart disease	**Diabetes**	**Cancer**
Smoker	30	50	40
Non-smoker	40	30	10

There is not a great deal wrong with this approach – it would identify the specific variables on which the three patient groups differ (and those on which they did not differ). One could also examine how the three patient groups differed from the others on any of the predictor variables. Since the analysis is based on chi-square, partitioning would help to test which groups differ from the others (Chapter 12) in terms of any of the predictors.

The obvious problem with the chi-square approach is that it handles a set of predictors one by one. This is fine if we only have one predictor, but we have *several* predictor variables. A method of handling all of the predictor variables at the same time would have obvious advantages. Predictor variables are often correlated and this overlap also needs to be taken into account (as it is with multiple regression – see Chapter 19). That is, ideally the *pattern* of variables that best predicts group membership should be identified.

In many ways, multinomial logistic regression is the more general case of binomial logistic regression described in Chapter 21. The dependent variable in multinomial logistic regression can have one of several (not just two) nominal values. Nevertheless the two forms of logistic regression share many essential characteristics. For example, the dependent variable is membership of a category (e.g. group) in both cases. Like binomial logistic regression, multinomial logistic regression uses nominal (category) variables. However, not all of the sophisticated regression procedures which are available for binomial logistic regression can be used in multinomial logistic regression. Because of this, multinomial logistic regression is actually easier than binomial logistic regression. Nevertheless, there is a disadvantage for the more advanced user, since there are few model-building options (no stepwise, no forward selection, no backward selection). This makes multinomial logistic regression simpler. Sometimes multinomial logistic regression is described as being rather like doing two or more binomial logistic regressions on the data. It could replace binomial logistic regression for the dichotomous category case – that is, when the dependent variable consists of just two categories.

Box 20.1	Focus on

Using score variables in log-linear regression

Although we concentrate on nominal or category variables as the independent or predictor variables in logistic regression in this chapter, this is because it is conceptually harder to deal with them than score variables as independent variables. So for pedagogic reasons, we have not considered score variables. Score variables can be used as the independent or predictor variables and can be mixed with nominal or category variables in logistic regression.

Conceptually, you should have no difficulty going on to using score variables in this way once you have mastered the material in this chapter and Chapter 21. You may have more difficulty running the analyses on SPSS since it uses somewhat idiosyncratic terminology to refer to the two types of variable and it is not even consistent between the binomial logistic regression and multinomial logistic regression.

20.2   Dummy variables

A key to understanding multinomial logistic regression lies in the concept of dummy variables. In our example, there are three values of the dependent variable, category *A*, category *B* and category *C*. These three values could be converted into *two* dichotomous variables and these dichotomous variables are known as dummy variables:

1. ***Dummy variable 1***   Category *A* versus categories *B* and *C*

2. ***Dummy variable 2***   Category *B* versus categories *A* and *C*

Dummy variables are as simple as that. The two values of each dummy variable are normally coded 1 and 0.

What about the comparison of category *C* with categories *A* and *B*? Well, no such dummy variable is used. The reason is simple. All of the information that distinguishes category *C* from categories *A* and *B* has already been provided by the first two dummy variables. The first dummy variable explains how to distinguish category *C* from category *A*, and the second dummy variable explains how to distinguish category *C* from category *B*. The third dummy variable is not used because it would overlap completely with the variation explained by the first two dummy variables. This would cause something called multicollinearity, which means that some predictors intercorrelate highly with each other. So, in our example, only two of the dummy variables can be used. Multicollinearity should be avoided in any form of regression as it is the cause of a great deal of confusion in the interpretation of the findings.

The choice of which dummy variable to omit in dummy coding is arbitrary. The outcome is the same in terms of prediction and classification whatever value is omitted.

If you are struggling with dummy variables and collinearity, consider the following. Imagine the variable gender which consists of just two values – male and female. Try to change gender into dummy variables. One dummy variable would be 'male or not' and the other dummy variable would be 'female or not'. There would be a perfect negative correlation between these two dummy variables – they are simply different ways of measuring the same thing. So one dummy variable has to be dropped, since it has already been accounted for by the other dummy variable. If there are more than two dummy variables, the same logic applies, although the dropped dummy variable is accounted for by several dummy variables, not just one.

20.3   What can multinomial logistic regression do?

Multinomial logistic regression can help in the following ways:

1. To identify a small number of variables which effectively distinguish between groups or categories of the dependent variable

2. To identify the other variables which are ineffective in terms of distinguishing between groups or categories of the dependent variable

3. To make actual predictions of which group an individual will be a member of (i.e. what category of the dependent variable) on the basis of their known values on the predictor variables.

What are we hoping to achieve with our multinomial logistic regression? The main things are:

1. Whether our predictors actually predict the patient categories at better than the chance level

2. The constants and regression weights that need to be applied to the predictors to optimally allocate the patients to the actual patient group

3. A classification table that indicates how accurately the classification is based on the predictors compared to the known category of patient

4. To identify the pattern of predictor variables which classifies the patients into their patient category most accurately.

This list is more or less the same as would be applied to any form of regression.

Some researchers would use a different technique (discriminant analysis or discriminant function analysis) to analyse our data (see Box 20.2). However, multinomial logistic regression does an arguably better job since it makes fewer (unattainable?) assumptions about the characteristics of the data. More often than not, there will be little difference between the two in terms of your findings. In those rare circumstances when substantially different outcomes emerge, multinomial logistic regression is preferred because of its relative lack of restrictive assumptions about the data. In other words, there is no advantage in using discriminant function analysis but there are disadvantages.

Box 20.2	Key concepts

Discriminant function analysis and logistic regression compared

Discriminant function analysis is very similar in its application to multinomial logistic regression. There is no particular advantage of discriminant function analysis, which is in some circumstances inferior to multinomial logistic regression. It could be used for the data in this chapter on different types of patients. However, it is more characteristically used when the independent variables are score variables. It would help us to find what the really important factors are in differentiating between the three groups of patients. The dependent variable in discriminant function analysis consists of the various categories or groups which we want to differentiate.

The discriminant function is a weighted combination of predictors which maximise the differentation between the various groups which make up the dependent variable. So the formula for a discriminant function might be as follows:

Discriminant (function) score
$= \text{constant} + b_1x_1 + b_2x_2 + b_3x_3 + b_4x_4 + b_5x_5 + b_6x_6$

The statistic Wilks' lambda indicates the contribution of each of the predictor variables to distinguishing the groups. A small value of lambda indicates the greater the power of the predictor variable to differentiate groups. The b's in the formula above are merely regression weights (just like in multiple regression) and x_1, etc. are an individual's scores on each of the predictor variables. As with multiple regressions, regression weights may be expressed in unstandardised or standardised form. When expressed in standardised form, the relative impact of the different predictors is more accurately indicated. In our example, there will be two discriminant functions because there are three groups to differentiate. The number of discriminant functions is generally one less than the number of groups. However, if the number of predictors is less than the number of discriminant functions, the number of discriminant functions may be reduced.

The *centroid* is the average score on the discriminant function of a person who is classified as belonging to one of the groups. If the analysis involves just two groups, there are two centroids. For a two-group discriminant function analysis there are two centroids. Cut-off points are provided which help the researcher identify to which group an individual belongs. This cut-off point lies halfway between the two centroids if both groups are equal in size. The cut-off point is weighted towards one of the centroids in the case of unequal group size. A classification table (in this context also known as a confusion matrix or prediction table) indicates how good the discrimination between the groups is in practice. Such a table gives the known distribution of groups compared to how the discriminant function analysis categorises the individuals.

> ## 20.4   Worked example

The data used are shown in Table 20.2. To make the output realistic, these 20 cases have been entered 10 times to give a total sample of 200 cases. This is strictly improper as a statistical technique, of course, but helpful for pedagogic reasons.

It is not feasible to calculate multinomial logistic regression by hand. Inevitably a computer program has to be used. Consequently, the discussion refers to a computer analysis rather than to computational steps to be followed. Figure 20.1 reminds us of the basic task in multinomial logistic regression. The predictors are scores and/or nominal variables. The criterion being predicted is always a nominal variable but one with more than two categories or values. Since nominal variables have no underlying scale by definition, the several nominal categories are essentially re-coded individually as present or absent. In this way, each value is compared with *all* of the other values. It does not matter which comparison is left out and, of course, computer programs largely make the choices for you. Figure 20.2 takes the basic structure and applies it directly to our study of patients in order to make things concrete. Remember that one dummy variable is not used in the analysis.

Table 20.2		Data for multinomial logistic regression						
	Age	**SES**	**Physical exercise**	**Alcohol consumption**	**Nutrition**	**BMI**	**Smoker**	**Type of patient**
1	younger	low	yes	low	low	high	no	heart disease
2	younger	low	yes	low	low	high	yes	heart disease
3	older	low	yes	low	low	high	yes	heart disease
4	older	high	yes	high	high	low	no	diabetes
5	older	high	yes	high	high	high	yes	heart disease
6	younger	low	yes	low	low	low	no	heart disease
7	older	high	no	high	low	high	yes	heart disease
8	older	high	no	high	high	low	no	diabetes
9	younger	low	no	high	high	low	yes	diabetes
10	older	high	yes	low	low	high	yes	diabetes
11	older	high	no	low	high	low	yes	diabetes
12	younger	high	no	high	low	high	no	heart disease
13	older	high	no	high	high	low	yes	diabetes
14	older	high	yes	low	high	high	yes	diabetes
15	older	low	yes	high	low	high	yes	diabetes
16	younger	high	yes	low	high	low	no	cancer patients
17	older	high	no	high	high	low	yes	cancer patients
18	older	low	yes	high	low	low	yes	cancer patients
19	younger	high	no	high	high	high	yes	cancer patients
20	older	low	no	high	high	low	no	cancer patients

etc.

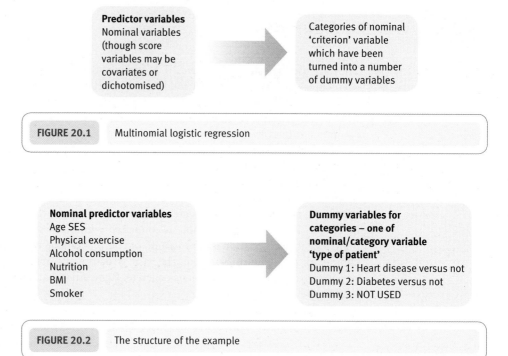

FIGURE 20.1 Multinomial logistic regression

FIGURE 20.2 The structure of the example

Our list of independent or predictor variables actually only includes two-value variables (binary or dichotomous variables). We could use more complex nominal variables as predictors. However, they would have to be made into several dummy variables just as the dependent variable is turned into several dummy variables.

Remember that the dependent variable in this case is the type of patient. There are three different types, categories or values of patient in the study. Hence there are two dummy variables listed (out of the maximum of three possible). Dummy variable 1 is heart disease versus not (not implies the patient is a diabetes or a cancer patient). Dummy variable 2 is diabetes versus not (not implies the patient is a heart disease or a cancer patient). The choice of which dummy variable to leave out of the analysis is purely arbitrary, makes no difference to the outcome, and, typically, is automatically chosen by the computer program.

20.5 Accuracy of the prediction

Once the analysis has been run through an appropriate computer program, a useful starting point is the classification table (that is, an accuracy assessment). Sometimes this is an option that you will have to select rather than something automatically produced by the program. The classification table is a crosstabulation (or contingency) table which compares the predicted allocation of the patients to the three patient groups to which they are known to belong. Usually, such tables include percentage figures to indicate the degree of accuracy of the prediction. Classification tables make a lot of sense intuitively and help clarify what the analysis is achieving. Table 20.3 is such a classification table for our data. We have yet to look at the calculation steps that allow this table to be generated. This comes later.

Table 20.3	Predicted versus actual category of patients			
Observed	Predicted to be a heart disease patient	Predicted to be a diabetes patient	Predicted to be a cancer patient	Percentage correct for row
Actually a heart disease patient	60	10	0	85.7%
Actually a diabetes patient	20	50	10	62.5%
Actually a cancer patient	0	30	20	40.0%
Column percentage	40.0%	45.0%	15.0%	Overall percentage correct = 65%

For the heart disease patients, the analysis is rather accurate. Indeed, the overwhelming majority of heart disease patients have been correctly identified. Hence, the row percentage correctly classified for heart disease patients is 85.7%. This calculation is simply the number of correctly identified heart disease patients (60) expressed as a percentage of the number of heart disease patients in total (70). So the accuracy for the prediction for heart disease is $60/70 \times 100\% = 0.857 \times 100\% = 85.7\%$.

None of the heart disease patients were predicted to be cancer patients, though some were predicted to be diabetes patients. The other two categories of patient could not be differentiated to the same level of accuracy. For the diabetes patients, 62.5% were correctly identified. The cancer patients were relatively poorly predicted – only 40% of cancer patients were correctly identified. Interestingly, the cancer patients are only ever wrongly classified as being diabetes patients; they are never wrongly classified as being heart disease patients.

So it would appear that the model (pattern of predictors of patient category) is reasonably successful at distinguishing the patient types. Nevertheless, the identification of diabetes and cancer patients is not particularly good. Obviously, if we were to persist in our research then we would seek to include further predictor variables that were better at differentiating the diabetes and cancer groups.

20.6   How good are the predictors?

Calculating multinomial logistic regression using a computer program generates a variety of statistical analyses apart from the classification table discussed so far. We need to turn to other aspects of this multinomial logistic regression output in order to identify just how successful each predictor is and what predictors should be included in the model. The classification table gives no indication of this since it does not deal with the individual predictor variables.

Is the prediction better than chance? At some point in the analysis, there should be a table or tables including output referring to, say, 'Cox and Snell' or 'Nagelkerke' or 'McFadden' or to several of these. These may be described as pseudo r-square statistics. They refer to the amount of variation in the dependent variable which is predicted by the predictor variables collectively. The maximum value of this, in theory, is 1.00 if the relationship is perfect; it will be 0.00 if there is no relationship. They are pseudo-statistics because they appear to be like r-square (which is the square of the multiple correlation between the independent and dependent variable – Section 19.3) but they are

Table 20.4	Pseudo *r*-square statistics	
		Pseudo-statistic
	Cox and Snell	0.756
	Nagelkerke	0.855
	McFadden	0.654

only actually analogous to it. One simply cannot compute a Pearson correlation involving a nominal variable with more than two values (categories). The nearer the pseudo-statistic is to a perfect relationship of 1.00 the better the prediction (just as it would be with a proper *r*-square). The value for 'Cox and Snell' is 0.756, the value for Nagelkerke is 0.855 and the value for McFadden is 0.654. So the relationship between the predictors and the criterion is quite good (see Table 20.4). We would interpret these values more or less as if they were analogous to a squared Pearson correlation coefficient.

Another table will be found in the computer output to indicate how well the model improves fit over using *no* model at all (Table 20.5). This is also an indication of whether the set of predictors actually contributes to the classification process over and above what random allocation would achieve. This is known as the model fit (but really is whether the modelled predictions are different from purely random predictions). This involves a statistic called −2 log likelihood which is discussed in Box 20.3. Often the value for the intercept is given (remember that this is a regression so there is a constant of some fixed value). Table 20.5 illustrates this aspect of the output. The chi-square value is calculated using the −2 log likelihood statistic. This amounts to a measure of the amount of change due to using the predictors versus not using the predictors. As can be seen, there is a significant change, so it is worthwhile using the model. (It is significant at the 0.001 level. That is, it is a change in predictive power which is significant at better than the 5% level or 0.05 level.)

There is yet another statistic that is worth considering – the goodness-of-fit of the model to the data. The model is not merely intended to be better than no model at all but, ideally, it will fit or predict the actual data fairly precisely. A chi-square test can be performed comparing the fit of the predicted data to the actual data. In this case, of course, the ideal outcome is no significant difference between the actual data and that predicted from the model. This would indicate that it is pointless searching for additional predictors to fit the model – assuming that the sample is fairly large so sampling fluctuations may not be too much of a problem. In this example, the model makes predictions which are significantly different from the obtained classification of the patient. The incomplete match between the data and the predicted data is not surprising given

Table 20.5	Model fitting information indicating whether the prediction actually changes significantly from the values if the predictors were not used			
Model components	**−2 log likelihood statistic**	**Chi-square for change**	**Degrees of freedom**	**Significance**
Intercept (i.e. constant) only	407.957			
Final model	248.734	159.224	14	0.001

Table 20.6	Goodness-of-fit of the actual patient category to the predicted patient category		
	Chi-square	**df**	**Significance**
Pearson goodness-of-fit statistic	228.010	22	0.001

the classification table (Table 20.3). This does not mean that the model is no good, merely that it could be better. Table 20.6 gives the goodness-of-fit statistics. Probably in psychology and the social sciences, it is unrealistic to expect any model to predict the actual data perfectly. Moderate levels of fit would be acceptable.

Box 20.3   Key concepts

Change in the −2 log likelihood

Logistic regression uses a statistic called −2 log likelihood. This statistic is used to indicate (a) how well both the model (the pattern of predictors) actually fits the obtained data, (b) the change in fit of the model to data if a predictor is removed from the model, and (c) the extent to which using the model is an improvement on *not* using the model. These uses are different although the same statistic is used in assessing them.

There is a similarity, however. All of them involve the closeness of fit between different versions of the classification table. Earlier in studying statistics, we would have used chi-square in order to assess the significance of these discrepancies between one classification table and another. Actually that is more or less what we are doing when we use the −2 log likelihood statistic. This statistic is distributed like the chi-square statistic. Hence, you will find reference to chi-square values close to where the −2 log likelihood statistic is reported. The −2 in the title −2 log likelihood is there because it ensures that the log likelihood is distributed according to the chi-square distribution. It is merely a pragmatic adjustment.

Just like chi-square, then, a zero value of the −2 log likelihood is indicative that the two contingency tables involved fit each other perfectly. That is, the model fits the data perfectly, dropping a predictor makes no difference to the predictive power of the analysis, or the model is no different from a purely chance pattern. All of these are more similar than they might at first appear. Similarly, the bigger the value of the −2 log likelihood statistic, the more likely is there to be a significant difference between the versions of the contingency table. That is, the model is less than perfect in that it does not reproduce the data exactly (though it may be a fairly useful model); the variable which has been dropped from the model should not be dropped since it makes a useful contribution to understanding the data; or the model is better than a chance distribution – that is, makes a useful contribution to understanding the pattern of the data on the dependent variable.

The statistic usually reported is the *change* in the −2 log likelihood. The calculation of the degrees of freedom is a little less straightforward than for chi-square. It is dependent on the change in the number of predictors associated with the change in the −2 log likelihood.

So which are the best predictors? It was clear from Table 20.4 that the predictors improve the accuracy of the classification. However, this is for *all* of the predictors. It does not tell us which predictors (components of the model) are actually responsible for this improvement. To address that issue, it is necessary to examine the outcomes of a number of likelihood ratio tests. Once again these use the −2 log likelihood calculation but the strategy is different. There is a succession of such tests that examine the effect of

Table 20.7	Likelihood ratio tests			
Predictor	−2 log likelihood of reduced model, i.e. without the predictor in the left-hand column	Chi-square	Degrees of freedom	Significance
Intercept (constant)	248.734			
Age	267.272	18.538	2	0.000
SES	249.454	0.721	2	0.697
Exercise	248.932	0.199	2	0.905
Alcohol	256.089	7.355	2	0.025
Nutrition	259.677	10.943	2	0.004
BMI	287.304	38.571	2	0.000
Smoker	263.914	15.181	2	0.001

removing *one* predictor from the model (set of potential predictors). The change in the −2 log likelihood statistic consequent on doing this is distributed like the chi-square distribution. Table 20.7 shows such a set of calculations for our data. Notice that in general little changes (i.e. the chi-square values are small) in a number of cases – SES, exercise and alcohol. Removing these variables one at a time makes *no* difference of any importance in the model's ability to predict. In other words, neither SES nor exercise level are useful predictors.

Other predictors can be seen to be effective predictors simply because removing them individually makes a significant difference to the power of the model. That is, the model with any of these predictors taken away is a worse fit to the data than when the predictor is included (i.e. the full model). While we have identified the good predictors, this is not the end of the story since we cannot say what each of the good predictors is good at predicting – remember that we have several (two in this example) dummy variables to predict. The predictors may be good for some of the dummy variables but not for others.

20.7 The prediction

So how do we predict to which group a patient is likely to belong given his particular pattern on the predictor variables? This is very much the same question as asking which of the predictor variables have predictive power. It is done in exactly the same way that we would make the prediction in any sort of regression, that is, we multiply each of the 'scores' by its regression weight, add up all of these products, and finally add the intercept (i.e. constant) (see Chapter 19 for this sort of calculation). In logistic regression we are actually predicting category membership or, in other words, which value of the dependent or criterion variable the patient has, i.e. a heart disease, diabetes or cancer patient? This is done mathematically by calculating something known as 'the logit' (see also Chapter 21 on binomial logistic regression). The logit is the natural logarithm of something known as the odds ratio. The odds ratio relates very closely and simply to the probability that a patient is in one category rather than the others. A key thing to note is that multinomial logistic regression, like multiple regression (Chapter 19), actually calculates a set of regression weights (*B*) which are applied to the logit. It also calculates a constant or cut-point as in any other form of regression.

Table 20.8 gives the regression values calculated for our data. There are a number of things to bear in mind:

1. The table is in two parts because there is more than one dependent variable to predict – that is, there are two dummy variables. If there were three dummy variables then this table would be in three parts and so forth.

Table 20.8	Constants and regression weights for predictors used					
Category	Predictor	*B*	Standard error	Wald statistic	Degrees of freedom	Significance
Heart disease – not	Intercept	−0.260	1.158	0.050	1	0.822
	Age (younger)	−0.159	0.678	0.055	1	0.814
	Age (older)	0			0	
	SES (lower)	0.575	0.735	0.612	1	0.434
	SES (higher)	0			0	
	Exercise (no)	−0.328	0.791	0.171	1	0.679
	Exercise (yes)	0			0	
	Alcohol (lower)	0.838	0.863	0.943	1	0.332
	Alcohol (higher)	0			0	
	Nutrition (yes)	−1.576	0.815	3.739	1	0.053*
	Nutrition (no)	0			0	
	BMI (high)	20.540	0.713	830.866	1	0.000*
	BMI (low)	0			0	
	Smoker (yes)	−18.570	0.000	∞	1	
	Smoker (no)	0			0	
Diabetes – not	Intercept	−0.314	0.813	0.150	1	0.699
	Age (younger)	−1.970	0.542	13.187	1	0.000*
	Age (older)	0			0	
	SES (lower)	0.086	0.562	0.024	1	0.878
	SES (higher)	0			0	
	Exercise (no)	−0.014	0.505	0.01	1	0.977
	Exercise (yes)	0			0	
	Alcohol (lower)	1.486	0.615	5.836	1	0.016*
	Alcohol (higher)	0			0	
	Nutrition (yes)	0.479	0.704	0.463	1	0.496
	Nutrition (no)	0			0	
	BMI (high)	0.652	0.582	1.255	1	0.263
	BMI (low)	0			0	
	Smoker (yes)	0.498	0.498	1.003	1	0.317
	Smoker (no)	0			0	

* Wald test is significant at better than the 0.05 level.

2. The dichotomous variables are each given a regression weight (B) value for each value. The value coded 1 has a numerical value which may be positive or negative. The other value is given a regression weight of 0 every time. That is, by multiplying the numerical value by 0 we are always going to get 0. In other words, one of the values of a dichotomous predictor has no effect on the calculation.

3. There is a statistic called the Wald statistic in Table 20.8. This statistic is based on the ratio between the B-weight and the standard error. Thus for the first dummy variable it is 0.055. This is not statistically significant ($p = 0.814$). Sometimes the output will be a little misleading since if the standard error is 0.00 then it is not possible to calculate the Wald statistic as it is an infinitely large value. Any value divided by 0 is infinitely large. An infinitely large value is statistically significant but its significance value cannot be calculated. The significant values of the Wald statistic indicate which of our predictors is statistically significant.

20.8   What have we found?

It is fairly self-evident that the features which distinguish the three groups of patients are as follows:

1. Heart disease patients (as opposed to diabetes and cancer patients) are less likely to have been low in nutrition ($B = -1.576$, the minus sign meaning that the reverse of nutrition is true). This is (only just) significant at 0.053. The heart disease patients were also more likely to be in the high BMI category ($B = 20.540$ and the sign is positive). This is much more statistically significant and the best predictor of all. Finally, the heart disease patients were – surprisingly – less likely to have been smokers. There is no significance level reported for this because the standard error is 0.000, which makes the Wald statistic infinitely large. Hence, a precise significance level cannot be calculated but really it is extremely statistically significant.

2. Diabetes patients (as opposed to heart disease and cancer patients) are more likely to be in the young group and to have low alcohol use.

The findings are presented in Table 20.9. There were two dummy variables so there are two dimensions to the table. This table probably will help you to understand why only two dummy variables are needed to account for the differences between three groups.

Table 20.9	Differentiating characteristics of the three patient types	
	Younger age group: Low alcohol consumption	Older age group: High alcohol consumption
Poor nutrition: low BMI, but smoker	diabetes	cancer
High nutrition: high BMI, but non-smoker		heart disease

20.9 Reporting the results

As with some other more advanced statistical procedures, there is no standard way of presenting the outcome of a multinomial logistic regression. One way of reporting the broad findings of the analysis would be as follows: 'A multinomial logistic regression was conducted using six dichotomous predictors to predict classification on the multinomial dependent variable patient type (cancer, diabetes, heart disease). The predictors were capable of identifying the patient group at better than the chance level. Two regression patterns were identified – one for heart disease versus the other two groups, the second for diabetes patients versus the other two groups. The pseudo-r^2 (Cox and Snell) was 0.76, indicating a good fit between the total model and data, although the fit was less than perfect. Heart disease patients were differentiated from the other two groups by having good nutrition and having a high BMI but not being smokers. Diabetes patients were significantly differentiated from the other two groups by being in the younger age group and having low alcohol consumption. Heart disease patients were correctly identified with a high degree of accuracy (85.7% correct). Diabetes patients were less accurately identified (62.5% correct). Cancer patients were more likely to be wrongly classified (accuracy 40.0% correct) but as diabetes rather than heart disease patients. The regression weights are to be found in Table 20.8.'

20.10 When to use multinomial logistic regression

Multinomial logistic regression is a very flexible regression procedure. The most important thing is that the dependent variable is a nominal (category) variable with three or more categories. It will work with a binomial dependent variable though it is probably better to use binomial logistic regression (Chapter 21) that has more advanced features in SPSS for this. The predictor variables can be any mixture of score variables and nominal (category) variables. Multinomial logistic regression is useful when trying to differentiate a nominal (category) dependent variable's categories in terms of the predictor variables. In the present example, the question is what lifestyle characteristics differentiate heart disease, diabetes and cancer patients?

20.11 When not to use multinomial logistic regression

There are few reasons not to use multinomial logistic regression where the dependent variable is a nominal (category) variable with three or more categories. The predictors used can be scores and nominal (category) variables, so it is very flexible in this respect.

In circumstances where binomial logistic regression is appropriate, this should be used in preference simply because SPSS has more powerful procedures for the two-category case.

20.12 Data requirements for multinomial logistic regression

The dependent variable should consist of three or more nominal categories. We would not advise the use of dependent variables with more than say five or six categories simply because of the complexity of the output. SPSS will cope with more categories – though the researcher may not cope with the output.

The independent variables ideally should not correlate highly (as in any regression) and it is wise to examine the interrelationships between the independent variables when planning which of them to put into the logistic regression analysis.

20.13 Problems in the use of multinomial logistic regression

Multinomial logistic regression can produce a great deal of SPSS output. However, much of it is not necessary and a good interpretation can be based on a limited number of tables. We find it particularly helpful to keep an eye on the classification table as this is a simple and graphic summary of the analysis.

SPSS procedures for multinomial logistic regression and binomial logistic regression are rather different in terms of how one goes about the analysis. This can cause confusion. Even the terminology used is different.

The major problem in our experience centres around stipulating which are score variables and which are nominal (category) variables – or failing to differentiate between the two. The worst situation is where SPSS believes that a score variable is a nominal (category) variable. The problem is that each value of the score variable is regarded as a different nominal category, so numerous dummy variables are created to the consternation of the researcher.

20.14 SPSS analysis

■ The data to be analysed

The use of multinomial logistic regression will be illustrated using the data described in Table 20.2. These data are from a fictitious study of the differences between heart disease, diabetes and cancer patients. This means that the categories of patient equate to a nominal or category variable with three different values. In this example all of the predictor variables – age, socio-economic status (SES), physical exercise, alcohol consumption, nutrition, Body Mass Index (BMI) and smoking – are nominal (category) variables with just two different values in each case. It must be stressed that any type of variable may be used as a predictor in multinomial logistic regression. However, the researcher needs to indicate which are score variables in the analysis.

■ Entering the data

These data are entered into SPSS in the usual way with each variable being represented by a column. For learning purposes, the data have been repeated 10 times in order to have a realistic data set for the analysis, but to limit the labour of those who wish to reproduce the analysis exactly.

In *all* multinomial logistic regression analyses, dummy variables are created by SPSS. This is always the case for the predicted variable (patient type in this case), but there may be also nominal (category) predictor variables with more than two categories. If this is the case, SPSS generates new variables (dummy variables) for inclusion in the analysis. So do not be surprised to find variables reported in the output which were not part of the data input. SPSS does not show the dummy variables that it creates in the data spreadsheet – they are referred to in the output, however. SPSS creates appropriate dummy variables for the dependent (criterion) variable automatically based on the number of different values (categories) of that variable. The predictor or independent variables are also dummy coded if they are defined by the researcher as being nominal (category or categorical) variables. Dummy variables are discussed in the chapter overview and in Section 20.2.

Step 1

Enter the data. Weight the cases with 'freq' (see Section 19.10 or 19.16).

	age	SES	Exercise	Alcohol	Nutrition	BMI	Smoker	Patient	freq
1	1	1	2	1	2	1	2	1	10
2	1	1	2	1	2	1	1	1	10
3	2	1	2	1	2	1	1	1	10
4	2	2	2	2	1	2	2	2	10
5	2	2	2	2	1	1	1	1	10
6	1	1	2	1	2	2	1	1	10
7	2	2	1	2	2	1	1	1	10
8	2	2	1	2	1	2	2	2	10
9	1	1	1	2	1	2	1	2	10
10	2	2	2	1	2	1	1	2	10
11	2	2	1	1	1	2	1	2	10
12	1	2	1	2	2	1	2	1	10
13	2	2	1	2	1	2	1	2	10
14	2	2	2	1	1	1	1	2	10
15	2	1	2	2	2	1	1	2	10
16	1	2	2	1	1	2	2	3	10
17	2	2	1	2	1	2	1	3	10
18	2	1	2	2	2	2	1	3	10
19	1	2	1	2	1	1	1	3	10
20	2	1	1	2	1	2	2	3	10

■ Stepwise multinomial logistic regression

Step 1

Select 'Analyze'
→ 'Regression'
→ 'Multinomial Logistic…'.

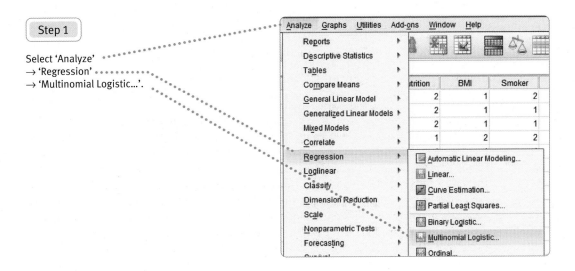

Step 2

Select 'Patient' and the arrow button beside
the 'Dependent:' box to put it there.
Select the other seven variables either
singly or together (excluding 'freq')
and the arrow button beside the
'Factor(s):' box to put them there.
Select 'Model...'.

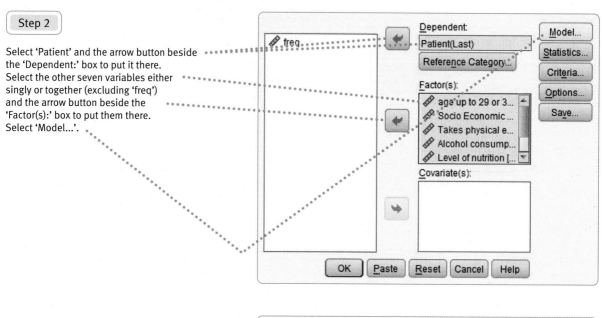

Step 3

Select 'Custom/Stepwise'.
Select the other seven variables
in turn and the arrow button beside
'Stepwise Terms:' to put them there.
Select 'Continue'.
Select 'Statistics...' in the previous box.

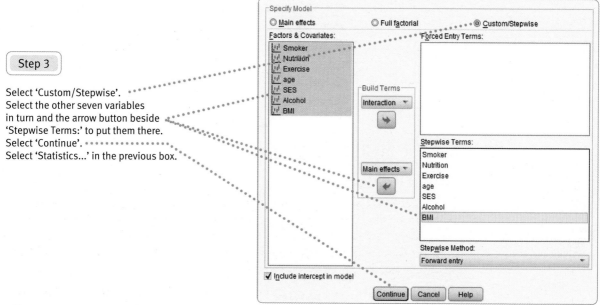

Step 4

Select 'Cell probabilities',
'Classification table' and 'Goodness-of-fit'.
Select 'Continue'.
Select 'OK' in the previous box.

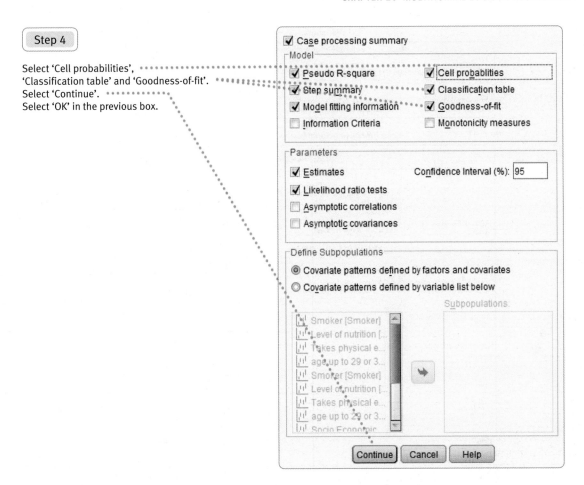

Interpreting the output

- The output for multinomial logistic regression is quite substantial. Of course, it is possible to reduce the amount of output but then the researcher needs to be clear just what aspects of the output are not necessary for their purposes. Since it is easier to ignore surplus tables than to redo the analysis, it is better to err on the side of too much output.

- It is a useful reminder to examine the table labelled Case Processing Summary. This provides a reminder of the distributions of the categories of each of the variables in the analysis. In our example all of the variables simply have two categories so no dummy variables need to be created. However, the predictor variables may have three or more categories, in which case SPSS will create appropriate dummy variables for all but one of the categories of that variable. (This does not apply to variables defined as a covariate which are treated as score variables.) There are, however, three different values of the criterion variable of patient type – heart disease, diabetes patients and cancer patients – and SPSS will create two dummy variables from these three categories.

Warnings

There are 37 (64.9%) cells (i.e., dependent variable levels by subpopulations) with zero frequencies.

Unexpected singularities in the Hessian matrix are encountered. This indicates that either some predictor variables should be excluded or some categories should be merged.

The NOMREG procedure continues despite the above warning(s). Subsequent results shown are based on the last iteration. Validity of the model fit is uncertain.

Case Processing Summary

		N	Marginal Percentage
type of patient	Heart Disease	70	35.0%
	Diabetes	80	40.0%
	Cancer	50	25.0%
age up to 29 or 30 and above	younger	70	35.0%
	older	130	65.0%
Socio Economic Status (SES)	low	80	40.0%
	high	120	60.0%
Takes physical excercise	low	90	45.0%
	high	110	55.0%
Alcohol consumption	low	80	40.0%
	high	120	60.0%
Level of nutrition	High	110	55.0%
	Low	90	45.0%
Body Mass Index (BMI)	High	100	50.0%
	Low	100	50.0%
Smoker	yes	130	65.0%
	no	70	35.0%
Valid		200	100.0%
Missing		0	
Total		200	
Subpopulation		19[a]	

a. The dependent variable has only one value observed in 18 (94.7%) subpopulations.

This table shows the distribution for each of the variables in the analysis. The patient distribution is circled.

- The Step Summary table essentially gives the sequence of variables entered into the stepwise multiple regression.

- Remember that in stepwise analyses the predictors are selected in terms of their (distinct) predictive power. So the best predictor is selected first, adjustments are made, the remaining best predictor is selected second, and so forth. There is a Step 0 which contains only the intercept of the regression line. Steps 1 to 4 in this example add in the strongest predictors in turn. The variable 'Nutrition' is added in Step 1, Age in Step 2, BMI in Step 3 and Smoker in Step 4. Each of these produces a significantly better fit of the predicted (modelled) data to the actual data. This can be seen from the lowering values of the −2 log-likelihood values (which are chi-square values) given in the table. Each of these changes is significant in this example, meaning that none of the predictors may be dropped without worsening the accuracy of the classification.

The model at Step 0 has no predictor variables. At Step 1 the variable Nutrition is entered. This is the best predictor available.

This table gives the order in which the predictor variables were selected.

Step Summary

Model	Action	Effect(s)	Model Fitting Criteria -2 Log Likelihood	Effect Selection Tests Chi-Square[a]	df	Sig.
0	Entered	Intercept	407.957	.		
1	Entered	Nutrition	330.132	77.825	2	.000
2	Entered	age	300.651	29.481	2	.000
3	Entered	BMI	274.195	26.456	2	.000
4	Entered	Smoker	258.708	15.487	2	.000
5	Entered	Alcohol	250.102	8.606	2	.014

Stepwise Method: Forward Entry

a. The chi-square for entry is based on the likelihood ratio test.

Alcohol is the last variable entered into the regression equation. The analysis proceeds no further after this in this example.

- The model fitting table gives the value of the −2 log-likelihood chi square for the fit of the model (i.e. the significant predictors plus the intercept). This value is significant in this case. It merely is an indication that the model (predictor variables) do not completely predict the actual data. In other words, the prediction is less than complete or partial. Clearly, there are other factors that need to be taken into account to achieve a perfect fit of the model to the data. This will normally be the case.

The Intercept Only model includes none of the predictor variables. The Final model is the one using the best set of predictors. Notice that there is a significant improvement in fit to the data by using the Final model.

Model Fitting Information

Model	Model Fitting Criteria -2 Log Likelihood	Likelihood Ratio Tests Chi-Square	df	Sig.
Intercept Only	407.957			
Final	250.102	157.856	10	.000

Goodness-of-Fit

	Chi-Square	df	Sig.
Pearson	230.126	26	.000
Deviance	246.629	26	.000

This table indicates how well the predicted data fits the actual data. There is a significant difference between the two – that is, the prediction is less than perfect.

● The table of the pseudo *R*-square statistics merely confirms this. The *R*-square statistic gives the combined correlation of a set of predictors with the predicted variable for score data. The pseudo *R*-square is analogous to this in interpretation but is used when it is not possible to accurately compute the *R*-square statistic itself as in the case of logistic regression. As can be seen, three different methods of calculation are used. They are all indicators of the combined relationship of the predictors to the category variable. A value of 0 means no multiple correlation, and a value of 1.00 means a perfect multiple correlation. Values of around 0.5 are fairly satisfactory as they indicate an overall combined correlation of the predictor variables with the predicted variable of around 0.7. (This is obtained by taking the square root of 0.5.)

Pseudo R-Square

Cox and Snell	.546
Nagelkerke	.617
McFadden	.365

This table gives three estimates of the 'multiple correlation' between the predictor variables and patient category membership. It is interpreted like a squared correlation coefficient. The values are moderate (1.00 would indicate a perfect classification) confirming that the prediction is less than perfect.

● The table of the likelihood ratio tests tells us what happens to the model if we remove each of the predictor variables in turn. The model is merely the set of predictors that emerge in the analysis. In this case we have four predictors as already described. In each case there is a significant decrement in the fit of the predicted data to the actual data following the dropping of any of the predictors. In other words, each of the predictors is having a significant effect and normally should be retained. Of course, should the researcher have good reason then any predictor can be dropped, though it is recommended that inexperienced researchers do not do this.

Likelihood Ratio Tests

Effect	Model Fitting Criteria -2 Log Likeliho od of Reduce d Model	Likelihood Ratio Tests Chi-Square	df	Sig.
Intercept	250.102	.000	0	.
Smoker	264.656	14.555	2	.001
Nutrition	273.076	22.975	2	.000
age	271.748	21.647	2	.000
Alcohol	258.708	8.606	2	.014
BMI	291.381	41.280	2	.000

The chi-square statistic is the difference in -2 log-likelihoods between the final model and a reduced model. The reduced model is formed by omitting an effect from the final model. The null hypothesis is that all parameters of that effect are 0.

a. This reduced model is equivalent to the final model because omitting the effect does not increase the degrees of freedom.

This is a very important table that indicates whether removing each of the predictor variables from the prediction reduces significantly the fit of the prediction to the actual data. As can be seen, in this case removing any of the four predictors adversely affects the fit of the predicted data to the actual data.

● The table of the parameter estimates basically gives the intercept and the regression weights for this multinomial regression analysis. The intercept value is clear at 0.88 for heart disease. But notice a number of things. The dependent variable (patient type) which has three categories has been turned into two dummy variables: heart disease (versus the other two groups) and diabetes (versus the other two groups).

This table gives the *B* weights that the computer will use in making its predictions. The *B* weights are useful to report but the researcher would not need to actually do any calculations involving them.

Parameter Estimates

type of patient[a]		B	Std. Error	Wald	df	Sig.	Exp(B)	95% Confidence Interval for Exp (B)	
								Lower Bound	Upper Bound
Heart Disease	Intercept	.088	.787	.012	1	.911			
	[Smoker=1]	-18.398	.654	791.747	1	.000	1.023E-8	2.839E-9	3.684E-8
	[Smoker=2]	0[b]	.	.	0	.	.	.	.
	[Nutrition=1]	-1.967	.606	10.535	1	.001	.140	.043	.459
	[Nutrition=2]	0[b]	.	.	0	.	.	.	.
	[age=1]	-.160	.621	.066	1	.797	.852	.252	2.878
	[age=2]	0[b]	.	.	0	.	.	.	.
	[Alcohol=1]	1.024	.672	2.323	1	.127	2.783	.746	10.380
	[Alcohol=2]	0[b]	.	.	0	.	.	.	.
	[BMI=1]	20.173	.000	.	1	.	5.765E8	5.765E8	5.765E8
	[BMI=2]	0[b]	.	.	0	.	.	.	.
Diabetes	Intercept	-.206	.596	.119	1	.730			
	[Smoker=1]	.488	.476	1.053	1	.305	1.629	.641	4.138
	[Smoker=2]	0[b]	.	.	0	.	.	.	.
	[Nutrition=1]	.380	.503	.572	1	.450	1.462	.546	3.917
	[Nutrition=2]	0[b]	.	.	0	.	.	.	.
	[age=1]	-1.955	.507	14.845	1	.000	.142	.052	.383
	[age=2]	0[b]	.	.	0	.	.	.	.
	[Alcohol=1]	1.481	.556	7.090	1	.008	4.399	1.478	13.087
	[Alcohol=2]	0[b]	.	.	0	.	.	.	.
	[BMI=1]	.613	.536	1.307	1	.253	1.846	.645	5.281
	[BMI=2]	0[b]	.	.	0	.	.	.	.

a. The reference category is: Cancer.
b. This parameter is set to zero because it is redundant.

When interpreting the output the values of the variable should be carefully checked. The *B* weight is −1.955 for the category 1.00 of the variable smoker; the other category is given the weight of 0.00. The value label 1.00 in this case means that the patient was a smoker. However, there is a negative value of *B*. This means that diabetes patients are partly distinguished from other groups by being smokers. This is a little confusing at first but is simply the way SPSS operates.

The standard error is 0.00 so the Wald value would be infinitely large. No significance level can actually be computed, although this variable is highly statistically significant.

● Remember that the number of dummy variables is given by the number of categories minus one. There are three patient categories so two dummy variables. The dummy variables are created by taking one of the three patient categories and contrasting this with the remaining patient categories. In our example, we have Heart disease versus Diabetes and Cancer patients, Diabetes versus Heart disease *and* Cancer patients, and Cancer patients versus Heart disease *and* Diabetes. The choice of which of the possible dummy variables to select is arbitrary and can be varied by selecting 'Custom/ Stepwise' in Step 3. Also notice that the variables have been given two regression weights – a different one for each value. However, one of the pair is always 0 which essentially means that no contribution to the calculation is made by these values. The significance of each of these regression weights is given in one of the columns of the table. Significance is based on the Wald value, which is given in another column. Do not worry too much if you do not understand this too clearly as one does not need to do any actual calculations.

● The classification table is very important and gives the accuracy of the predictions based on the parameter estimates. This crosstabulation table indicates what predictions would be made on the basis of the significant predictor variables and how accurate these predictions are. As can be seen, the predictions are very accurate for heart disease patients and to a lesser degree for the diabetes patients. However, the classification is poor for cancer patients.

The classification table indicates in a simple form how good the prediction is. As can be seen, the predictors are very good at predicting heart disease (85.7% correct). The predictors do a poor job at predicting cancer (only 40% of cancer patients correctly identified).

Classification

Observed	Predicted			
	Heart Disease	Diabetes	Cancer	Percent Correct
Heart Disease	60	10	0	85.7%
Diabetes	20	50	10	62.5%
Cancer	0	30	20	40.0%
Overall Percentage	40.0%	45.0%	15.0%	65.0%

- The observed and predicted frequencies table is probably most useful to those who have a practical situation in which they wish to make the best prediction of the category based on the predictor variables. The table gives every possible pattern of the predictor variables (SPSS calls them covariates) and the actual classifications in the data for each pattern plus the most likely outcome as predicted from that pattern. In other words, the table could be used to make predictions for individual cases with known individual patterns.

Observed and Predicted Frequencies

Smoker	Body Mass Index (BMI)	Level of nutrition	Alcohol consumption	Takes physical excercise	Socio Economic Status (SES)	age up to 29 or 30 and above	type of patient	Frequency Observed	Frequency Predicted	Frequency Pearson Residual	Percentage Observed	Percentage Predicted
yes	High	High	low	high	high	older	Heart Disease	0	1.302	-1.224	.0%	13.0%
							Diabetes	10	8.178	1.493	100.0%	81.8%
							Cancer	0	.519	-.740	.0%	5.2%
			high	low	high	younger	Heart Disease	0	3.375	-2.257	.0%	33.8%
							Diabetes	0	2.228	-1.693	.0%	22.3%
							Cancer	10	4.397	3.570	100.0%	44.0%
				high	high	older	Heart Disease	10	1.644	7.130	100.0%	16.4%
							Diabetes	0	6.531	-4.339	.0%	65.3%
							Cancer	0	1.825	-1.494	.0%	18.2%
		Low	low	high	low	younger	Heart Disease	10	8.581	1.286	100.0%	85.8%
							Diabetes	0	.857	-.968	.0%	8.6%
							Cancer	0	.562	-.772	.0%	5.6%
						older	Heart Disease	10	6.036	2.563	100.0%	60.4%
							Diabetes	0	3.627	-2.386	.0%	36.3%
							Cancer	0	.337	-.590	.0%	3.4%
					high	older	Heart Disease	0	6.036	-3.902	.0%	60.4%
							Diabetes	10	3.627	4.192	100.0%	36.3%
							Cancer	0	.337	-.590	.0%	3.4%
			high	low	high	older	Heart Disease	10	6.512	2.314	100.0%	65.1%
							Diabetes	0	2.476	-1.814	.0%	24.8%
							Cancer	0	1.012	-1.061	.0%	10.1%
				high	low	older	Heart Disease	0	6.512	-4.321	.0%	65.1%
							Diabetes	10	2.476	5.513	100.0%	24.8%
							Cancer	0	1.012	-1.061	.0%	10.1%
	Low	High	low	low	high	older	Heart Disease	0	.000	.000	.0%	.0%
							Diabetes	10	8.951	1.083	100.0%	89.5%
							Cancer	0	1.049	-1.083	.0%	10.5%
			high	low	low	younger	Heart Disease	0	.000	.000	.0%	.0%
							Diabetes	10	2.154	6.035	100.0%	21.5%
							Cancer	0	7.846	-6.035	.0%	78.5%
				high	older	Heart Disease	0	.000	.000	.0%	.0%
							Diabetes	10	13.195	-1.508	50.0%	66.0%
							Cancer	10	6.805	1.508	50.0%	34.0%
		Low	high	high	low	older	Heart Disease	0	.000	.000	.0%	.0%
							Diabetes	0	5.700	-3.641	.0%	57.0%
							Cancer	10	4.300	3.641	100.0%	43.0%
no	High	Low	low	high	low	younger	Heart Disease	10	10.000	.000	100.0%	100.0%
							Diabetes	0	.000	.000	.0%	.0%
							Cancer	0	.000	.000	.0%	.0%
			high	low	high	younger	Heart Disease	10	10.000	.000	100.0%	100.0%
							Diabetes	0	.000	.000	.0%	.0%
							Cancer	0	.000	.000	.0%	.0%
	Low	High	low	high	high	younger	Heart Disease	0	1.722	-1.443	.0%	17.2%
							Diabetes	0	3.524	-2.333	.0%	35.2%
							Cancer	10	4.754	3.322	100.0%	47.5%
			high	low	low	older	Heart Disease	0	.652	-.835	.0%	6.5%
							Diabetes	0	5.080	-3.213	.0%	50.8%
							Cancer	10	4.268	3.665	100.0%	42.7%
				high	older	Heart Disease	0	.652	-.835	.0%	6.5%
							Diabetes	10	5.080	3.112	100.0%	50.8%
							Cancer	0	4.268	-2.729	.0%	42.7%
				high	high	older	Heart Disease	0	.652	-.835	.0%	6.5%
							Diabetes	10	5.080	3.112	100.0%	50.8%
							Cancer	0	4.268	-2.729	.0%	42.7%
		Low	low	high	low	younger	Heart Disease	10	6.321	2.412	100.0%	63.2%
							Diabetes	0	1.237	-1.188	.0%	12.4%
							Cancer	0	2.441	-1.797	.0%	24.4%

The percentages are based on total observed frequencies in each subpopulation.

■ Reporting the output

There is no conventional method of reporting the findings succinctly for a multinomial logistic regression. If the technique has been used for previous studies in the chosen area of research then the reporting methods used in those studies might be adopted.

For the data analysed in this chapter, it is clear that there is a set of predictors that work fairly effectively in part. One way of reporting these findings would be as follows: 'Multinomial logistic regression was performed to establish what characteristics distinguish the three different types of patient. Out of the seven predictor variables included in the analysis, four were shown to distinguish the different types of patient to a degree. Heart disease patients were correctly identified as such in 85.7% of cases, diabetes correctly identified in 62.5% of instances, but cancer patients were correctly identified in only 40.0% of instances. Cancer patients tended to be misclassified as diabetes patients quite often. The predictors which distinguished heart disease from others best were being high in nutrition ($b = -1.967$), having a high BMI ($b = 20.173$) and being a smoker ($b = -18.398$). The latter is not reported as significant as such in the table. No significance is given. However, diabetes patients were best distinguished from the other two groups by age ($b = -1.955$) and alcohol consumption ($b = -1.481$).'

Key points

- The power of multinomial logistic regression to help identify differences among interesting – but different – groups of individuals means that it has far greater scope within research than has yet been fully appreciated.

- The unfamiliarity of some of the concepts should not be regarded as a deterrent. The key features of the analysis are accessible to any researcher no matter how statistically unskilled.

CHAPTER 21

Binomial logistic regression

Overview

- Binomial (or binary) logistic regression is a form of multiple regression which is applied when the dependent variable is dichotomous – that is, has only two different possible values.

- A set of predictors is identified which assesses the most likely of the two nominal categories a particular case falls into.

- The predictor variables may be any type of variable, including scores. However, in this chapter we concentrate on using dichotomous predictor variables.

- As in multiple regression, different ways of entering predictor variables are available. What is appropriate is determined partly by the purpose of the analysis. Blocks may be used in order to control for, or partial out, demographic variables, for example.

- Classification tables compare the actual distribution on the dependent variable with that predicted on the basis of the independent variables.

- Like other forms of regression, logistic regression generates B-weights (or slope) and a constant. However, these are used to calculate something known as the logit rather than scores. The logit is the natural logarithm of odds for the category. The percentage predicted in each category of the dependent variable can be calculated from this and compared with the actual percentage.

- As in all multivariate forms of regression, the final regression calculation provides information about the significant predictors among those being employed.

Preparation

Look back at Chapter 8 on simple regression, Chapter 12 on chi-square and Chapter 19 on multiple regression. Chapter 20 on multinomial logistic regression may be helpful in consolidating understanding of the material in this chapter.

21.1   Introduction

Binomial (or binary) logistic regression may be used to:

1. Determine a small group of variables which characterise the two different groups or categories of cases.

2. Identify which other variables are ineffective in differentiating these two groups or categories of cases.

3. Make actual predictions about which of the two groups a particular individual is likely to be a member of, given that individual's pattern on the other variables.

A simple way to understand binomial logistic regression is to regard it as a variant of linear multiple regression (Chapter 19). Binomial logistic regression, however, uses a dependent variable which is nominal and consists of just two nominal categories. By employing a weighted pattern of predictor variables, binary logistic regression assesses a person's most likely classification on this binary dependent variable. This prediction is expressed as a probability or using some related concept. Other examples of possible binomial dependent variables include:

- Success or failure in your driving test

- Suffering a heart attack or not

- Going to prison or not.

If the dependent variable has three or more nominal categories, then multinomial logistic regression should be used (Chapter 20). In other words, if there are three or more groups or categories, multinomial logistic regression is the appropriate approach. Often, but not necessarily, the independent variables are also binary nominal category variables. So gender and age group could be used as the predictor variables to estimate whether a person will own a car or not, for example.

Because the dependent variable is nominal data, regression weights are calculated which help calculate the probability that a particular individual will be in category *A* rather than category *B* of the dependent variable. More precisely:

1. The regression weights and constant are used to calculate the logit.

2. This in its turn is the natural logarithm of something called the odds.

3. Odds are not very different from probability and are turned into probabilities using a simple formula.

This is a little daunting at first but is not that difficult in practice – especially given that one rarely would need to calculate anything by hand!

You may find it helpful to work through the next section, on simple logistic regression. Studying this will introduce you to most of the concepts in binomial logistic regression without too much confusing detail and complexity. Simple logistic regression would not normally be calculated, since it achieves nothing computationally which is not more simply done in other ways.

21.2   Simple logistic regression

In this chapter we are looking at binomial logistic regression and applying it to predicting crime victimisation (i.e. people who are more likely to be a victim of crime). We will take a simple example of this which uses one independent variable (whether the individual is classified as unemployed or not – as opposed to, say, not in 'employment' but in education, retired or caring for children) and one dependent variable (whether or not the person has been a victim). Table 21.1 illustrates such data. The table clearly shows that people who are unemployed are much more likely to be victims than people who are not classified as unemployed. If a person is unemployed, the odds are 40 to 10 that they will be a victim. This equates to a percentage of 80% (i.e. 40/(40 + 10) × 100%). If a person is not unemployed then the odds are 15 to 30 that they will be a victim. This equates to a percentage of 33.33% (i.e. 15/(15 + 30) × 100%).

It would be a simple matter of predicting victimisation from these figures. Basically if a person is unemployed then they are very likely to be a victim of crime (80% likelihood) but if they have a job (or otherwise not classified as unemployed) then they are far less likely to be a victim (33% likelihood). Table 21.2 illustrates what we would expect on the basis of the data in Table 21.1. There is virtually no difference between the two tables – we have merely added the percentage of correct predictions for each row. That is how easy the prediction is in this simple case. Notice that we are more accurate at predicting victimisation in those people who are unemployed than we are at predicting no victimisation amongst those not classified as unemployed. That is how simple the prediction is with just a single predictor variable.

In logistic regression, simply for mathematical computation reasons, calculations are carried out using odds rather than probabilities. However, odds and probability are closely related (see Chapter 3). The odds of being a victim if the person is unemployed is simply the numbers victim divided by the numbers not victim. That is, the odds of being a victim if the person is unemployed are 40/10 = 4.0. On the other hand, if the person is not unemployed, the odds for being a victim are 15/30 = 0.50.

A simple formula links probability and odds, so it is very easy to convert odds into probabilities (and vice versa if necessary):

Probability (of being a victim) = odds/(1 + odds)
$$= 4.0/(1 + 4.0)$$
$$= 4.0/5.0$$
$$= 0.80 \ (= 80\% \text{ as a percentage})$$

It should be stressed that in reality things are even easier since, apart from explanations of logistic regression such as this, all of the calculations are done by the computer program.

Table 21.1	Tabulation of unemployed against being a victim of crime	
	Victim	**Not victim**
Unemployed	40	10
Not unemployed	15	30

Table 21.2	Classification table including percentage of correct predictions		
	Victim	**Not victim**	**Row correct**
Unemployed	40	10	80.0%
Not unemployed	15	30	66.7%

The concept of *odds ratio* occurs frequently in discussions of logistic regression. An odds ratio is simply the ratio of two sets of odds. Hence the odds ratio for being unemployed against not being unemployed is simply 4.0/0.50 = 8.0. This means that if a person is unemployed he is eight times more likely to be a victim of crime than a person who is not unemployed. Of course, there are other odds ratios. For example, if the person is not unemployed he is 0.50/4.0 = 0.125 times as likely to be a victim of crime than if he is unemployed. An odds ratio of 0.125 seems hard to decipher but it is merely the decimal value of the fraction 1/8. That seems more intuitively obvious to understand than the decimal. All that is being said is that there is eight times more chance of having outcome A than outcome B – which is the same thing as saying that there is an eighth of a chance of having outcome B rather than outcome A.

The actual calculations in logistic regression revolve around a concept known as the logit. This is simply odds or odds ratios expressed as their equivalent value in natural logarithms. So a logit is the natural logarithm of the odds (or odds ratio). Natural logarithms are explained in Box 21.1. For a short table of natural (or Napierian) logarithms see Table 21.3. Most scientific calculators will provide the natural logarithm of any number.

If we run the data from Table 21.1 through the logistic regression program, a number of tables are generated. One of the most important tables will contain a *B*-weight and a constant. These are somewhat analogous to the *b*-weight and the constant that are obtained in linear regression (Chapter 8) and multiple regression. For our data the *B* is 2.079 and the constant is −0.693. (If you try to reproduce this calculation using a computer program such as SPSS, be very careful, since programs sometimes impose different values for the cells from those you may be expecting.) The constant and *B*-weight are applied to the values of the dependent variable in order to indicate the likelihood of each of the two values occurring in offenders who are unemployed. Remember that the dependent variable is coded either 1 (if the offender has previous offences) or 0 (if the offender has no previous offences). The result of this calculation gives us the logit from which a probability of either outcome may be calculated, though normally there is no need to do so.

So, if we wish to know the likelihood of being a victim of crime, the dependent variable in our example has a value of 1. The logit (of the odds that the person will be a victim of crime) is calculated as

$$\text{logit} = \text{constant} + (1 \times B) = -0.693 + (1 \times 2.079) = -0.693 + 2.079 = 1.386$$

Table 21.3	Some odds and their corresponding natural logarithm values		
Odds (or odds ratio) or number	**Natural logarithm (logit)**	**Odds (or odds ratio) or number**	**Natural logarithm (logit)**
0.10	−2.30	1.50	0.41
0.20	−1.61	2.00	0.69
0.25	−1.39	3.00	1.10
0.30	−1.20	4.00	1.39
0.40	−0.92	5.00	1.61
0.50	−0.69	6.00	1.79
0.60	−0.51	7.00	1.95
0.70	−0.36	8.00	2.08
0.80	−0.22	9.00	2.20
0.90	−0.11	10.00	2.30
1.00	0.00	100.00	4.61

This value of the logit can be turned into odds using the table of natural logarithms (Table 21.3). The odds for a logit of 1.386 is 4.00. This is no surprise, as we calculated the odds for being a victim of crime earlier in this section using very simple methods. Expressed as a probability, this is 4.00/(1 + 4.00) = 4.00/5.00 = 0.80 = 80% as a percentage.

On the other hand, if the predictor variable has a value of 0 (i.e. the person is not likely be a victim of crime) then the calculation of the logit is as follows:

$$\text{logit} = \text{constant} + (0 \times B) = -0.693 + (0 \times 2.079) = -0.693 + 0 = -0.693$$

Again Table 21.3 can be consulted to convert this logit (natural logarithm of the odds) into the odds. We find that the odds for a logit of 0.693 is 0.50. Remember what this means. We have calculated the odds that a person who is not unemployed will be a victim of crime to be 0.50. We can express this as a probability by applying the earlier formula. This is 0.50/(1 + 0.50) = 0.50/1.50 = 0.33, or 33% as a percentage.

Thus, the probability of being a victim of crime (if the person is unemployed) is 0.67 (or 67%) and the probability of not being a victim of crime is 0.33 or 33%.

Unfortunately, binomial multiple regression is not quite that simple but only because it employs several predictor (independent) variables which may well be to a degree associated. Consequently, the prediction becomes much more complex and cannot be done without the help of a computer program, because it is very computationally intensive. But the main difference in practical terms is not great, since the user rarely has to do even the most basic calculation. Instead of one B-weight, several regression weights may be produced – one for each predictor variable. This merely extends the calculation a little as you will see later in this chapter.

Box 21.1	Focus on

Natural logarithms

We do not really need to know about natural logarithms to use logistic regression but the following may be helpful to those who want to dig a little more deeply. Natural logarithms are also known as Napierian logarithms. A logarithm is simply the exponential power to which a particular base number (which can be any number) has to be raised in order to give the number for which the logarithm is required. Let us assume, for example, that the base number is 2.00 and we want to find the logarithm for the number 4.00. We simply have to calculate e (the exponential or power) in the following formula:

$$2.00^e = 4.00$$

It is probably obvious that in order to get 4.00, we have to square 2.00 (i.e. raise it to the power of 2). So the logarithm to the base 2.00 for the number 4.00 is 2. Similarly, the logarithm of 8 to the base 2.00 is 3 and the logarithm of 16 is 4. Natural logarithms have as their base 2.71828. Table 21.3 gives some natural logarithms for a selection of numbers.

Natural logarithms are vital to the calculation of logistic regression because it is based on the Poisson distribution. Poisson distributions are largely used to calculate probabilities of rare occurrences in large populations. Multiple regression is based on the normal distribution; logistic regression is based on the Poisson distribution. One feature of logarithms is that they can be applied to any numerical measures in order to compact the distribution by making the large values relatively much smaller without affecting the small values so much. This can be seen in Table 21.3. Notice that if we take the odds ratios for 1 through to 100, the logit values only increase from 0 to 4.61. Also noteworthy is that the natural log of 1.00 (the point at which both outcomes are equally probable) is 0.0. In terms of the calculations, the main consequence of this is that the logistic regression B-weights have a greater influence when applied to a logit close to the midpoint (i.e. log of the odds ratio of 1.00) than they do higher on the natural logarithm scale.

21.3   Typical example

A typical use of binomial logistic regression would be in the assessment of the likelihood of being a victim of crime. Thus being a victim of crime could be assessed as a binomial (i.e. dichotomous) variable. In this case, the variable 'victim of crime' simply takes one of two values – the person has or has not been a victim of crime (Table 21.4). (If one, for example, counted the number of times each person was a victim of crime in that period, then regular multiple regression (Chapter 19) would be more appropriate since this would amount to a numerical score.) Decision-making about providing support and advice for victims is improved by knowing which of a set of variables are most associated with being a victim of crime. Such variables (i.e. independent variables) might include:

- Age (over 30 years versus 29 and under)

- Whether they were unemployed or not

- Whether they had substance abuse problems

- Whether they live in rented accommodation

- Whether they are married

- Whether they were a victim of a violent crime or not.

Data on these variables plus being a victim of crime are to be found in Table 21.5. There are only 19 different cases listed but they have been reproduced five times to give a 'sample' of 95 cases. This helps make the output of the analysis more realistic for pedagogic purposes, though statistically and methodologically it is otherwise totally unjustified. Nevertheless, readers may find it easier to duplicate our analysis on the computer because one block of data can be copied several times. The basic structure of our data for this regression analysis is shown in Figure 21.1.

Although we have selected binary (i.e. dichotomous) variables as the predictors in our example, score variables could also be used as predictors in binomial logistic regression. Equally, one could use nominal variables with three or more values, though these have to be turned into dummy variables for the purpose of the analysis (see Section 20.2). A dummy variable is a binary variable taking the value of 0 or 1. Any nominal (category) variable having three or more value may be converted into several dummy variables. More than one type of variable can be used in any analysis. That is, the choice of types of predictor variables is very flexible. One thing is not flexible – the dependent variable can only be dichotomous; i.e. only two alternative values of the dependent variable are possible.

As with any sort of regression, we work with known data from a sample of individuals. The relationships are calculated between the independent variables and the dependent

Table 21.4	Step 1 classification table		
	Predicted victim	Predicted non-victim	Percentage correct
Actually a victim	40	5	88.9%
Actually not a victim	5	45	90.0%

Table 21.5	Data for the study of crime victimisation (the data from 19 cases is reproduced five times to give realistic sample sizes but only to facilitate explanation)						
	Victim or not	Age	Unemployed	Substance abuse	Rented accommodation	Married	Violent offence
1	yes	younger	yes	no	no	no	yes
2	yes	older	yes	no	no	no	yes
3	yes	older	yes	yes	no	no	yes
4	yes	older	yes	yes	no	yes	no
5	yes	younger	yes	no	no	no	no
6	yes	younger	no	yes	yes	no	no
7	yes	older	no	yes	yes	yes	yes
8	yes	younger	yes	no	no	no	yes
9	yes	younger	no	no	no	yes	yes
10	yes	older	no	no	no	no	no
11	no	younger	no	yes	yes	no	no
12	no	older	no	yes	yes	no	no
13	no	older	yes	yes	yes	yes	yes
14	no	younger	no	yes	yes	yes	yes
15	no	younger	no	yes	yes	no	yes
16	no	younger	no	no	yes	yes	no
17	no	older	no	no	no	yes	no
18	no	older	yes	yes	yes	no	no
19	no	older	yes	yes	yes	no	no
etc.	yes	younger	yes	no	no	no	yes

Nominal predictor variables
Age
Unemployment
Substance abuse
Rented accommodation
Married
Victim of violent crime

Binary dependent variable
Victimisation

FIGURE 21.1	Structure of an example

variable using the data from this sample. The relationships (usually expressed as *B*-weights) between the independent and dependent variables sometimes are generalised to further individuals who were not part of the original sample. In our example, knowing the characteristics of persons who have been victims of crime, we would be likely to offer a greater degree of support to a particular person showing the pattern of characteristics which is associated with being a victim of crime.

Table 21.6	Data from Table 21.5 coded in binary fashion as 0 or 1 for each variable						
	Victimisation	Age	Unemployed	Substance abuse	Rented accommodation	Married	Violent offence
1	1	0	1	0	0	0	1
2	1	1	1	0	0	0	1
3	1	1	1	1	0	0	1
4	1	1	1	1	0	1	0
5	1	0	1	0	0	0	0
6	1	0	0	1	1	0	0
7	1	1	0	1	1	1	1
8	1	0	1	0	0	0	1
9	1	0	0	0	0	1	1
10	1	1	0	0	0	0	0
11	0	0	0	1	1	0	0
12	0	1	0	1	1	0	0
13	0	1	1	1	1	1	1
14	0	0	0	1	1	1	1
15	0	0	0	1	1	0	1
16	0	0	0	0	1	1	0
17	0	1	0	0	0	1	0
18	0	1	1	1	1	0	0
19	0	1	1	1	1	0	0
etc.	1	0	1	0	0	0	1

The terms independent and dependent variable are frequently used in regression. The thing being 'predicted' in regression is often termed the dependent variable. It is important not to confuse this with cause-and-effect sequences. Variations in the independent variables are not assumed to *cause* the variations in the dependent variable. There might be a causal relationship, but not necessarily so. All that is sought is an *association*. To anticipate a potential source of confusion, it should be mentioned that researchers sometimes use a particular variable as both an independent and a dependent variable at different stages of an analysis.

The data in Table 21.5 could be prepared for analysis by coding the presence of a feature as 1 and the absence of a feature as 0. In a sense it does not matter which category of the two is coded 1. However, the category coded 1 will be regarded as the category having influence or being influenced. In other words, if victimisation is coded 1 then the analysis is about predicting victimisation. If non-victimisation is coded 1 then the analysis is about predicting non-victimisation. You just need to make a note of what values you have coded 1 in order that you can later understand what the analysis means. If you do not use codes 0 and 1 then the computer program often will impose them (SPSS does this, for example) and you will need to consult the output to find out what codings have been used for each of the values. The coding of our data is shown in Table 21.6.

> **Box 21.2** **Focus on**
>
> # Score variables
>
> It is important to realise that score variables can be used as the independent or predictor variables in binomial logistic regression. In this chapter we concentrate on nominal (category) variables as independent/predictor variables to avoid cluttering the chapter too much. Score variables used in this way can be interpreted more or less
>
> as a binomial category/nominal variable would be, so do not add any real complexity. The difficulties come in relation to using a program such as SPSS to carry out the analysis when the user has to specify which predictor variables are score variables and which are category/nominal variables (see also Box 20.1).

21.4 Applying the logistic regression procedure

Logistic binary regression is only ever calculated using computers. The output largely consists of three aspects:

1. Regression calculations involving constant and B-weights as for any form of regression. Table 21.7 gives the constant and B-weights for our calculation.

2. Classification tables which show how well cases are classified by the regression calculation. These are to be found in Table 21.8.

| **Table 21.7** | Regression models for step 1 and step 2 |

	B	Standard error	Wald	df	Significance
Step 1					
Age (younger)	2.726	0.736	13.702	1	0.000
Unemployed – yes	1.086	0.730	2.215	1	0.137
Substance abuse – no	−9.362	59.982	0.024	1	0.876
Rented accommodation – no	21.459	76.318	0.079	1	0.779
Married – no	0.307	0.674	0.208	1	0.648
Violent offence – no	10.641	47.193	0.051	1	0.822
Constant	−13.056	47.199	0.077	1	0.782
Step 2					
Age (younger)	2.699	0.731	13.625	1	0.000
Unemployed – yes	1.153	0.708	2.648	1	0.104
Substance abuse – no	−9.428	59.946	0.025	1	0.875
Rented accommodation – no	21.375	76.395	0.078	1	0.780
Violent offence – no	10.475	47.362	0.049	1	0.826
Constant	−12.732	47.364	0.072	1	0.788

Table 21.8	Classification tables having eliminated the worst predictor		
	Not predicted victim	**Predicted victim**	**Percentage correct**
Step 1: *includes all predictor variables – age, unemployed, substance abuse, rented accommodation, married and violent offence*			
Not victim	45	5	90.0%
Victim	5	40	88.9%
			Overall correct 89.5%
Step 2: *married is dropped at this stage so age, substance abuse, rented accommodation and violent offence remain in the analysis*			
Not victim	45	5	90.0%
Victim	5	40	88.9%
			Overall correct 89.5%

The analysis terminated at this stage.

Table 21.9	Omnibus tests of model coefficients		
	Chi-square	**Degrees of freedom**	**Significance**
Step 1			
Step	70.951	6	0.000
Block	70.951	6	0.000
Model	70.951	6	0.000
Step 2			
Step	−0.210	1	0.647
Block	70.742	5	0.000
Model	70.742	5	0.000

3. Goodness-of-fit statistics which indicate, among other things, how much improvement (or worsening) is achieved in successive stages of the analysis. Some examples of these are presented in the text. Examples of these are in Table 21.9.

As with most forms of multiple regression, it is possible to stipulate any of a number of methods of doing the analysis. Entering all of the independent variables at one time is merely one of these options. Entering all predictors at the same time generally produces the simplest-looking computer output. To illustrate one of the possibilities, we will carry out *backwards elimination analysis* as our approach to the analysis of the data. There are several types of backwards elimination. Our choice is to use backwards stepwise conditional analysis which is one of the options readily available on SPSS. The precise mechanics of this form of analysis are really beyond a book of this nature.

In backwards elimination there is a minimum of three steps:

1. Step 0 includes no predictors. Since we know the distribution of values on the *dependent* variable – in this case victimisation – then this would help us make an

Table 21.10	Classification table based solely on distribution of being a victim of crime – the step 0 classification table		
	Best prediction: victim	Best prediction: not victim	% accuracy
Actually victim	0	45	0%
Actually not victim	0	50	100%
			Overall accuracy = 52.3%

intelligent guess or prediction as to whether persons are likely to be a victim of crime. Our study involves a sample of 95 persons. It emerged that 45 of them were victims of crime whereas the other 50 were not. Hence if we were to make a prediction in the absence of any other information, it would be that a person will *not* be a victim of crime since this is the commoner outcome. This is shown in Table 21.10. Such a classification table indicates the accuracy of the prediction. If we predict that no person will be a victim of crime, then we are 100% correct for those who are not victims of crime, and 0% correct (totally wrong) for those who do turn out to be victims of crime. The overall accuracy for the classification table (Table 21.8) is 52.6%. This is calculated from the total of correct predictions as a percentage of all predictions, that is, $50/95 \times 100\% = 0.526 \times 100\% = 52.6\%$.

2. Step 1 (in backwards elimination) includes all of the predictors. That is, they are all entered at the same time. This step is to be found in Tables 21.7 and 21.8. This is a perfectly sound regression analysis in its own right. It is the simplest approach in order to maximise the classificatory power of the predictors.

3. Step 2 involves the first stage of the backwards elimination. We obtain step 2 simply by eliminating the predictor which, if dropped from the step 1 model, makes no appreciable difference to the fit between the data and the predicted data (i.e. married – no). If omitting this predictor makes no difference to the outcome, it may be safely removed from the analysis. This is also illustrated in Tables 21.7 and 21.8. Dropping a variable means that the other values all have to be recalculated.

4. There may be further steps if it is possible to drop further ineffective predictors. The elimination of predictor variables in backwards elimination is not absolute. Instead, a predictor variable may be allowed back into the set of predictors at a later stage when other predictors have been eliminated. The reason for this is that the predictors are generally somewhat inter-correlated. As a consequence, the elimination of one predictor variable requires the recalculation of the predictive power associated with the other predictor variables. This means that sometimes a predictor which has previously been dropped from the analysis will return to the analysis at a later stage. There are no examples of the re-entry of variables previously dropped in our analysis – actually the analysis is now complete using our chosen method. Other methods of backwards elimination may involve more steps. There are criteria for the re-entry and dropping of predictors built into the statistical routine – the values of these may be varied.

The steps (step 0, step 1, step 2, etc.) could also be referred to as 'models'. A model is simply a (mathematical) statement describing the relationship of a set of predictors with what is being predicted. There are usually several ways of combining all or some of the predictor variables. Which is the best model depends partly on the data but equally on the researcher's requirements. Often the ideal is a model that includes the minimum set of predictors that are correlated with (or predict) the dependent (predicted) variable.

Table 21.9 gives the goodness-of-fit statistics for the step 1 and step 2 models to the step 0 model. The significant value of chi-square indicates that the step 1 model is very different from the step 0 model. However, there is very little difference between the step 1 and step 2 models. Dropping the variable marital status from step 1 to give the step 2 model makes very little difference to the value of the chi-square – certainly not a significant difference. The computer output can be consulted to see the change if a particular predictor is removed, though we have not reproduced such a table here. At step 2, having removed marital status makes a very small and non-significant change in fit. Indeed, marital status is selected for elimination because removing it produces the least change to the predictive power of the model. The chi-square value is −0.210 (the difference in the chi-square values), which indicates that the model is slightly less different from the step 0 model, but this chi-square is not significant (the probability is 0.647). Hence marital status was dropped from the model in step 2 because it makes little difference to the fit, whether included or not. The computer program then assesses the effect of dropping each of the predictors at step 2. Briefly no further predictors could be dropped without significantly affecting the fit of the model to the data. So there is no step 3 to report in this example.

Table 21.8 gives the classification tables for steps 1 and 2. (Step 0 can be seen in Table 21.10.) At the step 1 stage all of the predictors are entered. Comparing the step 0 and step 1 classification tables reveals that step 1 appears to be a marked improvement over the step 0 model. That is, the predictor variables in combination improve the prediction quite considerably. There are only 10 (i.e. 5 + 5) misclassifications and 85 (40 + 45) correct predictions using the step 1 model – an overall correct prediction rate of $85/95 \times 100\% = 89.5\%$. Those persons predicted not to be victims of crime on the basis of our predictors are, overwhelmingly, not likely to be victims of crime. At step 2, the classification table is exactly the same as for step 1. While the underlying model is clearly slightly different (see Table 21.7), in practical terms this is making no tangible difference in this case.

There is just one more useful statistic to be pulled from the computer output. This is known as the 'pseudo r^2' (see Section 20.6). It is roughly analogous to the multiple r^2 statistic used in multiple regression. It is a single indicator of how well the set of predictors predict. There are a number of such pseudo r^2. The Cox and Snell R-square and the Nagelkerke R-square are common ones. Several different ones may be given in the computer output. Although this is not shown in any of the tables, the value for the Cox and Snell R-square at step 2 is 0.525. This suggests a reasonably good level of prediction but there is clearly the possibility of finding further predictors to increase predictive power.

21.5   The regression formula

For most purposes, the above is sufficient. That is, we have generated reasonably powerful models for predicting the pattern of our data. The only really important task is making predictions about individuals based on their pattern on the predictor variables. If your work does not require individual predictions then there is no need for the following. Although we talk of prediction in relation to regression, this is often not the researcher's objective. Most typically they are simply keen to identify the pattern of variables most closely associated with another variable (the dependent variable).

The predictor variables in our example are as follows:

- Age – younger or older
- Unemployed or not
- Substance abuse or not
- Living in rented accommodation or not
- Marital status – married or not
- Victim of a violent offence or not.

The dependent variable is victimisation (or not).

It is important to recall that all of the variables were coded in binary fashion using the following. That is:

1. The variables were coded as 1 if the characteristic is present.

2. The variables were coded as 0 if the characteristic is absent.

By using these values, the predictors act as weights. It is important to note that multiplying by 0 means that we had nothing when we multiply values of 0 by their logistic regression weights. Computer programs such as SPSS usually recode binary variables for you in this way, though care needs to be taken to check the output to find out just how the recoding has been done.

The basic formula for the prediction is:

$$\text{Predicted logit} = \text{constant} + (B_1 \times X_1) + (B_2 \times X_2) + \text{etc.}$$

That is, the formula predicts the logarithm of the odds of being a victim of crime (victimisation) for an individual showing a particular pattern on the independent variables. X refers to the 'score' on a predictor variable (1 or 0 for a binary variable) which has to be multiplied by the appropriate regression weight (B). There is also a constant. It should be emphasised that this formula gives the predicted logit for a particular pattern of values on the independent variables. In other words, it is part of the calculation of the likelihood that a particular individual will be a victim of crime, though the predicted logit must be turned into odds and then probabilities before the likelihoods are known. It should be very clear from our step 2 model (Table 21.7) that the risk of being a victim of crime is greater if the person is young, is unemployed, is a substance abuser, is not living in rented accommodation and is not a victim of a violent offence.

Just what is the likelihood that an individual with a particular pattern on the predictor variables will be a victim of crime? Let us take a concrete example – an individual whose pattern is that he is young, is unemployed, is a substance abuser, is not living in rented accommodation and is not a victim of a violent offence. The first four of these are coded 1 if that characteristic is present. Not being a victim of a violent offence is coded 0. The formula for the predicted logit then is:

$$\begin{aligned}
\text{logit} &= -12.732 + (1 \times 2.699) + (1 \times 1.153) + (1 \times -9.428) \\
&\quad + (1 \times 21.375) + (0 \times 10.475) \\
&= -12.732 + (2.699) + (1.153) + (-9.428) + (21.375) + (0) \\
&= 3.067
\end{aligned}$$

This value for the logit of 3.067 translates approximately to an odds of 21.5 of being a victim of crime rather than not being a victim of crime with that pattern on the predictor variable. (That is, the natural logarithm of 21.5 is 4.067.) An odds ratio of 21.5 gives a probability of $21.5/(1 + 21.5) = 21.5/22.5 = 0.96$ or 96%. This is rather approximate as the calculation has been subject to a rounding error. So a person with this particular pattern on the predictor variables is extremely likely to be a victim of crime.

21.6   Reporting the results

The reporting of any regression is somewhat dependent on the purpose of the analysis. Consequently, only the broad outlines can be given here. The final model has been chosen, though there would be reason to choose some of the others in some circumstances. The following may be helpful as a structure for reporting one's findings. 'A binomial logistic regression was conducted in order to find the set of predictors which best distinguish between being a victim of crime or not. All the predictor variables were binary coded as was the criterion variable, victim. The analysis employed backwards elimination of variables. The final model to emerge included five predictors of victimisation – being young, being unemployed, history of substance abuse, not living in rented accommodation and not being a victim of a violent offence. This model had a pseudo r-square of 0.53 using the Cox and Snell statistic, which indicates that the fit of the model to the data possibly could be improved with the addition of further predictors. The success rate of the model was 90.0% for predicting not being a victim of crime and 88.9% for predicting being a victim of crime.'

21.7   When to use binomial logistic regression

Binomial logistic regression helps the researcher decide which of a set of predictor variables best discriminates two groups of participants: for example, which of our variables best discriminates male and female participants. More generally, it can be regarded as an example of a regression procedure but designed for situations where the dependent variable simply has two categories.

21.8   When not to use binomial logistic regression

There are no major circumstances that would argue against the use of binomial logistic regression except where there is just a single predictor variable. Also your predictor variables should not be highly correlated with each other, as in any regression. Avoid throwing every independent variable into the analysis without careful thought in advance. Usually it is better to be selective in the choice of predictors in any form of regression.

21.9   Data requirements for binomial logistic regression

The dependent variable should have just two nominal categories whereas the predictor variables can be any sort of variable including score variables. A participant may be only one category of the independent and dependent variable or contribute just a single score to score variables.

21.10   Problems in the use of binomial logistic regression

As with multinomial logistic regression, binomial logistic regression produces a great deal of SPSS output for most analyses, just a part of which may be useful to a researcher. Learning to identify the crucial aspects of the output is as essential here as with any other sort of SPSS analysis.

There is a confusing dissimilarity between how multinomial logistic regression and binomial logistic regression are computed in SPSS and they do not use consistent terminology.

Score variables can cause problems if the researcher fails to tell SPSS that a particular variable is not a nominal (category) variable but is a score. This is because SPSS will consider each different score mistakenly as a separate nominal category. Thus huge amounts of output may occur when the proper identification is not made.

21.11   SPSS analysis

■   The data to be analysed

The example we will be working with is a study of the variables that might be used to help assess whether a person is likely to be a victim of crime or not (see above). The data from the study are shown in Table 21.2. For pedagogical purposes and the convenience of those who wish to follow our steps on a computer, the 19 cases are reproduced five times. As can be seen, victimisation is a binomial category variable – in a given period of time, a person is either a crime victim or not. Since the purpose of our analysis is to find the pattern of variables that predict which of these two categories a person will fall into, this is an obvious set of data for binomial logistic regression.

■   Binomial logistic regression

Step 1

Enter the data. Weight cases by 'freq'.

	Victim	Age	Unemployed	Substance	Rented	Married	Violence	freq
1	1	1	1	1	1	1	0	5
2	1	0	1	1	1	1	0	5
3	1	0	1	0	1	1	0	5
4	1	0	1	0	1	0	1	5
5	1	1	1	1	1	1	1	5
6	1	1	0	0	0	1	1	5
7	1	0	0	0	0	0	1	5
8	1	1	1	1	1	1	0	5
9	1	1	0	1	1	0	0	5
10	0	0	0	1	1	1	0	5
11	0	1	0	0	0	1	0	5
12	0	0	0	0	0	1	1	5
13	0	0	1	0	0	0	1	5
14	0	1	0	0	0	0	1	5
15	0	1	0	0	0	1	0	5
16	0	1	0	1	0	0	0	5
17	0	0	0	1	1	0	0	5
18	0	0	0	0	0	1	1	5
19	0	0	1	0	0	1	1	5

Step 2

Select 'Analyze'
→ 'Regression'
→ 'Binary Logistic...'.

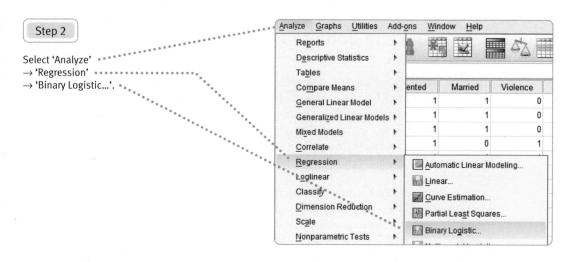

Step 3

Select 'Victim' and the arrow button beside
the 'Dependent:' box to put it there.
Select the other six variables (excluding
'freq') and the arrow button beside the
'Covariates:' box to put them there.
Select 'Categorical...'.

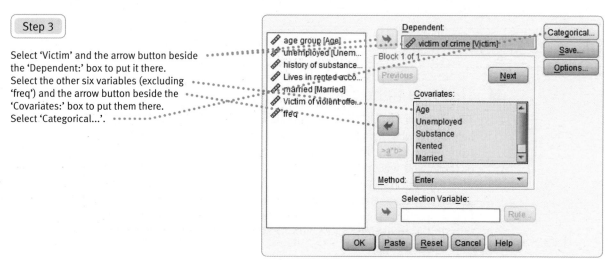

Step 4

Select all six variables (as they are nominal
variables in the example) and the arrow
button beside the 'Categorical Covariates:'
box to put them there.
Select 'Continue'.

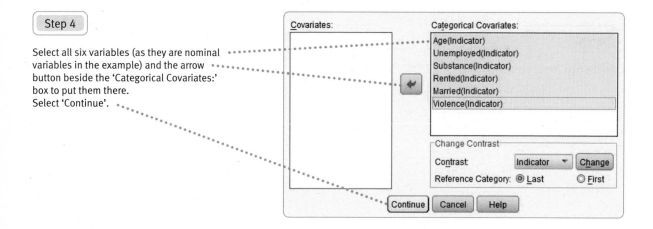

Step 5

Select the down-arrow button in the 'Method:' box, move the scroll bar to show 'Backward: Conditional' and select it. Select 'OK'.

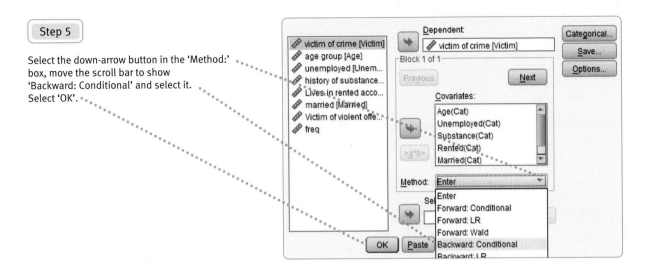

■ Interpreting the output

Case Processing Summary

Unweighted Cases[a]		N	Percent
Selected Cases	Included in Analysis	19	100.0
	Missing Cases	0	.0
	Total	19	100.0
Unselected Cases		0	.0
Total		19	100.0

a. If weight is in effect, see classification table for the total number of cases.

Dependent Variable Encoding

Original Value	Internal Value
No	0
yes	1

Check this table – it makes clear just how the dependent variable has been coded by SPSS (the Internal Value). In this case the values are the same as those we entered, but it is well worth checking, otherwise serious errors can be made.

Categorical Variables Codings

		Frequency	Parameter coding (1)
Victim of violent offence	violent offence	10	1.000
	not violent offence	9	.000
unemployed	Not unemployed	11	1.000
	Unemployed	8	.000
history of substance misuse	substance	11	1.000
	no substance	8	.000
Lives in rented accommodation	Not rented	10	1.000
	rented	9	.000
married	married	7	1.000
	not married	12	.000
age group	older (30 plus)	10	1.000
	younger	9	.000

> This table breaks down each variable and gives numbers in each category. Thus there are nine persons in the unweighted sample who are not victims of violent crime.

> Block 0 is before any predictors have been taken into account. Generally you can skip this section.

Block 0: Beginning Block

Classification Table[a],[b]

			Predicted		
			victim of crime		Percentage Correct
Observed			No	yes	
Step 0	victim of crime	No	50	0	100.0
		yes	45	0	.0
	Overall Percentage				52.6

a. Constant is included in the model.
b. The cut value is .500

> This table gives the actual numbers of victims and non-victims.

> The constant is more or less the same as the intercept in multivariate regression.

Variables in the Equation

		B	S.E.	Wald	df	Sig.	Exp(B)
Step 0	Constant	-.105	.205	.263	1	.608	.900

No predictors have been included
at this stage so there cannot be any
in the regression equation.

Variables not in the Equation

			Score	df	Sig.
Step 0	Variables	Age(1)	2.299	1	.129
		Unemployed(1)	21.159	1	.000
		Substance(1)	6.345	1	.012
		Rented(1)	31.714	1	.000
		Married(1)	.452	1	.501
		Violence(1)	.293	1	.588
	Overall Statistics		50.804	6	.000

Block 1: Method = Backward Stepwise (Conditional)

Block 1 contains the key variables.

Omnibus Tests of Model Coefficients

		Chi-square	df	Sig.
Step 1	Step	70.953	6	.000
	Block	70.953	6	.000
	Model	70.953	6	.000
Step 2[a]	Step	-.210	1	.647
	Block	70.743	5	.000
	Model	70.743	5	.000

Step 1 includes all of the predictors.

Step 2 and any later steps each involve the elimination of a variable – that is they are the backward elimination steps.

The 'Variables in the Equation' table (see below) indicates which predictors are in the model at each stage.

a. A negative Chi-squares value indicates that the Chi-squares value has decreased from the previous step.

Model Summary

Step	-2 Log likelihood	Cox & Snell R Square	Nagelkerke R Square
1	60.482[a]	.526	.702
2	60.692[a]	.525	.701

a. Estimation terminated at iteration number 20 because maximum iterations has been reached. Final solution cannot be found.

These are the indexes of the fit of the model to the actual data. The nearer the two (pseudo) R-square measures are to 1.0 the better the fit of the model at that step to the data. The smaller the −2 log likelihood value the better the fit of the model to the data.

Notice that the final model (Step 2) shows an improved fit – a variable has been allowed to re-enter the regression equation.

Classification Table[a]

			Predicted		
			victim of crime		
Observed			No	yes	Percentage Correct
Step 1	victim of crime	No	45	5	90.0
		yes	5	40	88.9
	Overall Percentage				89.5
Step 2	victim of crime	No	45	5	90.0
		yes	5	40	88.9
	Overall Percentage				89.5

a. The cut value is .500

This table indicates the accuracy of the classification table at each step. The overall accuracy remains constant throughout – what changes is the relative proportions of victims and non-victims correctly identified.

The least significant predictor in Step 1 is chosen for elimination in Step 2. Substance and Violence both have significances of 0.998 but Substance occurs first and is selected.

Variables in the Equation

		B	S.E.	Wald	df	Sig.	Exp(B)
Step 1[a]	Age(1)	-2.726	.736	13.702	1	.000	.065
	Unemployed(1)	-1.086	.730	2.215	1	.137	.337
	Substance(1)	19.362	8901.292	.000	1	.998	2.564E8
	Rented(1)	-41.459	11325.913	.000	1	.997	.000
	Married(1)	-.307	.674	.208	1	.648	.735
	Violence(1)	-20.641	7003.092	.000	1	.998	.000
	Constant	23.802	7003.092	.000	1	.997	2.174E10
Step 2[a]	Age(1)	-2.699	.731	13.625	1	.000	.067
	Unemployed(1)	-1.153	.708	2.648	1	.104	.316
	Substance(1)	19.428	8895.914	.000	1	.998	2.739E8
	Rented(1)	-41.375	11337.365	.000	1	.997	.000
	Violence(1)	-20.475	7028.411	.000	1	.998	.000
	Constant	23.542	7028.411	.000	1	.997	1.675E10

a. Variable(s) entered on step 1: Age, Unemployed, Substance, Rented, Married, Violence.

It is important to note that the regression weights are only applied to the value of the category variable coded as 1. So the negative regression weight for Violence(1) of −20.475 actually indicates that victims of violence are less likely to be victims overall. Great care is needed to know what codings are given to the different values of variables. This is made worse because variables not coded as 0 and 1 may be recoded by SPSS into those values.

Variables not in the Equation

			Score	df	Sig.
Step 2^a	Variables	Married(1)	.209	1	.648
	Overall Statistics		.209	1	.648

a. Variable(s) removed on step 2: Married.

This table gives the significance of the variables not included in the model.

■ Reporting the output

One way of reporting the findings of this analysis is as follows: 'Using the conditional backward elimination model, characteristics differentiating persons who were victims of crime or not were investigated. The final regression model indicated that younger people, those who were unemployed, those who were not living in rented accomodation, and those who were not victims of violent offences were more likely to be victims of crime. Age was a significant predictor at the 5% level. This Cox and Snell pseudo R-square was 0.53, indicating that the fit of the model to the data was only moderate. This model was almost equally accurate for victimisation (88.9% correct) as for non-victimisation (90.0%).'

Key points

● Given the power of binomial logistic regression to find the pattern of variables which are best able to differentiate two different groups of individuals in terms of their characteristics, it might be regarded as a fundamental technique for any study comparing the characteristics of two groups of individuals. In other words, it is much more effective to use logistic regression than to carry out numerous t-tests on individual variables.

● Binomial logistic regression has great flexibility in the variety of variables used so long as the groups being compared are just two in number.

CHAPTER 22

Log-linear methods

The analysis of complex contingency tables

Overview

- The analysis of nominal (category) data using chi-square is severely limited by the fact that a maximum of only two variables can be used in any one analysis. Log-linear can be conceived as an extension of chi-square to cover greater numbers of variables.

- Log-linear uses the likelihood ratio chi-square (rather than the Pearson chi-square we are familiar with from Chapter 12). This involves natural or Napierian logarithms.

- The analysis essentially examines the adequacy of the various possible models. The simplest model merely involves the overall mean frequency – that is, the model does not involve any influence of the variables acting either individually or interactively in combination. The most complex models involve in addition the individual effects of the variables (main effects) as well as all levels of interactions between variables. If there are three variables, there would be three main effects, plus several two-way interactions plus one one-way interaction.

- A saturated model is the most complex model and involves all of the possible components. As a consequence, the saturated model always explains the data completely but at the price of not being the simplest model to fit the actual data. It is essentially a conceptual and computational device.

Preparation

If you are hazy about contingency tables then look back to the discussion in Chapter 6. Also revise chi-square (Chapter 12) since it is involved in log-linear analyses. Log-linear shares concepts such as main effect and interaction with ANOVA which ought to be reviewed as general preparation (especially Chapter 14).

22.1 Introduction

In essence, log-linear methods are used for the analysis of complex contingency (or crosstabulation) tables. Data in Chapter 12 which were analysed using chi-square could be subjected to log-linear procedures although with no particular benefits. Log-linear goes further than this and comes into its own when dealing with three or more variables. Log-linear analysis identifies how the variables acting alone or in combination influence the frequencies in the cells of the contingency table. The frequencies can be regarded as if they are the dependent variable.

Some basic concepts need to be introduced:

1. ***Interactions*** Like analysis of variance (ANOVA), log-linear analysis uses the concept of interactions between two or more variables. The concept is a little difficult to understand at first. It refers to the effects of the variables that cannot be explained by the effects of these variables acting separately. Much of this chapter is devoted to explaining the concept in more detail.

2. ***Models*** A model in log-linear analysis is a statement (which can be expressed as a formula) which explains how the variables such as sex, age and social class result in the cell frequencies found in the contingency table. For example, one model might suggest that the pattern of frequencies in the contingency table is the result of the independent influences of the variable sex and the variable age. There are probably other contending models for all but the simplest cases. An alternative model for this example is that the data are the result of the influence of the variable social class *plus* the influence of the variable sex *plus* the combined influence of the variable sex interacting with the variable age. Table 22.1 gives the components of models for different numbers of variables in the contingency table. We will return to this later, but notice how the components include a constant (or the average frequency) *plus* the main effects of the variables *plus* interactive effects of the variables. Log-linear analysis helps a researcher to decide which of the possible models (i.e. which selection of the components in Table 22.1) is the best for the actual data. These different components will become clearer as we progress through this chapter. Model building can serve different purposes. Unless you have theoretical reasons for being interested in a particular model, then log-linear methods allow you to build up the model purely empirically.

3. ***Goodness-of-fit*** This is simply the degree of match between the actual data and those values predicted on the basis of the model. Chi-square is a common measure of goodness-of-fit. Chi-square is zero if the observed data are exactly the same as the expected (or predicted) data. The bigger the value of chi-square, the greater the *misfit* between obtained and expected values. In Chapter 12, a significant value of chi-square caused us to reject the 'model' specified by the null hypothesis. A good-fitting model would have a chi-square value approximating zero, whereas a badly fitting model would have a large chi-square value.

4. ***Pearson chi-square*** This is the version of chi-square used in Chapter 12 although common practice is simply to call it chi-square. The formula for the Pearson chi-square is:

$$\text{Pearson chi-square} = \sum \frac{(\text{observed} - \text{expected})^2}{\text{expected}}$$

The Pearson chi-square is used in log-linear analysis but it is not essential.

Table 22.1	Possible model components for different sizes of contingency table				
Component of model	**1**	**2**	**3**	**4**	**5**
Overall mean (equal frequencies)	yes	yes	yes	yes	yes
Main effects	A	A + B	A + B + C	A + B + C + D	A + B + C + D + E
Two-way interactions	–	A * B	A * B	A * B	A * B
			A * C	A * C	A * C
			B * C	A * D	A * D
				B * C	A * E
				B * D	B * C
				C * D	B * D
					B * E
					C * D
					C * E
Three-way interactions			A * B * C	A * B * C	A * B * C
				A * B * D	A * B * D
				A * C * D	A * B * E
				B * C * D	A * C * D
					A * C * E
					A * D * E
					B * C * D
					B * C * E
					B * D * E
					C * D * E
Four-way interactions				A * B * C * D	A * B * C * D
					A * B * C * E
					A * B * D * E
					B * C * D * E

5. *Likelihood ratio chi-square* This is the more common formula when doing log-linear analysis:

$$\text{Likelihood ratio chi-square} = 2 \times \sum \text{observed frequency} \times \ln\left(\frac{\text{observed frequency}}{\text{expected frequency}}\right)$$

The term ln is a symbol for *natural logarithm* (see Chapter 21). Although tables of natural logarithms are available, it is easier to obtain them from a scientific calculator (or the calculator built into Windows, for instance). Observed frequency refers to the obtained data, and expected frequency refers to the values expected according to the particular model being tested.

6. ***Differences between Pearson and likelihood ratio chi-square*** The formulae give slightly different values of chi-square for small sample sizes but converge as the sample sizes get large. Both formulae are often computed as measures of goodness-of-fit by computer programs for log-linear analysis. Nevertheless, it is best to concentrate on likelihood ratio chi-square in log-linear analysis because of its *additive* properties. This means that different components of chi-square can be added together to give the combined effects of different components of the chosen model. The Pearson chi-square does not act additively so cannot be used in this way, hence its comparative unimportance in log-linear analysis.

22.2   A two-variable example

The distinctive approach of log-linear analysis can take a little time to absorb. Its characteristic logic is probably best explained by re-analysing an example from Chapter 12. The study looked at the degree choice of male and female undergraduates (Calculation 12.1) and will be presented using the log-linear perspective. The data are given in Table 22.2 but they are exactly the same as the data in Table 12.7 in Chapter 12. The two variables were sex (male or female) and degree choice (business or medicine). In the (Pearson) chi-square analysis (Calculation 12.1) there is a sex difference in degree choice. Another way of putting this is that there is an interaction between a person's sex and their degree choice. (In Chapter 12, it was found that sex and degree choice acting separately were insufficient to account for the data. The expected frequencies in that chapter are the frequencies expected on the basis of sex and degree choice effects having separate and unrelated effects. In Chapter 12, a significant value of chi-square meant that the distribution of cell frequencies could not be explained on the basis of this independent influence of sex and degree choice. The different sexes had different preferences. This would be an interaction in terms of log-linear analysis.)

A log-linear analysis of the data in Table 22.2 would examine possible underlying models (combinations of the variables) which might predict the obtained data. Theoretically, there are a number of possibilities according to log-linear analysis:

1. ***Equal frequencies model*** This suggests that the observed cell frequencies are merely the total of cell frequencies divided equally between the cells. Since there are 119 observations in Table 22.2 and six cells, we would *expect* a frequency of 119/6 = 19.833 in each cell. Obviously this model, even if it fits the data best, is virtually a non-model.

2. ***Main effects model*** This suggests that the observed cell frequencies are the consequence of the separate effects of the variables. While this might seem an important possibility if you recall main effects for ANOVA, in log-linear analysis main effects

Table 22.2	Data to be modelled using log-linear analysis		
	Business degree	**Medicine degree**	**Neither**
Males	observed = 27	observed = 14	observed = 19
Females	observed = 17	observed = 33	observed = 9

are often trivial. The object of log-linear analysis is to account for the pattern of observed frequencies in the data. In Table 22.2 note that there are slightly unequal numbers of males and females (60 males and 59 females) but, more importantly, the choices of the different degree choices are unequal. That is, the different values of sex (male and female) and degree choice (business degree, medicine degree and neither) are not equally represented. For the main effect of sex, the inequality is small (60 males versus 59 females) but it is somewhat larger for the main effect of degree choice (44 choosing business degrees, 47 choosing medicine degrees and 28 choosing neither). The main effects merely refer to these inequalities which may be uninteresting in terms of the primary purpose of the analysis. In our example, a researcher is unlikely to be particularly interested in these main effects but much more interested if the interaction between sex and degree choice explains the data. In order for there to be *no* main effects, each of the categories of each of the variables would have to have the same frequency. This is rare in research.

3. *The interaction(s)* An interaction is the effect of the interrelationship between the variables. In the present example, because we have only two variables, there is just one interaction which could be termed sex × degree choice interaction. You will see from Table 22.1 that had there been more variables there would be more interactions to investigate. The number of interactions escalates with increasing numbers of variables (much as it does for ANOVA). Interactions interest researchers because they indicate the associations or correlations between variables.

The interactions and main effects are combined in log-linear analysis in order to see what main effects and what interactions are necessary to best account for (fit with) the observed data.

Log-linear analysis for this simple example involves the consideration of several different models.

■ Step 1: The equal frequencies model

In a manner of speaking this is the no-model model. It tests the idea that the cell frequencies require no explanation since they are equally distributed. This is *not* the same as the null hypothesis predictions made in Chapter 12 since these predicted not equal frequencies but *proportionate* frequencies according to the marginal totals. The equal frequencies model simply assumes that all of the cells of the contingency table have equal frequencies. Since we have a total frequency of 119 in the six cells of our analysis, the equal frequencies model predicts (expects) that there should be 119/6 or 19.833 in each cell as shown in Table 22.3. The likelihood ratio chi-square applied to this table is

Table 22.3	Contingency table for testing the equal frequencies model, i.e. the expected frequencies			
	Business degree	**Medicine degree**	**Neither**	**Total**
Males	observed = 27 expected = 19.833	observed = 14 expected = 19.833	observed = 19 expected = 19.833	
Females	observed = 17 expected = 19.833	observed = 33 expected = 19.833	observed = 9 expected = 19.833	
Total				119

Table 22.4	Calculation of the fit of the equal frequencies model			
Observed frequency	Expected frequency according to equal frequencies model	Observed ÷ expected	Natural logarithm of observed ÷ expected	Observed frequency × natural logarithm of observed ÷ expected
27	19.833	1.361	0.308	8.329
14	19.833	0.857	−0.154	−2.620
19	19.833	0.706	−0.348	−4.876
17	19.833	1.664	0.509	16.802
33	19.833	0.958	−0.043	−0.815
9	19.933	0.454	0.857	−7.111
				Total = 9.709

Likelihood ratio chi-square = 2 × total = 2 × 9.709 = 19.418

calculated in Table 22.4. Remember that the natural logarithms are obtained from a scientific calculator or one you find as a program on your computer. The use of natural logarithms is only important for understanding the basic calculation of log-linear.

The fit of the equal frequencies model to the data is poor. The likelihood ratio chi-square is 19.418. This is the amount of misfit of that particular model to the data. (It is also the amount by which the main effects and the interactions can increase the fit of the best model to the data.)

The differences between the values expected according to the model and what is actually found in the data are known as the *residuals*. The residuals can be used to assess the fit of the model to the data in addition to the likelihood ratio chi-squares. Often, residuals are standardised so that comparisons can be made easily between the different cells, in which case they are known as standardised or adjusted residuals. The smaller the residuals the better the fit of the model to the data.

■ Step 2: The saturated model

The log-linear analysis of this data could be carried out in a number of ways since there are a variety of different models that could be tested. In general we will concentrate on the procedures which would commonly be employed when using computer programs such as SPSS. Often these compute the *saturated model* for you. A saturated model is one which includes all of the possible components as shown in Table 22.1 which, consequently, accounts perfectly for the data. That is, the values predicted by the saturated model are exactly the same as the data. Any model based on all of the components by definition accounts for the data perfectly. Since there is always a perfect correspondence or fit between the observed data and the predictions based on the likelihood ratio chi-square for the saturated model, this chi-square is always zero for the saturated model.

Table 22.5 gives the data and the expected frequencies for the saturated model. Notice, as we have already indicated, that the observed and expected frequencies for any cell of the contingency table are identical for this model. We will not bother to do this calculation. It is worth noting that computer programs often routinely increase the observed values by 0.5. This is done to avoid undesirable divisions by zero in the calculation while making very little difference to the calculation otherwise.

Table 22.5	Contingency table for testing the saturated model			
	Business degree	**Medicine degree**	**Neither**	**Total**
Males	observed = 27 expected = 27.000	observed = 14 expected = 14.000	observed = 19 expected = 19.000	
Females	observed = 17 expected = 17.000	observed = 33 expected = 33.000	observed = 9 expected = 9.000	
Total				119

■ Step 3: Preparing to test for the main effects components of the model

The perfectly fitting model of the data (the saturated model) involves all possible components. It is not quite as impressive as the perfect fit suggests. We do not know what it is about our model which caused such a good fit. It could be the effects of sex, the effects of the type of degree, or the effects of the interaction of sex with type of degree, or any combination of these three possibilities. It could even mean that the equal frequencies model is correct if we had not already rejected that possibility. Further exploration is necessary to assess which of these components are contributing to the goodness-of-fit of the data to that predicted by the model. Any component of the model which does not increase the goodness-of-fit of the model to the data is superfluous since it does nothing to explain the data. (To anticipate a common practice in log-linear analysis, the corollary of this is also true: components are only retained if they *decrease* the fit of the model when they are *removed*.)

Usually in the initial stages of log-linear analyses using a computer, similar components of the model are dealt with collectively. That is, the main effects of sex and degree type are dealt with as if they were a unit of analysis. Had there been more than one interaction, these would also be dealt with collectively. At a later stage, it is usual to extend the analysis to deal with the combined components individually. That is, the data are explored in more detail in order to assess what main effects are actually influencing the data.

To reiterate what we already have achieved, we can say that we have examined two extremes of the model-building process: the saturated model and the equal frequencies model. We have established that the equal frequencies model is a poor fit to the data on this occasion (the saturated model is always a perfect fit). The misfit of the equal frequencies model to the data (likelihood ratio chi-square = 19.418) is the amount of improvement in fit achieved by the saturated model.

■ Step 4: Degree choice main effect

Main effects are one level of components in the saturated model. Understanding their calculation is fairly simple. Let us take the main effect of degree choice. In order to predict the frequencies in the data based solely on the effects of the different degree choice, we simply replace each cell by the average of the frequencies in cells referring to that degree choice. This in effect means that for our example we combine the data frequencies for the males and females who prefer business degrees and average this total by the number of cells involved (i.e. two cells). Twenty-seven males and 17 females prefer business degrees, so the total is 44, which is divided between the two cells involved in this

Table 22.6	Table of data and expected frequencies based solely on the main effect of degree choice			
	Business degree	**Medicine degree**	**Neither**	**Total**
Males	observed = 27 expected = 22.000	observed = 14 expected = 23.500	observed = 19 expected = 14.000	
Females	observed = 17 expected = 22.000	observed = 33 expected = 23.500	observed = 9 expected = 14.000	
Total	**44**	**47**	**28**	**119**

case. This gives us a predicted frequency on the basis of the main effects model for degree choice of 22.00 in each of the business degree cells. This is shown in Table 22.6. The predicted value for a medicine degree is 14 + 33 divided by 2 which equals 23.50. The predicted value for the 'neither' category is 19 + 9 divided by 2 = 14.00. Again these values can be seen in Table 22.6.

Now one can calculate the goodness-of-fit of this model simply by calculating the likelihood ratio chi-square for the data in Table 22.6. Just follow the model of the calculation in Table 22.4. The value of the likelihood ratio chi-square is 13.849. Compare this with the misfit based on the equal frequencies model (likelihood ratio chi-square = 19.418). It seems that there has been an improvement of 19.418 − 13.849 = 5.569 in the fit due to the degree main effect. (Remember that the bigger the likelihood ratio chi-square then the poorer the fit of the model to the data.) Because the likelihood ratio chi-square has additive properties, this difference of 5.569 is the contribution of the main effect of degree choice.

■ Step 5: Sex main effect

Because the frequencies of males and females in the data are nearly equal, there clearly is minimal main effect due to the variable 'sex' in this case. Nevertheless this minimal value needs to be calculated. A similar procedure is adopted to calculate the main effects of sex. This time we need to sum the frequencies over the three different degree choices for each sex separately and average this total frequency by the three degree choices. Thus the observed frequencies for males in each of the three different degree choice conditions is (27 + 14 + 19)/3 = 60/3 = 20. This gives a predicted value per male cell of 20. This is entered in Table 22.7. Similarly, the calculation for females is to sum the three observed frequencies and divide by the number of female cells. This is (17 + 33 + 9)/3 = 59/3 = 19.667. Again these values are entered in Table 22.7.

Table 22.7	Table of data and expected frequencies based on the main effect of sex			
	Business degree	**Medicine degree**	**Neither**	**Total**
Males	observed = 27 expected = 20.000	observed = 14 expected = 20.000	observed = 19 expected = 20.000	60
Females	observed = 17 expected = 19.667	observed = 33 expected = 19.667	observed = 9 expected = 19.667	59
Total				**119**

The likelihood ratio chi-square for the main effect of sex in Table 22.7 is 19.405. Compared with the value of 19.418 for the equal frequencies model, there is virtually no change, indicating the smallness of the sex difference in row frequencies. The improvement in fit due to sex alone is only 0.013.

■ Step 6: The main effects of degree choice plus sex

This can now be obtained. It involves taking each cell in turn and working out the effect on the frequencies of the degree choice and the sex concerned. This is done relative to the frequencies from the equal frequencies model (that is, 119/6 = 19.833 in every case). So, looking at Table 22.6, the expected frequency for a business degree is 22.000. This means that selecting a business degree cell increases the frequency by 22.000 – 19.833 = 2.167 as shown in Table 22.8. It may sound banal but in order to add in the effect of choosing a business degree cell we have to add 2.167 to the expected frequencies under the equal frequencies model. Similarly, choosing a medicine degree cell increases the frequency to 23.500 from our baseline equal frequencies expectation of 19.833. Selecting a medicine degree cell increases the frequency by 23.500 – 19.833 = 3.667.

In contrast, being in the 'neither' category tends to decrease the frequencies in the cell compared with the equal frequencies expectation of 19.833. From Table 22.6 we can see that the expected frequencies in the 'neither' column due to degree choice are 14.000, which is below the equal frequencies expectation of 19.833 as shown in Table 22.8. Thus, being a 'neither' cell changes frequencies by 14.000 – 19.833 = –5.833. That is, being neither decreases frequencies by –5.833. In order to adjust the equal frequencies expectations for the degree choice main effect we have to add 2.167 to the business degree cells, add 3.667 to the medicine degree cells and subtract 5.833 from (that is add –5.833 to) the 'neither' cells. This can be seen in Table 22.8.

We also need to make similar adjustments for the main effect of sex, although these are much smaller. Compared with the equal frequencies value of 19.833, the male cells have an expected frequency of 20.000 which is an increase of 0.167. In order to adjust the equal frequencies baseline of 19.833 for a cell being male we therefore have to add 0.167. This can be seen in Table 22.8. For female cells, the expected frequency is 19.667, a reduction of 0.166. In short, we add –0.166 for a cell being female. This is also shown in Table 22.8. (Of course, the additions and subtractions for the males and females should be identical, which they are within the limits of calculation rounding.)

Table 22.8	Table of expected (predicted) frequencies based on adding the main effects of degree choice and sex to the equal frequencies expectation			
	Business degree	**Medicine degree**	**Neither**	**Total**

Males	observed = 27
	expected = 19.833 + 2.167
	    + 0.167 = 22.167[a]
		observed = 14
		expected = 19.833 + 3.667
		    + 0.167 = 23.667[a]
			observed = 19
			expected = 19.833 + –5.833
			    + 0.167 = 14.167[a]
				60

Females	observed = 17
	expected = 19.833 + 2.167
	    + –0.166 = 21.834[a]
		observed = 33
		expected = 19.883 + 3.667
		    + –0.166 = 23.334[a]
			observed = 9
			expected = 19.883 + –5.833
			    + –0.166 = 13.834[a]
				59

Total				119

[a] These hand-calculated values are very approximate and do not correspond to the best values, for reasons discussed in the text.

At this point there is a big problem. That is, the values of the expected frequencies based on the main effects model gives the wrong answers according to computer output. For that matter, it does not give the same expected frequencies as given in the equivalent Pearson chi-square calculation we did in Chapter 12. Actually, the computer prints our expected frequencies which are the same as those calculated in Chapter 12. The problem is that we are not actually doing what the computer is doing. Think back to the two-way analysis of variance. These calculations worked as long as you have equal numbers of scores in each of the cells. Once you have unequal numbers, then the calculations have to be done a different way (and best of all by computer). This is because you are not adding effects proportionately once you have different cell frequencies. In log-linear analysis the problem arises because the marginal totals are usually unequal for each variable. This inequality means that simple linear additions and subtractions of main effects such as we have just done do not give the best estimates. That is in essence why a computer program is vital in log-linear analysis. Better estimates of expected frequencies are made using an iterative process. This means that an approximation is calculated but then refined by re-entering the approximation in recalculations. This is done repeatedly until a minimum criterion of change is found between calculations (i.e. between iterations). Computer programs allow you to decide on the size of this change and even the maximum number of iterations.

Now that we have some idea of how the adjustments are made for the main effects, even though we must rely on the computer for a bit of finesse, we will use the computer-generated values to finish off our explanation. Table 22.9 contains the observed and expected values due to the influence of the main effects as calculated by the computer's iterative process.

The value of the likelihood ratio chi-square for the data in Table 22.9 is, according to the computer, 13.841 (which is significant at 0.001 with $df = 2$). At this point, we can obtain the value of the sex*degree choice interaction. We now know the following:

1. The fit of the saturated model which includes main effects plus the interaction is 0.000.

2. The fit of the model based on the two main effects is 13.841.

3. The fit of the model based on the equal frequencies model is 19.418.

It becomes a simple matter of subtraction to work out the improvement in fit due to the different components. Thus:

1. The increase in fit due to the two main effects = 19.418 − 13.841 = 5.577.

2. The increase in fit due to the interaction = 13.841 − 0.000 = 13.841.

Table 22.9	Table of expected (predicted) frequencies based on adding the main effects of degree choice and sex to the equal frequencies expectation as obtained by the iterative computer process			
	Business degree	**Medicine degree**	**Neither**	**Total**
Males	observed = 27	observed = 14	observed = 19	60
	expected = 22.18	expected = 23.70	expected = 14.72	
Females	observed = 17	observed = 33	observed = 9	59
	expected = 21.82	expected = 23.30	expected = 13.88	
Total	**44**	**47**	**28**	

These numerical values are likelihood ratio chi-squares. Only the interaction is statistically significant out of these major components. The main effect of degree choice taken on its own would be statistically significant as it includes fewer degrees of freedom and has nearly the same likelihood ratio chi-square value. This is of no real interest as it merely shows that different proportions of people were choosing the different degrees. In short, the interesting part of the model is the interaction which is statistically significant. Formally, this model is expressed simply as:

constant (i.e. equal frequency cell mean) + degree main effect + A*B interaction

As the interaction is fairly simple, it is readily interpreted with the help of Table 22.8. So we can conclude that in order to model the data effectively we need the two-variable interaction. This we did in essence in Chapter 12 when interpreting the Pearson chi-square analysis of those data. Remember that the interaction is based on the residuals in that table (i.e. the differences between the observed and expected frequencies). As can be clearly seen, males are less inclined to choose medicine degrees than females but are more inclined to choose business degrees.

22.3   A three-variable example

Interactions when the data have three or more variables become a little more difficult to understand. In any case, only when there are three or more variables does log-linear analysis achieve much more than the Pearson chi-square described in Chapter 12. Consequently it is important to study one of these more complex examples. Even though log-linear analysis usually requires the use of a computer using the iterative procedures, quite a lot can be achieved by trying to understand approximately what the computer is doing when it is calculating several second-order and higher-order interactions.

Table 22.1 gave the possible model components of any log-linear analysis for one to five variables. It is very unlikely that anyone would wish to use log-linear analysis when they have just one variable, but it is useful to start from there just so that the patterns build up more clearly in the table. Computer programs can handle more variables than five but we are constrained by space and, moreover, log-linear analyses of 10 variables or more are both atypical of many research designs and call for a great deal of statistical sophistication – especially experience with simpler log-linear analyses.

Basically, the more variables you have the more components there will be to the model. All models consist of main effects plus interactions. The variables involved in model-building are those which might possibly cause differences between the frequencies in the different cells. These variables have to be measurable by the researcher too for them to be in the analysis. Also note that the more variables in a model, the more complex the interactions.

Our example involves three variables. If you look in the column for three variables in Table 22.1 you will find listed all of the possible components of the model for that data. In this column there are three main effects (one for each of the variables), three two-way interactions between all possible distinct pairs taken from the three variables, and one three-way interaction. The analysis is much the same as for our earlier two-variable example but there are more components to add in. In particular, the meaning of the interactions needs to be clarified as there are now four of them rather than just one. Remember that it is usual to take similar levels of the model together for the initial model fitting. Thus all the main effects are combined; all of the second-order interactions (two-variable interactions) together; all of the third-order (three-variable interactions)

Table 22.10	A three-way contingency table showing the relationship between sex, depression and substance misuse in a sample of prison inmates. The numbers in the cells are frequencies			
Variable B	**Variable C**	**Variable A Sex**		**Margin totals**
Depression	**Substance misuse**	**Female**	**Male**	
Depressed	Substance misuse	45	55	100
	No substance misuse	40	60	100
Not depressed	Substance misuse	55	45	100
	No substance misuse	80	20	100
Margin totals		**220**	**180**	**400**

together and so forth. Only when this analysis is done is it usual to see precisely which combinations at which levels of the model are having an effect.

Our example involves the relationship between sex, depression and substance misuse in a sample of prison inmates. The data are to be found in Table 22.10 which gives the three-way crosstabulation or contingency table for our example. The numbers in the cells are *frequencies*. Each of the variables has been coded as a dichotomy: (a) female or male, (b) depressed or not and (c) substance misuse or not. (Variables could have more than two categories but this is not the case for these particular data.) The researchers are interested in explaining the frequencies in the table on the basis of the three *variables* – sex, depression and substance misuse – acting individually (main effects) or in combination (interactions). This would be described as a three-way contingency table because it involves *three variables*. It is worth remembering that the more variables and the more categories of each variable, the greater the sample size needs to be in order to have sufficient frequencies in each cell.

Two of the possible models are easily tested. They are the equal frequencies and the saturated models, which are the extreme possibilities in log-linear analyses. The equal frequencies model simply involves the first row of Table 22.10 and no other influences. The saturated model includes all sources of influence in the table for the column for three variables.

■ Step 1: The equal frequencies model

The equal frequencies model is, in a sense, the worst-fit scenario for a model. It is what the data would look like if none of the variables in isolation or combination were needed to explain the data. The equal frequencies model merely describes what the data would look like if the frequencies were equally distributed through the cells of the table. As there are eight cells and a total of 400 observations, under the equal frequencies model it would be expected that each cell contains 400/8 = 50 cases. This model and the calculation of its fit with the observed data for which we are developing a model are shown in Table 22.11.

Just a reminder – the likelihood ratio chi-square is zero if the model fits the data exactly and increasingly bigger with greater amounts of misfit between the actual data and the data as predicted by the model. The chi-square value for the equal frequencies model is an indication of how much the variables and their interaction have to explain. The value of 44.58 obtained for the likelihood ratio chi-square on the equal frequencies model indicates that the data are poorly explained by that model. That is, there is a lot of variation in the frequencies which remains to be explained by other models than the equal frequencies model. Notice that the equal frequencies model only contains the mean

Table 22.11	The calculation of the likelihood ratio chi-square for the equal frequencies model			
Observed frequency	Expected frequency according to the equal frequencies model	Observed ÷ expected	Natural logarithm of observed ÷ expected	Observed frequency × natural logarithm of observed ÷ expected
45	50.0	0.90	−0.1054	−4.741
40	50.0	0.80	−0.2231	−8.926
55	50.0	1.10	0.0953	5.242
80	50.0	1.60	0.4700	37.600
55	50.0	1.10	0.0953	5.242
60	50.0	1.20	0.1823	10.939
45	50.0	0.90	−0.1054	−4.741
20	50.0	0.40	−0.9163	−18.326
				Total = 22.290

Likelihood ratio chi-square = 2 × sum of final column = 2 × 22.290 = 44.580

frequency which is one of the potential components of all models. The equal frequencies value is sometimes called the constant. If it is zero or nearly zero then the equal frequencies model fits the model well. Do not get too excited if the equal frequencies model fits badly, since the variation in frequencies between the cells might be explained by the main effects. To reiterate, main effects in the log-linear analysis are often of very little interest to social scientists. Only rarely will real-life data have no main effects in log-linear analysis, since main effects occur when the categories of a variable are unequally distributed. In our data in Table 22.10, the marginal totals for substance misuse and depression are the same, since equal numbers had been diagnosed with depression and substance misuse as had not. Nevertheless, there is a possible main effect for sex since there are more females in the study than males. Whether or not this sex difference is significant has yet to be tested. So whatever the final model we select, it has already been clearly established that there is plenty of variation in the cell means to be explained by the main effects acting independently and the two-way interactions of pairs of these variables plus the three-way interaction of all of the variables.

■ Step 2: The saturated model

This model involves all of the possible variables acting separately and in combination. It includes all components given in Table 22.1 for a given number of variables. For a three-way contingency table the saturated model includes the mean frequency per cell (i.e. constant) plus the main effects plus the three two-variable interactions plus the three-variable interaction. Predictions based on the saturated model are exactly the same as the data themselves – they have to be, since the saturated model includes every possible component of the model and so there is no other possible source of variation.

It is hardly worth computing the saturated model as it has to be a perfect fit to the data, thus giving a likelihood ratio chi-square of 0.000. A zero value like this indicates a perfect fit between the observed data and the expectations (predictions) based on the model. Remember that for the saturated model, most computer programs will automatically add 0.5 to the observed frequencies to avoid divisions by zero which are unhelpful mathematically. This addition of 0.5 to each of the frequencies is not always necessary, so some computer programs will give you the choice of not using it. Its influence is so negligible that the analysis is hardly affected.

■ Step 3: Building up the main-effects model

The process of building up a model in log-linear analysis is fairly straightforward once the basic principles are understood, as we have seen. The stumbling block is the calculation of expected frequencies when marginal frequencies are unequal. They are unequal most of the time in real data. In these circumstances, only an approximate explanation can be given of what the computer is doing. Fortunately, as we have already seen, we can go a long way using simple maths.

Table 22.12 contains the expected frequencies based on different components of the model. Remember that the expected frequencies are those based on a particular model or component of the model. The first column contains the data (which are exactly the same as the predictions based on the saturated model already discussed). The fourth column gives the expected frequencies based on the equal frequencies model. This has already been discussed – the frequencies are merely the total frequencies averaged over the number of cells.

The next three cells have the major heading 'Main effects' and there are separate columns for the main effect of sex, the main effect of depression and the main effect of substance misuse. The fourth column headed 'All' is for the added effect of these three main effects. How are these expected (predicted) values calculated? They are simply the averages of the appropriate cells. Thus for females, the four cells in Table 22.12 are 45, 40, 55 and 80 which totals 220. Thus if the cells in the female column reflect only the effects of being female then we would expect all four female cells to contain 220/4 = 55.00 cases. In Table 22.12, the expected frequencies under sex for the four female cells are all 55.00. Similarly for the four remaining cells in that column which all involve males, the total male frequency is 180 so we would expect 180/4 or 45.00 in each of the male cells.

Exactly the same process is applied to the depression column. Two hundred of the cases were depressed whereas 200 were not. Thus we average the 200 depressed cases over the four cells in Table 22.12 which involve depressed individuals (i.e. 200/4 = 50.00). Then we average the 200 non-depressed individuals over the four cells containing non-depressed individuals (i.e. 200/4 = 50.00). Because there are equal numbers of depressed and non-depressed individuals, no main effect of depression is present and all of the values in the depression column are 50.00.

Given that there are also 200 substance misuse and 200 non-substance misuse cases, it is not surprising to find that all of the expected frequencies are 50.00 in the substance misuse column too. The reasoning is exactly the same as for depression in the previous paragraph.

The combined main effects column labelled 'All' is easily computed for our example. It is simply the combined individual effects of the three separate main effects. So it is the effect of sex plus depression plus substance misuse. Thus being female adds a frequency of 5 compared with the equal frequencies model figure of 50.00, being depressed adds zero and indulging in substance misuse adds zero. For example, for the first row which consists of 45 females who had been depressed and had performed substance misuse, we take the equal frequencies frequency of 50.00 and add 5 for being female, + 0 for being depressed and + 0 for the substance misuse. This gives the expected figure of 55.00 under the 'all main effects' column.

To give another example, take the fifth row down where the data give a frequency of 55. This row refers to males who had been depressed and had performed substance

Table 22.12 The expected (or predicted) frequencies based on separate components of the model

Data	Details of cell			Equal frequencies model	Main effects				Two-way interactions			All
	Sex	Depression	Substance misuse		Sex	Depression	Substance misuse	All	Sex* Depression[a]	Sex* Substance	Depression* substance	
45	female	yes	yes	50.00	55.00	50.00	50.00	55.00	42.50	50.00	50.00	37.23
40	female	yes	no	50.00	55.00	50.00	50.00	55.00	42.50	60.00	50.00	47.77
55	female	no	yes	50.00	55.00	50.00	50.00	55.00	67.50	50.00	50.00	62.77
80	female	no	no	50.00	55.00	50.00	50.00	55.00	67.50	60.00	50.00	72.33
55	male	yes	yes	50.00	45.00	50.00	50.00	45.00	57.50	50.00	50.00	62.77
60	male	yes	no	50.00	45.00	50.00	50.00	45.00	57.50	40.00	50.00	52.23
45	male	no	yes	50.00	45.00	50.00	50.00	45.00	32.50	50.00	50.00	37.23
20	male	no	no	50.00	45.00	50.00	50.00	45.00	32.50	40.00	50.00	27.77

[a] An asterisk (*) between two or more variable names is one way of indicating interactions.

misuse. Being male subtracts 5.00 from the equal frequency value, being depressed adds nothing and the substance misuse also adds nothing. So our expected value is $50 - 5 + 0 + 0 = 45$, the expected value for all of the main effects added together.

■ Step 4: The two-variable interactions

The two-way interactions are not difficult to estimate either. The two-way interaction for sex*depression is obtained by combining together the substance misuse categories. In our example, there are some who have indulged in substance misuse and some who have not among the females who had been depressed. Of these depressed females, 45 had substance misuse issues and 40 had no substance misuse problems. Combining these two frequencies and averaging them across the two relevant cells gives us:

$$\frac{45 + 40}{2} = \frac{85}{2} = 42.5$$

This is the value that you see under the sex*depression interaction for the first two rows.

If you need another example, take the last two rows which have values in the data column of 45 and 20. These rows consist of the males who had not been depressed. One row is those who had performed substance misuse and the other those who had not done so. The two-way interaction of sex*depression is obtained by adding together the two different substance misuse categories and entering the average of these into the last two rows. So the frequencies are 45 and 20 which equals 65, which divided between the two relevant cells gives us 32.5. This is the value that you see for the sex*depression interaction for the final two rows.

What about the next interaction – sex*substance misuse? The calculation is basically the same. The only difficulty is that the rows corresponding to the cells we are interested in are physically further apart in the table. The sex*substance misuse interaction is obtained by combining the depression categories (i.e. the depressed and non-depressed). Let us take the females who had not been substance misusers. These are the second and fourth rows. If we look at the observed values in the data, these are frequencies of 40 and 80. The average of these is 60, and this is the value you find in the second and fourth rows of the sex*substance misuse interaction.

The depression*substance misuse interaction is calculated in a similar way – this time we combine the male and female groups for each of the four depression*substance misuse combinations. Take the depressed *and* substance misuse individuals. These are to be found in rows 1 and 5. The data (observed) values for these rows are 45 and 55. This averages at 50.00 – the value of the entry for this two-way interaction in the first and fifth rows. (Actually all of the rows for this particular column have the same value, indicating a lack of a depression*substance misuse interaction.)

The combined effects of the three two-way interactions cannot be seen directly from the table. This is because the values are based on an iterative process which involves several computational stages that are best done by the computer. The values in the last column of Table 22.12 are taken from SPSS computer output. Although we will not be showing this calculation here because of its complexity, we can show the essential logic although, as you will see, it gives slightly the wrong answers. All effects in log-linear analysis are additive so we should be able to combine the three two-way interactions in order to obtain the sum of the three two-way interactions.

This is quite simple. Compared with the equal frequencies mean frequency of 50.00 for each cell, what is the effect of each interaction? Taking the first row, we can see that the sex*depression interaction changes the score by –7.50 (i.e. 42.50 – 50.00), the sex*substance misuse interaction changes the score by 0.00 (i.e. 50.00 – 50.00) and the depression*substance misuse interaction changes the score by 0.00 (50.00 − 50.00). Adding these separate effects to the equal frequencies mean frequency of 50.00 we get:

50.00 + (−7.50) + 0.00 + 0.00 = 42.50

This at first sight is the wrong answer since it is nowhere near the 37.23 obtained from the computer.

What we have not allowed for is the fact that these interactions also include the effect of the main effects. The main effects for this row combined to give a prediction of 55.00 compared with the equal frequencies mean of 50.00. That is to say, the main effects are increasing the prediction for this row by 5.00. This would have to be taken away from the prediction based on the interaction to leave the pure effects of the two-way interactions. So our value of 42.50 contains 5.00 due to the main effects; getting rid of the main effects gives us the prediction of 37.50 based on the two-way interactions. This is pretty close to the 37.23 predicted by the model but not sufficiently so. The unequal marginal totals necessitate the adjustments made automatically by the iterative computer program. Had our marginal totals been a lot more unequal then our fit to the computer's value would have been much poorer. Simple methods are only suitable as ways of understanding the basics of the process.

If you would like another example of how the entries are computed, look at the final row of Table 22.12. The predicted values based on all the two-way interactions is 27.77. How is that value achieved? Notice that the two-way sex*depression interaction prediction is 32.50, which is 17.50 less than that according to the equal frequencies model prediction of 50.00; the sex*substance misuse prediction is 40.00, which is 10.00 less; and the depression*substance misuse prediction is 50.00, exactly the same. So to get the prediction based on the three two-way interactions together, the calculation is the equal frequencies mean (50.00) + (−17.50) + (−10.00) + 0.00 = 22.50, but then we need to take away the influence of all the main effects, which involves adding 5.00 this time. Thus we end up with a prediction of 27.50. Again this is not precisely the computer predicted value but it is close enough for purposes of explanation. Remember, it is only close because the main effects are small or zero.

What is the normal output of a computer program such as SPSS? The important point to remember is that it is usual to explore the model first of all as combined effects – the sum of the interactions, the sum of the main effects – rather than the individual components in the first analysis. For the data in Table 22.10 we obtained the information in Tables 22.13 and 22.14 from the computer by stipulating a saturated model.

Table 22.13	Tests of the increase in fit for the main effects and higher-order effects			
Level of effects	**Types of effect involved**	**Degrees of freedom**	**Likelihood ratio chi-square**	**Probability**
3	Three-way interaction	1	10.713	0.0011
2 (and above)	All the two-way interactions + the three-way interaction	4	40.573	0.0000
1 (and above)	All the main effects + the two-way interaction + the three-way interaction only	7	44.579	0.0000

Table 22.14	Tests that the levels of effect are zero			
Level of effects	**Types of effect involved**	**Degrees of freedom**	**Likelihood ratio chi-square**	**Probability**
1	All the main effects only	3	4.007	0.2607
2	All the two-way interactions only	3	29.860	0.0000
3	Three-way interaction only	1	10.713	0.0011

What do Tables 22.13 and 22.14 tell us? Remember that when we assessed the fit of the data based on the equal frequencies model we obtained a likelihood ratio chi-square value of 44.580. This large value indicates a large misfit of the model to the data. (The smaller the size of chi-square the better the fit.) Notice that this value of chi-square is exactly the same (within the errors of rounding) as the chi-square value in Table 22.13 for the contribution of the main effects, two-way interactions and the three-way interactions. Thus 44.580 is the improvement in the fit of the model created by including the three different levels of effect *together*.

If we take just the two-way and three-way interactions (omitting the main effects from the model), the improvement is a little less at 40.573 according to Table 22.13. Remember that the likelihood ratio chi-square is linear, so you can add and subtract values. Consequently, the improvement in fit due to the main effects is 44.579 – 40.573 = 4.006. Within the limits of rounding error, this is the same value as for the sum of all of the main effects in Table 22.14 (i.e. 4.007).

If we take only the three-way interaction in Table 22.13 (i.e. omitting the two-way interaction and main effects from the model), we get a value of 10.713 for the amount of misfit. This is the value given in Table 22.14.

Where does the value for the two-way interactions come from? We have just found that the value for the main effect is 4.006 and the value for the three-way interaction is 10.713. If we take these away from the chi-square of 44.580 we get 44.580 – 4.006 – 10.713 = 29.861 for the contribution of the two-way interactions to the fit (exactly as can be found in Table 22.14 within the limits of rounding error).

It looks as if a good model for the data can exclude the main effects which are failing to contribute significantly to the goodness-of-fit even though the value of the likelihood ratio chi-square is 4.007. Thus a model based on the two-way and three-way interactions accounts for the data well.

■ Step 5: Which components account for the data?

This analysis has demonstrated the substantial contributions of the two-way and three-way interactions to the model's fit to the data. Since there is only one three-way interaction in this case, there is no question what interaction is causing this three-way effect. There are three different two-way interactions for this model, not all of which may be contributing to the fit to the data. The way of checking for the relative influence of the different two-way interactions is to repeat the analysis but omitting one of the two-way interactions. This is easy to do on most computer programs. Doing this for the data in Table 22.10, we obtain the following:

- Based solely on sex*depression: chi-square = 15.036, $df = 4$, $p = 0.005$.
- Based solely on sex*substance misuse: chi-square = 36.525, $df = 4$, $p = 0.000$.
- Based solely on depression*substance misuse: chi-square = 44.579, $df = 4$, $p = 0.000$.

Working backwards, compared with the value of 44.580 for the misfit between the data and the equal frequencies model, there is no improvement in the fit by adding in the depression*substance misuse interaction, since the value of likelihood ratio chi-square does not change (significantly) from that value 44.580. This means that the depression*substance misuse interaction contributes nothing to the model fit and can be dropped from the model.

Considering solely the sex*substance misuse interaction, there is a moderate improvement in fit. The maximum misfit of 44.580 as assessed by the likelihood ratio chi-square reduces to 36.526 when the sex*substance misuse interaction is included. This suggests that this interaction is quite important in the model and should be retained.

Finally, using solely the sex*depression interaction, the likelihood ratio chi-square value declines to 15.036 from the maximum of 44.579, suggesting that the sex*depression interaction has a substantial influence and improves the fit of the model substantially.

It should be remembered that there is a main effect for sex in all of the above two-way interactions except for the depression*substance misuse interaction where it is not present. (Check the marginal totals for the expected frequencies to see this.) In order to understand just how much change in fit is due to the two-way interaction, we need to adjust for the main effect of sex which we have already calculated as a likelihood ratio chi-square of 4.007. So to calculate the likelihood ratio chi-square of the sex*substance misuse interaction we have to take 36.525 from 44.580, which gives a value for the improvement in fit of 8.054. This value is the improvement in fit due to the sex main effect and the sex*substance misuse interaction. So for the improvement in fit due to the sex*substance misuse interaction only we take 8.055 and subtract 4.007 to give a value of 4.048. This value is only roughly correct because of the unequal marginals involved, which means that a better approximation will be achieved through an iterative process.

Box 22.1	Focus on

Degrees of freedom

Using the computer means that you never need to actually calculate the degrees of freedom. However, if you understand their calculation from chi-square in Chapter 12, then you should have few problems with their calculation for log-linear. When reading degrees of freedom in tables, often they will include extra degrees of freedom for lower-level interactions or main effects. Adjustments may have to be made. Here are a few examples:

1. Total degrees of freedom are always the number of cells – 1.

2. Degrees of freedom for the equal frequencies model = 1.

3. Degrees of freedom for a main effect
$$= \frac{\text{total degrees of freedom}}{\text{number of different categories of the main effect}}$$

4. Degrees of freedom for the saturated model = 0.

Remember that the degrees of freedom for *all* of the main effects, for example, is not the same as the degrees of freedom for any of the main effects taken separately.

Table 22.15	The amounts of fit caused by different components of the model				

Model	Likelihood ratio chi-square	Degrees of freedom	Probability	Chi-square change
Saturated	0.000			–
All two-way interactions + all main effects (i.e. minus three-way interaction)	10.713	1	0.001	10.713[a]
Previous row less sex*depression	36.525	2	0.000	25.812[a]
Previous row less depression*substance misuse	36.525	3	0.000	0.000
Previous row less sex*substance misuse	40.573	4	0.000	4.048
Previous row less depression	40.573	5	0.000	0.000
Previous row less sex	44.579	6	0.000	4.006
Previous row less substance misuse	44.579	7	0.000	0.000

[a] Change significant at the 5% level.

Table 22.15 gives the results of an analysis starting with the saturated model and gradually removing components. If a removed component is having an effect on the fit, there will be a non-zero value for the chi-square change for that row, which needs to be tested for significance. The saturated model is a perfect fit (i.e. chi-square = 0.000) but taking away the three-way interaction increases the misfit to 10.713. This change (10.713 – 0.000) is the influence of the three-way interaction on the degree of fit. Taking away the interaction of sex*depression gives a chi-square change of 25.812, which indicates that the sex*depression interaction is having a big effect on the fit of the model.

When we take away depression*substance misuse there is a 0.000 chi-square change. This indicates that this interaction is doing nothing to improve the fit of the model. Thus the depression*substance misuse interaction may be dropped from the model.

Similarly the row of Table 22.15 where the main effect of depression is dropped has a zero likelihood ratio chi-square, indicating that the main effect of depression can be dropped from the model. Also the final row where the main effect of substance misuse is dropped also shows no change, implying that this main effect can be dropped from the model. Actually only two of the components are statistically significant at the 5% level so that the model could be built on these solely. Our model then becomes:

Mean frequency (i.e. equal frequencies mean) + sex*depression interaction
+ sex*depression*substance misuse interaction

■ Step 6: More on the interpretation of log-linear analysis

By this stage it should be possible to attempt fitting a log-linear model. Of course, a little practice will be necessary with your chosen computer in order to familiarise yourself with its procedures. This is not too technical in practice with careful organisation and the creation of systematic tables to record the computer output. If these things are not done, the sheer quantity of frequently redundant computer output will cause confusion.

Specifying the best-fitting model using likelihood ratio chi-squares is *not* a complete interpretation of the model. This is much as the value of Pearson chi-square in Chapter 12 is insufficient without careful examination of the data. An important concept in this respect is that of residuals. A residual is merely the difference between the actual data and the data predicted on the basis of the model. These can be expressed merely as the data value minus the modelled value. So residuals may take positive or negative values and there is one residual per cell. Not only this, since in a log-linear analysis you may be comparing one or more components of the model with the data, several sets of residuals will have to be computed, so you may be calculating different residuals for different components of the model or different models. Residuals can be standardised so that values are more easily compared one with another.

The good news is twofold. There is no difficulty in calculating simple residuals, and computers generally do it for you anyway as part of calculating the model fit. If you look back to Table 22.12, you can easily calculate the residuals by subtracting any of the predicted model values from the actual data. The residuals for the saturated model are all zero, of course, indicating a perfect fit. The residuals for the equal frequencies model are −5.00, −10.00, 5.00, 30.00, 5.00, 10.00, −5.00 and −30.00; that is, the value of the frequency for that cell in the data −50.000 in each case.

The other helpful thing when interpreting log-linear models is the estimated cell frequencies based on different components of the model. Remember that not only can you calculate these fairly directly but they are usually generated for you by the computer. The important thing about these estimated cell frequencies is that they tell you the trends in the data caused by, say, the interactions. For example, look at Table 22.12 and the column for the sex*depression interaction. You can see there that there are relatively few females who had been depressed and relatively more males who had been depressed in these data. It is best to compare these frequencies with the ones for the effects of the three main effects, since the interaction figures actually include the effects of the main effects. Thus this comparison removes the main effects from the interaction.

22.4 Reporting the results

With something as complex as a log-linear analysis you might expect that writing up the results of the analysis will be complex. Indeed it can be, and expect to write much more about your analysis than you would, for example, writing up the results of a correlation coefficient or a *t*-test. The purposes of log-linear analysis can be very varied, stretching from a fairly empirical examination of the data of the sort described earlier to testing the fit of a theoretical model to the actual data. Obviously there is no single sentence that can be usefully employed for describing the outcome of a log-linear analysis. Nevertheless certain things are very important. They are:

1. A table giving the data and the residuals for each of the models that you examine. Without this, the reader cannot assess precisely the form of the fit of the models to the data. Table 22.12 would be a useful format for doing this.

2. A table giving indications of the improvement in fit due to each component of the model. This will almost invariably be the likelihood ratio chi-square. Table 22.15 could be adapted to your particular data.

The text should discuss the final model which you have selected on the basis of your log-linear analysis. These could be expressed in terms of the components of the model which contribute significantly to the fit or, alternatively, as the lambda values mentioned in Box 22.2. Earlier in this chapter we indicated the models for our two examples in a simple form.

> ## Box 22.2 Focus on
>
> # Lambda
>
> Often in log-linear analysis, the models are specified in terms of lambda (λ). This is simply the natural log of the influence of each of the different sorts of component of the cell frequencies. Thus a model may be built up from a succession of lambdas. These are given superscripts to denote what type of effect is involved: λ^A is the main effect of variable A and λ^{A*B} is the effect of the interaction of variables A and B. So an equation involving these and other components might be:
>
> $$\text{Model} = \lambda + \lambda^A + \lambda^B + \lambda^{A*B}$$
>
> This simply means that we add to the natural logarithm of the equal-cell mean or constant (λ), the natural logarithm of the main effects of the variable A (remember that this has positive and negative values), the natural logarithm of the main effects of the variable B, and the natural logarithm of the interaction of the variables A*B.

> ## Box 22.3 Focus on
>
> # Hierarchical models
>
> Hierarchical models imply lower-order components and do not specify what these lower-order components are. Thus a hierarchical model may specify a four-variable interaction A*B*C*D. Any component involving A, B, C and D is assumed to be a component of that model. So the main effects A, B, C and D, the two-way interactions A*B, A*C, A*D, B*C, B*D and C*D, and the three-way interactions A*B*C, A*B*D, A*C*D and B*C*D are automatically specified as possible components in a hierarchical model. Notice that our examples employ a hierarchical approach.

22.5 When to use log-linear analysis

Log-linear analysis is used in exactly the same circumstances as a two-way chi-square to deal with the situation where the researcher has three or more nominal (category) independent variables which may be associated in some way. Many researchers prefer to collect data primarily in the form of scores so may never need log-linear analysis. Score data cannot be used in log-linear analysis.

Of course, it is tempting to think that nominal (category) data are simpler data than score data. This may encourage the less numerate novice researcher to employ nominal (category) data and thus snare themselves into the trap of needing log-linear analysis, which is among the more difficult statistical techniques to understand.

22.6 When not to use log-linear analysis

If any of your variables are score variables then they are not suitable for log-linear analysis. Be careful to consider quite what you need out of a log-linear analysis which could not be obtained by some other form of statistical analysis. For example, in the case of the study described in this chapter, does the researcher really want to know whether there is a difference between males and females in terms of their histories of substance misuse and depression? If this were the case, then binomial logistic regression (Chapter 21) or multinomial logistic regression (Chapter 20) might be capable of supplying the analysis required. One could even mix score and nominal variables in this instance. It is possible to use interactions with some forms of logistic regression.

22.7 Data requirements for log-linear analysis

Three or more nominal (category) variables are required – score variables may not be used. Be parsimonious in terms of the number of variables you include as each additional one adds significantly more complexity to the output.

22.8 Problems in the use of log-linear analysis

Log-linear analysis is not the simplest statistic to understand because of the variety of new and difficult concepts it introduces. It is probably unsuitable for total novices. So we would suggest that you do not contemplate using it until you have a more advanced level of statistical skill and experience in deciphering SPSS output. Only choose it when there is no alternative analysis that would do an equally good job.

22.9 SPSS analysis

■ The data to be analysed

The computation of a log-linear analysis is illustrated with the data in Table 22.16. This table shows the frequency of depression and substance misuse in 140 female and 160 male prison inmates. To analyse a table of data like this one with SPSS we first have to input the data into the Data Editor and weight the cells by the frequencies of cases in them.

Table 22.16	A three-way contingency table showing the relationship between sex, depression and substance misuse in a sample of prison inmates. The numbers in the cells are actual counts			

Depression	Substance misuse	Sex		Margin totals
		Female	Male	
Depressed	Substance misuse	20	30	50
	No substance misuse	40	25	65
Not depressed	Substance misuse	35	55	90
	No substance misuse	45	50	95
Margin totals		140	160	300

■ Log-linear analysis

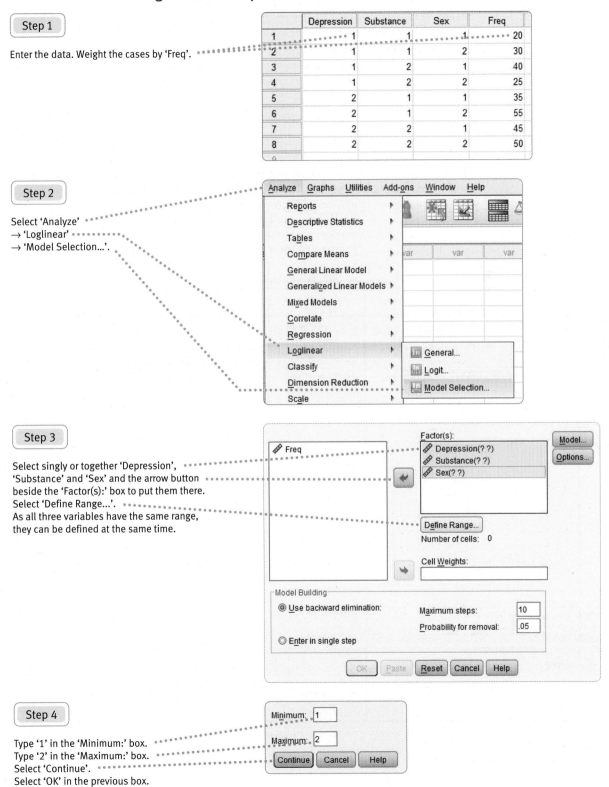

Step 1

Enter the data. Weight the cases by 'Freq'.

	Depression	Substance	Sex	Freq
1	1	1	1	20
2	1	1	2	30
3	1	2	1	40
4	1	2	2	25
5	2	1	1	35
6	2	1	2	55
7	2	2	1	45
8	2	2	2	50

Step 2

Select 'Analyze'
→ 'Loglinear'
→ 'Model Selection...'.

Analyze Graphs Utilities Add-ons Window Help

Reports ▶
Descriptive Statistics ▶
Tables ▶
Compare Means ▶
General Linear Model ▶
Generalized Linear Models ▶
Mixed Models ▶
Correlate ▶
Regression ▶
Loglinear ▶   General...
Classify ▶   Logit...
Dimension Reduction ▶   Model Selection...
Scale ▶

Step 3

Select singly or together 'Depression',
'Substance' and 'Sex' and the arrow button
beside the 'Factor(s):' box to put them there.
Select 'Define Range...'.
As all three variables have the same range,
they can be defined at the same time.

Freq

Factor(s):
Depression(? ?)
Substance(? ?)
Sex(? ?)

Model...
Options...

Define Range...
Number of cells: 0

Cell Weights:

Model Building
◉ Use backward elimination: Maximum steps: 10
   Probability for removal: .05
○ Enter in single step

OK Paste Reset Cancel Help

Step 4

Type '1' in the 'Minimum:' box.
Type '2' in the 'Maximum:' box.
Select 'Continue'.
Select 'OK' in the previous box.

Minimum: 1
Maximum: 2
Continue Cancel Help

■ Interpreting the output

- The likelihood ratio chi-square for the saturated or full model is 0.00000 which has a probability of 1.000. In other words, the saturated model provides a perfect fit for the observed frequencies and so is non-significant. The saturated model in this case consists of the three main effects, three two-way interactions and one three-way interaction. In general, the saturated model includes all main effects and interactions.

- However, the saturated model includes *all* components whether or not they individually contribute to explaining the variation in the observed data. So it is necessary to eliminate components in turn to see whether this makes the model's fit worse. If it does, this component of the model is kept for the final model.

- SPSS begins with the full model and eliminates each effect in turn to determine which effects make the least significant change in the likelihood ratio chi-square.

The likelihood ratio chi-square for the full or saturated model is zero and provides a perfect fit to the data.

Step Summary

Step[a]		Effects	Chi-Square[c]	df	Sig.	Number of Iterations
0	Generating Class[b]	Depression*Substance*Sex	.000	0	.	
	Deleted Effect 1	Depression*Substance*Sex	1.185	1	.276	3
1	Generating Class[b]	Depression*Substance, Depression*Sex, Substance*Sex	1.185	1	.276	
	Deleted Effect 1	Depression*Substance	.454	1	.501	2
	2	Depression*Sex	1.963	1	.161	2
	3	Substance*Sex	5.461	1	.019	2
2	Generating Class[b]	Depression*Sex, Substance*Sex	1.638	2	.441	
	Deleted Effect 1	Depression*Sex	2.272	1	.132	2
	2	Substance*Sex	5.770	1	.016	2
3	Generating Class[b]	Substance*Sex, Depression	3.910	3	.271	
	Deleted Effect 1	Substance*Sex	5.770	1	.016	2
	2	Depression	16.485	1	.000	2
4	Generating Class[b]	Substance*Sex, Depression	3.910	3	.271	

a. At each step, the effect with the largest significance level for the Likelihood Ratio Change is deleted, provided the significance level is larger than .050.
b. Statistics are displayed for the best model at each step after step 0.
c. For 'Deleted Effect', this is the change in the Chi-Square after the effect is deleted from the model.

This is the best-fitting model. It has a likelihood ratio chi-square of 3.91 which is not significant.

● The best-fitting model is presented last. In our example, this includes the interaction of substance misuse and sex and the main effect of depression. This model has a likelihood ratio chi-square of 3.91 (rounded to two decimal places), two degrees of freedom and a probability level of 0.271. In other words, it is not significant, which means that the observed data can be reproduced with these two effects.

These are the counts or frequencies for the data plus the expected frequencies under this model. The residuals are just the differences between the actual data and the data predicted by the model.

Cell Counts and Residuals

Depression	Substance	Sex	Observed Count	Observed %	Expected Count	Expected %	Residuals	Std. Residuals
Depressed	Substance Misuse	Male	20.000	6.7%	21.083	7.0%	-1.083	-.236
		Female	30.000	10.0%	32.583	10.9%	-2.583	-.453
	No Substance Misuse	Male	40.000	13.3%	32.583	10.9%	7.417	1.299
		Female	25.000	8.3%	28.750	9.6%	-3.750	-.699
Not Depressed	Substance Misuse	Male	35.000	11.7%	33.917	11.3%	1.083	.186
		Female	55.000	18.3%	52.417	17.5%	2.583	.357
	No Substance Misuse	Male	45.000	15.0%	52.417	17.5%	-7.417	-1.024
		Female	50.000	16.7%	46.250	15.4%	3.750	.551

There are two statistics used to test the goodness-of-fit of the final model. These are the likelihood ratio chi-square and the Pearson chi-square. The likelihood ratio chi-square is the test more commonly used because it has the advantage of being linear, so chi-square values may be added or subtracted.

Goodness-of-Fit Tests

	Chi-Square	df	Sig.
Likelihood Ratio	3.910	3	.271
Pearson	3.953	3	.267

● To interpret these two effects, we need to present the data in terms of a one-way table for depression and a two-way table for substance misuse and sex. We can do this using Chi-square . . . for the one-way table and Crosstabs . . . for the two-way table (see Chapter 12 and Section 12.7 for a review). These two tables are shown in Tables 22.17 and 22.18. The one-way table shows that more prison inmates have not been depressed than have been depressed. The two-way table indicates that males are more likely to indulge in substance misuse than females.

Table 22.17	Contingency table for depression		
	Depression		
	Observed *N*	**Expected *N***	**Residual**
Depressed	115	150.0	−35.0
Not depressed	185	150.0	35.0
Total	300		

Table 22.18	Contingency table for the interaction of substance misuse and sex				
	Substance misuse * Sex crosstabulation				
			Females	**Males**	**Total**
Substance misuse	Substance misuse	Count	55	85	140
		Expected count	65.3	74.7	140.0
		Residual	−10.3	10.3	
	Not substance misuse	Count	85	75	160
		Expected count	74.7	85.3	160.0
		Residual	10.3	−10.3	
Total		Count	140	160	300
		Expected count	140.0	160.0	300.0

- It is possible to see the contribution of each component to the final mode in the step just before the final step (step 4 in this example). These entries essentially indicate the change (reduction) in the goodness-of-fit chi-square if each component is taken away. Thus Substance*Sex has a likelihood ratio chi-square change of 5.770 which is significant (0.016). Depression has a value of 16.485 which is very significant (0.000). Obviously these two effects cannot be eliminated from the model because of their significant contribution.

- In a hierarchical model, components of an interaction may be significant. Since Substance*Sex has a significant contribution to the model, Substance and Sex may themselves be significant main effects. Select 'Model...' in the top right-hand corner of the 'Model Selection Loglinear Analysis' dialog box (Step 3 above). The window that appears will allow you to test these main effects by stipulating models containing only these particular main effects.

■ Reporting the output

One way of describing the results found here is as follows: 'A three-way frequency analysis was performed to develop a hierarchical linear model of substance misuse and depression in female and male prison inmates. Backward elimination produced a model that included the main effect of depression and the interaction effect of substance misuse and sex. The model had a likelihood ratio $\chi^2(3) = 3.91$, $p = 0.27$, indicating a good fit between the observed frequencies and the expected frequencies generated by the model. About 38% of the prison inmates had been depressed. About 53% of the males had misused substances compared with about 39% of the females.'

> ### Key points
>
> - It is recommended that before analysing your own data with log-linear, you reproduce our analyses in order to become familiar with the characteristics of your chosen computer program.
>
> - Confine yourself to small numbers of variables when first using log-linear analysis. Although computers may handle, say, 10 variables, you may find it difficult without a lot of experience.
>
> - Log-linear analysis can include score variables if these are treated as frequencies.

Recommended further reading

Agresti, A. (1996), *An Introduction to Categorical Data Analysis*, New York: Wiley, Chapters 1–4.

Anderson, E.B. (1997), *Introduction to the Statistical Analysis of Categorical Data*, Berlin: Springer, Chapters 2–4.

Appendices

Testing for excessively skewed distributions

The use of nonparametric tests (Mann–Whitney U-test, Wilcoxon matched pairs test) rather than parametric tests (unrelated t-test, related t-test) is conventionally recommended by some textbooks when the distribution of scores on a variable is significantly skewed (Chapters 10 and 11). There are a number of difficulties with this advice, particularly just how one knows that there is too much skew. It is possible to test for significant skewness. One simply computes skewness and then divides this by the standard error of the skewness. If the resulting value equals or exceeds 1.96 then your skewness is significant at the 5% level (two-tailed test) and the null hypothesis that your sample comes from a symmetrical population should be rejected.

A.1 Skewness

The formula for skewness is:

$$\text{Skewness} = \frac{(\sum d^3)N}{\text{SD}^3 \times (N-1) \times (N-2)}$$

Notice that much of the formula is familiar: N is the number of scores, d is the deviation of each score from the mean of the sample and SD is the estimated standard deviation of the scores (i.e. you use $N-1$ in the formula for standard deviation as described in Chapter 5). What is different is the use of cubing. To cube a number you multiply it by itself twice. Thus the cube of 3 is $3 \times 3 \times 3 = 27$. A negative number cubed gives a negative number. Thus the cube of -4 is $(-4) \times (-4) \times (-4) = -64$.

We will take the data from Table 5.1 in Chapter 5 to illustrate the calculation of skewness. For simplicity's sake we will be using a definitional formula which involves the calculation of the sample mean. Table A.1 gives the data in column 1 as well as the calculation steps to be followed. The number of scores N equals 9.

Table A.1	Steps in the calculation of skewness		
Column 1 Age (years)	**Column 2** Scores – sample mean	**Column 3** Square values in column 2	**Column 4** Cube values in column 2
20	$20 - 23 = -3$	9	-27
25	$25 - 23 = 2$	4	8
19	$19 - 23 = -4$	16	-64
35	$35 - 23 = 12$	144	1728
19	$19 - 23 = -4$	16	-64
17	$17 - 23 = -6$	36	-216
15	$15 - 23 = -8$	64	-512
30	$30 - 23 = 7$	49	343
27	$27 - 23 = 4$	16	64
$\sum \bar{X}$ = sum of scores = 207 $\bar{X}$ = mean score = 23		$\sum d^2 = 354$	$\sum d^3 = 1260$

For Table A.1,

$$\text{Estimated standard deviation (SD)} = \sqrt{\frac{\sum d^2}{N-1}}$$

$$= 6.652$$

Substituting this value and the values from the table in the formula for skewness we get:

$$\text{Skewness} = \frac{1260 \times 9}{6.652^3 \times (9-1) \times (9-2)}$$

$$= \frac{11\,340}{16\,483.332}$$

$$= 0.688$$

(Skewness could have a negative value.)

A.2 Standard error of skewness

The standard error of skewness involves calculating the value of the following formula for our particular sample size ($N = 9$):

$$\text{Standard error of skewness} = \sqrt{\frac{6 \times N \times (N-1)}{(N-2) \times (N+1) \times (N+3)}}$$

$$= \sqrt{\frac{432}{840}}$$

$$= \sqrt{0.514}$$

$$= 0.717$$

The significance of skewness involves a z-score:

$$z = \frac{\text{skewness}}{\text{standard error of skewness}}$$

$$= \frac{0.688}{0.717}$$

$$= 0.96$$

This value of z is lower than the minimum value of z (1.96) required to be statistically significant at the 5% level with a two-tailed test. Thus the scores are *not* extremely skewed. This implies that you may use parametric tests rather than nonparametric tests for comparisons involving this variable. Obviously you need to do the skewness test for the other variables involved.

For the related t-test, it is the skewness of the *differences* between the two sets of scores which needs to be examined, not the skewnesses of the two different sets of scores.

APPENDIX B

Extended table of significance for the Pearson correlation coefficient

Table B.1 gives both two-tailed and one-tailed values for the significance of the Pearson correlation coefficient. Ignoring the sign of the correlation coefficient obtained, your value has to equal or exceed the value in the table in order to be statistically significant at the level of significance stipulated in the column heading.

Table B.1 Extended table of significance for the Pearson correlation coefficient

Sample size	Two-tailed: 10% One-tailed: 5%	Two-tailed: 5% One-tailed: 2.5%	Two-tailed: 2% One-tailed: 1%	Two-tailed: 1% One-tailed: 0.5%
3	0.988	0.997	1.000	1.000
4	0.900	0.950	0.980	0.990
5	0.805	0.878	0.934	0.959
6	0.729	0.811	0.882	0.917
7	0.669	0.754	0.833	0.875
8	0.621	0.707	0.808	0.834
9	0.582	0.666	0.750	0.798
10	0.549	0.632	0.715	0.765
11	0.521	0.602	0.685	0.735
12	0.497	0.576	0.658	0.708
13	0.476	0.553	0.634	0.684

Sample size	Two-tailed: 10% One-tailed: 5%	Two-tailed: 5% One-tailed: 2.5%	Two-tailed: 2% One-tailed: 1%	Two-tailed: 1% One-tailed: 0.5%
14	0.458	0.532	0.612	0.661
15	0.441	0.514	0.592	0.641
16	0.426	0.497	0.574	0.623
17	0.412	0.482	0.558	0.606
18	0.400	0.468	0.543	0.590
19	0.389	0.456	0.529	0.575
20	0.378	0.444	0.516	0.561
21	0.369	0.433	0.503	0.549
22	0.360	0.423	0.492	0.537
23	0.352	0.413	0.482	0.526
24	0.344	0.404	0.472	0.515
25	0.337	0.396	0.462	0.505
26	0.330	0.388	0.453	0.496
27	0.323	0.382	0.445	0.487
28	0.317	0.374	0.437	0.479
29	0.311	0.367	0.430	0.471
30	0.306	0.361	0.423	0.463
31	0.301	0.355	0.416	0.456
32	0.296	0.349	0.409	0.449
33	0.291	0.344	0.403	0.442
34	0.287	0.339	0.397	0.436
35	0.283	0.334	0.392	0.430
36	0.279	0.329	0.386	0.424
37	0.275	0.325	0.381	0.418
38	0.271	0.320	0.376	0.413
39	0.267	0.316	0.371	0.408
40	0.264	0.312	0.367	0.403
41	0.260	0.308	0.362	0.398
42	0.257	0.304	0.358	0.393
43	0.254	0.301	0.354	0.389
44	0.251	0.297	0.350	0.384
45	0.248	0.294	0.346	0.380
46	0.246	0.291	0.342	0.376
47	0.243	0.288	0.338	0.372
48	0.240	0.285	0.335	0.368
49	0.238	0.282	0.331	0.365
50	0.235	0.279	0.328	0.361
51	0.233	0.276	0.325	0.358
52	0.231	0.273	0.322	0.354

→

Sample size	Two-tailed: 10% One-tailed: 5%	Two-tailed: 5% One-tailed: 2.5%	Two-tailed: 2% One-tailed: 1%	Two-tailed: 1% One-tailed: 0.5%
53	0.228	0.271	0.319	0.351
54	0.226	0.268	0.316	0.348
55	0.224	0.266	0.313	0.345
56	0.222	0.263	0.310	0.341
57	0.220	0.261	0.307	0.339
58	0.218	0.259	0.305	0.336
59	0.216	0.256	0.302	0.333
60	0.214	0.254	0.300	0.330
61	0.213	0.252	0.297	0.327
62	0.211	0.250	0.295	0.325
63	0.209	0.248	0.293	0.322
64	0.207	0.246	0.290	0.320
65	0.206	0.244	0.288	0.317
66	0.204	0.242	0.286	0.315
67	0.203	0.240	0.284	0.313
68	0.201	0.239	0.282	0.310
69	0.200	0.237	0.280	0.308
70	0.198	0.235	0.278	0.306
71	0.197	0.234	0.276	0.304
72	0.195	0.232	0.274	0.302
73	0.194	0.230	0.272	0.300
74	0.193	0.229	0.270	0.298
75	0.191	0.227	0.268	0.296
76	0.190	0.226	0.266	0.294
77	0.189	0.224	0.265	0.292
78	0.188	0.223	0.263	0.290
79	0.186	0.221	0.261	0.288
80	0.185	0.220	0.260	0.286
81	0.184	0.219	0.258	0.285
82	0.183	0.217	0.257	0.283
83	0.182	0.216	0.255	0.281
84	0.181	0.215	0.253	0.280
85	0.180	0.213	0.252	0.278
86	0.179	0.212	0.251	0.276
87	0.178	0.211	0.249	0.275
88	0.176	0.210	0.248	0.273
89	0.175	0.208	0.246	0.272
90	0.174	0.207	0.245	0.270
91	0.174	0.206	0.244	0.269

Sample size	Two-tailed: 10% One-tailed: 5%	Two-tailed: 5% One-tailed: 2.5%	Two-tailed: 2% One-tailed: 1%	Two-tailed: 1% One-tailed: 0.5%
92	0.173	0.205	0.242	0.267
93	0.172	0.204	0.241	0.266
94	0.171	0.203	0.240	0.264
95	0.170	0.202	0.238	0.263
96	0.169	0.201	0.237	0.262
97	0.168	0.200	0.236	0.260
98	0.167	0.199	0.235	0.259
99	0.166	0.198	0.234	0.258
100	0.165	0.197	0.232	0.256
200	0.117	0.139	0.164	0.182
300	0.095	0.113	0.134	0.149
400	0.082	0.098	0.116	0.129
500	0.074	0.088	0.104	0.115
1000	0.052	0.062	0.074	0.081

Table of significance for the Spearman correlation coefficient

Table C.1 gives both two-tailed and one-tailed values for the significance of the Spearman correlation coefficient. Ignoring the sign of the correlation coefficient obtained, your value has to equal or exceed the value in the table in order to be statistically significant at the level of significance stipulated in the column heading. Do not use the following table if you used the Pearson correlation coefficient approach described in Calculation 7.2. It is in most applications an approximation. The following table should only be used when the calculation has used the formula described in Calculation 7.3 and there are ties.

Table C.1	Table of significance for the Spearman correlation coefficient			
Sample size	Two-tailed: 10% One-tailed: 5%	Two-tailed: 5% One-tailed: 2.5%	Two-tailed: 2% One-tailed: 1%	Two-tailed: 1% One-tailed: 0.5%
5	0.900	–	–	–
6	0.829	0.886	0.943	–
7	0.714	0.786	0.893	–
8	0.643	0.738	0.833	0.881
9	0.600	0.683	0.783	0.833
10	0.564	0.648	0.745	0.858
11	0.520	0.620	0.737	0.814
12	0.496	0.591	0.703	0.776
13	0.475	0.566	0.673	0.743
14	0.456	0.544	0.646	0.714
15	0.440	0.524	0.623	0.688
16	0.425	0.506	0.602	0.665

Sample size	Two-tailed: 10% One-tailed: 5%	Two-tailed: 5% One-tailed: 2.5%	Two-tailed: 2% One-tailed: 1%	Two-tailed: 1% One-tailed: 0.5%
17	0.411	0.490	0.583	0.644
18	0.399	0.475	0.565	0.625
19	0.388	0.462	0.549	0.607
20	0.377	0.450	0.535	0.591
21	0.368	0.438	0.521	0.576
22	0.359	0.428	0.508	0.562
23	0.351	0.418	0.497	0.549
24	0.343	0.409	0.486	0.537
25	0.336	0.400	0.476	0.526
26	0.329	0.392	0.466	0.515
27	0.323	0.384	0.457	0.505
28	0.317	0.377	0.448	0.496
29	0.311	0.370	0.440	0.487
30	0.305	0.364	0.433	0.478
31	0.300	0.358	0.425	0.470
32	0.295	0.352	0.418	0.462
33	0.291	0.346	0.412	0.455
34	0.286	0.341	0.406	0.448
35	0.282	0.336	0.400	0.442
36	0.278	0.331	0.394	0.435
37	0.274	0.327	0.388	0.429
38	0.270	0.322	0.383	0.423
39	0.267	0.318	0.378	0.418
40	0.263	0.314	0.373	0.412
41	0.260	0.310	0.368	0.407
42	0.257	0.306	0.364	0.402
43	0.254	0.302	0.360	0.397
44	0.251	0.299	0.355	0.393
45	0.248	0.295	0.351	0.388
46	0.245	0.292	0.347	0.384
47	0.243	0.289	0.344	0.380
48	0.240	0.286	0.340	0.376
49	0.237	0.283	0.336	0.372
50	0.235	0.280	0.333	0.368
51	0.233	0.277	0.330	0.364
52	0.230	0.274	0.326	0.361
53	0.228	0.272	0.323	0.357
54	0.226	0.269	0.320	0.354
55	0.224	0.267	0.317	0.350

Sample size	Two-tailed: 10% One-tailed: 5%	Two-tailed: 5% One-tailed: 2.5%	Two-tailed: 2% One-tailed: 1%	Two-tailed: 1% One-tailed: 0.5%
56	0.222	0.264	0.314	0.347
57	0.220	0.262	0.311	0.344
58	0.218	0.260	0.309	0.341
59	0.216	0.257	0.306	0.338
60	0.214	0.255	0.303	0.335
61	0.212	0.253	0.301	0.332
62	0.211	0.251	0.298	0.330
63	0.209	0.249	0.296	0.327
64	0.207	0.247	0.294	0.324
65	0.206	0.245	0.291	0.322
66	0.204	0.243	0.289	0.319
67	0.202	0.241	0.287	0.317
68	0.201	0.239	0.285	0.315
69	0.199	0.238	0.283	0.312
70	0.198	0.236	0.280	0.310
71	0.197	0.234	0.278	0.308
72	0.195	0.233	0.277	0.306
73	0.194	0.231	0.275	0.303
74	0.193	0.229	0.273	0.301
75	0.191	0.228	0.271	0.299
76	0.190	0.226	0.269	0.297
77	0.189	0.225	0.267	0.295
78	0.187	0.223	0.266	0.293
79	0.186	0.222	0.264	0.292
80	0.185	0.221	0.262	0.290
81	0.184	0.219	0.261	0.288
82	0.183	0.218	0.259	0.286
83	0.182	0.216	0.257	0.284
84	0.181	0.215	0.256	0.283
85	0.179	0.214	0.254	0.281
86	0.178	0.213	0.253	0.279
87	0.177	0.211	0.251	0.278
88	0.176	0.210	0.250	0.276
89	0.175	0.209	0.248	0.274
90	0.174	0.208	0.247	0.273
91	0.173	0.207	0.246	0.271
92	0.172	0.205	0.244	0.270
93	0.172	0.204	0.243	0.268
94	0.171	0.203	0.242	0.267

Sample size	Two-tailed: 10% One-tailed: 5%	Two-tailed: 5% One-tailed: 2.5%	Two-tailed: 2% One-tailed: 1%	Two-tailed: 1% One-tailed: 0.5%
95	0.170	0.202	0.240	0.266
96	0.169	0.201	0.239	0.264
97	0.168	0.200	0.238	0.263
98	0.167	0.199	0.237	0.261
99	0.166	0.198	0.235	0.260
100	0.165	0.197	0.234	0.259
200	0.117	0.139	0.165	0.183
300	0.095	0.113	0.135	0.149
400	0.082	0.098	0.117	0.129
500	0.074	0.088	0.104	0.115
1000	0.052	0.062	0.074	0.081

Extended table of significance for the *t*-test

Table D.1 gives two-tailed and one-tailed significance values for the *t*-test. The value of *t* which you obtain (ignoring sign) in your calculation has to equal or be larger than the listed value in order to be statistically significant at the level of significance given in each column heading.

For the related *t*-test the degrees of freedom are the *number of pairs* of scores − 1.
For the unrelated *t*-test the degrees of freedom are the number of scores − 2.

Table D.1	Extended table of significance for the *t*-test

Degrees of freedom	Two-tailed: 10% One-tailed: 5%	Two-tailed: 5% One-tailed: 2.5%	Two-tailed: 2% One-tailed: 1%	Two-tailed: 1% One-tailed: 0.5%
1	6.314	12.706	31.820	63.657
2	2.920	4.303	6.965	9.925
3	2.353	3.182	4.541	5.841
4	2.132	2.776	3.747	4.604
5	2.015	2.571	3.365	4.032
6	1.943	2.447	3.365	3.708
7	1.895	2.365	2.998	3.500
8	1.860	2.306	2.897	3.355
9	1.833	2.262	2.821	3.250
10	1.813	2.228	2.764	3.169
11	1.796	2.201	2.718	3.106
12	1.782	2.179	2.681	3.055

Degrees of freedom	Two-tailed: 10% One-tailed: 5%	Two-tailed: 5% One-tailed: 2.5%	Two-tailed: 2% One-tailed: 1%	Two-tailed: 1% One-tailed: 0.5%
13	1.771	2.160	2.650	3.012
14	1.761	2.145	2.625	2.977
15	1.753	2.132	2.603	2.947
16	1.746	2.120	2.583	2.921
17	1.740	2.110	2.567	2.898
18	1.734	2.101	2.552	2.878
19	1.729	2.093	2.539	2.861
20	1.725	2.086	2.528	2.845
21	1.721	2.080	2.518	2.831
22	1.717	2.074	2.508	2.819
23	1.714	2.069	2.500	2.807
24	1.711	2.064	2.492	2.797
25	1.708	2.064	2.485	2.787
26	1.706	2.055	2.479	2.779
27	1.703	2.052	2.473	2.771
28	1.701	2.048	2.467	2.763
29	1.699	2.045	2.462	2.756
30	1.697	2.042	2.457	2.750
31	1.696	2.039	2.453	2.744
32	1.694	2.037	2.449	2.739
33	1.692	2.035	2.445	2.733
34	1.691	2.032	2.441	2.728
35	1.690	2.030	2.438	2.724
36	1.688	2.028	2.434	2.720
37	1.687	2.026	2.431	2.715
38	1.686	2.024	2.429	2.712
39	1.685	2.023	2.426	2.708
40	1.684	2.021	2.423	2.704
41	1.683	2.020	2.421	2.701
42	1.682	2.018	2.418	2.698
43	1.681	2.017	2.416	2.695
44	1.680	2.017	2.414	2.692
45	1.679	2.014	2.412	2.690
46	1.679	2.013	2.410	2.687
47	1.678	2.012	2.408	2.685
48	1.677	2.011	2.408	2.682
49	1.677	2.010	2.405	2.680
50	1.676	2.009	2.403	2.678
51	1.675	2.008	2.402	2.676

→

Degrees of freedom	Two-tailed: 10% One-tailed: 5%	Two-tailed: 5% One-tailed: 2.5%	Two-tailed: 2% One-tailed: 1%	Two-tailed: 1% One-tailed: 0.5%
52	1.675	2.007	2.400	2.674
53	1.674	2.006	2.399	2.672
54	1.674	2.005	2.397	2.670
55	1.673	2.004	2.396	2.668
56	1.672	2.003	2.395	2.667
57	1.672	2.002	2.394	2.665
58	1.672	2.002	2.392	2.663
59	1.671	2.001	2.391	2.662
60	1.671	2.000	2.390	2.660
61	1.670	2.000	2.389	2.659
62	1.670	1.999	2.388	2.658
63	1.669	1.998	2.387	2.656
64	1.669	1.998	2.386	2.655
65	1.669	1.997	2.385	2.654
66	1.668	1.997	2.384	2.652
67	1.668	1.996	2.383	2.651
68	1.668	1.995	2.383	2.650
69	1.667	1.995	2.382	2.649
70	1.667	1.994	2.381	2.648
71	1.667	1.994	2.380	2.647
72	1.666	1.994	2.379	2.646
73	1.666	1.993	2.379	2.645
74	1.666	1.993	2.378	2.644
75	1.665	1.992	2.377	2.643
76	1.665	1.992	2.376	2.642
77	1.665	1.991	2.376	2.641
78	1.665	1.991	2.375	2.640
79	1.664	1.990	2.375	2.640
80	1.664	1.990	2.374	2.639
81	1.664	1.990	2.373	2.638
82	1.664	1.989	2.373	2.637
83	1.663	1.989	2.372	2.636
84	1.663	1.989	2.372	2.636
85	1.663	1.988	2.371	2.635
86	1.663	1.988	2.370	2.634
87	1.663	1.988	2.370	2.634
88	1.662	1.987	2.369	2.633
89	1.662	1.987	2.369	2.632
90	1.662	1.987	2.369	2.632

Degrees of freedom	Two-tailed: 10% One-tailed: 5%	Two-tailed: 5% One-tailed: 2.5%	Two-tailed: 2% One-tailed: 1%	Two-tailed: 1% One-tailed: 0.5%
91	1.662	1.986	2.368	2.631
92	1.662	1.986	2.368	2.630
93	1.661	1.986	2.367	2.630
94	1.661	1.986	2.367	2.629
95	1.661	1.985	2.366	2.629
96	1.661	1.985	2.366	2.628
97	1.661	1.985	2.365	2.627
98	1.661	1.984	2.365	2.627
99	1.660	1.984	2.365	2.626
100	1.660	1.984	2.364	2.626
200	1.653	1.972	2.345	2.601
300	1.650	1.968	2.339	2.592
400	1.649	1.966	2.336	2.588
500	1.648	1.965	2.334	2.586
1000	1.646	1.962	2.330	2.581
∞	1.645	1.960	2.326	2.576

APPENDIX E

Table of significance for chi-square

Table E.1 gives one-tailed and two-tailed significance values for chi-square. The obtained value of chi-square has to equal or exceed the listed value to be statistically significant at the level in the column heading.

Table E.1	Table of significance for chi-square	
Degrees of freedom	**5%**	**1%**
1 (1-tailed)[a]	2.705	5.412
1 (2-tailed)	3.841	6.635
2 (2-tailed)	5.992	9.210
3 (2-tailed)	7.815	11.345
4 (2-tailed)	9.488	13.277
5 (2-tailed)	11.070	15.086
6 (2-tailed)	12.592	16.812
7 (2-tailed)	14.067	18.475
8 (2-tailed)	15.507	20.090
9 (2-tailed)	16.919	21.666
10 (2-tailed)	18.307	23.209
11 (2-tailed)	19.675	24.725
12 (2-tailed)	21.026	26.217

[a] It is correct to carry out a one-tailed chi-square only when there is just one degree of freedom.

Extended table of significance for the sign test

Table F.1 lists significance values for the sign test. Your value must be smaller than or equal to the listed value to be significant at the level stipulated in the column heading.

Table F.1	Extended table of significance for the sign test		
N	Two-tailed: 5% One-tailed: 2.5%	Two-tailed: 2% One-tailed: 1%	Two-tailed: 1% One-tailed: 0.5%
5	0		
6	0	0	
7	0	0	
8	1	0	0
9	1	1	0
10	1	1	0
11	2	1	0
12	2	2	1
13	3	2	1
14	3	2	1
15	3	3	2
16	4	3	2
17	4	4	2
18	5	4	3
19	5	4	3
20	5	5	3

→

N	Two-tailed: 5% One-tailed: 2.5%	Two-tailed: 2% One-tailed: 1%	Two-tailed: 1% One-tailed: 0.5%
21	6	5	4
22	6	5	4
23	7	6	5
24	7	6	5
25	7	7	5
26	8	8	6
27	9	8	6
28	9	8	7
29	10	9	7
30	10	9	7
31	10	10	8
32	11	10	8
33	11	10	9
34	12	11	9
35	12	11	9
36	13	12	10
37	13	12	10
38	13	12	11
39	14	13	11
40	14	13	11
41	15	14	12
42	15	14	12
43	16	15	13
44	16	15	13
45	16	15	13
46	17	16	14
47	17	16	14
48	18	17	15
49	18	17	15
50	19	18	15
51	19	18	16
52	20	18	16
53	20	19	17
54	20	19	17
55	21	20	17
56	21	20	18
57	22	21	18
58	22	21	19
59	23	21	19

N	Two-tailed: 5% One-tailed: 2.5%	Two-tailed: 2% One-tailed: 1%	Two-tailed: 1% One-tailed: 0.5%
60	23	22	19
61	24	22	20
62	24	23	20
63	24	23	21
64	25	24	21
65	25	24	22
66	26	25	22
67	26	25	22
68	27	25	23
69	27	26	23
70	28	26	24
71	28	27	24
72	28	27	24
73	29	28	25
74	29	28	25
75	30	29	26
76	30	29	26
77	31	29	27
78	31	30	27
79	32	30	27
80	32	31	28
81	33	31	28
82	33	32	29
83	33	32	29
84	34	32	30
85	34	33	30
86	35	33	30
87	35	34	31
88	36	34	31
89	36	35	32
90	37	35	32
91	37	36	33
92	38	36	33
93	38	36	34
94	38	37	34
95	39	37	34
96	39	38	35
97	40	38	35
98	40	39	36

→

N	Two-tailed: 5% One-tailed: 2.5%	Two-tailed: 2% One-tailed: 1%	Two-tailed: 1% One-tailed: 0.5%
99	41	39	36
100	41	40	37
200	88	86	81
300	135	132	127
400	183	180	174
500	231	228	221
1000	473	468	459

APPENDIX G

Table of significance for the Wilcoxon matched pairs test

Table G.1 lists significance values for the Wilcoxon matched pairs test. Your value must be smaller than or equal to the listed value to be significant at the level stipulated in the column heading.

Table G.1	Table of significance for the Wilcoxon matched pairs test		
Number of pairs of scores	Two-tailed: 10% One-tailed: 5%	Two-tailed: 5% One-tailed: 2.5%	Two-tailed: 1% One-tailed: 0.5%
6	2	0	–
7	4	2	–
8	6	4	0
9	8	6	2
10	11	8	3
11	14	11	5
12	17	14	7
13	21	17	10
14	26	21	13
15	31	25	16
16	36	30	20
17	42	35	24
18	47	40	28
19	54	46	33

Number of pairs of scores	Two-tailed: 10% One-tailed: 5%	Two-tailed: 5% One-tailed: 2.5%	Two-tailed: 1% One-tailed: 0.5%
20	60	52	37
21	68	59	42
22	76	66	47
23	84	74	54
24	92	81	60
25	101	90	67
26	111	98	74
27	121	107	82
28	131	117	90
29	141	127	99
30	153	137	108
31	164	148	117
32	176	159	127
33	188	171	137
34	201	183	147
35	215	195	158
36	228	208	169
37	242	222	181
38	257	235	193
39	272	250	206
40	288	264	219
41	304	279	232
42	320	295	246
43	337	311	260
44	354	327	275
45	372	344	290
46	390	361	305
47	409	379	321
48	428	397	337
49	447	415	354
50	467	434	371
51	488	454	389
52	508	474	407
53	530	494	425
54	551	515	444
55	574	536	463
56	596	558	483
57	619	580	503
58	643	602	524

Number of pairs of scores	Two-tailed: 10% One-tailed: 5%	Two-tailed: 5% One-tailed: 2.5%	Two-tailed: 1% One-tailed: 0.5%
59	667	625	545
60	692	649	566
61	716	673	588
62	742	697	610
63	768	722	633
64	794	747	656
65	821	773	679
66	848	799	703
67	876	825	728
68	904	852	752
69	932	880	778
70	961	908	803
71	991	936	29
72	1021	965	856
73	1051	994	883
74	1082	1024	910
75	1113	1054	938
76	1145	1084	967
77	1178	1115	995
78	1210	1147	1025
79	1243	1179	1054
80	1277	1211	1084
81	1311	1244	1115
82	1346	1278	1146
83	1381	1311	1177
84	1416	1346	1209
85	1452	1380	1241
86	1488	1415	1274
87	1525	1451	1307
88	1563	1487	1340
89	1600	1523	1374
90	1639	1560	1409
91	1677	1598	1444
92	1717	1636	1479
93	1756	1674	1515
94	1796	1713	1551
95	1837	1752	1588
96	1878	1792	1625
97	1919	1832	1662

Number of pairs of scores	Two-tailed: 10% One-tailed: 5%	Two-tailed: 5% One-tailed: 2.5%	Two-tailed: 1% One-tailed: 0.5%
98	1961	1872	1700
99	2004	1913	1739
100	2047	1955	1778
200	8702	8444	7944
300	20 101	19 628	18 710
400	36 294	35 565	34 154
500	57 308	56 290	54 318
1000	235 222	232 344	226 772

Tables of significance for the Mann–Whitney *U*-test

Table H.1 lists 5% significant values for the Mann–Whitney *U*-statistic (one-tailed test). Your value must be in the listed ranges for your sample sizes to be significant at the 5% level; i.e. to accept the hypothesis. In addition, you should have predicted which group would have the smaller sum of ranks.

Table H.2 lists 1% significant values for the Mann–Whitney *U*-statistic (two-tailed test). Your value must be in the listed ranges for your sample sizes to be significant at the 1% level; i.e. to accept the hypothesis at the 1% level.

| Table H.1 | 5% significant values for the Mann–Whitney *U*-statistic (one-tailed test) |

Sample size for smaller group	Sample size for larger group										
	5	6	7	8	9	10	11	12	13	14	20
5	0–4	0–6	0–8	0–9	0–11	0–12	0–13	0–15	0–16	0–18	0–25
21–25	25–30	32–40	36–45	39–50	43–55	47–60	50–65	54–70	57–75	75–100	
6	0–5	0–8	0–10	0–12	0–14	0–16	0–17	0–19	0–21	0–23	0–32
25–30	29–36	38–48	42–54	46–60	50–66	55–72	59–78	61–82	67–90	88–120	
7	0–6	0–11	0–13	0–15	0–17	0–19	0–21	0–24	0–26	0–28	0–39
29–35	34–42	43–56	48–63	53–70	58–77	63–84	67–91	72–98	77–105	101–140	
8	0–8	0–13	0–15	0–18	0–20	0–23	0–26	0–28	0–31	0–33	0–47
32–40	38–48	49–64	54–72	60–80	65–88	70–96	76–104	81–112	87–120	113–160	
9	0–9	0–15	0–18	0–21	0–24	0–27	0–30	0–33	0–36	0–39	0–54
36–45	42–54	54–72	60–81	66–90	72–99	78–108	84–117	90–126	96–135	126–180	
10	0–11	0–17	0–20	0–24	0–27	0–31	0–34	0–37	4–41	0–44	0–62
39–50	46–60	60–80	66–90	73–100	79–110	86–120	93–130	99–140	106–150	138–200	
11	0–12	0–19	0–23	0–27	0–31	0–34	0–38	0–42	0–46	0–50	0–69
43–55	50–66	65–88	72–99	79–110	87–121	94–132	101–143	108–154	115–165	151–220	
12	0–13	0–21	0–26	0–30	0–34	0–38	0–42	0–47	0–51	0–55	0–77
47–60	55–72	70–96	78–108	86–120	94–132	102–144	109–156	117–168	125–180	163–240	
13	0–15	0–24	0–28	0–33	0–37	0–42	0–47	0–51	0–56	0–61	0–84
50–65	59–78	76–104	84–117	93–130	101–143	109–156	118–169	126–182	134–195	176–260	
14	0–16	0–26	0–31	0–36	0–41	0–46	0–51	0–56	0–61	0–66	0–92
54–70	61–82	81–112	90–126	99–140	108–154	109–168	126–182	135–196	144–210	188–280	
15	0–18	0–28	0–33	0–39	0–44	0–50	0–55	0–61	0–66	0–72	0–100
57–75	67–90	87–120	96–135	106–150	115–165	125–180	153–195	144–210	153–225	200–300	
20	0–25	0–39	0–47	0–54	0–62	0–69	0–77	0–84	0–92	0–100	0–138
75–100	88–120	113–160	126–180	138–200	151–220	163–240	200–260	188–280	200–300	262–400	

Source: adapted from *Fundamentals of Behavioral Statistics*, New York: McGraw Hill (Runyon, R.P. and Haber, A., 1989) Table I The McGraw-Hill Companies.

Table H.2 1% significant values for the Mann–Whitney *U*-statistic (two-tailed test)

Sample size for smaller group	Sample size for larger group											
	5	6	7	8	9	10	11	12	13	14	15	20
5	0	0–1	0–1	0–2	0–3	0–4	0–5	0–6	0–7	0–7	0–8	0–13
25	29–30	34–35	38–40	42–45	46–50	50–55	54–60	58–65	67–70	67–75	87–100	
6	0–1	0–2	0–3	0–4	0–5	0–6	0–7	0–9	0–10	0–11	0–12	0–18
29–30	34–36	39–42	44–48	49–54	54–60	59–66	63–72	68–78	71–82	78–90	102–120	
7	0–1	0–3	0–4	0–6	0–7	0–9	0–10	0–12	0–13	0–15	0–16	0–24
34–35	39–42	45–49	50–56	56–63	61–70	67–77	72–84	78–91	83–98	89–105	116–140	
8	0–2	0–4	0–6	0–7	0–9	0–11	0–13	0–15	0–17	0–18	0–20	0–30
38–40	44–48	50–56	57–64	63–72	69–80	75–88	81–96	87–104	94–112	100–120	130–160	
9	0–3	0–5	0–7	0–9	0–11	0–13	0–16	0–18	0–20	0–22	0–24	0–36
42–45	49–54	56–63	63–72	70–81	77–90	81–99	90–108	89–117	104–126	101–135	144–180	
10	0–4	0–6	0–9	0–11	0–13	0–16	0–18	0–21	0–24	0–26	0–29	0–42
46–50	54–60	61–70	69–80	77–90	84–100	92–110	99–120	97–130	114–140	111–150	158–200	
11	0–5	0–7	0–10	0–13	0–16	0–18	0–21	0–24	0–27	0–30	0–33	0–48
50–55	59–66	67–77	75–88	83–99	92–110	90–111	108–132	106–143	124–154	132–165	172–220	
12	0–6	0–9	0–12	0–15	0–18	0–21	0–24	0–27	0–31	0–34	0–37	0–54
54–60	63–72	72–84	81–96	90–108	99–120	108–132	117–144	115–156	134–168	143–180	186–240	
13	0–7	0–10	0–13	0–17	0–20	0–24	0–27	0–31	0–34	0–38	0–42	0–60
58–65	68–78	78–91	87–104	97–117	106–130	116–143	125–156	135–169	144–182	153–195	200–260	
14	0–7	0–11	0–15	0–18	0–22	0–26	0–30	0–34	0–38	0–42	0–46	0–67
63–70	71–82	83–98	94–112	104–126	114–140	124–154	134–168	144–182	154–196	164–210	213–280	
15	0–8	0–12	0–16	0–20	0–24	0–29	0–33	0–37	0–42	0–46	0–51	0–73
67–75	78–90	89–105	100–120	111–135	121–150	132–165	143–180	153–195	164–210	174–225	227–300	
20	0–13	0–18	0–24	0–30	0–36	0–42	0–48	0–54	0–60	0–67	0–73	0–105
87–100	102–120	116–140	130–160	144–180	158–200	172–220	186–240	200–260	213–280	227–300	295–400	

Source: adapted from *Fundamentals of Behavioral Statistics*, New York: McGraw Hill (Runyon, R.P. and Haber, A., 1989) Table I The McGraw-Hill Companies.

APPENDIX I

Tables of significant values for the *F*-distribution

Table I.1 lists 5% significance levels for the *F*-distribution (one-tailed test). Your value has to equal or be larger than the tabled value to be significant at the 5% level for an effect to be significant.

| Table I.1 | 5% significance levels for the *F*-distribution (one-tailed test) | | | | | |

Degrees of freedom for error or within-cells mean square (or variance estimate)	Degrees of freedom for between-treatments mean square (or variance estimate)					
	1	2	3	4	5	∞
1	161.448	199.500	215.707	224.583	230.162	254.314
2	18.513	19.000	19.165	19.247	19.297	19.496
3	10.128	9.553	9.277	9.118	9.014	8.527
4	7.709	6.945	6.592	6.389	6.257	5.628
5	6.608	5.787	5.410	5.193	5.051	4.365
6	5.988	5.144	4.758	4.534	4.388	3.669
7	5.592	4.738	4.347	4.121	3.972	3.230
8	5.318	4.459	4.067	3.838	3.688	2.928
9	5.118	4.257	3.863	3.634	3.482	2.707
10	4.965	4.103	3.709	3.479	3.326	2.538
13	4.668	3.806	3.411	3.180	3.026	2.207
15	4.544	3.683	3.288	3.056	2.902	2.066
20	4.352	3.493	3.099	2.867	2.711	1.844
30	4.171	3.316	2.923	2.690	2.534	1.623
60	4.002	3.151	2.759	2.526	2.369	1.390
∞	3.842	2.996	2.605	2.372	2.215	1.000

Table I.2 lists 1% significance levels for the *F*-distribution (one-tailed test). Your value has to equal or be larger than the tabled value to be significant at the 1% level for an effect to be significant.

Table I.2	1% significance levels for the *F*-distribution (one-tailed test)					
Degrees of freedom for error or within-cells mean square (or variance estimate)	**Degrees of freedom for between-treatments mean square (or variance estimate)**					
	1	**2**	**3**	**4**	**5**	**∞**
1	4052.180	4999.500	5403.350	5624.580	5763.650	6365.860
2	98.503	99.000	99.167	99.250	99.300	99.500
3	34.117	30.817	29.457	28.710	28.238	26.126
4	21.198	18.000	16.695	15.977	15.522	13.464
5	16.259	13.274	12.060	11.392	10.967	9.021
6	13.745	10.925	9.780	9.149	8.746	6.880
7	12.247	9.547	8.452	7.847	7.461	5.650
8	11.259	8.650	7.591	7.007	6.632	4.859
9	10.562	8.022	6.992	6.423	6.057	4.311
10	10.045	7.560	6.553	5.995	5.637	3.909
13	9.074	6.701	5.740	5.206	4.862	3.166
15	8.684	6.359	5.417	4.894	4.556	2.869
20	8.096	5.849	4.939	4.431	4.103	2.422
30	7.563	5.391	4.510	4.018	3.699	2.007
60	7.078	4.978	4.126	3.650	3.339	1.607
∞	6.635	4.606	3.782	3.320	3.018	1.000

Table I.3 lists 10% significance levels for the *F*-distribution for testing differences between two groups (one-tailed test). This table is only to be used for determining whether an *F* value which is not significant at the 5% level for two groups is significant at the 10% level which is the equivalent to a one-tailed *t*-test. You should only do this if you have good grounds for predicting the direction of the difference between the two means. Your value has to equal or be larger than the tabled value to be significant at the one-tailed 5% level for the *t*-test.

Table I.3	10% significance levels for the *F*-distribution for testing differences between two groups (one-tailed test)
Degrees of freedom for error or within-cells mean square (or variance estimate)	**Degrees of freedom for between-treatments mean square (or variance estimate)**
	1
1	39.864
2	8.527
3	5.539
4	4.545
5	4.061
6	3.776
7	3.590
8	3.458
9	3.361
10	3.285
13	3.137
15	3.074
20	2.975
30	2.881
60	2.792
∞	2.706

APPENDIX J

Table of significant values of *t* when making multiple *t*-tests

Table J.1 gives the 5% significance values for two-tailed *t*-tests when you are making up to 10 unplanned comparisons. The number of comparisons you decide to make is up to you and does not have to be the maximum possible. This table can be used in any circumstances where you have multiple *t*-tests.

Table J.1	Table of significant values of *t* when making multiple *t*-tests									
Degrees of freedom	**Number of comparisons being made**									
	1	**2**	**3**	**4**	**5**	**6**	**7**	**8**	**9**	**10**
1	12.706	25.452	38.188	50.923	63.657	76.390	89.124	101.856	114.589	127.321
2	4.303	6.205	7.649	8.860	9.925	10.886	11.769	12.590	13.360	14.089
3	3.182	4.177	4.857	5.392	5.841	6.231	6.580	6.895	7.185	7.453
4	2.776	3.495	3.961	4.315	4.604	4.851	5.067	5.261	5.437	5.598
5	2.571	3.163	3.534	3.810	4.032	4.219	4.382	4.526	4.655	4.773
6	2.447	2.969	3.288	3.521	3.708	3.863	3.997	4.115	4.221	4.317
7	2.365	2.841	3.128	3.335	3.500	3.636	3.753	3.855	3.947	4.029
8	2.306	2.752	3.016	3.206	3.355	3.479	3.584	3.677	3.759	3.833
9	2.262	2.685	2.933	3.111	3.250	3.364	3.462	3.547	3.622	3.690
10	2.228	2.634	2.870	3.038	3.169	3.277	3.368	3.448	3.518	3.581
11	2.201	2.593	2.820	2.981	3.106	3.208	3.295	3.370	3.437	3.497
12	2.179	2.560	2.780	2.934	3.055	3.153	3.236	3.308	3.371	3.428
13	2.160	2.533	2.746	2.896	3.012	3.107	3.187	3.257	3.318	3.373
14	2.145	2.510	2.718	2.864	2.977	3.069	3.146	3.213	3.273	3.326

Degrees of freedom	Number of comparisons being made									
	1	2	3	4	5	6	7	8	9	10
15	2.132	2.490	2.694	2.837	2.947	3.036	3.112	3.177	3.235	3.286
16	2.120	2.473	2.673	2.813	2.921	3.008	3.082	3.146	3.202	3.252
17	2.110	2.458	2.655	2.793	2.898	2.984	3.056	3.119	3.174	3.222
18	2.101	2.445	2.639	2.774	2.878	2.963	3.034	3.095	3.149	3.197
19	2.093	2.433	2.625	2.759	2.861	2.944	3.014	3.074	3.127	3.174
20	2.086	2.423	2.613	2.744	2.845	2.927	2.996	3.055	3.107	3.153
21	2.080	2.414	2.601	2.732	2.831	2.912	2.980	3.038	3.090	3.135
22	2.074	2.406	2.591	2.720	2.819	2.898	2.966	3.023	3.074	3.119
23	2.069	2.398	2.582	2.710	2.807	2.886	2.953	3.010	3.059	3.104
24	2.064	2.391	2.574	2.700	2.797	2.875	2.941	2.997	3.047	3.091
25	2.064	2.385	2.566	2.692	2.787	2.865	2.930	2.986	3.035	3.078
26	2.055	2.379	2.559	2.684	2.779	2.856	2.920	2.975	3.024	3.067
27	2.052	2.373	2.553	2.676	2.771	2.847	2.911	2.966	3.014	3.057
28	2.048	2.369	2.547	2.670	2.763	2.839	2.902	2.957	3.005	3.047
29	2.045	2.364	2.541	2.663	2.756	2.832	2.894	2.949	2.996	3.038
30	2.042	2.360	2.536	2.657	2.750	2.825	2.887	2.941	2.988	3.030
31	2.039	2.356	2.531	2.652	2.744	2.818	2.880	2.934	2.981	3.022
32	2.037	2.352	2.526	2.647	2.739	2.812	2.874	2.927	2.974	3.015
33	2.035	2.348	2.522	2.642	2.733	2.807	2.868	2.921	2.967	3.008
34	2.032	2.345	2.518	2.638	2.728	2.801	2.863	2.915	2.961	3.002
35	2.030	2.342	2.515	2.633	2.724	2.797	2.857	2.910	2.955	2.996
36	2.028	2.339	2.511	2.630	2.720	2.792	2.853	2.905	2.950	2.990
37	2.026	2.336	2.508	2.626	2.715	2.788	2.848	2.900	2.945	2.985
38	2.024	2.334	2.505	2.622	2.712	2.784	2.844	2.895	2.940	2.980
39	2.023	2.331	2.502	2.619	2.708	2.780	2.839	2.891	2.936	2.976
40	2.021	2.329	2.499	2.616	2.704	2.776	2.836	2.887	2.931	2.971
41	2.020	2.327	2.496	2.613	2.701	2.772	2.832	2.883	2.927	2.967
42	2.018	2.325	2.494	2.610	2.698	2.769	2.828	2.879	2.923	2.963
43	2.017	2.323	2.491	2.607	2.695	2.766	2.825	2.875	2.920	2.959
44	2.017	2.321	2.489	2.605	2.692	2.763	2.822	2.872	2.916	2.955
45	2.014	2.319	2.487	2.602	2.690	2.760	2.819	2.869	2.913	2.952
46	2.013	2.317	2.485	2.600	2.687	2.757	2.816	2.866	2.910	2.949
47	2.012	2.316	2.483	2.598	2.685	2.755	2.813	2.863	2.907	2.946
48	2.011	2.314	2.481	2.595	2.682	2.752	2.810	2.860	2.904	2.943
49	2.010	2.312	2.479	2.593	2.680	2.750	2.808	2.857	2.901	2.940
50	2.009	2.311	2.477	2.591	2.678	2.747	2.805	2.855	2.898	2.937
51	2.008	2.309	2.476	2.589	2.676	2.745	2.803	2.853	2.896	2.934
52	2.007	2.308	2.474	2.588	2.674	2.743	2.801	2.850	2.893	2.932
53	2.006	2.307	2.472	2.586	2.672	2.741	2.798	2.848	2.891	2.929

Degrees of freedom	Number of comparisons being made									
	1	2	3	4	5	6	7	8	9	10
54	2.005	2.306	2.471	2.584	2.670	2.739	2.797	2.846	2.889	2.927
55	2.004	2.304	2.469	2.583	2.668	2.737	2.795	2.844	2.887	2.925
56	2.003	2.303	2.468	2.581	2.667	2.735	2.793	2.842	2.885	2.922
57	2.002	2.302	2.467	2.579	2.665	2.734	2.791	2.840	2.882	2.920
58	2.002	2.301	2.465	2.578	2.663	2.732	2.789	2.838	2.881	2.918
59	2.001	2.300	2.464	2.577	2.662	2.730	2.787	2.836	2.879	2.916
60	2.000	2.299	2.463	2.575	2.660	2.729	2.786	2.834	2.877	2.915
61	2.000	2.298	2.462	2.574	2.659	2.727	2.784	2.833	2.875	2.913
62	1.999	2.297	2.461	2.573	2.658	2.726	2.782	2.831	2.873	2.911
63	1.998	2.296	2.460	2.571	2.656	2.724	2.781	2.829	2.872	2.909
64	1.998	2.295	2.459	2.570	2.655	2.723	2.779	2.828	2.870	2.908
65	1.997	2.295	2.458	2.569	2.654	2.721	2.778	2.826	2.869	2.906
66	1.997	2.294	2.457	2.568	2.652	2.720	2.777	2.825	2.867	2.905
67	1.996	2.293	2.456	2.567	2.651	2.719	2.775	2.824	2.866	2.903
68	1.995	2.292	2.455	2.566	2.650	2.718	2.774	2.822	2.864	2.902
69	1.995	2.291	2.454	2.565	2.649	2.716	2.773	2.821	2.863	2.900
70	1.994	2.291	2.453	2.564	2.648	2.715	2.772	2.820	2.862	2.899
71	1.994	2.290	2.452	2.563	2.647	2.714	2.770	2.818	2.860	2.898
72	1.994	2.289	2.451	2.562	2.646	2.713	2.769	2.817	2.859	2.896
73	1.993	2.289	2.450	2.561	2.645	2.712	2.768	2.816	2.858	2.895
74	1.993	2.288	2.450	2.560	2.644	2.711	2.767	2.815	2.857	2.894
75	1.992	2.287	2.449	2.559	2.643	2.710	2.766	2.814	2.856	2.893
76	1.992	2.287	2.448	2.559	2.642	2.709	2.765	2.813	2.854	2.891
77	1.991	2.286	2.447	2.558	2.641	2.708	2.764	2.812	2.853	2.890
78	1.991	2.285	2.447	2.557	2.640	2.707	2.763	2.811	2.852	2.889
79	1.990	2.285	2.446	2.556	2.640	2.706	2.762	2.810	2.851	2.888
80	1.990	2.284	2.445	2.555	2.639	2.705	2.761	2.809	2.850	2.887
81	1.990	2.284	2.445	2.555	2.638	2.705	2.760	2.808	2.849	2.886
82	1.989	2.283	2.444	2.554	2.637	2.704	2.759	2.807	2.848	2.885
83	1.989	2.283	2.444	2.553	2.636	2.703	2.759	2.806	2.847	2.884
84	1.989	2.282	2.443	2.553	2.636	2.702	2.758	2.805	2.846	2.883
85	1.988	2.282	2.442	2.552	2.635	2.701	2.757	2.804	2.845	2.882
86	1.988	2.281	2.442	2.551	2.634	2.701	2.756	2.803	2.845	2.881
87	1.988	2.281	2.441	2.551	2.634	2.700	2.755	2.803	2.844	2.880
88	1.987	2.280	2.441	2.550	2.633	2.699	2.755	2.802	2.843	2.880
89	1.987	2.280	2.440	2.550	2.632	2.699	2.754	2.801	2.842	2.879
90	1.987	2.280	2.440	2.549	2.632	2.698	2.753	2.800	2.841	2.878
91	1.986	2.279	2.439	2.548	2.631	2.697	2.752	2.800	2.841	2.877
92	1.986	2.279	2.439	2.548	2.630	2.696	2.752	2.799	2.840	2.876

Degrees of freedom	Number of comparisons being made									
	1	2	3	4	5	6	7	8	9	10
93	1.986	2.278	2.438	2.547	2.630	2.696	2.751	2.798	2.839	2.876
94	1.986	2.278	2.438	2.547	2.629	2.695	2.750	2.797	2.838	2.875
95	1.985	2.277	2.437	2.546	2.629	2.695	2.750	2.797	2.838	2.874
96	1.985	2.277	2.437	2.546	2.628	2.694	2.749	2.796	2.837	2.873
97	1.985	2.277	2.436	2.545	2.627	2.694	2.748	2.795	2.836	2.873
98	1.984	2.276	2.436	2.545	2.627	2.693	2.748	2.795	2.836	2.872
99	1.984	2.276	2.435	2.544	2.626	2.692	2.747	2.794	2.835	2.871
100	1.984	2.276	2.435	2.544	2.626	2.692	2.747	2.793	2.834	2.871
∞	1.960	2.241	2.394	2.498	2.576	2.638	2.690	2.734	2.773	2.807

APPENDIX K

Some other statistics in SPSS Statistics

Some other statistical methods provided by SPSS Statistics but not described in this book are shown in Table K.1 in terms of their options on the 'Analyze' menu, submenu and dialog box options.

Table K.1 Some other statistics in SPSS Statistics

Analyze menu	Analyze submenu	Dialog box
Descriptive Statistics	Crosstabs . . .	Lambda
		Uncertainty coefficient
		Gamma
		Somers' d
		Kendall's tau-b
		Kendall's tau-c
		Risk
		Eta
Correlate	Bivariate . . .	Kendall's tau-b
Regression	Curve Estimation . . .	
	Ordinal . . .	
	Probit . . .	
	Nonlinear . . .	
	Weight Estimation . . .	
	2-Stage Least Squares . . .	
	Optimal Scaling . . .	
Loglinear	Logit . . .	

→

Analyze menu	Analyze submenu	Dialog box
Classify	TwoStep Cluster . . .	
	K-Means Cluster . . .	
	Hierarchical Cluster . . .	
	Discriminant . . .	
Dimension Reduction	Correspondence Analysis . . .	
	Optimal Scaling . . .	
Scale	Multidimensional Scaling . . .	
	Multidimensional Scaling [PROXSCAL] . . .	
	Multidimensional Scaling [ALSCAL] . . .	
Nonparametric	Binomial . . .	
Tests	Runs . . .	
	1-Sample K-S . . . (Kolmogorov–Smirnov)	
	2 Independent Samples . . .	Kolmogorov–Smirnov Z
		Wald–Wolfowitz runs
		Moses extreme reactions
	K Independent Samples . . .	Jonckheere–Terpstra
		Median
	2 Related Samples . . .	Marginal Homogeneity
	K Related Samples . . .	Kendall's W
		Cochran's Q
Survival	Life Tables . . .	
	Kaplan–Meier . . .	
	Cox Regression . . .	
	Cox w/ Time-Dep Cov . . .	

GLOSSARY

−2 log likelihood (ratio) test: Used in logistic regression, it is a form of chi-square test which compares the goodness-of-fit of two models where one model is a part of (i.e. nested or a subset of) the other model. The chi-square is the difference in the −2 log likelihood values for the two models.

***A priori* test:** A test of the difference between two groups of scores when this comparison has been planned ignorant of the actual data. This contrasts with a *post hoc* test which is carried out after the data have been collected and which has no particularly strong expectations about the outcome.

Adjusted mean: A mean score when the influence of one or more covariates has been removed especially in analysis of covariance.

Alpha level: The level of risk that the researcher is prepared to mistakenly accept the hypothesis on the basis of the available data. Typically this is set at a maximum of 5% or .05 and is, of course, otherwise referred to as the level of significance.

Analysis of covariance (ANCOVA): A variant of the analysis of variance (ANOVA) in which scores on the dependent variable are adjusted to take into account (control) a covariate(s). For example, differences between conditions of an experiment at pre-test can be controlled for.

Analysis of variance (ANOVA): An extensive group of tests of significance which compare means on a dependent variable. There may be one or more independent (grouping) variables or factors. ANOVA is essential in the analysis of most laboratory experiments.

Association: A relationship between two variables.

Bar chart: A picture in which frequencies are represented by the height of a set of bars. It should be the areas of a set of bars, but SPSS Statistics ignores this and settles for height.

Bartlett's test of sphericity: A test used in MANOVA of whether the correlations between the variables differ significantly from zero.

Beta level: The risk that we are prepared to accept of rejecting the null hypothesis when it is in fact true.

Beta weight: The standardised regression weight in multiple regression. It corresponds to the correlation coefficient in simple regression.

Between-groups design: Basically a design where different participants are allocated to different groups or conditions.

Between-subjects design: *see* Between-groups design.

Bimodal: A frequency distribution with two modes.

Bivariate: Involving two variables as opposed to univariate which involves just one variable.

Bivariate correlation: A correlation between two variables.

Block: A subset of variables which will be analysed together in a sequence of blocks.

Bonferroni adjustment: A method of adjusting significance levels for the fact that many statistical analyses have been carried out on the data.

Bootstrapping: A method of creating sampling distributions from the basic sample which is reproduced numerous times to approximate the 'population'. This allows repeated sampling and hence the calculation of sampling distributions for all sorts of statistics.

Boxplot: A diagram indicating the distribution of scores on a variable. It gives the median in a box, the left and right hand sides of which are the lower and upper values of the interquartile range. Lines at each side of the box identify the largest and smallest scores.

Box's M: A statistical test which partly establishes whether the data meet the requirements for a MANOVA analysis. It examines the extent to which the covariances of the dependent variables are similar for each of the groups in the analysis. Ideally, then, Box's *M* should not be significant. The test is used in MANOVA though its interpretation is complex.

Case: The basic unit of analysis on which data are collected such as individuals or organisations.

Categorical variable: A nominal or category variable.

Category variable: A variable which consists of categories rather than numerical scores. The categories have no particular quantitative order. However, usually on SPSS Statistics they will be coded as numbers.

Cell: The intersection of one category of a variable with another category of one or more other variables. So if a variable has categories A, B and C and the other variable has categories X, Y and Z, then the cells are A with X, A with Y, A with Z, B with X, B with Y, etc. It is a term frequently used in ANOVA as well as with chi-square tables (i.e. crosstabulation and contingency tables).

Chart: A graphical or pictorial representation of the characteristics of one's data.

Chart Editor window: In SPSS Statistics it is a window which can be opened up to refine a chart.

Chi-square distribution: A set of theoretical probability distributions which vary according to the degrees of freedom and which are used to determine the statistical significance of a chi-square test.

Chi-square test, Pearson's: A test of goodness-of-fit or association for frequency data. It compares the observed data with the estimated (or actual) population distribution (this is usually based on combining two or more samples).

Cluster analysis: A variety of techniques which identify the patterns of variables or cases which tend to be similar to each other. No cluster analysis techniques are dealt with in this book as they are uncommon in social science. Often factor analysis, which is in this book, does a similar job.

Cochran's Q test: A test of whether the frequencies of a dichotomous variable differ significantly for more than two related samples or groups.

Coefficient of determination: The square of Pearson's correlation coefficient. So a correlation of 0.4 has a coefficient of determination of 0.16. It is useful especially since it gives a numerically more accurate representation of the relative importance of different correlation coefficients than the correlation coefficients themselves do.

Common variance: The variance that two or more variables share.

Communality: The variance that a particular variable in an analysis shares with other variables. It is distinct from error variance and specific variance (which is confined to a particular variable). It mainly appears in factor analysis.

Component matrix: A table showing the correlations between components and variables in factor analysis.

Compute: In SPSS Statistics, this procedure allows the researcher to derive new variables from the original variables. For example, it would be possible to sum the scores for each participant on several variables.

Condition: One of the groups in ANOVA or the t-test.

Confidence interval: A more realistic way of presenting the outcomes of statistical analysis than, for example, the mean or the standard deviation would be. It gives the range within which 95% or 99% of the most common means, standard deviations, etc. would lie. Thus instead of saying that the mean is 6.7 we would say that the 95% confidence interval for the mean is 5.2 to 8.2.

Confirmatory factor analysis: A test of whether a particular model or factor structure fits a set of data satisfactorily.

Confounding variable: Any variable which clouds the interpretation of a correlation or any other statistical relationship. Once the effects of the confounding variable are removed, the remaining relationship presents a truer picture of what is going on in reality.

Contingency table: A frequency table giving the frequencies in all of the categories of two or more nominal (category) variables tabulated together.

Correlation coefficient: An index which gives the extent and the direction of the linear association between two variables.

Correlation matrix: A matrix of the correlations of pairs of variables.

Count: The number of times (frequency) a particular observation (score or category, for example) occurs.

Counterbalancing: If some participants take part in condition A of a study first, followed by condition B later, then to counterbalance any time or sequence effects other participants should take part in condition B first followed by condition A second.

Covariance: The variance which two or more score variables have in common (i.e. share). It is basically calculated like variance, but instead of squaring each score's deviation from the mean the deviation of variable X from its mean is multiplied by the deviation of variable Y from its mean.

Covariate: A variable which correlates with the variables that are the researcher's main focus of interest. In the analysis of covariance, it is the undesired influence of the covariate which is controlled for.

Cox and Snell's R^2: The amount of variance in the criterion variable accounted for by the predictor variables. It is used in logistic regression.

Cramer's V: Also known as Cramer's phi, this correlation coefficient is usually applied to a contingency or crosstabulation table greater than 2 rows × 2 columns.

Critical value: Used when calculating statistical significance with statistical tables such as those in the back of this book. It is the minimum value of the statistical calculation which is statistically significant (i.e. which rejects the null hypothesis).

Cronbach's alpha: A measure of the extent to which cases respond in a similar or consistent way on all the variables that go to make up a scale.

Data Editor window: The data spreadsheet in which data items are entered in SPSS Statistics.

Data handling: The various techniques to deal with data from a study excluding its statistical analysis. It would include data entry into the spreadsheet, the search for errors in data entry, recoding variables into new values, computing new variables and so forth.

Data View: The window in SPSS Statistics which allows you to see the data spreadsheet.

Degrees of freedom: The number of components of the data that can vary while still yielding a given population value for characteristics such as mean scores. All other things being equal, the bigger the degrees of freedom the more likely it is that the research findings will be statistically significant.

Dependent variable: A variable which potentially may be affected or predicted by other variables in the analysis. It is sometimes known as the criterion or outcome variable.

Descriptive statistics: Indices which describe the major characteristics of variables or the relationships between variables. It includes measures of central tendency (mean, median and mode for example) and measures of spread (range, variance, etc.).

Deviation: Usually the difference between a score and the mean of the set of scores.

Dialog box: A rectangular picture in SPSS Statistics which allows the user to select various procedures.

Dichotomous: A nominal (category) variable with just two categories. Gender (male/female) is an obvious example.

Direct Oblimin: A rotation procedure for making factors in a factor analysis more meaningful or interpretable. Its essential characteristic is that the factors are not required to be uncorrelated (independent) of each other.

Discriminant (function) analysis: A statistical technique for score variables which maximises the difference(s) between two or more groups of participants on a set of variables. It generates a set of 'weights' which are applied to these variables.

Discriminant function: Found mainly in discriminant (function) analysis. A derived variable based on combining a set of variables in such a way that groups are as different as possible on the discriminant function. More than one discriminant function may emerge, but each discriminant function is uncorrelated with the others.

Discriminant score: An individual's score on a discriminant function.

Dummy coding: Used when analysing nominal (category) data to allow such variables to be used analogously to scores. Each category of the nominal (category) variable is made into a separate dummy variable. If the nominal (category) variable has three categories A, B and C then two new variables, say A versus not A and B versus not B, are created. The categories may be coded with the value 1 and 0. It would not be used where a variable has only two different categories.

Dummy variable: A variable created by dummy coding.

Effect size: A measure of the strength of the relationship between two variables. Most commonly used in meta-analysis. The Pearson correlation coefficient is a very familiar measure of effect size. Also commonly used is Cohen's d. The correlation coefficient is recommended as the most user-friendly measure of effect size as it is very familiar to most of us and easily understood.

Eigenvalue: The variance accounted for by a factor. It is simply the sum of the squared factor loadings. The concept is also used for discriminant functions.

Endogenous variable: Any variable in path analysis that can be explained on the basis of one or more variables in that analysis.

Eta: A measure of association for non-linear (curved) relationships.

Exact significance: The precise significance level at and beyond which a result is statistically significant.

Exogenous variable: A variable in path analysis which is not accounted for by any other variable in that analysis.

Exploratory factor analysis: The common form of factor analysis which finds the major dimensions of a correlation matrix using weighted combinations of the variables in the study. It identifies combinations of variables which can be described as one or more superordinate variables or factors.

Exponent or power: A number with an exponent or power superscript is multiplied by itself by that number of times. Thus 3^2 means 3×3 whereas 4^3 means $4 \times 4 \times 4$.

Extraction: The process of obtaining factors in factor analysis.

F-ratio: The ratio of two variances. It can be used to test whether these two variances differ significantly using the F-distribution. It can be used on its own but is also part of the t-test and ANOVA.

Factor matrix: A table showing the correlations between factors and the variables.

Factor scores: Standardised scores for a factor. They provide a way of calculating an individual's score on a factor which precisely reflects that factor.

Factor, factor analysis: A variable derived by combining other variables in a weighted combination. A factor seeks to synthesise the variance shared by variables into a more general variable to which the variables relate.

Factor, in analysis of variance: An independent or subject variable but is best regarded as a variable on which groups of participants are formed. The variances of these groups are then compared using ANOVA. A factor should consist of a nominal (category) variable with a small number of categories.

Factorial ANOVA: An analysis of variance with two or more independent or subject variables.

Family error rate: The probability or significance level for a finding when a family or number of tests or comparisons are being made on the same data.

Fisher test: Tests of significance (or association) for 2×2 and 2×3 contingency tables.

Frequency: The number of times a particular category occurs.

Frequency distribution: A table or diagram giving the frequencies of values of a variable.

Friedman's test: A nonparametric test for determining whether the mean ranks of three or more related samples or groups differ significantly.

Goodness-of-fit index: A measure of the extent to which a particular model (or pattern of variables) designed to describe a set of data actually matches the data.

Graph: A diagram for illustrating the values of one or more variables.

Grouping variable: A variable which forms the groups or conditions which are to be compared.

Harmonic mean: The number of scores, divided by the sum of the reciprocal ($1/x$) of each score.

Help: A facility in software with a graphical interface such as SPSS Statistics which provides information about its features.

Hierarchical agglomerative clustering: A form of cluster analysis, at each step of which a variable or cluster is paired with the most similar variable or cluster until one cluster remains.

Hierarchical or sequential entry: A variant of regression in which the order in which the independent (predictor) variables are entered into the analysis is decided by the analyst rather than mathematical criteria.

Hierarchical regression: *see* Hierarchical or sequential entry.

Histogram: A chart which represents the frequency of particular scores or ranges of scores in terms of a set of bars. The height of the bar represents the frequency of this score or range of scores in the data.

Homogeneity of regression slope: The similarity of the regression slope of the covariate on the criterion variable in the different groups of the predictor variable.

Homogeneity of variance: The similarity of the variance of the scores in the groups of the predictor variable.

Homoscedasticity: The similarity of the scatter or spread of the data points around the regression line of best fit in different parts of that line.

Hypothesis: A statement expressing the expected or predicted relationship between two or more variables.

Icicle plot: A graphical representation of the results of a cluster analysis in which *x*s are used to indicate which variables or clusters are paired at which stage.

Identification: The extent to which the parameters of a structural equation model can be estimated from the original data.

Independence: Events or variables being unrelated to each other.

Independent groups design: A design in which different cases are assigned to different conditions or groups.

Independent *t*-test: A parametric test for determining whether the means of two unrelated or independent groups differ significantly.

Independent variable: A variable which may affect (predict) the values of another variable(s). It is used to form the groups in experimental designs, but it is also used in regression for the variables used to predict the dependent variable.

Inferential statistics: Statistical techniques which help predict the population characteristics from the sample characteristics.

Interaction: This describes outcomes in research which cannot be accounted for on the basis of the separate influences of two or more variables. So, for example, an interaction occurs when two variables have a significant influence when combined.

Interaction graph: A graph showing the relationship of the means of two or more variables.

Interquartile range: The range of the middle 50% of a distribution. By ignoring the extreme quarter in each direction from the mean, the interquartile range is less affected by extreme scores.

Interval data: Data making up a scale in which the distance or interval between adjacent points is assumed to be the same or equal but where there is no meaningful zero point.

Just-identified model: A structural equation model in which the data are just sufficient to estimate its parameters.

Kaiser or Kaiser–Guttman criterion: A statistical criterion in factor analysis for determining the number of factors or components for consideration and possible rotation in which factors or components with eigenvalues of one or less are ignored.

Kendall's tau (τ): An index of the linear association between two ordinal variables. A correlation coefficient for nonparametric data in other words.

Kolmogorov–Smirnov test for two samples: A nonparametric test for determining whether the distributions of scores on an ordinal variable differ significantly for two unrelated samples.

Kruskal–Wallis test: A nonparametric test for determining whether the mean ranked scores for three or more unrelated samples differ significantly.

Kurtosis: The extent to which the shape of a bell-shaped curve is flatter or more elongated than a normal distribution.

Latent variable: An unobserved variable that is measured by one or more manifest variables or indicators.

Level: Used in analysis of variance to describe the different conditions of an independent variable (or factor). The term has its origins in agricultural research where levels of treatment would correspond to, say, different amounts of fertiliser being applied to crops.

Levels of measurement: A four-fold hierarchical distinction proposed for measures comprising nominal, ordinal, equal interval and ratio.

Levene's test: An analysis of variance on absolute differences to determine whether the variances of two or more unrelated groups differ significantly.

Likelihood ratio chi-square test: A form of chi-square which involves natural logarithms. It is primarily associated with log-linear analysis.

Line graph: A diagram in which lines are used to indicate the frequency of a variable.

Linear association or relationship: This occurs when there is a straight line relationship between two sets of scores. The scattergram for these data will be represented best by a straight line rather than a curved line.

Linear model: A model which assumes a linear relationship between the variables.

LISREL: The name of a particular software designed to carry out *li*near *s*tructural *rel*ationship analysis also known as structural equation modelling.

Loading: An index of the size and direction of the association of a variable with a factor or discriminant function of which it is part. A loading is simply the correlation between a variable and the factor or discriminant function.

Log likelihood: An index based on the difference between the frequencies for a category variable(s) and what is predicted on the basis of the predictors (i.e. the modelled data). The bigger the log likelihood the poorer the fit of the model to the data.

Log-linear analysis: A statistical technique for nominal (category) data which is essentially an extension of chi-square where there are three or more independent variables.

Logarithm: The amount to which a given base number (e.g. 10) has to be multiplied by itself to obtain a particular number. So in the expression 3^2, 2 would be the logarithm for the base 3 which makes 9. Sometimes it is recommended that scores are converted to their logarithms if this results in the data fitting the requirements of the statistical procedure better.

Logistic or logit regression: A version of multiple regression in which the dependent, criterion or outcome variable takes the form of a nominal (category) variable. Any mixture of scores and nominal (category) variables can act as predictors. The procedure uses dummy variables extensively.

Main effect: The effect of an independent or predictor variable on a dependent or criterion variable.

Manifest variable: A variable which directly reflects the measure used to assess it.

Mann–Whitney Test: A nonparametric test for seeing whether the number of times scores from one sample are ranked significantly higher than scores from another unrelated sample.

Marginal totals: The marginal totals are the row and column total frequencies in crosstabulation and contingency tables.

Matched-subjects design: A related design in which participants are matched in pairs on a covariate or where participants serve as their own control. In other words, a repeated or related measures design.

Matrix: A rectangular array of rows and columns of data.

Mauchly's test: A test for determining whether the assumption that the variance–covariance matrix in a repeated measures analysis of variance is spherical or circular.

Maximum likelihood method: A method for finding estimates of the population parameters of a model which are most likely to give rise to the pattern of observations in the sample data.

McNemar test: A test for assessing whether there has been a significant change in the frequencies of two categories on two occasions in the same or similar cases.

Mean: The everyday numerical average score. Thus the mean of 2 and 3 is 2.5.

Mean square: A term for variance estimate used in analysis of variance.

Measure of dispersion: A measure of the variation in the scores such as the variance, range, interquartile range and standard error.

Median: The score which is halfway in the scores ordered from smallest to largest.

Mediating variable: One which is responsible for the relationship between two other variables.

Mixed ANOVA: An ANOVA in which at least one independent variable consists of related scores and at least one other variable consists of uncorrelated scores.

Mixed design: *see* Mixed ANOVA.

Mode: The most commonly occurring score or category.

Moderating or moderator effect: A relationship between two variables which differs according to a third variable. For example, the correlation between age and income may be moderated by a variable such as gender. In other words, the correlation for men and the correlation for women between age and income is different.

Multicollinearity: When two or more independent or predictor variables are highly correlated.

Multimodal: A frequency distribution having three or more modes.

Multiple correlation or R: A form of correlation coefficient which correlates a single score (A) with two or more other scores (B + C) in combination. Used particularly in multiple regression to denote the correlation of a set of predictor variables with the dependent (or outcome) variable.

Multiple regression: A parametric test to determine what pattern of two or more predictor (independent) variables is associated with scores on the dependent variable. It takes into account the associations (correlations) between the predictor variables. If desired, interactions between predictor variables may be included.

Multivariate: Involving more than two variables.

Multivariate analysis of variance (MANOVA): A variant of analysis of variance in which there are two or more *dependent* variables combined. MANOVA identifies differences between groups in terms of the combined dependent variable.

Nagelkerke's R^2: The amount of variance in the criterion variable accounted for by the predictor variables.

Natural or Napierian logarithm: The logarithms calculated using 2.718 as the base number.

Nested model: A model which is a simpler subset of another model and which can be derived from that model.

Nonparametric test: A statistical test of significance which requires fewer assumptions about the distribution of values in a sample than a parametric test.

Normal distribution: A mathematical distribution with very important characteristics. However, it is easier to regard it as a bell-shaped frequency curve. The tails of the curve should stretch to infinity in both directions but this, in the end, is of little practical importance.

Numeric variables: Variables for which the data are collected in the form of scores which indicate quantity.

Oblique factors: In factor analysis, oblique factors are ones which, during rotation, are allowed to correlate with each other. This may be more realistic than orthogonal rotations. One way of looking at this is to consider height and weight. These are distinct variables, but they correlate to some degree. Oblique factors are distinct, but they can correlate.

Odds: Obtained by dividing the probability of something occurring by the probability of it not occurring.

Odds ratio: The number by which the odds of something occurring must be multiplied for a one unit change in a predictor variable.

One-tailed test: A version of significance testing in which a strong prediction is made as to the direction of the relationship. This should be theoretically and empirically well founded on previous research. The prediction should be made prior to examination of the data.

Ordinal data: Numbers for which little can be said other than the numbers give the rank order of cases on the variable from smallest to largest.

Orthogonal: Essentially means at right angles.

Orthogonal factors: In factor analysis, orthogonal factors are factors which do not correlate with each other.

Outcome variable: A word used especially in medical statistics to denote the dependent variable. It is also the criterion variable. It is the variable which is expected to vary with variation in the independent variable(s).

Outlier: A score or data point which differs substantially from the other scores or data points. It is an extremely unusual or infrequent score or data point.

Output window: The window of computer software which displays the results of an analysis.

Over-identified model: A structural equation model in which the number of data points is greater than the number of parameters to be estimated, enabling the fit of the model to the data to be determined.

Paired comparisons: The process of comparing each variable mean with every (or most) other variable mean in pairs.

Parameter: A characteristic such as the mean or standard deviation which is based on the population of scores. In contrast, a statistic is a characteristic which is based on a sample of scores.

Parametric: To do with the characteristics of the population.

Parametric test: A statistical test which assumes that the scores used come from a population of scores which is normally distributed.

Part or semi-partial correlation: The correlation between a criterion and a predictor when the predictor's correlation with other predictors is partialled out.

Partial correlation: The correlation between a criterion and a predictor when the criterion's and the predictor's correlation with other predictors have been partialled out.

Participant: Someone who takes part in research. A more appropriate term than the archaic and misleading 'subject'.

PASW Statistics: The name for SPSS Statistics in 2008–9.

Path diagram: A diagram in which the relationships (actual or hypothetical) between variables are presented.

Pathway: A line in a path diagram depicting a relationship between two variables.

Phi: A measure of association between two binomial or dichotomous variables.

Pivot table: A table in SPSS Statistics which can be edited.

Planned comparisons: Testing whether a difference between two groups is significant when there are strong grounds for expecting such a difference.

Point-biserial correlation: A correlation between a score variable and a binomial (dichotomous) variable – i.e. one with two categories.

Population: All of the scores from which a sample is taken. It is erroneous in statistics to think of the population as people since it is the population of scores on a variable.

Post hoc test: A test to see whether two groups differ significantly when the researcher has no strong grounds for predicting or expecting that they will. Essentially they are unplanned tests which were not stipulated prior to the collection of data.

Power: In statistics, the ability of a test to reject the null hypothesis when it is false.

Principal component analysis: Primarily a form of factor analysis in which the variance of each variable is set at the maximum value of 1 as no adjustment has been made for communalities. Probably best reserved for instances in which the correlation matrix tends to have high values which is not common in social sciences research.

Probability distribution: The distribution of outcomes expected by chance.

Promax: A method of oblique rotation in factor analysis.

Quantitative research: Research which at the very least involves counting the frequency of categories in the main variable of interest.

Quartimax: A method of orthogonal rotation in factor analysis.

Randomisation: The assignment of cases to conditions using some method of assigning by chance.

Range: The difference between the largest and smallest score of a variable.

Ratio data: A measure for which it is possible to say that a score is a multiple of another score such as 20 being twice 10. Also there should be a zero point on the measure.

Recode: Giving a value, or set of values, another value such as recoding age into ranges of age.

Regression coefficient: The weight which is applied to a predictor variable to give the value of the dependent variable.

Related design: A design in which participants provide data in more than one condition of the experiment. This is where participants serve as their own controls. More rarely, if samples are matched on a pairwise basis to be as similar as possible on a matching variable then this also constitutes a related design if the matching variable correlates with the dependent variable.

Related factorial design: A design in which there are two or more independent or predictor variables which have the same or similar cases in them.

Reliability: Internal reliability is the extent to which items which make up a scale or measure are internally consistent. It is usually calculated either using a form of split-half reliability in which the score for half the items is correlated with the score for the other half of the items (with an adjustment for the shortened length of the scale) or using Cronbach's alpha (which is the average of all possible split-half reliabilities). A distinct form of reliability is test–retest reliability which measures consistency over time.

Repeated measures design: A design in which the groups of the independent variables have the same or similar cases in them.

Repeated-measures ANOVA: An analysis of variance which is based on one or more related factors having the same or similar cases in them.

Residual: The difference between an observed and expected score.

Residual sum of squares: The sum of squares that are left over after other sources of variance have been removed.

Rotation: *see* Rotation of factors.

Rotation of factors: This adjusts the factors (axes) of a factor analysis in order to make the factors more interpretable. To do so, the numbers of high and low factor loadings are maximised whereas the numbers of middle-sized factor loadings are made minimal. Originally it involved plotting the axes (factors) on graph paper and rotating them physically on the page, leaving the factor loadings in the same points on the graph paper. As a consequence, the factor loadings change since these have not moved but the axes have.

Sample: A selection or subset of scores on a variable. Samples cannot be guaranteed to be representative of the population, but if they are selected at random then there will be no systematic difference between the samples and the population.

Sampling distribution: The theoretical distribution of a particular size of sample which would result if samples of that size were repeatedly taken from that population.

Saturated model: A model (set of variables) which fully accounts for the data. It is a concept used in log-linear analysis.

Scattergram: *see* Scatterplot.

Scatterplot: A diagram or chart which shows the relationship between two score variables. It consists of a horizontal and a vertical scale which are used to plot the scores of each individual on both variables.

Scheffé test: A *post hoc* test used in analysis of variance to test whether two group means differ significantly from each other.

Score statistic: A measure of association in logistic regression.

Scree test: A graph of the eigenvalues of successive factors in a factor analysis. It is used to help determine the 'significant' number of factors prior to rotation. The point at which the curve becomes flat and 'straight' determines the number of 'significant' factors.

Select cases: The name of an SPSS Statistics procedure for selecting subsamples of cases based on one or more criteria such as the gender of participants.

Sign test: A nonparametric test which determines whether the number of positive and negative differences between the scores in two conditions with the same or similar cases differ significantly.

Significance level: The probability level at and below which an outcome is assumed to be unlikely to be due to chance.

Simple regression: A test for describing the size and direction of the association between a predictor variable and a criterion variable.

Skew: A description given to a frequency distribution in which the scores tend to be in one tail of the distribution.

In other words, it is a lop-sided frequency distribution compared to a normal (bell-shaped) curve.

Sort cases: The name of an SPSS Statistics procedure for ordering cases in the data file according to the values of one or more variables.

Spearman's correlation coefficient: A measure of the size and direction of the association between two variables rank ordered in size.

Sphericity: Similarity of the correlations between the dependent variable in the different conditions.

Split-half reliability: The correlation between the two halves of a scale adjusted for the number of variables in each scale.

SPSS: A statistical computer package which in 2008–9 was renamed PASW Statistics. In 2010 it was renamed SPSS Statistics.

Squared Euclidean distance: The sum of the squared differences between the scores on two variables for the sample.

Standard deviation: Conceptually, the average amount by which the scores differ from the mean.

Standard error: Conceptually, the average amount by which the means of samples differ from the mean of the population.

Standard or direct entry: A form of multiple regression in which all of the predictor variables are entered into the analysis at the same time.

Standardised coefficients or weights: The coefficients or weights of the predictors in an equation are expressed in terms of their standardised scores.

Stepwise entry: A form of multiple regression in which variables are entered into the analysis one step at a time. In this way, the most predictive predictor is chosen first, then the second most predictive predictor is chosen second having dealt with the variance due to the first predictor, and so forth.

Sum of squares: The total obtained by adding up the squared differences between each score and the mean of that set of scores. The 'average' of this is the variance.

Syntax: Statements or commands for carrying out various procedures in computer software.

Test–retest reliability: The correlation of a measure taken at one point in time with the same (or very similar) measure taken at a different point in time.

Transformation: Ways of adjusting the data to meet the requirements for the data for a particular statistical technique. For example, the data could be changed by taking the square root of each score, turning each score into a logarithm and so forth. Trial and error may be required to find an appropriate transformation.

Two-tailed test: A test which assesses the statistical significance of a relationship or difference in either direction.

Type I error: Accepting the hypothesis when it is actually false.

Type II error: Rejecting the hypothesis when it is actually true.

Under-identified model: A structural equation model in which there are not enough data points to estimate its parameters.

Unique variance: Variance of a variable which is not shared with other variables in the analysis.

Univariate: Involving one variable.

Unplanned comparisons: Comparisons between groups which were not stipulated before the data were collected but after its collection.

Unstandardised coefficients or weights: The coefficients or weights which are applied to scores (as opposed to standardised scores).

Value label: The name or label given to the value of a variable such as 'Female' for '1'.

Variable label: The name or label given to a variable.

Variable name: The name of a variable.

Variable View: The window in SPSS Statistics Data Editor which shows the names of variables and their specification.

Variance: The mean of the sum of the squared difference between each score and the mean of the set of scores. It constitutes a measure of the variability or dispersion of scores on a quantitative variable.

Variance ratio: The ratio between two variances, commonly referred to in ANOVA (analysis of variance).

Variance–covariance matrix: A matrix containing the variance of the variables (in the diagonal) and the covariances between pairs of variables in the rest of the table.

Variance estimate: The variance of the population of scores calculated from the variance of a sample of scores from that population.

Varimax: In factor analysis, a procedure for rotating the factors to simplify understanding of the factors which maintains the zero correlation between all of the factors.

Wald statistic: The ratio of the beta coefficient to its standard error. Used in logistic regression.

Weights: An adjustment made to reflect the size of a variable or sample.

Wilcoxon signed-rank test: A nonparametric test for assessing whether the scores from two samples that come from the same or similar cases differ significantly.

Wilks' lambda: A measure, involving the ratio of the within-groups to the total sum of squares, used to determine if the means of variables differ significantly across groups.

Within-subjects design: A correlated or repeated measures design.

Yates's continuity correction: An outmoded adjustment to a 2×2 chi-square test held to improve the fit of the test to the chi-square distribution.

z-score: A score expressed as the number of standard deviations a score is from the mean of the set of scores.

REFERENCES

Baron, L. and Straus, M.A. (1989) *Four Theories of Rape in American Society: A Street Level Analysis*. New Haven, CT: Yale University Press

Blalock, H.M. (1972) *Social Statistics*. New York: McGraw-Hill

Howitt, D. and Cumberbatch, G. (1990) *Pornography: Impacts and Influences*. London: Home Office Research and Planning Unit

Kerlinger, F.N. (1986) *Foundations of Behavioral Research* (3rd edition). Fort Worth, TX: Holt, Rinehart & Winston

Stevens, S.S. (1946) 'On the theory of scales of measurement', *Science*, Vol. 103 (2684), 677–680

The National Archives (2011) British Crime Survey Datasets. Available online at http://www.nationalarchives.gov.uk/catalogue/displaycataloguedetails.asp?CATID=7955&CATLN=3&accessmethod=5&j=1 (accessed 12 September 2011)

INDEX